Books of Poetry by ROBERT PETERS

(Note: An asterisk (*) following a title signifies that the book is out of print, except for a limited number of copies held by the author. These may be ordered directly from 9431 Krepp Drive, Huntington Beach, Calif. 92646.)

Songs for a Son. New York: Norton, 1967. paper, $2.75.

The Sow's Head and Other Poems.* Detroit: Wayne State University Press, 1968. boards only, $8.

Eighteen Poems.* private edition, paper, 1971, 1972, 1973. $5.

Byron Exhumed: A Verse Suite.* Fort Wayne, Ind.: Windless Orchard, 1973. $10

Red Midnight Moon.* Empty Elevator Shaft Press, 1973, with drawing by Don Bachardy. paper, $15.

Connections: In the English Lake District.* London: Anvil Press, 1973. paper, $3.

Holy Cow: Parable Poems. Berkeley: Red Hill Press, 1974. Small Press Distribution (1784 Shattuck Ave., Berkeley, CA 94709), paper, $2.50.

Bronchial Tangle, Heart System.* Granite Books, 1975. paper, $5.

Cool Zebras of Light.* Berkeley, Calif.: Christopher's Books, 1975. Most of remaining copies destroyed in a fire; $10

The Gift to Be Simple: A Garland for Mother Ann Lee, Founder of the Shakers. New York: Liveright, Inc., 1975. paper only, $2.50.

The Poet as Ice-Skater.* San Francisco: ManRoot Books, 1976. Parodies and poems to poets; paper, $5.

Gauguin's Chair: Selected Poems 1967-1974. Trumansburg, N.Y.: Crossing Press, 1977. cloth, $8.95; paper, $4.95.

Hawthorne. Fairfax, Calif.: Red Hill Press (poems adapted from Nathaniel Hawthorne's American Notebooks), 1977. paper, $4; case-bound, $15; case-bound but signed and numbered, $25; casebound with holograph poem and original etching by Carol Yeh, $45.

The Drowned Man to the Fish. St. Paul, Minn.: New Rivers Press (dist. by Small Press Dist., 1784 Shattuck Ave., Berkeley, Calif. 94709), 1978. paper, $3.

Ikagnak: The North Wind: With Dr. Kane in the Arctic. Pasadena, Calif.: Kenmore Press, 1978. Limited to 100 copies, hand-set, etc.; no longer available.

The Lost Ghabals of the 1st Century Persian Poet Harun abu-Hatim al-Farskin Recently Discovered.* Berkeley: Red Hill Press, 1979. Literary hoax; pamphlet, $5.

The Picnic in the Snow: King Ludwig II of Bavaria. Forthcoming late 1981, New Rivers Press, dist. by Small Press Distribution.

What John Dillinger Meant to Me. 120 poems on growing up in northern Wisconsin in the 1930's. Sea Horse Press, forthcoming late 1982: 307 West 11th St., New York, N.Y. 10014.

Shaker Light. Forthcoming, 1982; Bachy and Jazz Press: 11317 Santa Monica Blvd., Los Angeles, CA., 90025.

Brueghel's Pig, new and selected poems, Red Hill Press, forthcoming 1982, Small Press Distribution.

the
great american
poetry
bake-off

second series

by

robert peters

1982

the scarecrow press, inc.　　metuchen, n.j., & london

ACKNOWLEDGMENTS

For permission to reprint poetry excerpts and quotes, thanks to:

Atheneum Publishers, Inc. for Donald Justice's Selected Poems, copyright ©
1979 by Donald Justice (New York: Atheneum, 1979); and Mark Strand's
The Late Hour, copyright © 1978 by Mark Strand (New York: Atheneum,
1978). Both reprinted with the permission of Atheneum Publishers, Inc.

BackRoads/ROSS books for David Fisher's Teachings. Copyright © 1978.

Boa Editions for Michael Waters' Not Just Any Death. Copyright © 1979.

Bobbs-Merrill Co., Inc. for recipe quotes from Joy of Cooking, copyright ©
1931, 1936, 1941, 1942, 1943, 1946, 1951, 1952, 1953, 1962, 1963, 1964,
1975, by Irma S. Rombauer and Marion Rombauer Becker, reprinted by
the courtesy of the publisher, The Bobbs-Merrill Company, Inc.

Burning Deck Press for William Doreski's Half of the Map, copyright ©
1980; Russell Edson's With Sincerest Regrets, copyright © 1980; Harrison
Fisher's Text's Boyfriend, copyright © 1980; Barbara Guest's Biography,
Copyright © 1980; and Rosmarie Waldrop's When They Have Senses, copy-
right © 1980.

Carnegie-Mellon University Press for Peter Cooley's The Room Where Sum-
mer Ends. Copyright © 1979.

Cherry Valley Editions for Roxie Powell's Kansas Collateral. Copyright ©
1979.

The Common Table Press for Bert Meyers' Windowsills. Copyright © 1979.
Available from Hugh Miller, Bookseller, 216 Crown Street, Rm. 506,
New Haven, CT 06510.

Contact II for Elizabeth Marraffino's Blue Moon for Ruby Tuesday. Copy-
right © 1981.

Copper Beech for Henry Gould's Stone, copyright © 1979; and James Sche-
vill's Fire of Eyes, copyright © 1979.

Library of Congress Cataloging in Publication Data

PS
325
P43
1982

Peters, Robert, 1924-
    The great American poetry bake-off, second series.

    Bibliography: p.
    Includes index.
    1. American poetry--20th century--History and
criticism--Collected works. I. Title.
    PS325.P43   811'.5'09   81-18536
    ISBN 0-8108-1502-8   AACR2

Drawing on cover and section pages by Meredith Peters

ii

For: Jack Garlington

John Harris

Maurice Kenny

Tom Montag

Charles Plymell

Ron Sukenick

"Plan, if the meal is a hot one, to use recipes involving both the oven and top burners. Increase your limited heating surfaces with the use of electric skillets, steam tables or hot trays to hold food in good serving condition."

--Irma S. Rombauer and
Marion Rombauer Becker,
Joy of Cooking

TABLE OF CONTENTS

ix

PREFACE

The Joys of Cooking--A Critic's Perspective

In this book I continue the metaphor I developed in my first book of essays, The Great American Poetry Bake-Off (now in its second printing, Scarecrow Press, 1979). American poets compete for publishers, prizes, teaching positions, and fame via a metaphoric national Poetry Bake-off. The competition never seems to stop; and there is no single occasion when, Betty Crocker-like, poets participate in mad mixings and castings-forth of their culinary/poetic arts. Each poet does his best to concoct his delights, using special flavors and spices. Some present thinly-veiled imitations of prize-winning goodies purloined from other poets. Others, as I explained in the first Bake-Off, repeat recipes that guarantee awards--they simply repeat fail-safe dishes that have already won prizes.

As a critic of these goings-on, I continue to see myself as a Big Bad Wolf. I am not averse to nipping the heels of the sows, boars, shoats, rams, and ewes of poetry whenever they deserve it. Nor am I averse to dressing up in grandma's clothing in order to entice readers to a meal that they think is positive, but is actually the reverse. My mentors--Carlyle, Swinburne, Lawrence, Wyndham Lewis, Rexroth, and Bly ("Crunk")--were marvellous iconoclasts who employed humor as a vital critical tool. In general, however, irony and parody for such purposes remain much neglected.

I continue also to view the critical act as a sexual congress between the critic and his subject. If a critic can't raise a few hairs of affection or lust, he's failed, and reduces himself to being the non-controversial critic one finds in most journals today. * Such views recall those cheap sugar cookies

---

*For example, when I sent the editor of Credences my essay

(cont. on p. xii)

one buys in the supermarkets (Safe Ways). They produce a
sugar rush, but rot your teeth. My new collection is meant
to be a smorgasbord of ragouts, bouillabaisses, casseroles,
and chopped-liver dishes. Towards this end, it has seemed
appropriate to go to that grandmother of all cookbooks, the
Joy of Cooking, for appropriate head-quotes. I am grateful
to the publisher for permission to use these, as a garnish
for the whole.

I wish to be clear about my critical principles. I try
for a catholicity of taste, and find room for a variety of verse
modes and poets. Hence, I admire the finely-tooled poems of
Donald Justice, Cynthia Macdonald, and Carolyn Stoloff. At
the same time, I like the experimental work of Jerry Ratch
and Rosmarie Waldrop; the urbane poems of James Schuyler
and John Ashbery; the cerebral yet deeply-felt work of Robert
Duncan; Leland Hickman's welter of language and emotion;
and the punk efforts of Jack Skelley and Opal Nations. A
critic, I believe, should write on those poets he is unable to
praise as often as he writes on those he can praise. Coda
recently interviewed some poets on the question of reviewing
peers. The consensus? No poet should write negatively of
other poets. Smacks of doctors and lawyers, right? The
American Poetical Association--the APA!

Poetry is many-faceted; and there is much aborting
of original talent for the sake of sanitized deliveries. The
critic must declaim against mediocrity wherever he finds it
--in the National Poetry Series, the American Poetry Review,
the Wesleyan series, and the Pulitzer, Lamont, and similar
competitions, where prizes, reportedly, are awarded to the
friends and protégés of former winners. Critics must shake
the scented gauntlet at mindlessly-revered poets who have
come to write badly, or who ape their former selves, or who
"translate" poems from languages they can't read. These are
all essential tasks, and they are Augean ones. Since it is
unlikely that the critic may divert the river Alpheus through
these stables, he must lay to with his pitchfork, casting
as much offal as he can through the windows.

Nor do I care whether the poet I review is famous or

(cont. from p. xi) on Ashbery for possible publication in
his magazine, he informed me that his new position as cura-
tor for the University of Buffalo archives requires that he
maintain tastes reflecting the exalted reputation of those holdings.

not. One of my functions is to highlight young or hitherto
neglected talents. My essay on Alfred Starr Hamilton attempts
to correct some of the disgraceful neglect of a national treas-
ure.

Above all qualities, I desire energy in poetry. I am
unhappy with work that reports in enervated and boring fashion
the interminable prosaic actions of "I." Also suspect are
poems that editorialize; I prefer to work out implicit meanings
for myself. Poems that sentimentalize over children, dead
relatives, lost youth, primitive folk gone sour, and slippery
nature-transcendentalisms dismay me--as does that fashionable
bit of tatting, the modern Memento Mori Poem, in which a
recumbent poet, generally middle-aged, reviews some of the
tepid events of his life, meditates on a seashell or a eucalyp-
tus tree, and, with much self-pity, considers his eventual de-
mise. Also enervated are those gray poems, esoteric myth-
loaded Olsonesque argosies with their paper sails and sawdust
contraband.

My division of this new Bake-Off more or less follows
the pattern of the first book. Part I consists of essays de-
voted to single poets and a critic. These are like entrees
for the feast--beefy. The pieces on Kenneth Koch and John
Ashbery are experimental. The former employs a collage
method and interweaves passages from Ronald Firbank's nov-
els with commentaries on Koch. The essay on Ashbery is
arranged as a dialogue between Dick and Jane, that primer-
pair, who are incestuously married, and while sipping straw-
berry margaritas on their Southern California patio at sunset,
try to say something simple about "Litany." Throughout this
new book, my aim has been to find some theme or thrust
that will enable readers to see poets in a new and helpful
light: I compare Cynthia Macdonald to Diane Arbus, Alfred
Starr Hamilton to Charles Ives, and Robert Duncan to a med-
ieval jongleur (a kind of hermaphroditic high-born Lady of
Poetry). For seeing the stark failure of James Dickey's The
Strength of Fields, I invent a concept of hare-and-tortoise
poetry. I blast Paul Fussell's woefully benighted (I think)
handbook on poetry--one used throughout the country in litera-
ture and writing classes.

A gathering of essays follows in Part II, of an amus-
ing, and perhaps even outrageous sort. One explores the
reasons (vanity, friendship, career-seeking) that lead poets
to dedicate poems to people. The next attempts to show how
dreary the opening lines of poems have become--I scrutinize

Edward Field's A Geography of Poets. Another essay considers the pretentious practice some poets have for dating their poems, sometimes including the exact hour as well as the place. Then follows a parody of the interviews one finds in Coda in which the editors take some seemingly momentous topic and invite poets to spew forth. My question addresses the impact of baseball on American poetry. I might also have considered these burning issues: Should poets use middle names? Should book-jackets carry blurbs? Why must brief biographies of male poets include that they are married and record the number of children they have sired?

The fifth essay records my discovery of the ancient Persian verse form the ghabals, lost for centuries, and written only by Persian goat-boys up to the age of seventeen. I hope to generate a new school of verse written by poets exhausted by having nothing new of their own to say. (Since this essay first appeared in Paul Vangelisti and John McBride's Invisible City, I have received numerous, often hilarious, ghabals from poets around the country.) Next appear sections of Pioneers of Modern Poetry, a book I wrote with George Hitchcock in the late sixties. The book appeared under the Kayak imprint, saw several printings, and is now unavailable. We intended, among other things, to expose the excesses of the Projective Verse School.

Part III, in the nature of hors-d'oeuvres, features a number of short pieces, some no more than a paragraph in length. A critic can often make a crucial point about a writer or about a book briefly, better than he can in a longer essay. My model is Kenneth Rexroth, who over the years has managed to say more about literary works in a couple of pages than other critics have in books.

Part IV contains pieces that resemble salads, a mix of greens and condiments. I characterize a pair of movements --New Wave and the Beats. I consider two magazines--the tenth anniversary issue of Invisible City and The Mouth of the Dragon, the latter treated as an episode in the novel of the editor's life. I scrutinize the National Poetry Series (few of my essays have generated so much heat) and the Giorno Sound-System records. I also sample books by three small presses --Copper Beech, Momentum, and Burning Deck.

Part V returns to essays on single poets and another critic, Helen Vendler. I also include two interviews, one conducted by mail with William Matthews, and one of my own published this past year in Gargoyle. Appreciative pieces appear on Josephine Miles, Judith McCombs, Wendy Rose, James Schuyler, Rosmarie Waldrop, and Lew Welch. Not so appreciative ones focus on George Quasha, Aram Saroyan, Mark Strand, and David Wagoner. I provide a frank assessment of Helen Vendler's Part of Nature, Part of Us, an overly cautious work. Like Paul Fussell, Vendler is an ossifier of taste. For readers who may wish to ferret out some of my poetry, I have included a list of titles, indicating which books are still in print and where they may be ordered. Also, since so many of the books I review here are from obscure presses, I supply a list, with publishers' addresses, and costs, insofar as I have that information.

I am dedicating this volume to some editors who have helped my criticism over the past few years. Tom Montag, of Margins, first gave me the opportunity to write the essays I pleased, as often as I pleased. His loyalty remains constant. Ronald Sukenick, founder of the American Book Review, and his editorial staff (Charles Russell, Suzanne Zavrian, Rochelle Ratner, and John Tytell) have all along supplied nurturing and good advice. Maurice Kenny, of Contact II, provides an important forum for me, and has allowed me to speak my mind. So has Charles Plymell of North-East Rising Sun. Jack Garlington, of Western Humanities Review, has published several essays, making witty, concise suggestions. Finally, John Harris of Bachy has been, and continues to be, an enthusiastic supporter of my efforts, and keeps his store, Papa Bach Books, wellstocked with Bake-Offs. He has also printed some of my more controversial essays in Bachy. Not one of these editors agrees with everything I say; I alone am responsible for any errors of taste and judgment.

Irma S. Rombauer recommends that as a cook beats his batter he increase his velocity and add some sugar at the same time. While I perform a few highspeed beatings herein, I hope that my readers, including those who find themselves the subjects of these essays, may also taste some sweetness.

Robert Peters
Huntington Beach, CA
June 1981

PART ONE

"Do not let the knife drag, as
this will distort the layering."
  --Irma S. Rombauer,
  Joy of Cooking

DICK AND JANE AT HOME IN SOUTHERN CALIFORNIA:

John Ashbery's "Litany"

Note: I employ Dick and Jane, those primer
siblings, to symbolize my critical approach to
John Ashbery's new poem. I've sent the pair
to college (Jane to Vassar, Dick to law school
--from which he's dropped out to be a plumber)
and, astonishingly enough, married them. Moth-
er, Father, Spot (the dog trained to bark out critics'
names) and Puff the kitten are dead. And Baby, a
non-poetry lover, lives with her husband and her
Baby in Newport Beach, California; she plays a
lot of golf. I owe a debt also to Gary Trudeau,
and keep hearing Joanie, Jr. and pals talking
more than I want them to. I am, I stress, try-
ing to say something new about Ashbery's work.
I hope to make the MLA bibliographies.

Dick and Jane are seated on their Southern California
beach patio. Dick is tanned and bare-chested. Jane is wear-
ing a flowered bikini. Behind them, as background, is a
terraced vegetable garden, an apricot tree, a Santa Rosa plum,
and a Japanese persimmon tree, and three hummingbird feed-
ers. On the glass-topped patio table is a copy of The Ameri-
can Poetry Review for July/August 1979.

JANE: Slow down, Dick. You're drinking your straw-
berry margarita too fast. What's the matter?

DICK: This big chunk of Ashbery's new poem, Litany
II. I've read so much twisted, self-indulgent, opaque com-
mentary on his work I'm afraid to trust myself now reading
him on my own.

JANE: Don't be upset, dear; and stay away from the libraries.

DICK: Well, I've had it!

JANE: I know you're passionate about poetry, Dick. Ever since you decided to be a plumber and realized that poetry, too, begins with "p," you've been an aficionado. I think that's the word. Sometimes I wish you hadn't dropped out of law school.

DICK: Right as always, Janie. And now that I own two of my own plumbing companies, I have more time than ever to sit here at home and read verse. I might even try writing some myself some day--"Poems for Plumbers...."

JANE: Seriously, Dick, can you really say anything utterly simple about Ashbery? He is complex. He makes my head spin. I could never get through his books in those lit courses I took at Vassar. I preferred playing tennis to reading the tennis court oath....

DICK: Well, I'd like to give it a try, to say something about Litany that Spot, if he were still alive, would understand. And he would understand. (He sighs.) Remember how we taught him to bark Derrida?

JANE: Yes, and Brooks, Krieger, Lentricchia, Bloom, Frye, Barthes....

DICK: Look, Jane. Replenish our margaritas, and since Litany II is arranged for two voices, why don't I read the left column while you read the right one.

JANE: Good idea, Dick. That's what the maestro intended.

They read the entire sixteen pages aloud, together. As they near the end, a gorgeous rust-colored sunset appears. An intense smog layer produces a spectacular refraction of setting rays.

DICK: Janie, you seem to be pouting.

JANE: I'm jealous. You seem so carried away. Ever since we decided to step out of those dreadful primer pages and grow up, you've seemed at times to prefer poetry to me....

DICK: Dear, that's not fair. Every titillation I feel from a well-directed iamb, or a cruelly spavined dactyl, means that I have enlarged my feelings for you. I love you more because I love poetry more....

JANE: I'm sorry. I won't be jealous now. Your very Benthamite answer soothes me.

DICK: Remember when Baby saw his first airplane? All he could say was "See. See." Well, Ashbery's poems are something like that biplane whizzing over. "See, See" is about all you can say, until you inspect the aerofoils, cooling systems, lift angles, propeller rpms of the Ashbery craft.

JANE: Certainly the various technical manuals, those ubiquitous helps for deciphering the Ashbery airplane, haven't helped much--most of them simply launch their own criticism aircrafts and do their own barn-storming stunts....

DICK: Isn't most criticism a matter of stunts? So little of it illuminates literature as it was conceived and written. Actually, APR has two such pieces pretending to illuminate Ashbery....

JANE: You're stalling, love.

DICK: OK. Here goes. First off, Ashbery's poetry strikes me as inspired babbling.

JANE: That doesn't sound flattering.

DICK: He allows us hardly a moment to breathe while he spins off his talk--delicious often, yes. Even his metaphysics emerges in a wash of words. He's the most tidal poet we have writing today ... a poet of many estuaries.

JANE: Metaphysical, as well as tidal?

DICK: Well, he speculates on God--even uses the word. He sees time as a horizontal rather than a vertical process. If there are no vertical processes (lines), nothing runs up to an enthroned deity. Time, Ashbery says, is therefore seamless. There is neither beginning nor end. We swim along in our particular portion of the onward sweeping time-wave. It all sounds like good A. C. Swinburne's "The Triumph of Time," or "By the North Sea," or "Thalassius."

JANE: That's simple?

DICK: I think I understand the concept better as an image than I do the simple-minded metaphysics of most religions. It is earth-located and earth-struck. There's no sense that we are to spin off into an empyrean, to a palace where God is enthroned and eternity prevails.

JANE: I wish I were a child again and didn't have to deal with such thoughts.

DICK: If it helps, much of the time Ashbery evokes a return to childhood. In the depths of the blackest night, he writes, our "blanket buries us in a joyous tumult." We are children again, and as our child-like joy increases, our sorrow "is precipitated out."

JANE: Sounds a bit like old Wordsworth, doesn't it? Child as father of the man. Impulses from a vernal wood. And it's Biblical too: "Except as ye are little children," or however it goes.

DICK: I dig the Wordsworthian allusion, Jane. I see a lot of old William in Ashbery--and some of that other old William, Blake. The child is again father of the man. And what I earlier called babbling--and I am not being pejorative-- is of that Wordsworthian tradition. Isn't The Prelude one extended stretch of terrific babbling? Poetry is speech. Sometimes it is a speech gone loquacious, where the writer seems to be feeling his way towards some truth. You assume also that the world makes sense only as you perceive it--the solipsistic Romantic ego. You feel various distresses, Byronic displacements, Shelleyan exaltations, Keatsian triumphs over sputum, blood, and expectorated lung cells. The imperfections of the world are enormous--putting literature aside. We feel threatened. We begin to sing (a kind of inspired babbling), as a means of stilling our fears. If we face an immense nothingness, a universal void, why not try filling it with our own songs. The faster we sing, and the louder, the better our chances of commanding the void.

JANE: But 150 years have passed since the Romantics. You make Ashbery sound like a fashionable Existentialist--and except for a handful of poets (Kinnell comes to mind, and perhaps Merwin) the mode is passé.

DICK: Kinnell is a latter-day Existentialist then.

Where Beckett preferred silence and dead space in his plays, Ashbery doesn't want to stay silent for a second. Where Kinnell constructed rhetorically controlled and fashioned meditations against absurdity and meaninglessness, and asserted the vigor of his own gigantic will against suffering and existence, Ashbery cultivates much looser forms as a means for inveighing against a God-absent, Sisyphean universe. He chatters away, writing, as he says, "Poems that are as inexact as mathematics. "

JANE: Well, that's a conundrum if I ever heard one.

DICK: I gather that he refers to the purity of math. His babble-poems aim for a similar purity. When they achieve it, something turns right in his reader's psyche. He's a fine restorative poet.

JANE: In a prayer section of Litany--in fact, the whole poem is a kind of prayer--he asks to receive some "shrewd, regular knowledge" to counteract the obsolescence of the universe. He describes himself as one hungering "so much for something to calm his appetite. " And he doesn't mean food, but rather some "positive chunk" of a kind of faith, counteracting "the freedom of too much speculation. "

DICK: His freedom directs him to the metaphoric edge of the universe where he sits beside us with his legs dangling over the abyss, babbling his poetry, filled with recollections of childhood, of memories of friends, and with various topics--environmental pollution, death, sex, eternity, the fiction of poetry, Casey at the bat, and the role of criticism.

JANE: You make Litany sound pretty disorganized....

DICK: In a sense it is a pot-pourri, an extended prayer with much else sandwiched in between the prayer-moments. It helps to think of musical compositions. Major and minor themes interweave, disappear, and emerge again later in modified form. Whitman wrote this way--euphonic and threnodic. "Out of the Cradle Endlessly Rocking" is an amazingly successful orchestrated poem. Walt seemed to have had the individual voices of an orchestra in mind.

JANE: You'd say then that Ashbery rejects all notions of the neo-critical, well-made poem?

DICK: Yes. His mode is far more expansive, Whitmanic, Blakean, Swinburnian.

JANE: He seems to say that like the universe itself, our minds host fluctuating events--memories, thoughts, passions. Nothing is the only absolute, it seems: "The way to nothing, " he writes, "is the way to all things. "

DICK: Yes, and since we are part of that "riddle of the skies" (the "meaningless / rolling and lurching" of the universe), our minds, too, like a busy ocean inside our heads, surges, falls, lifts, ebbs, all in a thematic chaos. The free interplay within the mind creates insights amidst the babblings --double voices, if you will, of the sort we are given in Litany II.

JANE: Yet, the babblings, as you call them, are important as a necessary part of the whole verbal sea birthing flashes of silvered meanings.

DICK: Yes. For Ashbery, writing poems is a process, a discovering rather than a formalized, structured presentation of thoughts and ideas.

JANE: A bunch of chintz at the window?

DICK: I'm afraid so. And there are many kinds of poems in Litany. Some are almost Alexander Pope-ian. Others wield long Whitmanic free-verse lines and motifs. There is even an Edward Lear-like creature--a non-being beast in a pen. There is camp/faggot verse--"Honey, it's all Greek to me. " And there are several Walter Paterian moments-- "filaments of silence. " And, finally, there are allusions to the Bible, well-known older poems, and nursery rhymes. And, often, he's very witty indeed.

JANE: Oh, Baby would have loved him!

DICK: One of his best moments is a parody of the Biblical style--and he conveys one of his major ideas, that our conscious inquiries must fail, for our minds must always lack justified right margins.
As in a life with only one fixed margin, what goes on in a poem between vague limits, are elusive flappings, constrictions, and expandings:

> And so
> I say unto you: beware the right margin
> Which is unjustified; the left
> Is justified and can take care of itself,
> But what is in between expands and flaps
> The end sometimes past the point

Of conscious inquiry, noodling in the near
Infinite, off-limits.

JANE: He seems to be saying that by observing the
failure of our minds to proceed from point A to B to C, with-
out meandering, he appeals to a host of readers. Our minds
are fallible and jumpy. And yet, poets from Chaucer for-
ward have been trying to show us otherwise--the well-made
poem is an unfortunate perversion of how our minds work...
a deceit even....

DICK: Well, you may be over-drawing a bit, Jane.

JANE: I know that Ashbery does reach me.... And
I'm thinking, too, that if one wants to be metaphysical, you
could see his left margins as fixed situations given by God,
society, family. The right approximate our free will....

DICK: Perhaps, but that's a bit schoolish.... I like
parallels with photography better than these stale metaphysical
connections.

JANE: Well, that sure is a parallel he suggests him-
self. He begins Litany II: "I photographed all things. " A Whit-
manic turn, don't you think? Encyclopedic? He says he has
encompassed a totality of experience....

DICK: It's a modern image though. Ashbery may be
the Edward Steichen of American poetry.

JANE: Or the Cecil Beaton?

DICK: He says in Litany that he doesn't much like
portraits of people--we see too much of our boring selves in
others. He prefers landscapes--more of that later. He feels
apparently that photography records elusive hints of almost
Shelleyan meaning out there in the aether. "Preludes" is the
word he uses.

JANE: Or, is it up there in the aether?

DICK: Whatever, wherever. Much of Litany is a
series of poem-snapshots. There are so many superb sec-
tions, individual pictures, separate visual poems....

JANE: And yet, I wouldn't call Litany a poem exactly
rich in visual detail.

DICK: True. The pictures, briefly given, seem occasions for ideas and feelings. And you can have fuzzy pictures, can't you? He rubs vaseline over the lens of his verse quite often.

JANE: I guess you're right. A Watteau shimmer can say a lot more than a Chardin glow. It depends on how reflective and meditational you want to be, I suppose.

DICK: Yet, his picture-poem passages are important.

JANE: They keep his meditational matter from being overly abstract.

DICK: Yes. In a fine free verse lyric passage (again, in the manner of Walt Whitman), "I have heard that in spring the mountains change," landscape generates reflections. The picture/poem produces a quick triumph:
What seemed
Reckless, incoherent, even filthy at times
Is now the shortest distance....

JANE: Photographs are a form of seeing, obviously. And as we turn over the album pages/portions of Litany, a serial poem unfolds.

DICK: That's a useful term, the serial poem. It lacks the negative connotations of babbling. But serial implies a dulled Warholian repetition of themes and motifs--and I don't see that that's what Ashbery does.

JANE: You're right.

DICK: Again, like the photograph album, the poem presents us with "snapshots" of life and feelings we want to linger over, while there are others we spin swiftly past. Pictures then for resting the eye/mind. Memories evoking many intensities and responses.

JANE: One of his gifts, it seems to me, is that of evoking some person or event from the past with a sudden vitality--almost as an epiphany....

DICK: His sense of the picture assists his metaphysics. One of his powerful images is of modern man "chewing on darkness like a rind," finding in his arts "comfort" during those terror-inducing existential spaces--the "crevices between us."

JANE: He's afraid, I gather, that he won't find the objects (pictures) he needs to revitalize his seeing.   If he can't find them he won't be able to rift those terrible crevices. Art, he hopes, can still redeem the universe....

DICK: Yes, and he says then he'll end up repeating himself, as we repeat ourselves in the routines of our lives. In an impressive section, "We fucked too long," he makes himself clear.   After sex, his lovers decide it's "too late to stay home," so they go off to see a film they've already seen a dozen times.   They have come to feel they are the movie. The movie life is better than their own away from the film. How dreadful: We must move, Ashbery insists, to "other living experiences."   It's too easy to play possum with life.

JANE: I suppose that his fascination with photography, albums, memories of childhood, movies, social nostalgia, reflect the promptings of his own nature to play ostrich.

DICK: His modesty helps.   I feel he never preaches at me.   He shares my existential dark, my own ostrich needs. He is witty, too, and that also helps.   And he has an ingratiating casual manner:
>
> Anyway, I am the author.   I want to
> Talk to you for a while, teach you
> About some things of mine, some things
> I've put away, more still that I remember
> With a tinge of sadness....

JANE: That's moving.   I'd like to meet him.   He could be sitting here right now sharing a margarita, and talking about his work.

DICK: Don't be fooled by him though.   He does have ulterior motives.   He wants us to "get something out of life." As he enriches his own perceptions by writing, so our perceptions are enriched by reading him.   He's concerned, he says, that we share this quest together: "Otherwise the night has no end."   Our fatigue, another of his favored concepts, is his fatigue as well.

JANE: He invites us to wonder with him....

DICK: And to wander....

JANE: I suppose that's why he uses allusions to pop culture, occasional slang and four-letter words, and allusions

to commonplace things like coffee pots, taxis, and dancing.
Here's a marvellous brief parody of some bad pop song:
    The lovers saunter away.
    It is a mild day in May.
    With music and birdsong alway
    And the hope of love in the way

DICK: When he satirizes, parodies, or burlesques he's
never vicious. And that helps us in--we are amused at the
same time that we see the absurd in what has amused him.

JANE: Yes, there are splendid, funny moments amidst
the ashes, cinders, pain.

DICK: Getting away from the deep-image, or object
poem is a great help. Get off the still-life, he urges:
"those oranges / And apples, and dishes, what have they
to do/With us....?" Plenty, he says, paradoxically. But
we need the relief of turning from them, to broad landscapes
of the mind--paintings and photographs of capes and peninsulas,
of sea-vistas, some depicting ravenous gales. These great
scapes our spirits enter and pass through--"We can see / Into
them and come out on the other side...."

JANE: You're implying that what you've said is a
metaphor for his poetry? The expansive forms he uses, the
symphonic forms, are like landscapes. A poem by Neruda,
Bly, James Wright, or Creeley is like a still life--such poems
speak to us with a painful immediacy. But, Ashbery implies,
we need much more than hurt-confrontations with images.

DICK: Ashbery returns poetry to those old nineteenth-
century landscape poems by the Romantics, and by Tennyson,
Arnold, and Swinburne. We move gracefully through them.
Visions require space; jolts of recognition do not. To medi-
tate on an abandoned pair of peasant's shoes, or a sick hawk
sitting on one's back porch, is not the same as losing one's
self, meditating on a vast sea-scape. Ashbery's visions re-
semble clouds tumbling, blandly floating, rent. Vision-clouds
are ephemeral and elusive.

JANE: We're back to those margins again. We can
count on the left being set for us--the right never, unless we
use hand-set type or a word processor.

DICK: Well, this may be one of Ashbery's main contributions to the shape of the poem in our time--the return to the expansive poem. The poem is now no longer a tight, controlled "verbal construct."

JANE: And it may explain why although so few people seem to understand his poems well, they do buy his books and give him all the prizes.

DICK: Let's be clear. Let's say a poem has a duration in time of miles. In other words, to read all of <u>Litany</u> II would consume the minutes it would have taken us to walk two miles. Well, as we proceeded, we thought of the path or road intensely for twenty yards or so. Then our minds wandered, went off elsewhere, after some flower, cloud, or bird. Then we returned to the specifics of the path. Finally, our journey ended, and so did the poem. We know that we began at point A and are now at a different point B. We can describe some of the landscape we've covered, but not all of it.

JANE: Yet, we are satisfied. We've understood enough of the poem-scape to make sense--so that what we haven't understood doesn't bother us.

DICK: Our old notions of needing to translate poems into exact ideas or prose equivalents no longer obtains. And, obviously, as elusive as much of Ashbery is, he must be getting through to many readers. This poem, the landscape poem, may explain some of his fascination for readers and prize-givers.

JANE: And his modesty helps, too. As we've said, he's right in there with us, swimming, as he inelegantly calls it, in "the piss and destruction." When we paint wooden tulips, so does he.

DICK: And he's so right about our lives being collections of <u>perhapses</u>, <u>almosts</u>, and <u>only ifs</u>. Our ground is "soaked with tears." <u>Transversals</u> (another of his words) define our personal lives. And it's impossible to say where we are or how far we've come. Our ecstasies are "unfinal."

JANE: There's a kind of dignity here--and I respond keenly, in a way I never did in all those lit courses at college. Ashbery lets me know how much I only seem to know about myself, and my life.

DICK: Are you implying that he's a kind of sexless poet?

JANE: How did you jump to that?

DICK: Well, you hint, I feel, at his androgyny--something appeals to females in his poetry, and to males. I think of Richard Hugo as highly male, Charles Bukowski as blatantly so, Wakoski and Rich as overtly female.

JANE: Well, reading poetry together, Dick, explains why we've been so happy for so long. Those early years, when we braved our mother and dad by marrying, and when you were plumbing but not reading poetry, those were difficult times.

DICK: I'm glad they're over. But, as I was saying, one of Ashbery's appeals is that he can't be faulted by women for being sexist, or by men for being effeminate. His love-makers are of an indeterminate sex--which means we can read into them whatever combinations we wish.

JANE: I respond to his gentleness. I feel he welcomes me into his confidence. I'm not saying he wants to touch my breasts, or that he wants me to stroke his penis ... there's a winsomeness ... child-like perhaps.

DICK: I must stop you, Jane. Remember our own sexual frivolities when we were kids? Remember our lurid doctor games?

JANE: OK. I'm wrong there. But Ashbery doesn't threaten me sexually--that's all I'm saying. Like Whitman, he encompasses the sexes....

DICK: You don't think his allusions to boys and meat are a bit kinky? Or take that wonderful passage on what appears to be gay cruising and its dangers, rendered into throw-away, camp end-rhymes:

> The sleeve detaches itself from the body
> As the two bodies do from the throng of gay
> Lovers on the prowl that do move and sway
> In the game of sunrise they play
> For stakes no higher than the gray
> Ridge of loam that protects the way
> Around the graveyard that sexton worm may
> Take to the mound Death likes to stay

> Near so as to be able to slay
> The lovers who humbly come to pray
> Him to pardon them yet his stay
> Of execution includes none and they lay
> Hope aside and soon disappear.

JANE: Well, what can I say? That is fun. A romp of bad verse? But his "field full of people in gentle raiment," contains all manner of genders. I stand by what I said. His prowling lovers enjoy the "contagious" air--they seem special, as all lovers do; and as they walk by the sea, "the waves stand on tiptoe around the ball / of land where they all are." And isn't that lovely? It's so tender. The music in that poem, in the absence of a bird of paradise, celebrates the circle that rounds the lovers, and their sweet sounds.

DICK: The poem points ahead, finally, to "A new chapter," which we enter "confused and possibly excited." It is a new chapter, all the same, and that's what counts.

JANE: Both voices seem to chime together here; you've given voice B its due. Voice A provides a closing meditation on Love and Happiness.

DICK: I gather that these two voices are facets of Ashbery's consciousness moving simultaneously. On the whole, Voice A seems more reflective and conceptual, more concerned with public issues. B strikes me as more intimate, personal, more conversational. We have a long chunk of a major poem, done in a binary mode, musical, in which two voices in the same mind proceed together. At a recital, we would hear both voices simultaneously, deriving numerous latching points from both during the course of the hearing.

JANE: Do you still feel that babbling describes Litany II?

DICK: Yes, I stand by my word. There's a great intelligence in this poem. It's a stunning technical achievement, with much variety, and a compassionate voice. I feel better that he babbles both with me and for me, giving meaning to the void of existence. I prefer his gentle humor, affection, playfulness, and intensity to reams of the grim, self-pitying poems seemingly everywhere today.

JANE: They are the fashion.

DICK: Ashbery proves again that poetry may confront deep themes and issues and remain engaging and moving.

JANE: I look forward to reading the entire poem.

DICK: I don't know though that we'll take the time to read it all aloud.   How many miles will we be able to walk?

JANE: Well, we might just do it anyway.   If you won't, I'll sell your pipe wrenches.

YOUTH-AN-AGIA: NURTURED FANTASIES:

Dennis Cooper's Idols*

The two most despised groups of people in America
are adolescents and senior citizens. The popular image of
the young as walking genitals and of the aged as dotty, rigid,
and senile--the men bearing by-pass scars, the women ar-
thritic and filled with fetid love--seem more right-on than
right-off. Before you are overly incensed, reader, I hasten
to say that these feelings are not mine. I have always ad-
mired adolescents, though I have never felt tempted to take
them to bed--their feelings are so ill-concealed. As for the
old, on reaching 57 myself, I now join that crowd of folk
qualified to live in Sun City and Leisure World. How the
juices still rage and flow around these aging bones!

Do you know of many significant poets who have cele-
brated aging? The only one I recall is Yeats, who saw a
scarecrow with trappings and despised the tin-can of an aging
frame tied to a still sexual self. Until recently, I knew of
no poets who capture the rich fantasy life of the adolescent,
in poetry worthy of the name. Leonard Cohen's self-pitying,
beaver-shot, teenybopper poems don't quite make it. But
Dennis Cooper's new poems, Idols, do. This is Cooper's
first full-length book. He is the innovative young editor of
a small-mag, Little Caesar, published in Los Angeles.

A couple of reviews, already out, find Cooper's poems
distasteful--thereby possibly revealing the reviewers' fears of
that rambunctious teen-ager still lurking in themselves. Idols
is, I find, a seasoned book--the poems are varied and skill-
fully crafted, and the motif of adolescent sexual yearning is
not all that unconnected with the fantasies of adolescents grown
old. While Cooper lives out his own delights in Los Angeles,
he has been touched by a brand of poem popular with younger
poets elsewhere, who have taken that eternal adolescent Frank
O'Hara as their master, and who also adore the winsome pa-

---

*Reprinted by permission from San Francisco Review of Books
(April 1980), pp. 21-22.

laver of John Ashbery, James Schuyler, and Kenward Elmslie.
They celebrate, it seems, trivial thoughts and emotions; a sigh
is as good as a blistering Miltonic fart, a cute Jackie Curtis
joke is a big "Ha! Ha!" in the face of a grossly pointless uni-
verse. Cooper adds his own dimensions of sexual violence,
and an unprettified sexual exploitation, a kind of promiscuous
usury. His poems often read as if they were written exclu-
sively for the eyeballs of a hot visitor, or for the nearest
friend who knows the jokes. At times they are nurtured on
pop art, comic-strip, and masturbation literature.

The point Cooper seems to make is that we live in
comic-book, hydrogen bomb disaster times. This, of course,
is not news; and it's appropriate that our poems sound like
balloon inserts in our favorite gross funny-papers. As a cul-
ture, we've never matured. Although illusions of power and
success may say we have arrived, we haven't. We remain
disgustingly adolescent, victims of a post-pubescent retarda-
tion, snivelling, without dates to the Junior prom. Cooper
captures this scary drift well. We are pathetic souls.

Nor does Cooper spare himself and his own fantasy
life. He is frank about his sexuality, his hustles, his loves
fashioned from "pornos / stuffed under a mattress, in crouch-
ed / down old movie halls." His idols include the famous
and the not-so-famous: a series of teen-age gods with first
names only appear, as do various turn-ons who are well-
known--Peter Frampton, John F. Kennedy, Jr. , the Cassidy
brothers.

For "Some Adventures of John F. Kennedy, Jr, "
charged with erotic overtones, Cooper borrows from trashy
papers and pop mags/rags ("The Star, " "The Enquirer, ") to
evoke the stunning lad's difficult growing up. The poem, in
13 parts, is impressive. We observe John, Jr. trying to
shuck the awful burden of celebrity-hood. All he recalls of
his dad is that he was "a big guy." Told by others of the
assassination, he decides that JFK was a "god. " When he's
mugged in Central Park, Jackie finds John Jr. "shaking, in-
coherent":

Seeing her holiness
He leaps into her arms.

What this kid needs
is a malt, a Stones concert,
and a hundred dollars.
Things, surprisingly, he can have.

Another episode takes John to an ice-cream parlor. A man who loved his dad gives him his seat. A clerk dumps eight scoops of stuff on his plate instead of the two he ordered. In Nice, he swims madly, upsetting his mom who, like all mothers, tries to slow her kid down. In London, dressed in punk style, he wanders unobserved, grateful for his freedom. At home, aged fifteen, he sleeps behind guarded doors, while the guards have sexual fantasies about him. In Amsterdam he meets a whore. Left on an island by himself, on a self-survival course, he matures some, abandoning his former "girlish" state. In school, he writes a poem in the mode of William Carlos Williams, and receives an A+ from the professor. His poem is called "I'm Going Nowhere":

> I never thought anyone died,
> especially not me,
> then my father and uncle got it from maniacs
> and Ari kicked the bucket the hard way,
> and I've started thinking of my own death,
> when will it come and how,
> by some madman out to end the Kennedys?
> I hope so, and that it happens
> before I have a chance to show my mediocrity.
> I know that's clumsy rhythm
> but what have I got to lose, man?...

At a Robert Kennedy Tennis Match, Howard Cosell turns his "wit" on John, sycophantically declaring him "Handsome / like his father." John flunks 11th grade, dreams he's Travolta, and that the Bee Gees are the three wise men who'll bring him through. In the final poem, a movie producer wants him to play his dad. But John has, it turns out, merely "an average mind," and lacks charisma. When he's asked if he wants to play his father, John says: "It's better than playing his son." John prepares to leave the office:

> The producer sees him go. He thinks,
> "Nice ass but nothing upstairs," and
> sits back, imagining sex, knows John's
> sperm would taste like <u>something</u>.

Cooper loves the celebrity trapped in funk. John Jr. is an ordinary lad damaged by circumstance. But there is more to the image. John touches the residual adolescent in us--don't we wish we had been so lucky, so glamorous, so blessed--even if tragic? J. F. K. himself opened hot spigots of feeling the American male couldn't handle; so Oswald shot him. Cooper's lengthy poem can be read as a meditation on that homophobia; the father's incredible sexual magnetism reappears full-blast in the son.

Our addiction for celebrities, particularly those who have died young (Valentino, James Dean, Marilyn Monroe, John Lennon) is evidence of our own failures to grow up. They've died for us; they've preserved their youth forever ageless. Their deaths, like their presences when they were alive, we've managed to insulate against the violent and the gross. We sanitize our idols--and never accept that if we got them into bed we'd find pure mortal odors and blemishes. Cooper does not sanitize his idols; and because of this, many of his poems are disturbing, viz., a prose-poem, "Mike Roberts," ostensibly a piece of a porn novel depicting the sodomic violations and murder of youth. In another poem, after sex with one of the Cassidy brothers, the poet wanders sniffing the Cassidy odor still redolent on his fingers.

Cooper ruthlessly exposes our fawning subservience to cult figures as a means for salving our personal failures and pains:

> Forgetting bitter parents, pissed off boyfriends
> and even poems that won't jerk into the cosmos,
> we reach for a TEEN BEAT, flip its pages to
> Shaun (the All American Boy) or Leif (angelic
> surfer) or Lance (cute class clown) or Scott (dark
> and mysterious). We wet our lips and feel our
> favorite moving nearby.

Illusion is poignantly real. No matter how dope-ridden or perverse, our idols must be sanitized. At 19, Shaun Cassidy, "hard to spot among his fans," is "the reddest apple on the perfect tree."

Cooper celebrates not-so-famous persons, too. Various stunning youths, known by their first-names only, wander through IDOLS, exposing themselves in various postures of enticement. They are like figures in an art gallery. We admire them, may even surreptitiously touch them, but we don't take them home. Idols. Other males Cooper does take home, but not always with the resultant joy he expected. The pornographic and the violent are always possible. One of the best of these poems is "BL." BL (Boy Love), a boy men hire, is too young to know what sex is. The poet exclaims:

> I want to kill
> the men who
> paid his way,
> who kiss his
> bug-mouth
> and poke
> at his farts,
> lean back from
> him burping ...
> ... the same
> guys who should
> tell him to
> get lost, scram,
> when he teases
> them, but who
> aim at it, turn
> fools in his
> presence, as if
> he were the
> true love
> ahead, and
> not the wild
> crush far behind.

Another of Cooper's themes is that one so dear to
old A. E. Housman: of youth fading into the ugliness of aging,
of athletes (sexual and sports-ground) dying young.   Cooper's
"Tom" is a once-stunning youth who hustles himself by using
photographs taken in his teens.   When men sleep with him
and find a "man" instead of a "boy, " they're saddened, finding
they have "pawed the remains. "   The final stanza says it
well: our frenetic clasping of "youth" is a way of clinging to
a residue of our own youth.   The claspers, worshipping,

> ... draw the beauty
> from youth and it refills
> like some mysterious bar.

One final motif indicts the straight world as much as
it does the homosexual world.   Sexual cannibalism is a dismal
spiritual feeding on others.   Going down on young lovers is
totemic.   Youth juices are transformed into energy for older
bodies.   We are often vampires, and the borderlines between
the eater and the eaten get confused.   It's a painful theme.

IDOLS, then, directs us to areas of our own psychic
hurt we'd prefer to cover up like a cat about its business.

We pretend that soiled underwear, the smells of the unwashed body don't turn us on. We pretend that the garlic-lilac stench of sex in our nostrils and on our tongues is something we never savor. But we do savor, Cooper insists; and we can never be fully healthful, or beautiful, sexual creatures until we cease despising the raunchy in ourselves. In "A Picture," Cooper takes a scalpel to the hypocrisies of the sanitary-self. The events transpire in a gay baths, a Boschian metaphor (meat-a-phor), I feel, for the world at large:

> I was never caught...
> that way and like it even now, in the back
> row of the Male Man Theater where an old
> guy's fist pumps under my lap jacket,
> or in the room at the baths where men fuck
> and others watch, using what they see
> like strangers do their wives. And we are
> happy crowded in like this, brushing
> against one another at the watering hole,
> sniffing each other's asses like food.
> We look the way dogs do when they want to screw,
> a shiny blankness in our one-track eyes.
> A quake hits our looks where the handsome get
> ugly and the ugly monstrous. We let words
> out like farts we can't control. We stink
> to the lowest heavens, talk like dime-novels,
> and we eat from each other like cannibals,
> piss snob cannibals who'll eat only caviar.

Cooper hits us where we live, as the cliché goes. IDOLS is a disturbing book. Cooper is a young poet of startling gifts.

THE PHENOMENON OF JAMES DICKEY, CURRENTLY:

James Dickey's The Strength of Fields*

James Dickey is a much decorated ace among American poets. He has retracted his poem-wheels sufficiently often and gone winging off into the blue to earn his place in that Poetry-Pilot Sky Hall-of-Fame. And, if he never decides to publish another line, or to rev up another poem/engine, his reputation is secure. But he does keep writing. The Strength of Fields, out from Doubleday, contains about fifty pages of new poems and about forty pages of what Dickey calls "Free-Flight Improvisations from the Un-English," which are poems based very loosely on a series of foreigners: Montale, Jarry, Po Chu-yi, Lautréamont, Aleixandre, and Yevtushenko, among others. Since these "improvisations" are special, the result of a mixed engineering, so to speak, I shall simply recommend them and in my remarks concentrate on those poems that are entirely Dickey's own.

Nowadays, the public that notices poetry at all assumes that Dickey has succeeded Robert Frost as Poet Laureate of America. This is at best a tacitly bestowed accolade, since there is no formal office as such; the fame transpires when either Time magazine features some poet on its cover, or the President invites a poet to read a poem aloud at his inauguration. As everyone knows, Dickey read a poem at Carter's inauguration, and that poem is the title poem of this new volume. Well, the English have appointed Laureates for years, nay for centuries, and until recently have awarded a butt of good sack as a prize. (Did Carter present Dickey with a fifth of good Bourbon?) Moreover, these English Laureates, apart from Wordsworth and Tennyson, are renowned for their mediocrity. So it is probably just as well that we have no official Poet Laureate of America.

*Reprinted by permission from Western Humanities Review (Spring 1980), pp. 159-166.

Which brings me to The Strength of Fields, published now, some three years after Dickey read the poem for Carter. Just how good a poet is Dickey today--assuming that this volume reflects the best that he is capable of now? I hope to explore this matter in some detail, realizing that to fuss about Dickey at all will undoubtedly resurrect a host of Confederate troops, supported by University of South Carolina cheer-leaders, to march out here and lay waste my Southern California gardens, fields, domicile, books, and life. But I am sufficiently perplexed by what happens to our immensely successful poets to brave the dangers of strafing and mayhem. I mean to be entirely constructive in what is about to follow.

1.

Poems may be seen as either tortoises or hares. Their Aesopian progress towards a goal (the end of the poem) may wreak strange transformations: The tortoise may metamorphose into a hare along the way, or vice versa. Projective verse apologists have sufficiently explained how useful the hare is as an image for the poem racing helter-skelter through the open-field towards its burrow, and to safety. The hare is energy, madness, quick-spinning poem-life. The tortoise, on the other hand, is slow, plodding, apt to take his sweet time in a straight path along some sandy road. He may even stop to rest within the spaces of a single line of verse. More of this later; for it helps, I think, to describe James Dickey's new work.

2.

Most of these new poems, with a pair of exceptions, instead of soaring off easily into the empyrean, skim the tops of trees and occasionally crash. They generate weakly, and, to shift metaphors, they are like tortoises plodding along, testing their way, being maddeningly self-indulgent, as they rest after every 3 or 4 words. Also, Dickey now reflects what I call Momentosity, an easy metaphysics, a yanking of the poem into Significance, which doesn't always work. It's as if Dickey feels that a poet as famous as he is is obligated to say Big Things--the poet as a Shelleyan universal Sky-Pilot for Mankind. Further, he frequently has trouble moving his poems, in their causal dispositions across the page, past the middle. By grabbing onto some vague concept, he tries to propel the poem on to its landing (hand-thrown rather than jet-flown projectiles). Finally, there's a sentimentality based in part on his affection for the male world of men's feelings (the only women in the book are either dead or are memories), recollections of military service, guitar-strummings, jogging, and football. The fact that he still manages some good poems containing the old high-octane revved magic makes us regret there aren't more such poems. As a poet who himself owes a good deal to Dickey, I sincerely hope that this book is merely a hiatus in his career; obviously, there is evidence in The Strength of Fields that there are good things still to come, possibly.

3.

The title poem, read at Carter's inauguration, has trouble launching itself. Language is a problem; the first line informs us that a small town "always" has a "moth-force," once we are "given the night." I'm confused. Does a moth's force drive the moth to fling itself suicidally into light? I thought that earth-anchored small towns were incapable of leaving their earth-moorings and wafting towards glimmering bulbs. Perhaps, though, if you are a lonely man walking the fields outside town, the street-lamps seen from across the fields are like moths--but doesn't a firefly rather than a moth cast a winking light? "Moth-force" is a phrase that sounds good rather than means much. Dickey separates these lines with white turtle space, indenting freely, forcing us to assemble his lines as a meditational act of sorts--we linger over "moth-force"; we linger over "night" (pretty frayed sentimental image); we linger over "field-forms," and we linger over a "solar system" floating on above this walking/thinking man as "town moths." Stars as moths? Stars as fire-flies? I'm lost. The tortoise underpaces me.

Dickey's attempt to develop an Idea also seems enervated. All men are around his walking man, including dead ones, he says--although they are "not where he is exactly now." But they are nevertheless still with him, just as "the strength of fields" is with him. Race consciousness? A kind of cosmic significance labors to be born, as this Ur-Mensch type, symbolizing the poet perhaps, in his night wanderings, quests after the metaphysical. A passing train, one of the sentimental motifs in the poem, appears, shedding its melancholy, hunger, loneliness, and "long-lost grief."

Dickey's conundrum, posed on behalf of his walker (and

us) is--what should we do with our lives? A good Laureate-
esque conundrum. He prays to "Dear Lord of all the fields"
for an answer. In another inflated, sentimental turn, he
hopes his good ambulating man will find his "secret blooming"
by taking help from the dead who lie under the pastures. How
did these dead get there? I thought people were buried in
cemeteries even in small towns. And who says the dead have
nothing better to do than worry about our individual destinies,
taking time out from their Eternity-Canasta games to prod us
and guide us? Does Dickey have in mind a general image of
rot, as Walt Whitman does in "Earth's Compost?"

   Dickey next imagines the ocean as a possible answer-
giver (thanks again to Whitman). Hundreds of miles off,
ocean fumbles in its "deep-structured roar," a roar like that
of nations in struggle with a "profound, unstoppable craving
... for their wish." Well, what is this wish? Some variety
of manifest destiny? And aren't profound and unstoppable
hollow attempts to jerk the poems towards meanings only
vaguely felt by the poet? "Hunger, time and the moon," an-
other triad of frayed abstractions, indented way over to the
right, don't provide an answer either. The repetitions of the
three prepositional phrases beginning with on are like running
a dull bit of film over again, hoping that to recreate the
scene all over may ignite the fuel to blast the poetry-ship off
into space. It doesn't happen, alas, and Dickey's observa-
tion that "it" has to begin "with the simplest things" recalls
some of Robert Frost's shibboleths (see "Directive"), but
lacking Frost's sense of the specific and the graphic. The
poem concludes with our wandering mensch aware--as if there
were any other choice--that his life belongs to the world.
Knowing this now, he promises "to do what he can". The
poem flakes off into the ether.

   "Remnant Water," an ecology poem, is another piece
with generator trouble. It, too, begins with pretty quiescent,
tortoise-phrases slabbed out on the page. Variations on thin,
again, and water seem to be the sparks meant to ignite the
fuel. But it's a weary tortoise. Half-way through there are
some effective touches, as dead fish emerge through the
"scum-gruel" of the dying lake. Unfortunately, the presence
of what seems to be a lone Indian lamenting the death of his
tribe and his fish dying doesn't quite make it as either an
image of then or now.

   A pair of poems, fairly ripping with energy, are
among the best of Dickey's poems. The first, "The Voyage of

the Needle, " has much of Dickey's old magic.   The main
metaphor really works.   A child, carrying one of his moth-
er's sewing needles, draws bath-water, and climbs in.   As
he lies there with the needle floating, attached to its paper,
the paper soaks up, separates from the needle which remains
floating on the skin of the water.   The image turns towards
Dickey's adult life and his memories of his mother.   If by
some simple miracle from beyond the grave, she can drive
her needle through the skin of the magical water to its death,
to prick her son with pain, his love for his family will re-
store itself, and be as weightless as the needle floating on
the water.   In a superb turn, he craves for the needle to
pierce his lips, as he lies (now a fifty-year-old man) lip-
level in the bath.   He imagines thorns bursting into rain on
his mother's grave.

"False Youth: Autumn: Clothes of the Age" is an-
other successful piece.   It opens with precise, interesting
detail: The poet enters a barbershop in Georgia, wearing a
cap made of three red foxes.   His hair is long, and he wears
a denim jacket with a huge eagle embroidered on the back of
it by his son's old-lady.   He strikes the barbers as a middle-
aged hippy.   As a matter of fact, the barber at the last chair
says that he hates "middle-aged hippies. "   Dickey plays cow-
ard and replies that he does too, hoping, I gather, in a very
human way, to deflect criticism.   As he leaves, dressed in
his "false youth, " he turns so that they will be sure to have
a good look, "a lifetime look, " at his eagle's single word:
poetry.   There's no shallow writing here, no pushing towards
pompous metaphysical abstractions, no forcing of feelings that
aren't earned.

4.

The difficulties Dickey has beginning poems (one of the
worst starts is this obfuscated opening for the very first poem:
"That any just to long for / The rest of my life, would
come... ") is symptomatic of an underlying problem I find in
many of these poems--a problem I call Momentosity.   As I
have already suggested, the title poem, read at Carter's in-
auguration, suffers from this malady.   In an ambitious "Two
Poems of the Military, " the first poem is particularly instruc-
tive, since it contains evidence that Dickey can still yank up
that old jock-strap and chase the hare through the fields.   But,
alas, he goes slack when he tries to net that Big Statement.
He reminds me of Matthew Arnold, who in early middle-age
quit writing poetry for essays--he could no longer, apparently,

sustain his special melancholy without puffing out abstractions he didn't feel. In one of Arnold's poems, "A Summer Night," he begins to conclude an otherwise nicely detailed, felt poem with this hollow ejaculation: "Plainness and clearness without shadow of stain! / Clearness divine! / Ye heavens...." Instead of blowing our socks off and addling our brains, Arnold soporifically and tepidly lets us down. The metaphysics is shallow stuff rubbed between the muses' fingers into syllable ash.

Dickey's "Haunting the Maneuvers," the first of these paired poems, begins tautly and originally. He's declared "dead" during maneuvers. He lies "dead" on a spread of pine-needles, observing the needles as they point up compasslike into the night. They are whiter than his own skin. Great. But then Dickey gets into trouble. This luminosity dissolves into:

> O those who are in this
> With me, I can see nothing
> But what is coming   can say
> Nothing but what the first-killed
> Working hard all day for his vision
> Of war says best: the age-old Why
> In God's name Why
> In Louisiana, Boys   O Why
> In Hell are we doing this?

The rhetoric is sentimental, stagey, and turtle-slow. Instead of shedding its clothes, as a good poem should, revealing itself specific and bare, this one hides itself in the swaddling of a stuffed military uniform. The poem comes off as an attitude.

Another seemingly ambitious poem, this one too for a public occasion, the Phi Beta Kappa Poem, Harvard, 1970, creaks and groans towards Momentosity. Dickey does, however, make intriguing use of lines and phrases by the poet Joseph Trumbull Stickney (1874-1904). Dickey calls his form a "dead-living dialogue." There are also several specific echoes of Whitman's poems. The piece is an odic lament over our polluted environment. The speaker, at Zuma Beach, California, with guitar (that sentimental image of Appalachian love, male tenderness, poverty, and healthy ecologies), laments the Los Angeles smog and the off-shore drilling threatening the beaches. The sun seems about to die. As Dickey sings and strums, thanks to Whitman, he becomes a child again (Whitman sang sans guitar on Paumanok Beach): "I

playing from childhood also / Like the Georgia mountains
the wind out of Malibu whipped her / Long hair into 'Wild-
wood Flower'.... "

    His singing-meditation seems to alleviate his pain that
California by tomorrow may be the deadest world of all. He
is a bit comforted by knowing that there is a celestial uni-
verse towards which his thoughts now leap easily, as if they
are mullet leaping in a dying stream. In a Dylan Thomas-
esque "country of death," things, I gather, are somehow
righted and Dickey can jangle his guitar-strings and vocalize
with his dead ancestors and lost poet-pilot predecessors. An
Existentialist Abyss all by itself doesn't necessarily make for
good poetry, and despite the skillful interplay Dickey manages
between Stickney's lines and his own, when Stickney's "mys-
terious truth" turns Dickey's own thoughts wild, he hymns
pretty warmed-over abstractions, calling on "the shapeless
and very / Music of the universal / Abyss." One wonders:
If Stickney's poems were better would they have generated
a better poem from Dickey? Phrases like "solitude," "the
quality of life," "better or worse," and "death changed for-
ever" plod along like dull tortoises. The poem concludes as
the poet wanders the beach "mumbling" to the dead Stickney
in the musical "key of A," seeking rainbows in the oil on the
beach. A good dab of kerosene would wipe the tar-oil from
our heels and perhaps dissolve the poem.

5.

    One of Dickey's great gifts, both in his fiction and his
poetry, is an uncanny ability to convey feelings occurring be-
neath the skin--withdrawing a barbed arrow-head from one's
chest; brain-ache; the slowly engulfing misery of lungs filling
with water; the physicality of another person's self entering
yours. In "The Rain Guitar," one of the best of these new
poems, these qualities exist. He's in England, sitting by a
weir in the rain, with his guitar, watching the water-grass
wave. His own life, as he sits there in the wet and cold, is
like eel-grass which tries to move down stream, but has all
the necessary motions but one, the one that will move it with
the current's flow. A peg-legged fisherman approaches.
Dickey begins to play his guitar. The Englishman is pleased.
Dickey plays faster, as he soaks with rain. The guitar show-
ers its sound as the fisherman casts his line and taps his
wooden-leg on the cobbles, in time with Dickey's strumming
and singing. He's playing Australian renditions of British
marching songs. Both men are air force--and, hence, are

buddies of sorts. So far, so good. The male world is neatly intact, as a sharing. The poem, though, comes apart in the middle. The guitar seems to represent a kind of plain-folks music-making, a charmer uniting men on some basic male level. One imagines the mountain-women in the background frying chicken, making crazy-quilts, minding their bare-footed siblings. Now, in England, a buck dance settles over the weir. It's Ephiphany-Time! Momentosity pulls its head out of its shell! There's an old Cathedral in the background, out of view, hidden in the English town. Whole worlds of tradition and metaphysical meanings waft through as the men reminisce over their war adventures. Dickey is now singing so well he has "mouths" all over him. The Englishman pounds his wooden leg, keeping time. Memories of Burma, the South-west Pacific, and North Georgia all chime together, drawing down "Cathedral water." The rain itself, thus, is mystical, falling as it does from some Cathedral in the sky. For me, the poem works well without the Cathedral; it's a bit like having the Mormon Tabernacle Choir on cue.

Dickey's male world, as a dominant motif, appears again in "For the Death of Lombardi" which celebrates the tough, famous sports figure dead of cancer. Football heroes keep us "men," Dickey informs us, much as General George Patton kept us "men" by creating his armies and driving them forward. Lombardi hypnotized us, so that we never knew for sure, and we know even less now, as we sit watching sports events on the tube, whether he freed us to be men or not. Yes, J. D. , what of another side of the impact of sports heroes? their fostering of easy angers, cry-babyhood, bribery and shucked false grades at colleges and universities? But Dickey's poem isn't meant to go deep: He provides the easy sentiment to go with our Budweisers and Coors: "We're with you all the way / You're going forever, Vince. "

Finally, "For the Running of the New York City Mara-thon" should please both hare and tortoise, since it is a natural for some jogging magazine. Again, Dickey delays the poem by re-running the first scene of a poem-movie: "If you would run / If you would quicken...." It's as if he can't generate the poem. And the dependence on Whitman's ejacu-lations ("O my multitudes") doesn't work. Dickey is best, as always, when he's detailing experience: He sees jogging suits plastered with bright emblems, parkas and hoods worn in hot weather, odd hairpieces, Zulu plumes. Once the marathon starts, Dickey conveys a sharp sense of the race; but he can't resist an easy sentimental mysticism: We are all runners, he seems to say; and as we move "farther into the dark" we cast shadows. A trite Existentialism? The poetry-darkness trap? An empty concept? As the runners stumble to their goal, Dickey stumbles over crippled language: We "breast our own breathless arrival...." Repetitions of me are little more than tortoise breaths. And, almost as a sop to jogger-readers, he concludes that we are all winners--in the race of life?

6.

It is indeed difficult to render so negative an assessment of a poet who has as greatly enriched American poetry as has Dickey. He has inspired by being the rare iconoclastic writer who writes, publishes, and finds his audience without the blessings of Establishment (read "Eastern") poetry enclaves. Dickey is where he is pretty much on his own, which makes witnessing what seems a deterioration in his work particularly painful.

Momentosity will probably always be with us, as long as our poets feel obliged to see themselves as legislators for mankind and believe that success in the mass market obligates them to serve as wisdom-platitude figures. And there are other traps, given such renown. Certainly, the need to keep writing and publishing, even if one has nothing much to say, is real. And success in the mass markets and on the movie screens leads the writer to believe that he must not stir from the themes he's known for--in Dickey's case the southern roots, the macho interests, the World War II experiences, the feelings of once-vigorous males now aging. When experiences seem to have written themselves out, it's time to move on. His publisher, obviously, deserves a good wrist-slap: If a poet will bring in some bucks, publish whatever he writes. His avid public will buy, the investor will be pleased--so we'll publish, publish, publish, abrogating our editorial responsibilities. Just charge plenty for the book, and make it pretty. Well, I for one, as an avid Dickey fan, will be cautious from here on.

LATTER-DAY PRE-RAPHAELITE: ROBERT DUNCAN

Essays on Duncan: Scales of the Marvelous,
edited by Robert J. Bertholf and Ian W. Reid*

Those of us who admire Robert Duncan's poetry will
welcome Scales of the Marvelous, for it presents useful in-
formation about Duncan, assembling much hitherto scattered,
and at the same time provides valuable commentaries on his
work. Most of the contributions are sufficiently conjectural
to leave us free to create our own Master-of-Rime.

My personal Duncanesque Poet is a Lady in a medieval
tower who has withdrawn her bridge, forcing us to interpret
and admire from afar. Occasionally, some perceptive soul
will throw down his own bridge and dash madly into the castle,
overcome the retainers, and proceed up those stone stairs to
the tower where the Lady waits in all her brocades, wearing
a chaplet of roses, ready to bestow her favors. Around her
are mounds of books for her arcane researches, a complete
set of first editions of Oz, and piles of her own manuscripts.
There is also a picture of Alice lifting her skirts--Alice B.
Toklas, not Alice in Wonderland.

When I view this Lady who inspires poet-critic knights
to untold feats of verbal courage, I do not confuse her with
Tennyson's Lady of Shalott, a kindred soul who, as a pure
art-for-art's sake creator, has shut herself off from all direct
experiences with life. Duncan's Lady is wise and fey, and
knows much about the ravenous world outside and the encyclo-
pedic lore underpinning much of that world. She's not about
to stare at a flesh-and-blood knight and die; she'll devour
him in her own way. She stirs up hungers in our blood for
the long-gone courtly days when poets sang and cantered for
their Muse/Lady, who was herself pure and free of syphilis
sores, impetigo, bed-lice, and armpit odors. By contrast

*Reprinted by permission from The Three Penny Review (Sum-
mer 1980), pp. 15-17.

with her ancient Greek counterparts, the Muses, our Lady is splendidly clothed: she's a figure of tapestries.   Her wrist and exposed throat are probably far more erotic than her entire body would be if she were standing naked before a court full of jongleurs and crazy poets dressed in silver.

This image of Poet-as-Lady is not as misguided as it may seem.   Look at all the references to ladies, medieval settings, magicians, courtly love business, and mixed sexualities in Duncan's work.   No American poet since Pound is so versed in poetic tradition, going back to the days of the Provençal poets and before.   Duncan seems to hold that poetry is a rarefied, aristocratic, initiatory act transpiring outside the vicissitudes of on-going political strife and change.   He uses the images of the jongleur, the Master-of-Rime, and the Lady to produce the ambience of this ancient tradition; this is his way of insisting that poetry transcends history and human pettiness.   The Lady, then, as Inspiritor of Poetry is to Duncan what Duncan becomes to contemporary poets influenced by him.

The metaphor of the medieval conveys Duncan's sense of Poetry's exalted role--as does his language, consciously archaic as it often is.   And, if he invokes the ancient jongleurs, can Dante be far behind?   We see Dante, with his big nose (to be reincarnated later on George Eliot's face), wearing his funny cap with the earflaps, his thumb in a book he wishes Duncan to read, waiting to take Duncan with him through the Infernal on the way to Paradise.   Bridging as he does the medieval and the Renaissance worlds (as did Chaucer, another of Duncan's mentors), Dante symbolizes Art as Religious Event, as Visionary World.

I stress this (and I am not simply delaying a discussion of the individual contributions to Scales of the Marvelous) because somehow this primary connection between Duncan and the bygone world, largely prettified and sanitized and enameled though it is, is crucial for understanding Duncan's poetry.   It is barely touched on in this book.   Duncan strikes me as something of a latter-day pre-Raphaelite, a free-verse, projective Dante Gabriel Rosetti--a poet who was himself a translator of Dante, Blake enthusiast, student of the arcane and the mystical, practitioner of the different arts.

The essays in Scales of the Marvelous fall roughly into three groups: reminiscences, overall considerations of Duncan's work, and analyses of individual books and groups

of poems. The reminiscences are the least valuable of the
contributions: They are too brief, and they have a sentimen-
tal unctuousness about Duncan and his private life. Joanna
and Michael McClure explain that Duncan's workshop in San
Francisco during the 1950s "was a divine milieu." Helen
Adam's adulation is most disappointing: Her own gifted work
is intimately tied to Duncan's (they are Rosicrucian soulmates),
and we might hope for more than an extolling of his "genius."
In a valuable reminiscence, Hamilton and Mary Tyler recount
their friendship with Duncan during the forties, when he was
writing The Years as Catches. R. B. Kitaj's "Etching of
Robert Duncan" positions Kitaj in that world of the fifties,
with Jonathan Williams, Creeley, and Duncan. Lou Harri-
son's "Note" on Duncan and music remains disappointingly
just that. Since the title of this anthology includes the word
scales (I assume that the reference is to music, and not to
fish or those over our eyes), there remains a need for fuller
treatment of Duncan and music, both actual and implied.

The remaining contributions are in general more ambi-
tious. Before making extended comments on four of them--
Denise Levertov's, Jayne Walker's, Ian Reid's, and Michael
Davidson's--I will briefly mention each of the others.

Don Byrd charts some of the thorny connections be-
tween Pound, Olson, and Duncan--a valuable piece. Eric
Mottram examines metaphors in Roots and Branches in a
rather stultified academic tone. Thom Gunn writes on the
homosexual motif in Duncan, and demonstrates what I have
sensed throughout Duncan's work--that he largely eschews the
overtly autobiographical, preferring layered meanings reaching
through several levels of time and space. Nathaniel Mackey's
description of the "Uroboric impulse" is somewhat overwhelm-
ed by quoted matter, and he is basically a pretty wooden writ-
er (viz., his gargoyle-esque term "Uroboric" means that Dun-
can's work reflects "a need or desire to root his experience,
artistic or otherwise, in an assurance of precedent provided
by those who have gone before"). By contrast, Gerrit Lansing
says as much in two pages as Mackey says in sixteen. Sean
V. Golden's "Duncan's Celtic Mode" is an informed romp
through the arcane; one learns something here. The final
essay, by Mark Johnson and Robert de Mott, explores connec-
tions between Duncan and Whitman--a fertile "field" indeed--
but fails to deliver much beyond a few general observations.

Denise Levertov's lengthy "memoir and critical tribute"
nicely bridges the reminiscences and the critical pieces. Lev-

ertov details the intense sharing, largely via letters, that
transpired between her and Duncan over more than twenty
years. She quotes from his letters, and we see the shaping
of an important poetics between them. Being younger, Lever-
tov saw herself as Duncan's pupil. His poems formed for
her, she says, "a kind of trans-Atlantic stepping-stone." She
was grateful to find "that old, incantatory tradition" in Duncan;
for as a young English poet she had sought an alternative to
the "dull and constipated attempts at a poetry of wit and in-
tellect" characterizing British poetry right after World War
II. Duncan, she found, seemed to make her own impending
emigration to America "more possible, more real." Yet the
roles they played for and with one another were not always
easy. As her own aesthetics formed, she grew through con-
flicts with Duncan rather than submissions to him. "A men-
tor," Levertov observes, "is not necessarily an absolute
authority, and though Duncan's erudition, his being older than
I, his often authoritative manner, and an element of awe in
my affection for him combined to make me take, much of the
time, a pupil role, he was all the more mentor when my own
convictions were clarified for me by some conflict with his."
Her perceptions of Duncan as man and artist are chillingly
apt--his aesthetics of the object, "the presented thing," as he
called it, come clear. She was somewhat in awe of his so-
phistication, the "almost encyclopedic range of his knowledge,"
and his living in "a literary and sexual ambience I didn't even
know existed." Their first contact in the early fifties was
"almost a disaster," she says, and she objectively describes
the occasion. Throughout the friendship, Levertov seems to
have been overly serious: She suspected Duncan was critical
of her when he was really being playful, and she often felt
inferior when confronted by his intellect. Her account of the
cooling or falling-off of their friendship in the early seventies,
when she involved herself with the anti-war movement is
poignant.

Writing in a more technical vein, Michael Davidson
discusses Duncan's multi-layered responses to Olson's open-
field theories of composition. He writes easily and percep-
tively about these complex issues: the hermeneutic as a
means for Duncan to grasp the origins of language; Duncan's
sense of the poem as an enactment rather than a reflection of
cosmic and natural orders; and Duncan's fondness for Dante,
Blake, and Whitman, all of whom seemed willing to allow the
poem to command them, rather than the other way around.
Davidson is incisive and convincing in presenting Duncan as a
receiver of the poem, to whom the poem dictates, discovering

its own necessary language and fields of relevance. Duncan
emerges as a Romantic who employs language "as a series of
transparent signs" leading towards lost Edenic or Atlantean
civilizations. He desires "a new prosody," one undetermined
before the actual writing of the poem. Through the almost
alchemical changes, transpiring between the poet's brain, the
objects he observes, and the mystical and hermeneutic ab-
stractions he entertains, the poem's shape or form is deter-
mined. The poet invents persons to assist him: the "Master
of Rime," a parallel of Nietzsche's Zarathustra, a woman
"who resembles the sentence," a Lion who is the creative
imagination. Poems become "language-events"; feeling, in
Whitehead's sense, lures the poet along towards a "hurt and
healing" love. "A Poem Beginning With a Line By Pindar"
is central to Duncan's poetics and cosmology, and Davidson
is brilliant in his commentary on it, demonstrating how the
poem circles around "those old stories" until it locates the
"scene" of the writing.

Jayne L. Walker's tracing of Gertrude Stein's influence
is one of those essays where a couple of summarizing sen-
tences might have said most of it. For the specialist reader,
though, Walker usefully details the history of Duncan's interest
in Stein and his fascination with her incoherent language.
Walker concludes (rightly, I think) that Duncan's imitations
of Stein are consciously experimental: "He was never com-
pletely converted to her theoretical and epistemological pre-
mises." When he imitates Stein by employing words that "ex-
plode into multiplicity"--words loaded with historical meaning
and with their prior uses in literary tradition--he operates
"in opposition to her theoretical premises." A problem with
Walker's paper is that she possibly gives Duncan credit for
too much originality; I don't see where Duncan's "assault on
the structure and functions of language" is all that "radical."
More radical than Stein's? Joyce's? And what of E. E.
Cummings? (The latter is never mentioned--and yet it seems
to me that the Lady of Cummings's Mystical Verbiological
Mythicizing-Poeticizing was as radical, if not more so, than
Duncan's.) And one can argue that a collage technique, no
matter how imaginatively employed or how brilliant its con-
tents, is still an easy way of avoiding the kinds of connections
and transitions the poet has to make in lengthy traditional
poems. The defense for open-field poetry is that an under-
current of themes suffices as a structure; also, that initiates
on their knees before the Lady of Myth and Verse in her
Tower will understand without having the connections clarified
(only the humdrum worry about such matters).

As his contribution toward de-mystifying Duncan, Ian
W. Reid develops the idea of "plural texts. " He decides that
we are "co-poets" with Duncan, in a "collaborative response. "
Once again, we are told of Duncan's obsession with ritual and
verse, with music and dance, with our "tribal" sense of hearth
and home, and with "communal consciousness. " It seems to
be this latter phenomenon that allows us to co-poet (if there
is such a verb). According to Reid, Duncan as myth-maker
is primarily a "retrospective one" who seeks a return "to
first things. " (Can you think of any myth-makers who aren't
retrospective?) Reid does say some insightful things about
the war poems Duncan wrote during the sixties: He points
out that they are not "anti-war poems but war poems, studies
in struggle, " in which the Vietnam War is present, "a ganglion
of pain, " a current manifestation of war, that "abiding social
and spiritual reality which brings to poetry a mythic dimen-
sion. " But, finally, it seems to me that Reid is trapped by
Duncan's intellectuality into an even more prodigious display
of learning: The poet and critic dance together, on opposite
sides of the room, furiously twirling their Loie Fuller drapes
and spinning madly through brain-fields of the arcane. For-
tunately, when I return to Duncan's poetry I find that his
energy, zest, and marvelous passion are still intact.

There are pitfalls to writing projective verse, obvious-
ly--pitfalls that no one in this volume says much about. These
critics assume that Duncan is a major (which he is) and nearly
faultless (which he is not) poet: His Lady's skirts are never
rent, her maquillage never runs, and she never mistakenly
mouths a word askew. It seems to me that any poet who
thinks that he becomes a transcriber for his poem rather than
a direct shaper of it may be in big trouble. According to
this belief, the poem underway determines its own "field, "
and the poet--almost as if he is an automatic writer--must
pursue. If the bunny is excitable, the "poem" will take many
jumps and bumblings through the gorse, furze, and blackberry
shrubs. If the bunny is simply out there sniffing the air, hop-
ing for another bunny in heat and relishing life, obviously his
"field" won't be as pulsating and disturbed and helter-skelter.
By this standard, every shape and direction a poem assumes
must be good because the poet received and transmitted it.
I'm afraid, folks, that it ain't necessarily so.

Another pitfall is erudition. Duncan, one senses, has
mastered much that his followers have not, and any trivial,
esoteric bit of information they may possess about pygmies,
skuas, the diets of seers in ancient Egypt, the positions of

planets during the burning of Rome, etc., becomes instant
expertise. And even Duncan, as masterful as he is, can at
times write preciously; strange orts crumble from the Lady's
ruby lips. The collage method at times lacks cement (and I
find this true of moments in the highly-praised Pindar poem).
Even Homer nodded, as they say.

My various fussings about some of the essays in Scales
of the Marvelous should not dissuade readers from buying and
reading it; it has numerous strengths. It is the second vol-
ume in a series published by New Directions called "Insights:
Working Papers in Contemporary Criticism" (the first was on
John Hawkes). "Working Papers" nicely reflects the spirit
of the Duncan volume. Robert Bertholf and Ian Reid have
done their assembling and editing pretty well. Obviously, I
would have liked the weaker pieces left out and the reminis-
cences strengthened. I would like to have seen more of an
objective assessment of Robert Duncan, less adulation and
worship. The editors seem to view their book as part of
an on-going exploration of Duncan and his work. The state-
ments made here by the contributors, then, are not to be
seen as final. This is the first such book on Duncan; hope-
fully, it will generate other, better ones. My guess is that
the Lady in her Tower will be delighted with this current set
of courtiers. In Scales of the Marvelous there are several
fine breachings of her moat.

WHERE THE BEE SUCKS*:

A Meditation on Robert Duncan's "Night Scenes"†

As Roland Barthes said, The need to say "I love you"
is a lack. In Robert Duncan's trio of "Night Scenes" that
lack/need drives a young poet out into New York's glaring
neon streets. There he wanders the homosexual world of
quest, pursuit, and connection. He is fear-ridden--there are
cruising police cars everywhere. The time seems to be the
mid or late fifties--before minority protest movements, when
gays were routinely attacked and beaten by fag-haters and en-
trapped by the police. In this heralding, courageous poem
Duncan creates Whitmanic music; each of the three movements
are strategic improvisations on a young homosexual's coming
to maturity.

1: Confrontation

An "up-riding" moon attached to a line flowing from a
lion's mane--created by traffic lights. Ascension: an image
of stunning visual beauty tied to earth and moving through the
sky. Street lights symbolize the hustling transpiring along
"sexual avenues" of threat and motion. These avenues, "whale-
shark dark," push up blunt noses of loneliness. They seem
subterranean, at psychological levels below the lions of the
street with their brilliant lighted manes. In neon-glow nests
and shadows hidden in the "whale-shark dark" the young man
moves.

Neither surface lion nor whale-shark depths swallow
him. Consummating his cravings for other males releases
Eros--his mistrusts and guilt feelings recede. The warm
male hand going to his throat says No; the vigorous male hand
caressing his groin says Yes. God's face, he knows, has

---

*Reprinted by permission from Little Caesar, 11 (1981), pp.
225-228.
†This poem appears in Roots and Branches, New Directions:
New York, 1964.

rarely blessed the homosexual. The "divine" glimmers ac-
cusingly from the windows of cruising police cars. Protect
society! Procreate more soldiers, police, fathers!

Duncan, the first poet in America to publish "cock-
sucker" in a poem, is the courageous poet of the Barthesian
letter Z, that letter of deviance and reactive energy. Homo-
sexual drives demand lightning dashes through streets rife
with police and gangs of queer-beaters. A pull of incredible
forces: a straight line sails to the moon; a zigzag of denial
and fear jolts its way through the streets.

2: Celebration

The penis is a sperm fountain-stamen. Duncan's cele-
bration is a collage-music of lover/lovers in a "grand chorale"
of sexual being. A marvelous panegyric, improvisational, on
the bliss of male sex. The hero's life-line no longer zigzags
--it becomes a direct Whitmanic current "forth-flowing" from
"green lovers" in "a fearful happiness." The hitherto inex-
perienced youth sees in the eyes of his lover a resolute mysti-
cal eye. Opposites spring forth, twined, as a "light toward
the knotted tides of dark." The lovers inspire the "Prince
of Morning" to open "a door of Eros." Filled with sperm,
sated with bliss, the Prince "falls" into wisdom. From the
Beast (copulation) emerges Beauty.

Duncan's turn to a lyric mode (to an aubade, of sorts)
is a celebration. "maiden hours" dance, "circling" to slow
the lovers' ecstasy. Archaic, semi-medieval allusions bor-
rowed from Provençal love-poetry and from Shakespeare's
The Tempest suggest timelessness. Morning "steales upon
the night." Darkness dissolves. The lovers' "rising sences/
Begin to chace the ignorant fumes that mantle/Their cleerer
reason." Homosexual love, transcendent, sweeps ignorance
and guilt away. Loving another man releases our total sex-
uality. This is the fresh music developed from "the first
melody" of the first movement of "Night Scenes." And yet,
another paradox: The very core of sexual ecstasy is female,
Duncan seems to say.

A Shakespearean innocence blesses the lovers--the
Cowslip and the Sucking Bee. The nurturing flower is the
lover. Duncan's youth enters the flower--"Where the Bee
sucks there suck I." Semen-honey sweeps up the stamen,
primal, as "the mothertides of the first magic," Adamic,

when Adam, as yet alone, discovered masturbation, and flow-
ers, and the mystery of generation.

We are all, in a sense, Adam in our penis-wisdom--
a lover's mouth is far superior to our own hand.   The lover
knows "I am not I"; I am a texture of blent sexual identities.
As I suck, my lover's penis "lifts lifewards."   The "spirit
of the hour" descends.   And it doesn't matter that my lover is
anonymous.   There's no lessening of intensity, of becoming.
All longing and incompletion dissolve as I shape my throat
around my lover's "single up-fountain of a/single note...."
The resultant "grand chorale" of identities is fugal, not frugal.

3:   Transcendence

A professor, said Barthes, completes his sentences.
I assume then that a poet does not complete his, preferring
elipses, smoke-hints, fumings at the mystical gates, collage-
effects arranged from other poets (medieval lyricists, Shake-
speare, Andre Breton).   The beaker bubbles over.   Brain
zephyrs waft bubbles along the moon's track, towards the
golden harpstrings of the sun.

Part Three of "Night Scenes" is just such an evocation
via the overheard, rather than the heard joys of a resplendent
maleness.   Nothing effeminate here.   Food and labor ("circu-
lations of food and rays") illuminate "the torsos of men and
trucks in their own light, steaming."   A gargantuan celebra-
tion, Whitmanic.   The poem is a male body.   The sinuous
lines of flexed sweating muscles straining in fields and ware-
houses create sexual cathedrals for the mind.   If Part Two
of "Night Scenes" is a resolving of our female selves, this
part, since the female/male elements are now synchronized,
reflects a new freedom--to love men for their utter maleness
without guilt and recrimination.   The rosy slit of the penis
symbolizes the heart's meat-dream, and is the "opening in
Paradise."   Yet, no matter how firm the contours of a
muscle, they somehow remain nervously, femininely delicate.

Duncan's youth seems to reject his earlier dreaming
and is no longer a closeted homosexual.   His courageous con-
frontations in the streets have released him from guilt and fear.
The males he enjoys now are not the males of fantasy dis-
guised by the artifice of his imagination--he doesn't require
medieval or Shakespearean escape motifs.   A modern poet,
André Breton, provides clues.   The image of Breton's parvis,

or forecourt, of the poet's imagination/temple, stimulates a fresh vision of potent males. The mystical Byzantine Queen of art is now an essentially sterile figure: Penises are no longer glowing tapers, nor are the gorgeous flanks of strong men lion-flanks. One's sexual cravings are not diluted into mystical feelings and imagery. Thoroughly open treatments of homosexuality in art are possible now--the disguises aren't necessary. The Queen, therefore, becomes the Zolaesque queen of the belly of Paris--a "temple of produce" is her palace "of transport and litanies." In her Outer Court, half-nude men are seen "mounting and dismounting" trucks (and one another). The Queen savors that primal beauty (music) engendered by the loins of men loving men. In these modern environs the poet is at home, unshackled, free. His heart "smokes." His fumblings through the zigzag streets have reached the moon. What an incredible interweaving of allusion, fantasy, realism and art! Robert Duncan's "Night Scenes" is a pioneering poem, merely one of an impressive gathering of his works on sexual themes.

ON LEAVING THE CARNIVAL:

David Fisher's Teachings

David Fisher's topics vary: childhood; brief excursions
into memories of a European visit; a step over into other
voices--those of a bear, a teacher of Emerson, Jean Cocteau.
Pain is a norm to be endured. Sanity is at best fragile. Ex-
perience teaches by knuckling us down. Intellection is a form
of possum-playing. Fisher's lyric gifts are considerable. He
can handle tight forms as well as he can spin out more dis-
cursive, fragmented pieces.

In "The House" a child lies awake late at night, full
of the day's memories: "turnips warm from the fields," a
"hog-nosed snake in the mailbox," the schoolbus, school, and
the smell of paste and construction paper, the "big boys"
smoking on the steps of the gym. The house whispers to him
that he is "too little"; he is like "the dog with his head in the
smokehouse, / none of this is yours." The boy turns his
pillow over, to the cool side, and remembers seeing dogs
sleeping in a hard dirt yard, a blackwidow spider in an old
shoe by an apple tree, and blooming hollyhocks. The house
interrupts his reveries with a harsh truth: "Not yours, never
yours." Even those memories we think we possess, we don't.
We are pushed towards madness. Fears of coming tragedies,
so near the surface in most of Fisher's poems, plague him.
He knows that his father is not "breathing right," and that his
mother sometimes presses her hand to her side in pain. He
helps his mother with her bread-machine, as his father snores
in front of the TV. Later, his mother sits reading a catalogue.
Fisher wants to ask his father something, probably about pain
and death; but there is no communication. Again, sleepless,
he hears the house whisper that tomorrow he'll "still be too
little" to matter to anyone. He won't have "time to under-
stand." Nothing, the house persists, "will ever belong to
you." Chilling. The drift of this poem recalls some of those
awful, scary German tales--Strewelpeter, Wilhelm Busch.

Fisher then evokes his grandfather, as he waited for death
in a mental hospital--"frail and bearded in a nightgown / pro-
vided by the legislature, " sleeping upright because he was
afraid to die.   Strengthened, the boy now asserts his own
size against the negative pressuring of the house:

> ...I am not so little,
> not so little as
> the dog who climbs the ladder
> and jumps into the blanket,
> or the yellow chick
>
> that died in the brooder,
> or the fawn whose eyes
> the raven took.   I am not too little.

The house is silent.   The boy falls asleep as an owl on the
rooftree hoots and "dark lines of geese cross the moon. "

"The Bear" is a remarkable tour-de-force presented
as a parable.   Society trains a bear (us) to perform in a
carnival (life).   When the bear falls from a train, in transit
to a new town, the bear is plunged into what should be his
natural habitat, a forest.   Freed of restraints, he learns
survival through pain.   He adapts, but never completely; for,
often, in the depths of a forest, he performs one of his ear-
lier carnival turns.   Much of the poem is from the bear's
point of view.   Here he discovers ants:

> The forest is veined with trails,
> he does not know which to follow.
> The wind is rising, maple leaves turn up
> their silver undersides in agony, there is a
> smell in the air, and the lightning strikes.
> He climbs a tree to escape.   The rain
> pours down, the bear is blue as a gall.
>
> There is not much to eat
> in the forest, only berries,
> and some small delicious animals
> that live in a mound and bite your nose.

He meets hunters, and is jolted by their cruelty.   Pain, again,
is experience:

> The bear moves sideways through a broom-straw
>   field.
> .He sees the hunters from the corner of his eye

> and is sure they have come to take him back.
> To welcome them, (though there is no calliope)
> he does his somersaults, and juggles
> a fallen log, and something
>   tears through his shoulder,
> he shambles away in the forest and cries.
> Do they not know who he is?

Like many of the personae of Teachings, the bear is nearly
destroyed by entering a strange, yet, ironically, natural
terrain. In human terms, Fisher's characters skirt madness
while coping with life. The lessons for both master and pupil
are harsh and cruel.

Fisher's teacher--he appears in several poems--is
well-equipped to teach. He has the necessary pain-wisdom,
and displays an ironic humor while facing threats. As a
teacher, however, he is not always effectual. Like the bear,
he is adept at certain routine gymnastics. He performs some
classroom tricks with flair. His class learns the proper his-
tories of pestilence and disease; but, despite all his efforts,
they persist in learning it backwards. When he diagrams the
structure of tragedy, he's disappointed that the students don't
respond. He quits teaching, retires to his father's grubby
farm, makes his own beer, wears a miner's helmet to bed
(but still has his bad dreams), and contemplates the visual
beauty of winter: "The landscape is set forth / like the best
blue china.... Outside, on the cold roof of my Nash, / I
hear the frosty clatter of goat hooves." The teacher is alone.
His woman has abandoned him, leaving behind an old stocking
which he fills with hops, concocting his own beer.

Winter is an important motif in Teachings. In another
poem, "Snow," as the poet drives with his wife from Cam-
bridge to New Haven, he recalls an experience in the Black
Forest, when he was in the U. S. Army:

> ... A truck is coming towards us.
> I lose control and float through the
> curve, drifting slowly across
> the center line in front of the
> oncoming truck. ...

As he returns to the present, the snow falls softly, described
in a lovely image: "the snow comes in soft parabolas, / lift-
ing into the windshield." A sudden violence shatters the mood:

A pheasant flies through the
windshield, and lies dead
in your arms, the snow melting
from its wings, the tiny bits of glass
in the quivering body. The snow
pours in through the broken windshield,
and piles our coats like fur.

Since he can't see, the speaker takes off his glasses and
hands them to his wife to clean. Their small red car skids
off into a drift.

Such crashings are Fisher's metaphor for life. Won-
der and fear, pleasure and pain, affection and separation are
so intimately connected they induce terrible screechings, gen-
erating madness--which is the dominant theme of Teachings.
Surviving, merely surviving, is hopelessly difficult. When
memories compound the viciousness of one's daily life, there
is little hope. Memories turn hostile, leaping out to destroy
us when we find ourselves isolated from other human beings.
Few poets have explored this frightening territory so well.
There's no fakery, no workshop writing, no tatting in Fisher's
book. And Susan Fisher's drawings, stark and lyrical, en-
hance the whole. I do, though, have two complaints: I want-
ed the book to be longer, and I would have preferred more
lyrics. Fisher might have reserved the translations and
prose pieces for another book. Also, I guess I am old-
fashioned enough to want pages numbered. If publishers want
to be different, why don't they try lettering the pages, or
cook up a series of symbols--paw-prints, stars, bits of sand,
faded leaves--for marking the pages. These quibbles aside,
Teachings deserves the important prize it has won--the first
winner of the William Carlos Williams prize, given by the
Poetry Society of America to the best small press book of
the year. Williams would have applauded this choice.

SMUGGERY, SKULDUGGERY, BUGGERY, PLUGGERY:

Paul Fussell's Poetic Meter & Poetic Form*

Poetic Meter & Poetic Form is a little creature left
over from the sixties when academics dressed in those ill-
matching suit coats and pants--the pants tailored of some
flimsy cloth that wrinkled easily around the crotch, glistened
in the seat, and hung like badly contoured drapes from the
waist, secured there with a thin belt too small for the loops.
We all knew what was happening down the street, behind the
palm trees, by the rivers, and in the dorms--dope, free sex,
pig-screaming, riots. Some of us in academe threw a string
of beads around our neck, wore heavy sand-dollar medallions,
let our hair grow, and began to abandon those sleazy slacks
for Levi's. We began also to read a stream of poets con-
sidered gross, unwashed, threatening to poetic tradition, by
professors afraid that a horde of tree-branch bearing students
might invade the corridors and sit there disrupting classes.
But, for most academicians, it took a lot of guts to drop their
Fruit-of-the-Loom boxer shorts and move past those rest-
less, nasty hordes, with their Dylan coiffures, Joplinesque
Salvation Army clothes, and Morrison obscenities. They kept
right on teaching meter, Chaucer, scansion, Milton, metrical
variations, Pope, as if nothing were happening. They changed
their shapeless trousers less often; there were some nights
they had to sleep on campus, to protect their files. The as-
sortment of outrageous crotch-wrinkles and shiny-contoured
buttocks merely showed their dedication to the hoary cause
of tradition, sanity, and a Liberal Education. Hooray for
Francis Bacon, Gerard Manley Hopkins, John Stuart Mill,
Cardinal Newman, and Matthew Arnold! Down with Ginsberg,
Bukowski, Snyder, Wakoski, Sanders, Levy, McClure, etc.

Random House has reissued Paul Fussell's Poetic
Meter & Poetic Form, first published in 1965, in a revised

*Reprinted by permission from The Independent (October 1979),
pp. 31-34.

edition. According to Fussell, he has added a new chapter
on free verse, provided additional examples (almost always
from traditional poets), and brought the suggestions for fur-
ther reading up to date. It is an elegant book, designed to
help "aspiring writers to produce passable verses" and to
assist "aspiring readers" in cultivating more sensitivity "to
the rhythmical and formal properties of poetry." Fussell is
after "an appropriately skilled audience of an exacting art."
I wouldn't normally bother to review a revised edition of a
book--except that this one is symptomatic of others ubiquitous
to college courses throughout the country--they are out of
date, malicious, bigoted. As a practicing poet myself--and
an academic--I hunger for more enlightened, judicious books
explaining poetry to fledgling students.

Fussell's book reflects class values: yes, class in the
sense of freshman, sophomore, etc; but class also in the
sense of bourgeois. He's like a writer who draws his skirts
up above his ankles, hoping to evade the murk and offal of
proletariat streets, his academic robes secured by a cincture
embossed with "TRADITION." I can't see his shoes--they
probably have buckles though.

II

It's a truism to say that in order to protect what you
love from what you hate, you clutch what you love, extend your
elbows and chant your distastes. This I feel Fussell does.
He is more than adequate when he explains how the various
traditional meters and forms work--he's readable and useful.
Terrific. Just delete most of the chapter on free verse. His
distaste, generally stated, for American poetry written since
the mid-fifties upsets me. I want to tuck Poetic Meter &
Poetic Form in between the Lady of Shalott's cheek and
tresses, as she arranges herself in her shallop, and send it
with her flitting down to Camelot to die. I find the book ul-
timately retrogressive, prejudiced, and damaging to the ideals
of fairness and open-mindedness usually held to be sacred to
teaching. My fear is that this book represents what the
majority of books used in undergraduate literature courses
maintain--that the poetry of the last 30 years is not worth
much attention, except to despise and denigrate. Projective
verse is never mentioned. If traditional poetry is Chanticleer
puffing his feathers, greeting a glorious sun-rise, this new
poetry is a rooster bedraggled by mud and dung, blear-eyed,
his clarion crow reduced to an ugly squawk.

I am not saying that I mindlessly approve of free-verse --it can be formless, ego-obsessed, and journalistic. Chaucer knows! The excesses are atrocious! And I love traditional forms, and maintain enough of the academic in my blood to desire that the poet streams unite again in a single sparkling river of form/experiment. Since I've written in most modes from traditional to free, I have learned much about whatever craft I have from some of these free-verse poets Fussell so blithely dismisses. I want all poets read and judged in a disinterested, balanced way--with their defects described, their strengths extolled.

Fussell allows the vexed boil of his distaste to spew its virulence at the close of the newly-written chapter on "Free Verse." He laments the plethora of bad verse around today, without actually naming many of the writers. He seems to dismiss a sort of universal "them." The characteristics of this verse he sees are as follows: vague surrealist imagery, unmetered colloquial idioms, and a set of clichéd values, viz., youth is better than age, acute perceptions are better than dulled, Johnson and Nixon were criminals, sex is fine, the CIA is a menace, women are mistreated, contemporary history appears "entropic," etc. Most contemporary free-verse lacks what Fussell calls a "subtle dynamics." "A group of words arranged at apparent haphazard is as boring as tum-ti-tum." There's tradition of the meandering poem, derived from Whitman, which Fussell incisively delineates. At their best, these poems are "vignettes of imagistic kinesis." Samples are Whitman's "Cavalry Crossing a Ford" and Cummings's "All in green went my love riding." And, Fussell adds, with a nod towards living free-verse writers: "Robert Bly's free-verse horses, as well as his free-verse automobile drives, are in the tradition." Fussell is perceptive about what free-verse should do, theoretically. My experience is that more contemporary poets writing in the mode are fine craftsmen, in exactly the ways he deems essential. Has Fussell read Wakoski at her best, say The George Washington poems? What of Bukowski in the early books? Duncan's Roots and Branches? Ashbery's "The Skaters?" Why does he ignore the whole phenomenon of Projective Verse? You may like it or not, but it's been around for 30 years, influencing all manner of American poets good and bad. The limitations of Fussell's notions become patently clear in his final chapter. It seems obvious that he has not himself written much poetry, or he would understand the writing process better. He opines that poems can't be written outdoors where the wind blows papers about and where you don't have the use of a dictionary. Poems, he says, are written at desks. Well, that just ain't true. I've done lots of writing outdoors; for example, my Gift to Be Simple: A Garland for Ann Lee (Liveright/Norton 1975) was largely written lying prone on the diving board at Yaddo one summer. And wasn't Wordsworth in the habit of writing poems sitting under some person's elm or yew tree? And even Coleridge spun off a good one sitting in a lime-tree bower. The list can be extended.

Another of Fussell's dicta--he quotes Northrop Frye-- is that poetry "can only be made out of other poems." Frye is, of course, that old darling of academic critics and theorists, that cool Canadian who has done so much to keep the muse's chastity belt chained and padlocked. To be fair to Fussell, he is partly right: I have frequently complained in print of the ignorance of many poets of any tradition preceding them. It often seems the ideal to appear completely primitive and stupid. But I do at the same time want to keep the option open for the appearance of some singular talent who knows little or nothing of tradition to emerge from some madhouse or outhouse and zap us with splendid poems, created ex nihilo. Shades of Christopher Smart and Alfred Starr Hamilton!

Finally, two more of Fussell's disarming rules: "The individual talent is speechless without the convention." And: "The poet expresses himself by reflecting his uniqueness of the solid backboard, as it were, of the conventional." Pin the tail on which donkey?

III

I have been severe with Fussell's book because, given his reputation, his mass publisher, and the prejudiced, lazy ignorance of most college instructors regarding free-verse poetry, I fear Poetic Meter & Poetic Form, revised edition, will thwart many young readers and potential poets from making their own determinations of the poetry around them. If they blindly accept Fussell's notions--and he has a reputation--they will assume that reading Bly, Duncan, Bukowski, Wakoski, Eshleman, Creeley, Ashbery, Ginsberg, Jonathan Williams is a waste of time. They will sneer rather than explore, despise rather than determine what is valuable in free-verse poets. If I had the space, I could isolate numerous passages from these writers rich in cadence and complex motion.

It seems to me that Fussell chokes the kitten before
he allows it to purr. He locks the zoo before the beast is
brought inside. He knows pudding will be sour before he takes
a taste. Acolytes come to us--poets and teachers--sufficiently
prejudiced. Why not encourage them to develop open-minded-
ness and some disinterestedness? We urgently need theorists
who have cast off the smelly ultra-conservative vestments of
the sixties, and who are willing to adopt the sometimes mad-
dening, self-indulgent, outrageous poetry-clothes/costumes of
the late seventies.

ALFRED STARR HAMILTON:

An American Treasure*

I was unaware of Alfred Starr Hamilton's poetry until
a friend recommended that I obtain the beautiful Jargon Press
edition of The Poems of Alfred Starr Hamilton and read it.
Jonathan Williams published the book in 1970 (it is still in
print), edited by Geof Hewitt, one of David Ray's students.
In the 1960s Ray was teaching at Cornell and editing Epoch.
Hamilton sent carboard cartons full of poems and stories to
Ray (I've seen four or five of these stuffed boxes myself--
all of manuscripts unpublished). Ray kept them, believed in
what he saw, published a sampling in Epoch, and interested
Hewitt in this eccentric man's work. Hewitt finally persuaded
Williams to sit down and read the poems. The result was the
Jargon Press edition, the only sizeable collection of Hamilton's
work anywhere. As Williams says on his jacket blurb: "We
are living in the Badlands. Dorothy's ruby-slippers would get
you across the Deadly Desert. So will these poems."

Hamilton was born in Montclair, New Jersey, in 1914,
graduated from high school, and was a catch-as-catch-can
worker from 1932-1940. He was drafted into the Army, went
AWOL, and was Dishonorably Discharged. As Hewitt notes,
Hamilton sometimes signs his name, adding D. D. as a pri-
vate joke. When The Poems appeared, Hamilton was unem-
ployed, living in a rented room on a thousand dollars a year,
cooking his frugal meals on a hotplate, and doing little else
but writing poems. Shortly after the Jargon Press edition,
Jonathan Williams wrote a guest essay for the New York
Times Book Review about Hamilton. This resulted in a flurry
of interest in the poetry and in Hamilton's welfare. Numerous
people contributed cash to help him out.

Trying to characterize Hamilton's poetry is like trying
to report the color of a chameleon just before he changes hues.

*Reprinted by permission from Little Caesar 12: Overlooked
& Underrated; A special issue edited by Ian Young. Winter
1981/82, pp. 121-130.

Whatever one says about Hamilton seems <u>almost</u> true: He is
an American Primitive, a Grandpa Moses of American poetry
--let's start there.   When we examine the poems, though, we
see that he is more sophisticated than a Grandpa Moses could
ever be--and he is far less detailed and object-enamored.
Further, his grammar isn't always bad, just some of the
time; and he doesn't fit the image of your basic Sunday poet-
farmer busy shovelling manure and pitching hay.   While he
doesn't use many literary allusions (among the rare ones are
<u>Alice in Wonderland</u> and Thoreau), his allusions are some-
times literary--if that makes sense.   Here, for example, in
a simple poem, "Sphinx," Hamilton provides an unexpected
conceptual, literary turn:

THE SPHINX

The sphinx said;
I wanted no hurt
I wanted no pain ever again
I wondered if that was all that was ever meant
And ever happened.

In "Sheets," he improvises on a mundane act, as a primitive
poet might, without using literary models.   The simple task
of ironing becomes a metaphor for his fashioning the moon in
his own image.   Have you ever thought, dear house-wife or
house-husband, of ironing the moon?   Hamilton has, and pro-
duces a stunning visual image of fantasy and affection.   He
invites us to see the poem on its own terms, via his imagina-
tion, which evokes TV cartoons: quick dissolves of forms
into other forms (the fox pursuing road-runner suddenly be-
comes a juggernaut), and a resultant hilarity, a tonic disrup-
tion of our sense of what ought to be.   Here is the poem:

SHEETS

How wonderfully the moon was to have been ironed
last night
And carefully kept the moon in its place
And last night I ironed the moon
And lifted the daffodil back on top of the daisy
And folded the daffodil back on top of the moon
And carefully carried the moon upstairs
And kept the moon in the daffodil closet
Last time I ironed the moon.

One of several poems on angels (he seems to live with them
as easily as old Emanuel Swedenborg did) is a good example
of his irreverent care for normal syntax.   He opens with a

conditional phrase and concludes the poem without ever completing it. The poem remains open-ended. I guess the angel will understand; and since that's most important, Hamilton sees no need to finish it up for inferior mortals who can't think as angels. He warns the angel that if he comes collecting dust in the city he'll be contaminated:

THAT HAS BEEN TO THE CITY

> If you're an angel
> that has been sent to the cleaners
>
> More often than
> a farmer has been sent to gather the harvests
>
> but if you're an angel
> that has been to the city to gather its dust

The popular cliché "sent to the cleaners" might suggest a poet-Grandpa Moses at work; but the implications of the poem are sophisticated; nothing puerile, jejune takes over, as it would in a primitive poet, say in Julia Moore, that Sweet Singer of Michigan.

Well, if Hamilton is not a Grandpa Moses, perhaps he's a Munchkin Prince dropped to earth from Munchkin-land where he's been regaling Billie Burke with his verses. An informed Munchkin might write some of these poems--childlike arcane riddles, delightful non-sequiturs requiring an agile fantasy to decipher them, a splendid play of language--including puns, juxtaposed objects radically evoking one another, sudden jabs of a Rocky Horror Show pain. A golden sun, in one poem, evokes a housewife's golden dishwashing suds: "golden sun's suds." Manpower "is M. P. H. faster than manure-power." "Thank your iron stars, bub" becomes "an iron sea bubble." In "Chinaware" broken dishes become the occasion for a Beware poem; for the broken pieces as they become broken angels are the pieces of our own broken lives:

CHINAWARE

> But they are the fallen angels
> That fell downstairs
> I picked some of them up
> I left the pieces behind
> Others were whole
> But others were more like ourselves
> I wanted these most of all

> Some of the broken parts of our lives that are never
> To be put back together again

Often, one of these Munchkin motifs is a playful sketch fraught
with chilling overtones. The arrangement of the brief poem
"White Mice" is not what we would expect--he's left out some
lines; that's how it sounds. But has he? No. The first line
sets a locale, "in back of the stars." The last two lines jump
logically way ahead to an army of mice who don't seem to
come from "in back of the stars," but rather from somewhere
out in space. The event of the poem, the mice "invading the
moon," excites Hamilton, and he dashes ahead, as a child
might, anxious to express the vivid, off-the-wall image that's
just moved into his head. The title here, as it happens in
so many of Hamilton's poems, is actually the first line of the
poem:

WHITE MICE

> Somewhere in back of the stars,
> But the white mice invading the moon tonight
> Must have come from the Milky Way

Hamilton suits the role also of a Cole Porter, of a
composer of popular songs, unembarrassedly improvising on
the old romantic clichés of June, moon, spoon. Hamilton is
no Emily Dickinson listening to lugubrious Protestant hymns,
risking ear damage from those persistent rhymed tetrameter
quatrains. When Hamilton uses popular music motifs (these
relate also to his fondness for the pop-folk saying or cliché),
he spins them around or stands them on their head, making
them his own. "Swan in June" is an example of his wry use
of pop-song motifs:

> The moon is a swan in June
> The moon can paddle and paddle
> And be the moon all night long.

"June Silver" also owes something to pop music. But how
refreshingly lyrical and original Hamilton is: Images of black
and blue silver, and images of motion, result in a childlike
spontaneity, with a hint of hurt (black and blue):

JUNE SILVER

> I wanted you to know of
> The black June bug
> That buzzed silver

But I wanted you to know of
June silver, of blue silver
During the month of June

I wanted you to know
I rocked in a rocking chair
And all along the silvery vines

I wanted you to know I knew
Of a boy who rocked on top of a rocking horse
And up and down the wiry plains

I wanted you to know of
Blue silver, of black silver
During the month of June silver

In "Walden House," by evoking the spirit of Thoreau, he nicely plays off his penchant for fantasy against reality. Here, at least, it seems that the latter wins out: Hamilton loves mom's apple pie and can tell you the variety of the apples she's used; but he also loves that fantastic, goo-piled pie in the Munchkin sky:

WALDEN HOUSE

Are you a fierce nomad?
Are you a friend of sword and disaster?
Do you know of the only star in heaven?
Do you know of only the sun's daily sword
That pushed the scorched wagon wheels forward?
Are you a goldhunter?
Are you a Scythian mountebank?
Are you a plainsman who fled the plains?
Will you recross the deserted desert airways?
Or are you a Walden traveler?
Do you have your meals at the Walden House?
Do you read your wanton heels to your shoemaker?
Are you a city traveler?

The riddle form, used effectively here, is one of Hamilton's hallmarks. The answers are open, and anything is possible, depending upon the freedom of your imagination, and your willingness to risk that imagination. The lines themselves could easily be adapted for music by some nasal-voiced, country-western plucker.

If the composer of pop songs seems a useful parallel, an even better one is that great iconoclast-composer Charles

Ives. Hamilton is the Charles Ives of American poetry. Ives' cacophonies resemble Hamilton's cacophonies of syntax, grammar, and imagery. And the latter's use of puns and blatantly frayed folk materials would have appealed to Ives, who in sophisticated ways took the prosaic and the mundane from small town American life and made them his own--the brass bands, the popular tunes, the patriotic songs. And, like Hamilton, Ives was always his own man, quite indifferent to the world out there that ignored him. Hamilton keeps himself entirely removed from the American poetry Rat Race; he sends his work nowhere, apparently, except to Epoch magazine.

One more parallel may help to fix our elusive Hamilton butterfly, a parallel with Christopher Smart (1722-1771), the English poet who wrote incredible poems from a madhouse where he was incarcerated most of his life. His Jubilate Agno, with its famous section "For I will consider my cat Jeoffry," has a marvellous fey spirit and inventiveness. His cat becomes a cherub: "For he is of the tribe of Tiger. / For the Cherub Cat is a term of the Angel Tiger." His angels find affinities with Hamilton's; and the latter's use of the serial style, the questions and refrains, and the wise-child, all suggest Smart. Nothing is too illogical or bizarre for either poet. Stellar washings flood through brains, outdistancing readers who expect logical progressions in poems. We follow these poets along the conch-like trammelings of their free-spirited minds; and if we fail to reach the Munchkin castle, or Cat-Jeoffry Heaven, it's our fault. By drawing this parallel, I do not say that Hamilton was consciously imitating Smart, or that he even knows Smart's work. What I am saying is that a tradition exists for the poetry Hamilton writes; and if we are to appreciate his contributions, anything we can do to place him in a tradition may prevent us from dismissing him as an inept, hopeless eccentric.

So far, I have focused on Hamilton's playful side. My attempt to evoke other lives and personages in order to understand him has been playful. But there is a telling sense of the tragic and the frustrating in his work; despite all the stars and the angels and the miracles of colors and forms changing before one's amazed and startled eyes, he never pretends either that God's in his Heaven or that all's right with the world. In "Stalk" he says that he hopes to leave "a doubt in the mind of mankind." And, in "A Crust of Bread," he wonders about his being a poet--he always wanted to be a bird. His concern is for the pains of birds, even for the despised starling--he cares "first of all" that they are fed. In "Travel

Along," he warns us that our fantasies may lull us into be-
lieving we are doing more than just "rolling along" through
life only half-awake. His pure iconoclasm and distaste for
a hostile society erupts in "Rhododendron": "I could have
written on the back of a parchment leaf /The story of our
terrible municipal lives." The personal pain aroused by his
dishonorable discharge appears in several poems. In one,
"False Faces," he berates G. I. beer as a form of poison
ivy:

> "Even Himmler who'd accused us of rape
> Gasped at ivy 3. 2. American poisoning"

In "Deign to Design," a chilling sense of lost hope accretes
around the image of a steel pin, possibly a part of the sol-
dier's rifle:

> If
> it's
> a
> steel pin
>
> It
> isn't
> to
> dig your grave with
>
> If
> it's
> dug
> already

In the following pair of poems, his personal bitterness is a
vivid loathing; the Army has him fast by the buttons:

> IT'S ARMY BALONEY
>
> Is hatred baloney?
> And getting one's teeth into it
> And getting one's teeth out of it
> And never forgiving any of them for any of it

> HOLD FAST, ARMY BUTTONS
>
> Ironically, those are brass buttons
> that are made of holdfast iron

> Dumbfounded, those are brass knuckles
> to have been tied to just straitjackets
>
> Those are a tyrant's muscles
> to your best vest buttons

We may take our pick of which of these figures is the
real Alfred Starr Hamilton--Grandpa Moses, the Prince of
the Munchkins, Cole Porter, Charles Ives, or Christopher
Smart. That no single figure entirely works is evidence, I
think, of his elusive originality. He isn't likely to stand up to
show us the real Hamilton. Like a good pixie (or leprechaun)
he'll keep leaping aside once you think you've grabbed him.
Perhaps, though, that's how a true "gentleman of our dark-
ness" is supposed to behave. In one of his best poems,
"Guardian," he does stay still long enough to write a poem
about the poet (himself) as a beautiful rooster, guardian
of the dawn; Bo-Peep's pasture land is brought into tune and
harmony, and the world, through the illusions of the poem,
is temporarily secure:

GUARDIAN

> Contrast Rooster's white feathers
> With the greater surrounding darkness,
> But he sings with all his blue might;
> An iconoclast of old scoffs at the ghosts of
>   the pastures,
> Bespeaks of himself, stalks and struts in the
>   eerie morning moonlight;
> But he sings with all his white might,
> Because truthfully he is our gentleman of the
>   darkness,
> And out in Bo Peeps pasture land, and morning
>   miles away,
> He is the savior, He is the guardian of the new
>   dawn.

ON SLAVES AND MASTERS:

Leland Hickman's Tiresias: Great Slave Lake Suite*

To opt entirely for the autobiographical in so ostensibly
personal a book as this (the protagonist throughout the suite
is "Lee Hickman") is tricky.   When you've decided you've
picked a pineapple, you see that you've actually grabbed a
pumpkin; or, the moment you've seen the protagonist as an
invention, you're not so sure.   "Hickman" ends up having the
normal pair of balls.

Great Slave Lake Suite has to be one of the most ambi-
tious poems of growth and sexual history ever attempted by
an American poet.   As a work in progress, it begins some-
where in the middle and has not concluded.   Hickman may be
writing this poem for the rest of his life.   It recalls a spate
of earlier writers--Whitman, Joyce, Shelley, Hopkins, Dylan
Thomas, Thomas Wolfe.   Yet, it is more than a pastiche of
echoes.   Hickman's turbulent, even torrential, energies of
emotion and language make the work entirely his.

The Great Slave Lake lies in the remote reaches of
Canada's Northwest Territory; and Hickman goes there with
a guide-friend to camp and fish.   Their progress into the
wilderness occasions reflections and memories of "Lee's"
adolescence and young manhood.   He grew up in Bakersfield,
California.   His father, vicious and remote, bestowed far
more whippings than embraces.   Early boyhood homosexual
experiences, as well as later ones in New York City, are
sharply described.   And there's a moving liaison with a wo-
man Ginny, who is finally mistreated.   Hickman demolishes
her apartment and takes off, occasioning suffering and pain
all around.

There's an uncanny undercurrent of violence through-
out Great Slave Lake Suite; in fact, the thin skin over pus-

*Used by permission of Small Press Review (July 1981) pp.
6-7.

tules about to erupt is a dominant theme, as are the recal-
citrance and obstreperousness of Lee the child continuing on
in the adult Lee: He seems to anticipate the sexual and
other punishments he'll receive for being naughty. His lovers
are often images of daddy with fist or board raised, ready to
smash the buttocks of his quivering son.

Hickman writes in the rhapsodic imperative mood. In
fact, this mood dominates. Here is one moment:

> ... in
> shitsong in self wallow I
> beg you beat me let me swallow you & strict eyes of my Lion please
> search me how to kill.
> this furious beating beggd,
> judgd abject we go,
> daredevil Lee & Lion tailgating, los feliz western in brea gardner, scatter
> my limits, boundspreadeagled, drunken, druggd, gaggd, home.

His father's whippings seem to have set cruel perimeters for
the son's psyche. Throughout the suite, his pleas for
whippings are intense. One has the feeling that Lee will
never finish the business with his brutal father. Here is
another powerful moment. The Lion as incredible sex-master
fuses shortly (I think) with the man in the tie, another aloof,
inaccessible sex-tormenter. Lee lies

> in subtle husht boy-thin
> body beneath numinous ill gaze under lamplight, undoes
> cufflinks, tie, I reach out to touch, no you can never touch me,
> doffs
> shirt shoes socks unbuckles belt-
> buckle my cock up bright o hoist me higher in my harsh malign
> fire this
> ragged rasa for stern aloof beauty whose
> tight black slacks inch low down slow over hard rock silence....

Even in passages of a diffused beauty, as in this re-
collection of his childhood when he stayed overnight with an-
other lad, the powerful, assertive adjectives suggest a vol-
canic psychic tension trying to play itself out--a kind of
shucking of his puberty. The intimacy he feels for David is
realistic, keen, and sensuous:

> I climb into David's damp bed.
> I gaze at bony ribcage rise, fall, sleepwarm
> skin so moongray sweaty. in kidsnore,

inch by inch slithering under shushthin
sheet until held breath hovers over
kidstink pajamaflap & my stretcht tongue
quivers, feathertipt, tickles kidsalt.
he stirs he sleeps, these brave cubscout
lips slip soft-snapdragon-tight on
wiggleless pollywog, sweetpea-pale,
hairless, nutless. I sneak to the pillow.
    David asleep. mouth open. moist
    blue eyelids. blind, still.

As in a musical suite, here, too, themes recur. One
motif is primary, and is shaded off into Anglo-Saxon diction--
an apostrophe/imperative to the old Tiresias of ancient legend:
"Sothsegger, sothsegger, scry...." Tiresias is the inspirer
of the poem and a sightless (but seeing) guide to Hickman's
passing through joys and horrors of puberty and adult homo-
sexuality. The imperatives, recurring often, serve to place
the poem in an old tradition of powerful visionary poetry. I
think the device works.

Tiresias, of course, was the ancient prophet who had
the temerity to watch Athena (or, Artemis, in some forms of
the tale) taking a bath. For his gaucherie he was struck
blind; but, pitying him, the gods gave him the gift of prophecy,
with the codicil that none of his prophecies would be believed.
He himself was born of magic, and sprang from the dragon's
teeth sown by old Cadmus. He is an image of the poet in a
hostile society. As a Shelleyan "legislator for mankind" his
prophecies go unheeded. Tennyson, in a great monologue, has
Tiresias proclaim a warning, also ignored by his audience,
that "the tyranny of one" is "prelude to the tyranny of all."
And, further, "the tyranny of all" leads "backward to the
tyranny of one." In part, Hickman sees himself as a Tiresian
figure, as poet and homosexual, a pariah to the mainstream of
his culture. Until all conditions of love are honored, he in-
sists, and the voice of the poet is valued in the land, tyrants
of prejudice and persecution (popular opinion) and its crippling
edicts (issued by the government, and by repressive social
and religious groups) will persist.

I read Great Slave Lake Suite taking notes, making con-
siderations. And I am left with some crucial questions: Will
the completed poem incorporate sufficient physical details of
the Canadian wilderness to balance the vividness of the scenes
recollected from American places? We see a few Indians and
a lake; but the Canadian setting remains elusive and sketchy.

Despite the book's having been nominated for the prestigious Los Angeles _Times_ yearly book-awards for poetry, will _Tiresias_ find the readers it deserves? Since the publisher is one of our small presses, distribution will be a problem. Also, the open and persistent homosexuality and the lavish invention of the diction may dissuade readers. I am not saying that I approve--reading Hickman requires the focus one expends on the best poetry. Here is one bravura passage, for example, amazing for its piling of charged word on charged word, all moving towards what strikes me as an intense self-exorcism:

> forlorn in a severance rain from root,
> then to slave austerely to wail down insanity into my singing rages
> pleading stop stop me enthralld
> by avidya's big boot death grum fugue death dry fountain death pig pouf
> turdblossom cringing anonymous slurp I
> beg trappt braying hate me dont hate me this is my
> song. . . .

And as for the sado-masochism, that is an element most of us possess to one degree or another, I would guess: The pecking orders we arrive at in our jobs and professions; the frequency with which we hang our metaphoric tails between our legs and avoid direct eye contact with someone we feel is better than we are. Gerard Manley Hopkins celebrated the condition in his slave/master relationship to Jesus, whom he pled with to come and lay his Lion-limb firmly on his quivering body. An ecstatic submission.

Hickman's testament is visceral, haunting, and generously spread. He creates passages of an overwhelming beauty. His _Suite_ is worth great care.

THE CHILD IN THE HOUSE:

Donald Justice's Selected Poems*

Flawless poets are hard to criticize. And the casual figure Donald Justice promotes--a constant throughout a career noted for its slim output--does not invite us to quarrel with him, or to shake the poetry-bunny very hard by its ears. Justice's modesty is rare in American writing, where poet-egos clamor for attention in the kudzu fields of Georgia, the cornfields of Iowa, the scrub pines of Long Island, the sculpture saltmarsh of San Francisco, and the hepatitis-tainted breakers of Bolinas. The critical attention poets receive often seems in direct ratio to the loudness of their personal racket. A Donald Justice who murmurs in a quiet room, echoing the sighs of potted ferns, who willingly steps aside for noisier and more flamboyant younger poets, seems almost too diffident by comparison with the screamers. It's easy to ignore nice guys; they give you the impression that they won't dislike you if you do. It has been too easy for critics to accept Justice's passivity--his "Self Portrait as Still Life" (emphasis mine) says it.

Justice is in love with mirrors and windows. His often Matisse-like views are curiously de-peopled; he is the poet of the scene framed and contained, the poet of the non-event: his persons are either dead, have moved away, or are sitting about quietly like fumed oak cupboards, beds, or escritoires. Justice is fond of positioning people in stasis. "The Missing Person" utilizes both mirror and hollow-man. A "person" turns himself into the authorities as a missing person. He tries to complete a questionnaire, but is unable to: His life has been a series of blank spaces. He hopes a mirror will help him out; but all he sees is "what is missing"--himself. Justice's mirrors never distort; they are of

*Reprinted by permission of American Book Review, Vol. 4, no. 2 (January-February 1982), p. 15.

the parlor, not the fun-house.   While they may not tell one
very much, they reflect back images you may not care to
see.

Justice's non-person spends much of his time waiting.
He shuts his eyes seeking to imagine a dark interior "where
something might still happen. "   Suicide is always a possibility.
(One of Justice's best poems is "The Suicides, " commemo-
rating half a dozen self-slaughterers.) He sees an open razor
on a marble washstand, hears drips, but does not know whe-
ther it is water or blood. He waits for something to move
him.

A superb poem of departure (on a disappearance from
life and from the poem), "Variations for Two Pianos, " turns
on this refrain: "There is no music now in all Arkansas. "
Thomas Higgins, piano teacher at a small college full of
"brash, self-important brick, " has departed the state, taking
his pianos with him.   Whether Higgins has died or has simply
moved elsewhere hardly matters.   What does is the original,
rather winsome music of the poem.   The ambiguity is part
of the fun.

Another small masterpiece is "Anonymous Drawing. "
Notable is the absence of the painter from art history.   Ano-
nymity seems to be a condition desired by Justice for his
ideal poet-artist, a desire expressed in various ways through-
out his book.   Justice's anonymous Perugian artist and his
portrait of a Negro holding the reins of his master's horse
is lost to posterity, as is the person intended as the center
of the scene, the nobleman owning both horse and slave.
The problem, Justice speculates, occurs off-stage where the
nobleman was busy tending to some estate matter or to his
toilette.   Irritated by the delay, the painter settles the score
by proceeding with the picture before the nobleman arrives.
Even if the latter were now to rush up all wet and panting,
he would be too late.   The poem, a wonderful tour-de-force,
is in wildly varied free-verse couplets, an impressive dis-
play of craftsmanship.   Both Renaissance painter and noble-
man are hollow-men, abstractions seen only by their being
absent and missing.

The phenomenon of the poet distilled (bleached) from
his poems turns on a hoary aesthetic concept, that art en-
dures while life is brief.   With Justice, though, the idea is
more Shelleyan than classical.   Enamored (and often bemused)
by his sedentary graying self, Justice invites more whimpers

than he does bangs. He is more Cynaraean than he is grandly
philosophical; viz., Ernest Dowson, that superb but limited
cameo lyricist of the English 1890s, whom Justice resembles.
Justice appears as an unabashed Romantic in many ways; his
tremulous psyche dominates most of his poems, and his world
turns on his own ego. Even when his will is grayest, it re-
mains a presence, if somewhat hollowed. And his playful
"chance" poems (see "The Success," "The Assassination,"
"The Confession," and the pair of sonatinas from Departures)
interestingly imply the absence or anonymity of a writer who
remains nonetheless paradoxically present, as an "arranger"
or first-secretary to the aging muse.

One of the clichés of contemporary self-help psychology
is that by playing passive and self-effacing we are really
masking sizeable egos. Hence, a seeming weakness becomes
a strength of the sort that dominates others. In Justice,
moments of private rage and venom are almost non-existent;
they would ruffle the bushes of his self-concealment. And
yet there is one poem, "The Furies," where Justice trashes
critics who disliked his first book.

The final poem of the book, "Childhood," appearing in
a book for the first time, should probably be read at the out-
set by a reader coming to Justice new. The poem begins as
Justice spins a child's globe of the world, an action which
triggers other early recollections: His grandfather peels
oranges on a spread-out Sunday paper, on top of the Katzen-
jammer Kids; he remembers drowsy afternoons when he sat
"ignored" among his relatives, observing the "myriad tiny
suns" in the deep, polished mahogany chairs. At an ornate
movie palace, a locale for delicious solitudes, the painted
ceiling was a real sky fraught with stars. The distant glow
of the everglades ablaze suggested a "smoky rose of ob-
livion," a consummation somehow the child seems to have
wished, devoutly, like ceasing upon a midnight with no pain,
a release from the awful boredom of childhood.

Justice's fascination with his child may suggest the old
Wordsworthian notion of the child as father of the man. Jus-
tice's child is not, however, the father of the man; he is ra-
ther somehow the man. The child lives intact, inside the
man, as a still vibrant presence who knows prolonged illness,
loneliness, and stiff hours practicing the piano. Yet, he knew
physical comfort and the amenities of a solidly middle-class
family. Meaning in the boy's life occurred through music,
fantasy (viz., the eyes in the mahogany) and rhymes and songs.

The cadences of the latter must have reassured him, enrich-
ing his fantasies in his isolated world.   Important vestiges of
that music remain throughout Justice's work.   "Counting the
Mad, " an early poem, is an echoing of one of the most fa-
mous of all children's poems, "This little pig went to market. "
But there are startling differences: madmen in straightjackets,
catatonic folk, and other incarcerated persons convinced that
they are birds and dogs.   These people never get out to go to
market.   What the mad retain is the power to cry NO   NO
NO   NO (all the way home) against their keepers' brutaliza-
tions and the horrors rampant within their own psyches.   This
is a stunning use of a simple form for complex purposes.

The fate then the mad most loathe, as does the child
in his empathy for the mad, is that they may grow into "or-
dinary" men.   This fate Justice's child seems to have escaped.
At points, Justice the craftsman touches the cryptic beauty of
that earlier adult-child poet Robert Louis Stevenson.   Steven-
son's garden of verse is a parallel writing out of the life of a
gifted child, bed-ridden with a lingering disease, isolated
from playmates, and forced to depend on his own devices to
fight self-pity and boredom.

The assembling of a poem for Justice is an order of
game--viz. , his fondness for villanelles, rondeaux, odes, and
sonatinas.   Even practicing the piano, another recurring
motif, is a child's enterprise of endless repetitions teaching
patience, craft, and an architectonics of form and emotion.
During these practice sessions, Justice informs us in his
homage to Wallace Stevens, he avoided "the darker notes, "
thereby perpetuating the cycle of the child who rebels, who
must be pursued and caught and whipped down the street
("but gently") home.   The man, then, still cries out after all
these years for someone to care enough to seek him in some
vacant weed-filled lot where he waits out of bounds, risking
punishment--harsh evidence that he is loved.

Boy and man merge beautifully in "Men at 40. "   While
it may be impossible to accept Justice's idea that to be forty
is to be on the threshold of senility, the motif works if one
sees the child in this aging male, forced to be older than his
years.   Again, Justice finds the image of a mirror useful.
Men gazing deep into mirrors "rediscover" themselves as they
were as boys imitating their fathers, tying neckties and shav-
ing.   As these males gaze at their boy-selves, they are filled
with the "twilight sound" of crickets, which burgeons into a
crescendo overwhelming the woods "behind their mortgaged
houses. "

Finally, Justice is a poet who loves the old folks, and seems comfortable remembering them as they parallel his own aging. Justice's poet seems like a child alone among a houseful of self-preoccupied, aging adults. Even as a young poet, Justice seemed fascinated by old men and ladies. He reminds one of Alfred Tennyson who as a fairly young man assumed the identities of the aged Ulysses and Tithonus to reflect his private angst. In The Summer Anniversaries (some of the poems were probably written before Justice was thirty) aging ladies wait at their twilit windows for a lover to appear. One expects old John Crowe Ransom to wing up the path. But the lover never comes. In another poem, old men hang out in a freezing park in Florida; they are like thermometers "stuck ... at zero everlastingly." One poem reviews various dead members on the poet's family tree--"a simple chinaberry" tree, Justice modestly says, among the vast oaks of more pretentious and considerable families.

To step further into his own aging is for Justice an easy matter. He sees himself as a thin man who falls asleep and becomes a horizon. In "Fragment: To a Mirror," he is as bland as the bland facade of the glass he gazes into. In his sanitized revery there's a trick of mirrors: The mirror reflects a fragment of a Miami beach-scape, much as one would see it through the window of a painting by Matisse, of a scene at Antibes. The vision evokes a memory of a boyhood spent in Miami where the landscape was full of exotic flowers and trees. The primary motif of "Mirror" is a state of semi-nothingness, which the aging poet confronts in his mirror. The end he desires is "rest," the oblivion preceding his eventual death. His "Variations on a Text by Vallejo," which begins "I will die in Miami in the sun," actually treats his demise whimsically. Donald Justice dies, but his dog keeps on quivering beneath a chair, afraid of a storm; his son keeps on reading without speaking; his wife continues to nap. As the gravediggers cover him over with black Miami marl, they spit and turn abruptly away, "out of respect."

Like his Tremayne, in "The Mild Despair of Tremayne" and "The Contentment of Tremayne," Justice loves armchair mordancies, as he calls them. These are those vaguely depressing thoughts occasioned by meditating on one's mortality and by a distaste for direct confrontations with life. Tremayne asks little, and is grateful for the dim street-light still shining outside his room window, and for the "pale rectangles" of meaning formed thereby. Throughout his wasting, glimmers the face and form of that precocious child, antidote

to the illness, isolation, and indifference of adults experienced
by that child.

The most powerful of all Justice's poems on the child-
adult is "Heart," the first poem in Night Light. The poet
seems to want to extricate the child who has taken residence
inside his heart. He wants to reason with the child, to con-
vince him that it is time for each to go his separate way.
Justice sees himself as an "antique, balding spectacle" who
stammers, as the child once did, "with all the seedy inno-
cence of an overripe pomegranate." For the time being, as
he hears the child beating his little fist against the walls of
his heart, wanting to break out, Justice recalls the times
he's had to walk the streets to retrieve his child, restoring
him to his safe parlor inside the heart, a presence the poet
seems to need, both for the sanity of his person and the health
of his verse. Once again, at the end of the poem, Justice
allows the child permission to flee the man, thereby perpetua-
ting the cycle of the child who rebels, who must be pursued,
caught, and whipped down the street ("but gently") home.
Alas, the adults who might miss him seem either dead, pre-
occupied, or incapacitated.

To write so insistently on aging, death, and passive
memory, as Justice does, is to risk boring the reader. An
easy melancholy has been fashionable in verse since Shelley's
charnel-house days, and numerous poets still use the mode.
What saves Justice are his skill at honing old forms, his
sense of humor (which I read as yet more evidence of his
general diffidence towards himself and his art), and by his
use of the persistent child inside him. The latter serves as
a window onto the poet's adult self--or, more accurately, as
a mirror situated in the poet's heart from which the child
casts images from the past forward, and stimulates the poet's
stark personal meditations. The image, I feel, better almost
than any other, illuminates Justice's work.

LIFE IS BETTER OFF THE FLOOR:

Kenneth Koch's The Burning Mystery of Anna in 1951*

"If we go on as we go on," Mrs. Thoroughfare com-
    mented as dinner
was ceremoniously announced, "we'll be almost too
    ornate!"--Valmouth

"I know your creative taste! I rely on you."--Con-
    cerning the Eccentricities of Cardinal Pirelli.

"Come nearer, Charlie. Is that ink, on your head,
    I see?"
"Probably.... Father often wipes his pen in my
    hair."--Valmouth

"Oh! help me, Heaven," she prayed, "to be decorative
    and to do right!"
--Mademoiselle de Nazianzi, The Flower Beneath the
    Foot. †

1.

Mlle de Nazianzi's prayer could suffice as a prayer also
for Kenneth Koch as he appears in The Burning Mystery of
Anna in 1951. His decorative thrust, in the first poems
here, is paradoxically a kind of reductionism--he writes some-
where in between baby primer talk and what sounds like Ger-
trude Stein babbling. The ornateness results from his trying
to sound cute; he's a Carol Channing of poetry, a damosel
Ronald Firbank would have greatly admired. (Wasn't Chan-
ning really Firbank in drag?) If the hairs in your nose (with
or without inkstains) could write poems, some of these are
what they might be like. At the same time, like Mlle de

*Reprinted by permission from Bachy, No. 18 (1981), pp.
  315-317.
†Headquotes from Ronald Firbank's novels.

Nazianzi, Koch seeks to "do right." He's obsessed with meta-
physical matters, attracting attention by a generous use of
tag words: "things," "these things," "maybe," and "perhaps"
are examples. But he doesn't go quite as far as Firbank's
Cardinal Pirelli does, "attempting to attract attention, in in-
fluential places, by the unnecessary undulation of his loins,
and by affecting strong scents and attars." Perhaps Koch
lacks real daring. He does a bit of hoofing though--in an
ambitious, only partially successful, sequence of nine free-
verse sonnets, where he discovers that "living and creating
are a kind of tap dancing." Fred or Ginger? Ginger or
Fred?

In "Our Hearts," this "sonnet" sequence, Koch loves
the effete effect. ("I'm tired, true, child," says Firbank's
Primate about to chase a naked choir boy around the church;
"but not of jasmine.") Koch sees, not very originally, that
we are born into, walk around in, examine, and think of the
"Mystery" of life, until eventually we find ourselves in love
"or in some crazy religion, in a church at sunset." An
adolescent preoccupation. As Lady Parvula de Panzoust says:
"I can't bear to think of the man I love under some cow's
chidderkins." But the dance, whether under or over the
dairy-cow's choice parts, is Koch's primary motif: We should
all be dancing, not just tripping here and there in pursuit of
our favorite husky farmer-milkmen, rich and mauve aristo-
crats, or Russian dairy-girls. We need a few band-aids for
the committed life, to see us through the vicissitudes, so that
we shall all enjoy Firbankian lilac-life passages: " 'I want
mauve sweetpeas,' she listlessly said."

Trying to say things simply is one of these band-aids;
but, alas, while yum-yum, yum-yum simple ways may be
"immensely enjoyable," they are not often the explanations
we require. Playfulness is another band-aid: "The sun is
a basket of wash / Let down for our skin, and germs are
all around us like cash," Koch writes. And, Ecstasy, if
we can develop same, helps us patch over wounds. Unlike
the Marchioness of Macarnudo who realizes that her "joie de
vivre is finished," but is amazed still by how she "goes on,"
our elan exists so that we can be happy. In the sixth sonnet
Koch develops a winsome set of lines that read like multiple
choice test questions. The playfulness leads to one of his
best examples of G. Stein-writing:

> It is the problem of living and not being the first one
> And yet wanting to do as much as that first one, and,
> because

there is all that train behind one, more.

Even though the riot police are outside the window, despite
our knowing we are in some vanguard of life, we can still
play it safe and feel zippy. We don't have to go out into the
streets, and we can avoid many of the germs in the air.
Yes, and we can keep hoping to find the answer, one so
elusive we really don't know what the question is! " 'Why
can't they all behave?' the Cardinal asked himself plaintively,
descrying Lucrezia, his prized white squirrel sidling shyly
towards him. "

2.

" 'T'were far better often to be a primrose in the
wilderness than a
polyanthus in a frame. "--Mrs. Tooke, Valmouth.

When he writes best, Koch manages to anchor the con-
ceptual nicely to the literal. In "The Simplicity of the Un-
known Past" he creates a diptych of alternating moments--out-
side the window, inside the window. The poem works, fasten-
ing to a closing image of a farm machine starting up. On the
other hand, "Fate" is one of his worst, most-mannered, most
trivial poems. The tone is dizzy, coy, sweet; one craves
for a good fart to humanize the chummy giggliness of the
scene. ("I can't explain," says Firbank, "but I adore all that
mauvishness about him. ") Everything is mauve, that Oscar
Wildean tint for the precious and esoteric. What Firbank
sensed (and said) that "the chic" is "such a very false reli-
gion, " Koch doesn't always see. Koch's poem with its Winnie
the Pooh-esqueries chatters on about friendly dos with Larry
Rivers, Frank O'Hara, John Ashbery, and Jane Freilicher.
Nothing much happens; in fact, I gather that some of the
poem's charm is supposed to froth up from the seeping capil-
laries of a brain that can't remember much of anything that
was said, except a kind of intimate baby talk: The friends
seem to lick one another all over; each line is another scented
saliva-swirl. ("The Marchioness will be birched tomorrow,
and not today. ") Koch gives us information we need of a lit-
erary movement only after everything else, including laundry
slips and restaurant receipts, are published--gossip, dizzy
imprecisions: "autobiography all / The time plowing for-
ward...." Ahem. And some readers and historians will won-
der whether that Yale crowd was that much of a movement
anyhow--perhaps it was more in the nature of a briefly daz-

zling gigue.   Whatever.   Pretty slim furrows from the plough,
folks, not much of that old plough-down sillion-shine.   Here
is one of the cartoon-balloon moments:

> And John said Um hum and hum and hum I
> Don't remember the words Frank said Un hun
> Jane said An han and Larry if he
> Was there said Boobledyboop so always
> Said Larry or almost and I said
> Aix-en-Provence me new sense of
> These that London Firenze Florence
> Now Greece and un hun um hum an
> Han boop Soon I was at Larry's....

"Fate" is a very occasional ode!

3.

> "What I want is an English maid with Frenchified
> fingers"--Queen Thleeanouhee in The Flower Beneath
> the Foot.

The title poem, "The Burning Mystery of Anna in 1951"
has eight parts, held together most loosely by the mauve rib-
bon of adolescent sexuality.   Koch seems to have been a bit
delayed in his growing up.   Most of the parts occur in France.
Most are touched with Koch's characteristic wispy cravings
for the non-events in his life.   And the Laureate of the Non-
Event I dub him, a Possum Player Cum Life.   As Firbank
notes, "You can't judge of Egypt by Aïda"; and, so, dear
reader, you can't judge of France by "The Burning Mystery
of Anna."   Koch's ego is the primary subject--and his almost
desperate craving to be liked and accepted.   And I don't know
whether this was who he was in the fifties; or, if he is still
that way, charming the panties and jock-straps off us via his
immense cheer and feyness.   Please remember that he seems
to see his poems as part of his "autobiography / all the time
ploughing forward."   He's playful, too.   ("Are you ready for
your Quail, sir?"--Cardinal Pirelli.)   He imitates Creeley:
"Wandering along through the twisting streets of the city /
One day as I was, as is my habit."   He plays also with a
primeresque, humoresque manner: "It was a sunny morning.
/ Sunny sunny sunny sunny sunny."   Occasionally there's a
note of pain, but one that seldom hurts much--viz., the germs
in "Our Hearts"; and here a "keen bursitis" lights up a window.

Koch is bright, biking with his French girlfriend
through Cezanne country. He seems to want to be what he
thinks the French want: a Boy-Intellectual (the opposite of
the American Boob-Boy). ("The Cardinal answered, delib-
erating if a lad of such alertness and perception might be
entrusted to give him a henna shampoo.") Various non-events
occur. Koch's insights into the starchlessness of himself are
refreshingly unsparing. " 'The mistress, I presume, is with
the scourge,' the butler announced."

4.

" 'I could almost envy the fleas in the Cardinal's
vestments,' Sister Ursula declared. "--The Flower
Beneath the Foot.

The major portion of The Burning Mystery of Anna,
excluding the prose diary-like pieces on Morocco, are potent
contrasts to the flipping-flitting about of "flitter-mice" (we
call them "bats") poems early in the book. Koch now aban-
dons (or develops beyond) his earlier "vaguely distraught air
of a kitten that had seen visions" (Firbank describing Felix
Ganay, Chief-dancing-choir-boy) towards a winning maturity.
Even a poem as ridden with abstractions--here a few flitter-
mice would help--he moves with impressive flair among im-
ages of shadow/light, and develops a marvellous image of a
lioness of language who via the shadows between her teeth in-
forms her newly-roaring cub of the vicissitudes of life.

Brilliant, and unreservedly so, is "The Problem of
Anxiety." As King William, "tucking a few long hairs back
into his nose," said to his Son the Prince, "We had always
thought you too lacking in initiative," and was proved wrong
(the Prince married a black woman), so we too, thinking that
Koch would remain fey and playful only, were wrong. Il
Penseroso and The Anatomy of Melancholy come to mind--
there's an old-fashioned quality about Koch's lengthy "Anxiety."
The poem takes off from what sounds much like a bright un-
dergraduate essay on the theme--and as it grows intimate and
loquacious, it leans out into its own music and power. There's
a Mary Worth situation about a man who gives up the presi-
dency of a bank for a girl, and a soap tycoon who can make
tons of money if he doesn't tell his investors that a big ship-
ment of soap is arriving. He examines (at times hilariously)
these anxiety inducers: causes of anxiety for Artists and for
Businessmen--the general sense of mortality and impending

doom; feeling that one is no good; the fear of failing at some-
thing. The important thing is to keep yourself off the floor--
anxiety can throw you down there and leave you writhing. Koch
seems really to care that we triumph over anxiety (all six
causes). And he is engaging as he turns the knife towards
himself at the end, by sharing the anxiety (welling) he feels
writing the poem: "Well, my /Headache is worse now and
on both sides, still mild though, and I am not on the floor."

"The Boiling Water" is also good. Koch's imagination
is in top form as he takes a commonplace event and spins
relevancies. (" 'It's queer, dear, how I'm lonely!' he ex-
claimed, addressing the ancient Zurbarans flapping austerely
in their frames.") Koch's inventions of language and insight
are vital and alert. His Primer Style works, and his caring
affectionate voice is a real tonic for the reader. I shall
think of this poem each time I boil water for my coffee, or
attempt to bring one of my own poems to a boil. ("My tongue
is over-prone perhaps to metaphor.") Koch asks a germane
question: "Who put the boiling potentiality into water?" The
water is always "serious" when it is boiling. "At the Post
Office one day she had watched a young man lick a stamp.
His rosy tongue had vanquished her."

5.

> "Alighting like some graceful exotic bird from the
> captivity of a dingy cage, Lady Parvula de Panzoust
> hovered a moment before the portal as much to
> manipulate her draperies, it seemed, as to imbreathe
> the soft sweet air."--Valmouth.

Koch's final poem, the longest in the book, is "To
Marina." There's an undercurrent here, present in earlier
poems, about loving "rosy tongues" from a distance; but, be-
cause of one's personal feelings of sexual inadequacy, there's
a failure to act daringly--the result, a possum-playing, to be
regretted later. Koch details his passionate oscillations (and
a few osculations) around (and with) a Russian girl he knew
in the 1950s in New York City. He "wasn't ready" for her.
He hurts with love, frustration, his injured sense of beauty
in the world, his penchant for saying no. His ego is the
central theme ("Thus will egotism, upon occasion, eclipse
morality outright."--Cardinal Pirelli). His "abject stupidity"
seen from the perspective of twenty-six years, irritates him,
flooding him with renewed pain. Koch manages an amazing im-
mediacy: the books they read, the girl's seriousness, Koch's

wish that everything be pleasant, scenes in a Chinese restaurant, in a friend's apartment. He writes numerous poems to Marina over the years. She's a kind of useful Muse ("The illustrious Eva /Schnerb/ ... only closed her notebooks towards Dawn, when the nib of her pen caught fire. "--Flower) In pain, Koch hangs onto a chair to keep from collapsing. His humor saves him, as flashes of Koka-Koka Humor appear: "I love you," he declares, "as a sheriff searches for a walnut"--which means about as much, I guess, as Gertrude Stein's "The envelopes are on all the fruit trees. " He recalls Marina's special broken English; he makes her feel "nawble" (noble). Koch's free-verse style is arranged in loosely structured stanzas: "I would never rush my art, especially wif you. No; oh no. You, my dear, are my most beautiful triumph!" --Mrs. Yajnavalkya to Mrs. Tooke. Koch writes with urgency as a poet possessed, exorcising feelings too-long haunting and suppressed. His poem crackles. Powerful emotions oscillate through the closing section, resolving the hurt and guilt he has harbored over the years. This is Koch at his best. "To Marina" is a moving poem. Here Koch "concentrates" his roses, achieving energy and power. *

In conclusion, then, I find this book a maddening composite of the self-indulgent and the fine. As a totality it fails (the Moroccan work is alas, for me, an unfortunate interruption). Yet the poems on anxiety, boiling water, and Marina are among the best of Koch's poetry. I wish he had waited for more poems like these, before publishing the book. Why is it that poets of renown sometimes feel that they are absolved from publishing books with the kind of integration and force we expect from lesser-known poets? They rush gatherings of works full of disharmonies and irregularities into print. Where are their editors? Koch's ego, clad in Firbankian mauve, steps too far ahead of the poet too often--for my taste, at least.

---

*Cardinal Pirelli, just before his fatal nude pursuit of the naked choir boy, has been reading the Arabian Nights: " 'If only Oriental literature sprawled less, was more concise!' he observes. 'It should concentrate its roses,' he told himself, glancing out, inquiringly, into the nave. "

THE DIANE ARBUS OF AMERICAN POETRY:

Cynthia Macdonald's (W)Holes*

Various artists have taken the motif of the monster, the retarded human being, the carnival freak and the sexual outcast as a vivid, sometimes brutal means of shocking us into truths about ourselves. Bosch and Brueghel were there early, as were the great Cologne masters of the Middle Ages. Their inspirations were religious, their pictures intended to ready us for Eternity as the apocalypse approached. There were later artists--Flaubert, Hugo, Constantin Guys (the aquarelles of monsters and devils invading Paris by night), James Ensor (the great tableaux of skeletons and masked carnival figures), Soutine (his portraits of mad men and women and flayed fowl and beasts), and Francis Bacon (floggings of the human body and soul).

Renowned also for a similar art, and for the tragedy of her life, is Diane Arbus. Her photographs seem to be an important influence on, or inspiration behind, Cynthia Macdonald's new poems. Macdonald features this quotation from Arbus: "Nothing is ever the same as they said it was. / It's what I've never seen before that I recognize." By evoking freaks, hermaphrodites, and carnival figures, Macdonald acknowledges Arbus's vision. The result is in homage to, rather than in slavish imitation of, the photographer. Macdonald's earlier books, Transplants and Amputations, make clear that her world is a vast carnival of dwarfs, cripples, hunchbacks, and variously smashed persons. She has an unforgettable power, and plays upon our own non-freak willingness to snicker at those less fortunate than ourselves. By doing so we are trapped in our own snickerings. The question then becomes: Who are the real freaks? Well, folks, we may just be. Macdonald seldom makes the reader's chore easy. You will linger over these poems, deciphering, worry-

*Reprinted by permission from Meridian (April 1980), pp. 4-6.

ing, no matter how sure you feel you know where you are.
She entices us by her impressive techniques; she is often
bizarrely funny: "Siamese sextuplets/ heroic couplets." And
she likes puns: an ice-storm creates a "frieze" on a building.
She spins off couplets and nursery rhyme forms with a be-
guiling glee. She is a master of "telling" line breaks.

W(Holes) itself has two sections: a sequence of twenty-
one poems, followed by a long collage-sequence on the roles
of women called "Burying the Babies."

The opening poem, "Francis Bacon, the Inventor of
Spectacles, is the Ringmaster," sets her various modes--the
intelligent but funky use of a figure from the past to illumi-
nate and comment on the present; the collage design; puns--
spectacles are both eyeglasses and opera, stage and film pro-
ductions. The poem is, for me, a grisly little fable: All
Mouth is just that, a ravenous mouth possessing an attached
"rudimentary bag." All Mouth finds itself/herself (it seems
hermaphroditic) pregnant. Soon All Ear is born. All Mouth
has moved towards self-completion. Twenty years elapse.
All Ear is lonely. He tries to sing, as his mother did, and
he fails. He "wills" himself to transform--to create another
being from himself, as he had been created from All Mouth.
He decides against an All Nose, because he thinks he couldn't
stand the smell. So out of a drop of his blood All Eye is
born. All Eye joins the carnival (of life?). The poet is the
barker, who details what All Eye (image for All Poet?) sees
inside itself. "Image and imagination" occur in the depth of
those "indivisible" inward eyes. All Eye (All Poet) sees "to
the edge of self (all those translucent pronouns)/ And beyond
into the dark quarter of the circle." Macdonald reports her
frank, unsparing visions from that dark quarter.

"The World's Fattest Dancer" stuffs herself with
chocolates and "larded guinea hens" and entertains the public.
Also, her tiny mouth, immersed as it is in all that fat, pre-
vents anyone from kissing her, even with a nibble. "The
Mother of the Sun" seems to be an ode for Diane Arbus, who
was a suicide. "Queen Diane," a circus queen, after giving
birth to the Sun Prince, leaves the circus; and when the son/
sun brings his own baby to see her, when she kisses the
grandson/grandsun she is consumed by his flames and sails
through the sky as a new meteor. She is now "the star of
her own show."

In "Celebrating the Freak" we may experience self-
discovery, having confronted something of the misshapen and

bent in ourselves. Macdonald urges, set "the freak flags
flying." We can even order the freak best-suited for us
from a freak catalogue. The following cluster of poems dis-
plays a few of these freaks. "The Siamese Sextuplets" is
grisly and hilarious. "The Kilgore Rangerette Whose Life
Was Ruined" reviews the history of the former cheerleader's
life-mishaps. She trips herself during an important game.
She hugs her grandmother too hard right after the latter's
surgery. She spoils a Christmas concert by giggling. Finally,
cheer-leading days over, she winds up as the only bag-lady in
Dallas. She has a baby, Billielou, whom she carts around in
her bag of rags. She loves the kid, melting with motherly
pride as the baby's fingers curl around her thumb "like little
tongues." Edvard Munch, the painter, is also a freak; he has
a driving secret passion for Edvard Grieg, the composer.
"Florence Nightingale's Parts" is a brilliant tour-de-force
about the famous angel with the lamp. Nightingale's rigid,
compulsive hair-parting parallels the rigidity of her Crimean
hospital-keeping. The poem, of course, also refers to her
sexual parts, and her starved life. Florence ironically de-
clares: "I am seen as austere. I am not." She sees dis-
order as a form of death. Parting life into severe halves
allows her to reject and to accept decisively. During her
final illness (she died at 90), her hair fell out. Being bald
made no difference, Macdonald writes; she simply "parted
her skin."

Other freaks include a birdwatcher who entices the
birds to his porch so that he can watch from indoors, en-
tirely cozy, un-rained and un-defecated upon. A lady base-
ball pitcher dreams of marriage, kids, Spode china, and
sees herself tragically, in a wonderful image, as a china
pitcher fully crazed and sitting empty on a shelf. There is
a series of family freaks: a glass full of objects symbolizes
a family's distortions. Modern lovers in an icy relationship
reconnect at a lobster dinner. Before serving the creatures,
the woman keeps the smelly lobster in her bureau drawer
wrapped in an expensive linen handkerchief. Two final poems
round off Part I: the first is on the birth of the ultimate hu-
man freak--Hermaphroditus, offspring of Hermes and Aphro-
dite. The second is about a twelve-foot statue of a hunchback
carved by an Austrian in 1520 who becomes an image for re-
bellious women who pick a baby full of holes. Will this mo-
saic baby (a play on Moses, too, I suspect) be the new Mosaic
Hunchback? The poem dovetails into the thirty-page con-
cluding poem, "Burying the Babies."

"Burying the Babies" is primarily about women in a male-dominated society. The inspiration is a brief passage from one of Mark Strand's poems: he admonishes--"Let us hurry/ Let us save the babies." Macdonald's tone throughout is wonderfully sardonic, as exploited women (if I read the poem accurately), conditioned through history to be passive and vapid, finally take the lives of their children into their own hands, let them die, and are ready to bury them in coffins (old telescope boxes described in an old children's book, Common School Classics, 1846). In this sequence, Macdonald intersperses her own verse passages between telling culls from various older poems, biographies, letters, female-behavior manuals, a director's book for a Japanese puppet theater, elephant joke lore, old movies (Lifeboat), farm manuals. In general, there is a tight weaving of part to part, of collage moment to poem. An important word may thread over from one passage to the next; and puns are employed vigorously throughout for thematic continuity and effect--crewel and cruel, seagull and gullible, dining room and dying room. Here is one passage of extended puns:

> The babies are all right. Pretend-
> ing to write.
> What else to do with a play pen?
> Each is alone, rapt, except for the
> near-twins
> Who are sibyls, able to tell what
> will hold
> Water by stirring the cauldron.
> Syllables swim up ...

Also, some motifs recur--trying to hold water cupped in a hand is one; another, obviously, is of the babies themselves, and the various things that happen to them. One of the most effective of Macdonald's central images is the mermaid. Mermaids arise from the Mare Fecundatatis. Why? Because "A woman is born a mermaid so she can picket/ For the rights of both women and fish." And, a bit earlier:

> A woman is born a mermaid so her
> husband knows
> She cannot run away once he lands
> her.
> A woman is born a mermaid so she can
> swim,
> Carrying plates of water vegetables
> and fish

> To her father who stretches under a
> red-and-white-striped
> Umbrella at the beach. A woman is
> born a mermaid
> So that she will win only sack races
> And, once in a while, the egg and
> spoon.
> A woman is born a mermaid so there
> will always be
> Scales available for weighing flour
> and justice.

I find this passage an effective statement of rage against the exploitation of women. Because the rage is artfully presented through the mermaid image, its effectiveness is greater than if it had been baldly shouted out. Macdonald jabs with considerable force.

And there are other facets to this theme: One woman is used by a strongman to show his strength: Queen Caroline accompanies her King on the road to battle and simply stops in the pebbles and grass to suckle her current child (she had 16). An old woman in a lavender robe, who loved going to movies and collecting free china, sets herself on fire as she sorts through the memorabilia and trash of her life. A modern woman married to an M. D. persuades her husband to sew her maidenhead back--"Hymen's Protection. "

These individual women constitute Woman: old, young, whores, queens, lesbians (G. Stein), mermaids, pregnant women, mothers, estranged wives. They hold children in their laps, exhibit freak-babies born with wings ("angels") in museums, sit with children on the beach, check their babies in coatrooms, gaze into their dead babies' "grave faces, " check the babies in their playpens to see if they are still alive, and finally, arrange them in their coffins for burial.

Now, where does Mark Strand fit into all this? It's possible that his brief admonition to save the babies is nothing more than a stimulus for Macdonald's poem. It is also possible that "Burying the Babies" is one angry woman's response to an arrogant male who assumes for himself a woman's prerogative--the disposition of her babies in life and death. I prefer to see Macdonald's vibrant poem as a scream in this direction--saving humanity by saving the babies won't suffice. Lysistrata and her women withheld sex; Macdonald's women bury their babies. Where now can men turn to resolve the nightmare of their own creating? Into their shunned female selves?

RECIDIVIST OF VERSE:

Paul Mariah's Selected Poems: This Light Will Spread*

Some male poets are Zeus types.   Their poems spring
full-blown from their brains.   Other poets are Neptunes
birthing poems from the froth and spume of their creative
ejaculations.   Both sorts feel responsible for their progeny.
They must see to it that they are well-placed (published) in
the world.   Each poem, including those already published
(generally in obscure places), never cease to be a worrisome
responsibility.   The life of a book of poems is brief; an out-
of-print condition is a kind of death, a being out-of-life condi-
tion.   And those poor little creature-poems who never find a
slot in the world at all must twist rancorously inside the
poet's brain or genitals.   The occasion of a Selected Poems
allows a poet to resuscitate poems out-of-print, and to launch
hitherto unpublished pieces.   A good poet needs to know which
of his waifs deserve a place in the world, and which should
be kept, like Kaspar Hauser, in a dark cellar, on bread and
water.

The occasion for these musings is the recent appear-
ance of Paul Mariah's This Light Will Spread, a gathering
of poems written over fifteen years (1960-1975).   According
to his count, about half of them are appearing for the first
time in print.   This massive collection has been ignored by
reviewers and the poetry world in general.   My guess is that
they don't really know how to treat it--Mariah is not your
safe, palliating, comfort-inducing poet.   He writes out of a
searing life: three years spent in an Illinois state prison
where he was incarcerated for sexual deviation; a decade of
activist causes, political and sexual, during the late fifties
and sixties when he participated in the protests of San Fran-
cisco and Berkeley, worked with Kay Boyle and Robert Dun-
can, and was an interviewer for the Kinsey Institute; twenty

*Reprinted by permission from American Book Review (May-
June 1980), p. 12.

years of immersion in the gay world of San Francisco, and
twelve years as a counsellor at various half-way houses; and,
finally, a dozen years as a courageous publisher of an influ-
ential literary magazine ManRoot and ManRoot Books. He has
featured Jean Genet, James Broughton, Jack Spicer, Amnesia
Glasscock, David Fisher, Cocteau, Cavafy, among others.
He has also published numerous lesbian and gay writers who
have had few if any quality outlets for their work. In short,
he has been a vibrant force in the ongoing cultural life of the
country. His progeny are numerous, and they come in vari-
ous guises, hues, and tones. The name Mariah, incidentally,
is a pseudonym, and is a wry comment on police and their
paddy-wagons, as well as a play on being a social pariah.

Let's take a closer look at his poetry. The opening
prison sequence, even without the much-printed Persona non
Grata (its exclusion is a mistake, I think), is the most valua-
ble and moving part of the collection. These derive from
Mariah's own incarceration, when he taught himself to write
poetry and served as a prison librarian and tutor to inmates
who were unable to read or write. Obviously, experience in
itself does not make for good verse--craftsmanship, intelli-
gence, compassion--all are needed. And these poems possess
these qualities. His lyric voice is assured, poignant, and at
times playful. And he moves us beneath the skins of his in-
mates; we feel his Genet-world as the prisoners make clan-
destine love, endure shake-downs, marry one another with
rings made of cafeteria spoons, suffer solitary confinement,
and develop thin scars over wounds that never heal. Like
Genet, Mariah transforms this grotesque maiming world into
an existentialist metaphor for decency and loving in the face
of injustice, brutality, and terror. "Shakedown and More,"
in almost painfully cramped, projective-verse lines and
rhythms, evokes both fear and love:

> Silver is missing
> From the messhall;
> All
>
> Prisoners suspect.
> Cells torn open
> Like wounds
>
> Setting out
> In search of
> The germ,

The spoon stolen,
Each frisked
As he returns

To his cell.
Shakedown for
Contraband.

All known hands
Are checked
For shivs.

One lives in
Terror that it's
Not marked

For him.   Still
It may be found
As a ring on

Newly wedded hand
Or as a worse attack
A knife in the back.

Here is a portion of a moving panegyric "Muse Elek-
trique" written for a Puerto Rican prisoner Mariah taught and
loved.   He writes in the man's idiom:

The wife is dead.   You live yr life in rivers
That flow thru yr veins.   My senses, name-givers.

The parent living has not told you there embedded in
        rock,
Living Fossil, that yr father is dead.   In Puerto Ric

O bottle slashed him in too-drunken quarrel.   You've
        sensed
Absence: the father, the wife, the teacher.   I often
        glanced

At you studying under my teacherguise while the class
Workt assignments, and the guards pit-pattered ass

From room to room, cell to cell, no matter where I
        look always
I find you lockd in the closet mind that plays

Teacher. What delight we found in that lockd closet!
I aftercelebrated you in a series of Christmas Sonnets

The closest thing to giving I could give. Penniless.
            You played
Handball on cloistered days. We, with finesse,
            splayed

Each other in the shower when we could. Now we
            are older,
Growing together: you there, I here. In slower, so
            much slower

Tones I am giving up my life to live
Among my bones. You, Isolate, do not know that I've

Written these lines for you. My letters seized,
My poems contraband. I write this in silence....

This prison sequence should be read with Mariah's Persona
non Grata, that small classic of American prison literature,
still in print after numerous editions, and available from
ManRoot Books.

Several poems written to an Army Deserter connect
nicely with the prison group, and reveal another aspect of
Mariah as social outcast--lover, though here unconsummated,
of another social outcast. As love poems, carried on in let-
ters and poems, these are exquisitely tender and moving:

My hands are invisible now
Around you
Around your shoulders
As you look thru the bars.
The Moon is not looking.

She is fogged out ...
Of the city I had to go
The pressure on my head
The bust coming
Felt the siege
But my knowing
Wouldn't stop you.

You could not trust the season
Of sage, the feelings.
The thrust of words.

The reality of them
Guards you thru this
Imprisoned night.

The "Bay Poems" have many surprises. There are tender
love poems--"All Things Soft" is memorable; social poems:
"Mamaism" extols the blacks for having what whitey lacks,
Mamaism and Dadaism: "it's a tar-baby world." In the
hilarious "For Sale / Coldwell, Banker" Mariah settles a
score with the telephone company. Perched on top of an
abandoned building near the San Francisco-Oakland freeway
sits a phone booth. For three months it's been there. Mari-
ah decides not to drop in a dime to tell the company where the
booth is: "You never listen to outside voices / Unless they
plug you with dimes." Moreover, Pacific Telephone does not
service poets: "Poetry is not Big Business."

In the "Bay Poems" there are also various takes on
other writers who have influenced Mariah's work: Duncan (he
was for a time in Duncan's poetry workshop), Spicer, Olson,
Gertrude Stein. His "homage" to Stein is a successful tour
de force, a writing to Stein and a writing like her. The
poem to Olson is a bit preachy and insufficiently outrageous.
"Yr Night Mare," to Duncan, brilliantly apes Duncan's ob-
sessions with weird mythical figures ("Gllave," who "bridled
the Golden Three"), esoteric mental gymnastics, the role of
the poet as vates ("What the Irish call FILI, a seer"), and
Duncan's penchant for verbal encrustations ("gold torques and
honey-cakes"). "Stringing the Lights," also from this section,
is one of the most moving of all Mariah's poems: We learn
of our vulnerability as invisible strings wind about our heads
and then unwind. When it's "almost too late / to measure
the pulling on strings" we manage to "collect ourselves / to
see how whole we are."

"The Gay Heretic" poems, I am sure, have prevented
this book from getting the attention it should. Yet, many of
these poems, because of Mariah's numerous public readings,
have achieved a wide Bay Area fame. No gay person be-
lieves that the terrible struggle for tolerance is won. There
are signs that the straight world, because of some enlightened
souls, real-politics, and a few anti-discrimination laws, is
at least moving towards some notion, if not of a necessary
co-existence between homosexuals and straights, at least to-
wards more tolerance. Sure, gays have a right to exist, but
only if they stay in their Greenwich Village and Castro Street
ghettos. It's the old idea: "Out of sight, out of mind." Do
your thing, but don't tell us about it.

The gay writer who seeks to inform and educate the straight world may run into trouble.   John Rechy, for example, is faulted for his frank presentations of homosexual life.   Critics in the straight press seem to feel smeared with urine and offal.   These same critics, though, seem to admire Genet's works a lot; he's rarely sexually explicit and employs symbols of roses and lilies and saints, borrowed straight from Roman Catholic liturgy, to sanitize degradation and misery.   Somehow his prison/sexual experiences become more palatable to the world at large.   They sound the way good literature should.

I grant that the ingredients of a stew are not the stew--the slowly simmering tastes and aromas are.   And Rechy is faulted for merely presenting the ingredients for a "Sexual Outlaw Stew," leaving it to us to throw them into a pot, add the wine and spices, and create our own dish.   Genet seems to do all this for us; so we simply dig in and feast. Rechy resembles Truman Capote and Norman Mailer who write documentaries (a kind of journalism) and call them "novels."

I am not implying that Mariah is a writer of gay life documentaries.   But there is a problem, and as a writer myself who happens to be gay (as distinct from being a gay writer), I am puzzled by the reticence of the straight world to want to know of this other world that contains some 10 percent or more of their brothers.   There are times, yes, when Mariah fails to see that a good romping sex poem is only that, and that a really good poem should be more.   His outrageous "Figa," is more; a good poem can really wake you up with a good plunge.   He does generate larger meanings--and a longer essay would explore his fascination with the art/ poetry of French surrealist poets.   His primary theme, underlying all the pyrotechnics of his sense of craft, is loving via erotic self-discovery.   Making vigorous love to a lover, from all angles, in all weathers of fragrance and stench, is a creative act.   Deviance is beside the point.

Recall Mariah's stay in prison.   See the prisoner as outlaw.   See the poet as outlaw.   See the poet returning again and again to outlawed sexual acts.   See the poet returning to the "crime" of writing poems in a culture hostile to the spiritual and the sensitive.   In Mariah's world, we begin to discover loving via some basics--the soles of other men's feet, the heft of their testicles, their firm/soft throats, the stubble of their beards.   Magnificent shootings and spurtings

of the spirit and body occur that the world knows too little
of.   Obviously, what I have just written is in the nature of
a polemic.   I intend it to be that, and realize that I have
probably managed to dissuade some readers from taking a
look at Mariah's Selected Poems.   There's no other poet
around quite like him.   The fact that he is here should be
vigorously noted.   And that's what I have tried to do.

PART TWO

"The nuts should never be
ground in a meat grinder,
which simply crushes them
and brings up the oil."
    --Irma S. Rombauer,
    Joy of Cooking

ON DEDICATING POEMS TO INDIVIDUALS*

Poems are written to commemorate friendships and loves, to borrow luster from some revered, more-established poet, and to evoke the memory of some departed parent or other relative. Occasionally, poets appear for whom dedications are an unhappy addiction. For the sake of delicacy, I shall not name names; but recently I saw a book of some 50 poems--all but ten bore dedications. All of us who write, at one time or another, have published pieces for members of our families, for famous people, and for persons of no particular distinction other than that they are acquaintances.

Most of the time these poems lock the general reader out of the poem--he/she is spying at sentiments meant for one, and only one, person's eyes. In my more iconoclastic moments, when I do come across these poems, I stifle the impulse to send same back to their authors, complaining that the authors presume too much. If a poem carries an intimate dedication, why publish it in the first place?

Well, I won't play stupid; there are several reasons for such behavior. The chief one is probably _vanity_. When a poet publishes a poem signed to John and Jane Doelicker, to show appreciation for a groovy weekend in the country, or to Carolyn and Fred Anonymous for letting him, the poet, rock Fred Jr. to sleep, or to Barry X-ray for that splendid fishing trip, or to Michael, Grace, or David, one-night sex-stands lacking last names but so vivid in bed they deserve commemorative poems--when a poet publishes poems to such folk he displays his _vanity_ by assuming that he, poet, is making these folk immortal.

Isn't all poetry, once it's published in even the most obscure journal, possibly immortal? One hundred and fifty years from now, when Fred and Carolyn, John and Jane, etc.,

*Reprinted by permission from Northeast Rising Sun (Fall/Winter 1980), pp. 11-12. Also reprinted as "Poetry Left Better Un-named," in Contact II (Winter/Spring 1982), pp. 7-8.

are little more than bones or hanks of hair, some enterprising graduate student hot for a dissertation topic may unearth these poems and once more expose their fragile contents to the light. Moreover, if the poet has become famous, the most obscure dedicatee becomes a figure for inquiry and for footnotes.

Obviously, though, vanity isn't the whole explanation. Whereas other mortals say "thanks" with a pint of home-made jam, an afghan, a birdhouse, or a coffee-table book on James Ensor's art, the poet gives what he is best able to craft--a POEM! Affection and social decency prompt his dedication.

Yet, while jam passes through your bowels, afghans wear out, and birdhouses come unglued and smeared with bird offal, the poem, once it is printed, may persist. And since poems belong with "the finer things of life," they have a possible lasting power beyond the fragility of the single words they contain. So, dedicatees are thrilled to see their names in print. Many even mount a copy of the poem in their bathroom.

There's another kind of dedication, one a bit more suspect than these I've been discussing. Here a certain self-seeking strikes the gong of hoped-for success. Included are those battalions of poems dedicated to prestigious poets (some personally known by the authors, most not). The dedicator may be hoping that his dedication of a poem to James Wright, James Dickey, or Anne Sexton (even the dead ones get into the act) will help him get his poems published, eventually in book form. What editor, I ask you, wouldn't look twice, even at a lousy poem, if he saw Galway Kinnell's or Jonathan Williams's name attached to it? To be fair, a young poet may simply be acknowledging a debt of gratitude to a writer who has inspired and influenced him. Swell! Too often, though, these dedications fit the pattern of namedropping: and, for some of us who spend a lot of time reading poetry, they are turn-offs.

Dedications are also made to non-poet celebrities-- dead politicians, victims of social injustice (Che Guevara, for example), famous actresses and actors (Mansfield, Monroe, and Dean), and dancers (Duncan). I have less quarrel with these dedications than I have with those to family and friends, and to poets. I don't discern the same self-seeking.

To help clear the air, I make this modest proposal: Have a committee of concerned poets, sponsored probably by the more alert membership of the Poetry Society of America and the less fascistically inclined of those poetfolk in Boulder, draft an agreement, to be signed by all publishers of poets, and by all poets listed in the Poets and Writers Directories, that there be an agreed-on ratio of dedications to the overall number of poems published by any poet in any given year. Perhaps, as a rule of thumb, no more than one dedication should occur for every 20 poems. Another possibility is to create a tradition whereby a final page of a book contains all the dedications crowded together in a single paragraph of small type. Friends and lovers can still find their names and be thrilled. The Committee (supra) may also want to restore that wonderful old nineteenth-century practice of the anonymous dedication: "To _____."

WHAT'S MY OPENING LINE?

or,

A Mathematics for the Muse*

"But was the language alive?"--Robert Friend

Examining only the first lines of poems is possibly in that category of act known as the superficial. It's akin to a doctor's taking your pulse but not your temperature, or to his thumping your chest but not proceeding to your nether parts where the trouble is; or, it's like a vet's dropping flea powder behind a poodle's ear when the whole creature is infested; or, finally, it's like a bright student who supplies the opening sentence of an essay and asks you to intuit what he or she knows from that sentence.

So, I am aware that what I am about to do implies some risk. I shall try to be fearless though, in the interests of serving poetry and the fledgling writers of verse who may see this essay. For my purposes, I have taken Edward Field's recent anthology A Geography of Poets (Bantam) since it is an ambitious presentation of poets known and unknown from all over the country. Moreover, since everybody in the book was alive last year when the book appeared, we have a guarantee of sorts that the poems reflect a pretty good spectrum of poetry writing as it occurs these days.

Until I started copying first lines and classifying them, much as old Charles Darwin classified his beetles and finches, I had no idea that they would group themselves as neatly as they do. I suspect that much of the monotony of contemporary poetry is due to the monotony of lines generating poems. In general, there is an ubiquitous declarative, plain-language,

*Reprinted by permission from Bachy, No. 18 (1981), pp. 310-313.

detrital opening.   Eschewed is the old-fashioned rhetorical-verbiage start, the overt alliterative line, and the highly in-spired opening moment we associate with the ancient ode or epic start--"Arms and the man I sing," "Lost midway this path of life in a dark wood," "Of man's first disobedience ..," etc.   Modern launchings often read as lifts from newspapers, or from letters back to dear old granny on the farm, or from tacky autobiographical details.   I hope that my examples (I mean to be entirely scientific) will startle poets into testing out their first lines before they freeze them in print.   If they sound stupid and self-indulgent they probably are.

I realize that I will be accused of being unfair for not presenting entire opening verse sentences rather than first lines.   I hereby throw down a scented glove.   My challenge runs this way: Since most contemporary poets using the fashionable free-verse modes swear by their line-breaks as necessary, pregnant, and even beautiful, they should gladly submit to such scrutiny.   Obviously, a sentence cut off in mid-air, as most of my examples are, do often sound ridicu-lous without their lower parts, legs, feet and slippers.   Some unintentional double-entendres occur: One poet offers her man some "head."   Some sound far more self-important and pompous than they should.   Others do manage to intrigue us over what is to come.   My apologies to any poet (and many are my friends) who may be offended by finding his/her line parading around sans fig leaf.   Like all good satirists, I can only hope that my bolus will effect cures, and that future poems by some of these poets will have less questionable be-ginnings.   And, as you will see for yourself, the more pres-tigious the poet, the sappier some of these lines are.   There are moments, too, where they wonderfully evoke one another, making comments and completions never intended by the poets, their critics, the gods, or anyone else.

To be entirely fair, I should encourage another critic to return to an earlier anthology--say to one by Selden Rod-man, Oscar Williams, or Louis Untermeyer, and make a similar study.   We may find that all along opening lines, in general, have been lousy.   At the same time, we may find some stunning empirical evidence for evaluating the merits of poetry then and now.   The more data and related instru-ments of measurement we can develop the better.   Since poets as a gens are pretty self-obsessed, we need to remove their work from the scramblings of the critical market-place, and freeze, dissect, classify, and analyze--much as the Dar-winians examined their flora, fauna, and insectivora.   I cau-

tion though against using any laser-beam, or related, tech-
nology--the state of our poet-science is not ready.   Rudimen-
tary steps first, please! We are in our infancy.   I turn now
to the major classes of opening lines, with examples and in-
terpretative commentaries.

Reportage

Reportage is one of the more frequently used devices.
Some of the assumptions here are 1) Poetry is for plain
folks--so throw out anything that might smack of the literary
or traditional, 2) We limit our subject matter pretty much to
our families and friends, and to the often humdrum events of
our lives.   This confusion of poetry with journalism is en-
demic for much current writing.   Whether this mode will
ever disappear remains to be seen.   I doubt that it will;
American poetry will continue to sound like a vehicle of
thousands of gears and parts all indistinguishable as to func-
tion--although colors, sizes, and manufacturers may vary.

There are two main types (sub-classes) of reportage.
In the first, the poet tells you about people other than him-
self.   In the second, he tells you about himself.   Here are
some examples of Type A.   Notice how beautifully Simpson's
line squints at Soto's grandmother and Ortiz's sister.   Hitch-
cock lets us know that Kinnell's bear is doing more than defe-
cating or eating blackberries.   Finally, Dickey delivers Gild-
ner's bitch.   I have grouped the lines that tie-in with one an-
other:

>"My oldest sister wears thick glasses" (Simon J.
>   Ortiz)
>"Grandma lit the stove" (Gary Soto)
>"Her face turned sour" (Louis Simpson)
>
>"A black bear sits alone" (Galway Kinnell)
>"He sits in a deckchair reading Colette" (George
>   Hitchcock)
>
>"The boxer bitch is pregnant" (Gary Gildner)
>"Next door they've finally brought home the new
>   baby. " (William Dickey)

Type B, Personal Reportage, falls neatly into five sorts, all
of them possibly suspect unless they predict some devastating
irony or drama to be worked out in the poem as a whole.   It

is almost impossible to detect much lyrical beauty in any of
these lines--although some of them scan pretty regularly.
Here are the five kinds:

a.   What I Look Like: Here we have a choice of
physiognomies.   For evocativeness, I prefer Le Sueur's:

> "I have a wide, friendly face" (Paul Zimmer)
> "I am a crazy woman with a painted face"(Meridel
>   Le Sueur)

b.   What I'm Doing: This one allows for a delicious
poetic license--unless you can imagine the poet composing his
poem as he bends over a stump or stares out at the trees:

> "I bend over an old hollow cottonwood stump. . . . "
>   (Robert Bly)
> "I am looking at trees" (W. S. Merwin)

c.   What I'm Really Like: These starts don't always
help us.   King, Ortiz, and Stafford are pretty straightforward,
except that one might want to see Stafford's love for flat
country as a paradigm for some of his poetry.   Browne's
"green books" aren't very helpful though--Graham Greene's
novels?   Books Browne hasn't read and which, therefore, re-
main green?   Or, has he literally painted all his books green
as part of a decorating scheme?   I like the ambiguity.

> "I like a man around" (Linda King)
> "I happen to be a veteran" (Simon J. Ortiz)
> "In scenery I like flat country. " (William Stafford)
> "In my house I keep green books" (Michael Dennis
>   Browne)

d.   My guilts and traumas: This sub-class does over-
lap somewhat with a larger class I shall call "problems. "   I
include them here because they seem to deal frankly and
overtly with some basic autobiographical fact the poet requires
us to know at the outset.   I assume that Haines never became
a cauliflower--which may be a metaphor for his having left
Alaskan snow and ice (cauliflowers are either white or polar-
bear-piss yellow).   Norse deals with his frustratingly potent
gay feelings for an elusive Mr. Right of the Golden Calves.
Meltzer supplies a religious turn: centuries of Jewish reli-
gious life confront him, and we are anxious to know what he
has done wrong.   Kunitz's speaker makes us wonder on whose
side he is, and how heavy the guilt trips are.

"I wanted to be a cauliflower" (John Haines)
"A pair of muscular calves" (Harold Norse)
"The Rabbi is before me. " (David Meltzer)
"My mother never forgave my father" (Stanley Kunitz)

e. Irrefutable Facts About Me: These might be
placed under sub-group "c", but they do seem better separated
off. Whittemore's event, entirely factual, is so casual that
we assume it means little more than what it says. Or, was
he setting himself up to write poems in French forms? May
Swenson's bit of news about herself is indeed shocking--and
refreshing. Mei-Mei Bersenbrugge's first line nicely begins
with first things--honkings? Alta's confession, unfrosted with
guilt, seems almost metaphysical and, as such, anticipates
McClure's scream of joy, a scream all poetry and art worthy
the name moves towards--the intense, personal apotheosis:

"At breakfast I had french toast. " (Reed Whittemore)
"I took my cat apart" (May Swenson)
"I was born the year of the loon" (Mei-Mei Berssen-
    brugge)
"I'm frigid when i wear see thru negligees" (Alta)
"I HAVE INHERITED THE UNIVERSE!" (Michael
    McClure)

Placings

A few poets try to energize their poem-starts by
placing themselves in unexpected locales. I admire such
poems because they begin as if they were more than journalis-
tic drivel. The rarest and most free-wheeling is Nathan's
appearance in the Indian Ocean. Barker and Lawson write
while borne aloft. Huff is ethnic and earth-located. Brinnin's
panegyric to suburban life (actually a threnody on Dachau)
turns more melancholy in Levine's line and achieves violence
in Barker's, although the violence is that of movie illusion.
In all these cases, we refreshingly share the poet's locale,
where he was when the poem was conceived:

"I come sailing through the Indian Ocean" (Leonard
    Nathan)
"Here in the open cockpit" (David Barker)
"We're up in a balloon" (Paul Lawson)

"Sitting down near him in the shade" (Robert Huff)

"Such a merry suburb!" (John Malcolm Brinnin)
"In a coffee house at 3 am" (Philip Levine)
"On these sunny steps / they stabbed Sal Mineo"
(David Barker)

Flamboyancies

Flamboyant openings are intended to draw us into the
poem via sheer style alone, or by saying something outrageous
to arouse (or offend) our grosser instincts, or our socio-
political sense. Of the three sub-groups here, the first is
the most traditional: Wagoner and Jong love alliteration. I
do wish though that the sibilants had rolled less trippingly
from their lips. Duncan is much less serpentine--his joy is
cathartic; naming is a celebration, and the dance of syllables
provides a special pleasure. Ashbery employs sibilants to
evoke memories of delicious breakfasts past:

"On sloping, shattered granite, the snake man"
(David Wagoner)
"Stiff as the icicles in their beards, the Ice Kings"
(David Wagoner)
"A man so sick that the sexual soup" (Erica Jong)
"Most beautiful! the red-flowering eucalyptus"
(Robert Duncan)
"A pleasant smell of frying sausages" (John Ashbery)

Here is a pair of much less-daring examples of alliteration:

"The planet that we plant upon" (Knute Skinner)
"There was a brightness in the branches" (Ron
Loewinsohn)

The second sub-group includes beginnings meant to
jar us by presenting human universals in semi-tragic or gross
conditions--scroti, abortions, etc:

"They [genitals] droop like sad fuchsias from our
bodies" (Henry Carlile)
"Cell by cell the baby made herself. . .
(George Oppen)
"My sweet-faced, tattle-tale brother was born blind"
(Mona Van Duyn)
"After she finished her first abortion" (Judy Grahn)

In sub-group three fall those lines boasting a funky,
folksy, or intimate touch, singly and in combination. Their

colloquial tone frequently suggests the anti-poetic. Genital and breast orientations provide zippy beginnings for Ochester, Stetler, Barker, and Koch. Sometimes these starts are surreal (Edson) and funny (Broughton):

> "Ordinarily I call it 'my cock,' but" (Ed Ochester)
> "Karl, my friend, caught the crabs" (Charles Stetler)
> "I know those tits. They are" (David Barker)
> "Happy the man who has two breasts to crush against
>   his bosom" (Kenneth Koch)

> "He had hitched a chicken to a cart" (Russell Edson)
> "In Zen you can't yen for anything" (James Broughton)

Imperatives

Since poets are so inclined to be assertive, even bossy, I was surprised to find so few poems opening with imperatives. This may, of course, reflect the wisdom of the editor who eschewed commanding poems in favor of those of a more congenial sort. But, there are a few. Wagoner tells us to "stand still," Meinke says "stop," alta, with a little help from Contoski, informs us how to behave once we have followed Meinke's command. Field is about to show us what to do when those drums appear at the door. Bronk hates turn-on stuff and waxes nicely metaphysical.

> "Stand still. The trees ahead and bushes beside you"
>   (David Wagoner)
> "STOP: if you're racing at night" (Peter Meinke)
> "hunger for me hunger hunger for me" (alta)
> "Kiss the one you love." (Victor Contoski)
> "When the drums come to your door" (Edward Field)
> "Yes, look at me; I am the mask it wears" (William
>   Bronk)

Ejaculations and Apostrophes

The ejaculation as a starter is also rare in this anthology, demonstrating, I would guess, how far behind we have left the English Romantics and the writers of Neo-classical odes. I find only these three instances of the orotund apostrophe. Kuzma's line would seem to have sexual overtones; his sex life seems no longer to move as it once did. Rakosi is nicely ambiguous--a circle of friends? a circle of early poets presided over by <u>rare</u> Ben Jonson? a fairy-circle of mushrooms on a lawn? Rukeyser's line may be read as a refreshing comment on my entire study.

> "Oh to be moving as we once were" (Greg Kuzma)
> "o rare circle" (Carl Rakosi)
> "O for God's sake" (Muriel Rukeyser)

You Do This, You Do That

One of the most pretentious of all openings is the "You do this, you do that" opening. Not only has this method afflicted starts but entire poems. I am happy to report only a scattering of such starts in A Geography of Poets--evidence, I hope that this once immensely popular form (nourished by workshops) is on the wane. The device was useful particularly for evoking dead people--particularly dead fathers and grandmothers once hated by the poet. Sometimes historical figures are addressed. What sounds so phony most of the time is that the persons are told what they once knew they did--and if they are stone-dead and unresurrected, the effect is of talking to a tombstone. Here are the examples:

> "When you walked down the stairs / to touch my root" (Steve Orlen)
> "You drive down MAIN STREET" (Jim Heynen)
> "As you are walking / down the street" (William J. Harris)
> "You remember the name was Jensen. She seemed old." (Richard Hugo)
> "You raise the ax" (Ai)
> "You follow, dress held high above / the fresh manure" (Lucien Stryk)
> "you know" (Charles Bukowski)

Direct Address

A related form, and one of the most common, is the Direct Address opening. Here the poet zeroes in on a listener, often with dramatic effect, often for getting even with a parent or lover who has caused torment, often to commemorate a lost or departed person, showing thereby the poet's enviable sympathies. There seem to be three subspecies here, or sub-classes. The first treats sexual matters. Interestingly, the examples together create a brief short story of sexual favors and vengeances:

> "Do you love me?   I asked. "   (Gerald Locklin)
> "darling here's my head"   (Judith Johnson Sherwin)
> "Haunt him, Mona!   Haunt him, demon sister!"
>   (Larry Rubin)

The second sub-class addresses parents and siblings.
Kumin remembers her mother's girlhood.   Scott reassures
his parent that her life-teaching was not in vain.   De Frees
establishes a meaningful relationship with a son who may have
good reason to doubt her affection.   Ai arraigns her man for
abandoning her in a truck.   Huff, enamored of passing years,
addresses an old ventriloquist, an image perhaps of the seamy
life of the poet himself.   Dickey says goodby to his teeth,
items even more intimate and necessary than parents in one's
life.   Shelton brings a dear-departed up to date.   Aubert,
almost divining Dickey's problem, blames Jean for the loss
of incisors and bicuspids.   Did Jean, Dickey's mom, feed
him too much refined sugar?

> "Mother my good girl / I remember this old story"
>   (Maxine Kumin)
> "Mother Dear, I am being careful. "   (Herbert
>   Scott)
> "It's right to call you son.   That cursing alcoholic"
>   (Madeline De Frees)
> "You keep me waiting in a truck"   (Ai)
> "Four years ago, dear old ventriloquist"   (Robert
>   Huff)
> "Now you are going, what can I do but wish you"
>   (William Dickey)
> "Five years since you died and I am"   (Richard
>   Shelton)
> "you should have, jean, stopped them"   (Alvin
>   Aubert)

The third sub-class (the reader may wish to flesh this
one out with examples from other anthologies) flashes certain
political apostrophes (Knight), lines directed to people in gen-
eral (Corso), and apostrophes to devils and supernatural en-
tities (Clifton):

> "And, yeah, brothers"   (Etheridge Knight)
> "Folks, sex has never been"   (Gregory Corso)
> "Demon, Demon, you have dumped me"   (Lucille
>   Clifton)

The Pregnant Problem/Question

We arrive finally at lines preoccupied with stating a
problem the poet is obliged to work out.   Since poems tradi-
tionally deal with strivings and spiritual struggles, we would
expect to see numerous examples here.   For, as philosophers
and linguists keep pointing out, the age-old problems vex us
and snow-white hairs upon our heads.   Nor are the re-
sponses helpful in one generation helpful in a later one.   If
time is but the stream we go a-fishing in, as Thoreau said,
we keep dropping different baits, hoping to lure the bass of
ultimate wisdom into our nets.   What the starts and castings
from A Geography of Poets show is our dismal failure to re-
solve these preoccupations.   These lines work from the meta-
physical concern down to the most mundane of difficulties.

Finkel and Di Prima, by asserting the whoeverness
of self, symbolize the first sub-class.   Ammons supplies a
more responsible grip on the issue by declaring his intention
to pursue both unity and difference.   By simply not seeing
the point, Alan Dugan actually absolves himself from questing.
Miller Williams shows more courage, framing his conclusions
around an image of banging.   Watson, at least, is in motion
as he moves through "invisible glass"--a nicely Wonderlandian
metaphor.   Gregor, again, is in a dilemma over which role
to choose in the face of the Existentialist abyss.   Shapiro
merely responds by assuming there is a "dawn"--question-
begging, I think, since the case may be, however tragically,
that we are in an eternal dusk, and one which no amount of
poetic querying or haggling will resolve:

>   "Whoever I am...." (Donald Finkel)
>   "who is the we, who is" (Diana Di Prima)
>   "I want to know the unity in all things and the
>   difference" (A. R. Ammons)
>   "I never saw any point" (Alan Dugan)
>   "No one knows what the banging is all about"
>   (Miller Williams)
>   "Was I moving through the invisible glass"
>   (Robert Watson)
>   "If I could choose a role" (Arthur Gregor)
>   "What dawn is it?" (Karl Shapiro)

A second class of line develops the problem of lost
cultures and societies in trouble--problems of a different or-
der than the strictly metaphysical.   Bloch worries specifically
about lost tribes.   Schulman evokes the Cassandra-wail, via
some consciously stilted writing, in the manner of a nineteenth-

century translation of the Oresteia. This is the only instance
I find of an overt imitation of a dead style in Field's anthology.
From Heyen's line we can't be sure of the folk needing to be
saved--the implication seems to be that since we can't save
ourselves why should we try to save others? Tate seems to
provide a telling epitaph for our own age, seen from the
scary perspective of a forthcoming era, one uncannily antici-
pated by Josephine Miles' line: "Shall I pull the curtains...."

> "What happened to the ten lost tribes" (Chana
> Bloch)
> "What happened to Cassandra? She who cried"
> (Grace Schulman)
> "I do not think we can save them" (William Heyen)
> "They didn't have much trouble" (James Tate)
> "Shall I pull the curtains against the coming night?"
> (Josephine Miles)

The most frequent problem line (and the third sub-class)
is the personal rather than the grandiose line. Extremely
solipsistic at their worst, and generally anemic in imagination,
these lines work best when they transcend self-pity, contain
surprises, or are humorous. A series of these, again,
counter-point one another. Poverty is the theme for Howard
Moss who is awakened by his refrigerator to the issue of
having and not having. James Wright comes on with a whistle
in the wind. Corman dips back into his personal history, as
does Rutsala, to find contrastingly poignant material situations
--an encapsulation perhaps of growing up in America during
the late twenties and early thirties. Nathan's question, as
refreshingly literal as it is, is confusing, we can't tell wheth-
er he himself is impoverished, or whether he's well-off.
Does he merely hope to experience poverty by simply wearing
a poor dude's shirt?

> "The argument of the refrigerator wakes me."
> (Howard Moss)
> "I still have some money" (James Wright)
> "I had so little" (Cid Corman)
> "We had more than / we could use" (Vern Rutsala)
> "What is it like to have just one shirt" (Leonard
> Nathan)

Other lines of a highly personal-problem sort treat
prognancy, alcohol, and pseudonyms:

> "I have this bulging belly because" (Ann Darr)

"If I needed brandy alone/there would be no prob-
lem" (Keith Wilson)
"I was content with the pseudonym" (Vassar Miller)

Coda

As I pull the curtains on this perhaps needlessly
arcane but scientific excursion into the very core of poetry,
I can only hope that poets will think more about their opening
lines. Do your first lines sound silly taken all by themselves?
Do line-breaks really matter, so that you risk writing non-
sense if you observe the breaks and read individual free-
verse lines as if they were single-line poems? Are you too
much enamored of the ephemeral and the tackily solipsistic?
Have you done well to abandon a style that may sound literary
merely because it sounds like one of your grandfather's?
If you are writing journalism (which much poetry seems to
be) why should you expect your scribblings to endure longer
than the daily newspaper? Other questions will come to
mind, I am sure. Obviously, there are other kinds of begin-
nings not in evidence in Geography: the nonsense line, for
example, or the language-syllable line which makes no sense
as ordinary syntax, or the overtly scatalogical line, or the
baldly parodic line. Please, reader, contribute your own
kinds to the list.

I hope I have performed a basic and useful chore by
examining this host of poem-beginnings. I can foresee similar
studies of second, third, and fourth lines. The consumma-
tion of all such studies would be, of course, a monumental
Arithmetic of Poetry, or a Muse's Math, which would in-
deed take the teeth out of Jonathan Williams' first-line com-
mand: "Stop all the literary shit" or provide a stunningly
affirmative answer to Robert Friend's opening query: "But
was the language alive?"

POETRY AND BASEBALL: IS THERE ANY CONNECTION?

Poll of Poets Leaves Foolish Question Up in the Air Over Second
Base, A Satirical Pop Fly--in the manner of the <u>Coda</u> Interview*

From Aristotle's day to this, intellectuals have argued
about the nature of poetry and the influences on it--influences
from the poet's unconscious as well as from the tangible daily
world.   Today, the U. S. literary world is split fatuously be-
tween baseball addicts and despisers of the game.   Towards
resolving what is probably a tempest in the shower-drain,
we have invited a handful of poets to register their feelings
about the noxious sport, in alphabetical order to avoid tan-
trums of envy.

We dedicate the piece to Jonathan Williams, an aficion-
ado of baseball who eschews the team effort and largely goes
it alone, whacking balls into the stratosphere with great zest
and abandon, all the while performing linguistico-boogies on
the names of players and teams, and on arcane lore relative
to the sport.   We further supply this bit of window-dressing,
by way of prelude, recollected by our editor, Robert Peters,
from the folk-wisdom of an old aunt: "I like baseball 'cause
that seam down the back of the player's pants always lies
true to the crack of his ass. "--Aunt Bobbie Lustall, Spring
Green, Wisconsin, 1939.

JOHN CINDERBERRY:

First of all, I don't know.   I never thought of myself
as having much of a relationship to baseball, or baseball
players.   Every hour of my life is surrounded by a lot of
things that don't add up to anything, and these sprout up as
part of a situation I'm writing.   I prefer skating to baseball.
I begin with the figure of a baseball arcing through the air,
on an only partly explicit trajectory.   I end now with a figure

*An abbreviated version of "Poetry and Baseball" is scheduled
to appear in <u>Pulp-Smith.</u>

8 cut starkly in a cake of ice, by a skate. This may be a
geography--if you want to call it that. But you'll have to for-
give me. I'd rather write on the hollow handle of a paper
knife, or on one of the last Czar of Russia's ornamental Eas-
ter eggs.

ROBERT REALLY:

[To be read in a clipped Projective-Verse mode, in an un-
mistakable monotone]

     I wouldn't feel much at ease playing baseball with other
poets, or writing poems about baseball, unless doing so would
result in something like a whole experience with LSD. Yet,
the free-running player winging into home plate, or dashing be-
tween bases (the idea of stealing bases has possibilities) is
the unexpressed question mark some poets (including myself)
love. A poem has to be an echo of something, if only an _if_.
And _if_ there's a baseball team upon your roof reciting Chau-
cer and waiting to fuck your nagging wife, that's fine with me.
To be insistent, rather than make an accumulating statement,
an inning, after all is a kind of canto, isn't it?

JAMES HICKEY:

[Read with a deep Southern accent, crescendoing]

     I'm against it. It's for sissies, and suggests to me
a faggotry of the poetic art. You do a series of dances in
your baseball uniform, you play with a ball about the size
of a dog gonad, and when you sock a ball into that baseball
mitt, it whunks almost as if you've rammed home a sodomic
thrust. I'm for football. There's more beef on the hoof in
football. And when those bodies collide! It's the stuff of
cavemen jetting ever greater poet republics! Vince Lombardi
is my ideal for the perfect poem. Great goddamn! When a
poem like Vince Lombardi comes through the kudzu you'd bet-
ter tackle it and hold on tight, chew his jugular if you must,
or wrench off his nuts--anything to keep a-holt.

ALLEN GINSENG SATSANG:

[Chant, accompanied with Hindu temple finger-bells]

     My data is [sic], as always, half-conscious; yet it

serves as a cosmic flashlight for my nubile-baby, pubescent-navelquest introspections, Himalayan and western. The game, I think, lacks any Hebraic ghostpresence however, is hardly a trip to impel you out toward the cosmic spaces very far, or very fast. Om, Om, Om---!

DONALD VESTIBULE:

[Adopt a casual, chummy, mid-Western tone of mild self-amazement]

I have a wicked self, and that self loves baseball. A baseball game is runic, as a poem is, in the sense you can't flatter it. I feel especially wicked when I am being runic; that's how I felt as an apologist for American verse when I was resident in England, where the persona (myself) seemed, I am sure, awfully insular to the British because of my preference for baseball over cricket. Where would American poetry be without poets to share baseball? There'd be nobody to put in all my anthologies but women.

RICHARD H. MORPHEME:

[To be read with passion, yet with an unmistakable spread of great self-importance--the reading style is the man, etc.]

If you catch the lagoon of my drift, or attempt to paddle about on limpid waters propaedeutically, you will sense that baseball, a noun, requires an adjective steamy, in solution, en gelée, even when, of course, those who struggle adversely with their balls (poems) turn their distaste into Chautauquas of distress. New men. New methods. The locus of baseball, an impenetrable patina of pretty things, and hence of verse, is a refusal of, a languid wrestling of, or at least an insistence on, encouraging moisture to stream along the deepest and most noisome body trenches, flooding the poems with anti-human acceptations--the fans in the stands, towards a logorrheic fungoid growth, having both furred tongue and speech. I remind you of Thomas Aquinas' proposition that Willa Cather was never at home except with muskrat bites. I don't mean to have bad manners, rather hope to formulate an implication, a bravery of attitude, a valorization of baseball separated by an anacoluthon full of despondent sailors.

ERIKA AGING:

I resent, with a mastiff bitch's anger, baseball. Women are mere contraries here, and are seldom allowed to stretch their queyntes over those well-placed diamonds. To my calme observation (do believe mee this), too many American male bards now approaching deeply middle-age affect cute baseball caps whilst allowing their poems (and miserable shrunken cod-pieces) to dangle toward their trencher-side. Their scribblings often sound as if they were strummed on a single high-stretcht lute string--no more. These ambitious bauds have greatly reduced testosterone levels, faint lecherous humours, are woefully shy before all women (except their mothers), and pursue strange meats. I have done.

GALWAY FIRTH:

[To be read in a tone of some Existential distress]

Unless while you are playing the game--it doesn't matter in what position--and are in enough pain to make you grit your teeth, to test your limits; and unless, at that endurance peak, you don't exclude animals, plants, and stones from your interior life, a connection resembling the one a skunk or a porcupine has for another skunk or porcupine, baseball won't affect your poetry much one way or the other. Yet, now that I think of it, if, at the end of a long, hot game, poet-teams could be persuaded to throw their sweat-drenched jockstraps, caps, and uniforms into a heap, at the edge of a woods outside some New Hampshire hamlet, the porcupine and bear and other creatures who'll appear to drink sweat-nectar might suffice to generate a whole new school of totemic animal poems. It's a thought.

DIANA W. KOSKI:

The "team sense" irritates me. I've always wanted to read my poems to a baseball team of poets, right after they've finished a game: Iowa 7, New Hampshire 3. Since baseball is so matter of fact, it fits my matter-of-fact sense of poetry very well. Also, when you were young, game-playing was a good way of starting poems. Neither George Washington nor the King of Spain played baseball, nor even knew of it. Well, if I, naked, wearing only oranges, diamonds, and peaches around my neck, walked into a team's locker room, they probably wouldn't look up--they'd be so stuck on one another. That's when I'd scream at them to stand there jocked while I showed them some real poetry! I'm sure they won't be so contemptuous of women when I'm through with them!

ADRIENNE POOR:

I refuse to answer the question, since so far as I can tell a male asks it.

THE LOST GHABALS OF THE
1st CENTURY PERSIAN POET
HARUN abu-HATIM al-FARSKIN
RECENTLY DISCOVERED*

When a poet's wellsprings dry, the possibility of dis-
covering some long-buried poet or poetic form excites him,
as a means of recharging his own creative energies, or of
slaking his creative urge, until he can once again write, in-
spired by his own watery muses.

A year ago, struck with a horrid fallow period, sterile
and distraught, feeling utterly worthless, I stumbled onto an
amazing discovery: In an upper New York State library, I
came upon an entirely forgotten Persian shepherd poet of the
first century (first quarter) A. D. , Harun abu-Hatim al-Farskin.
How incredible that in an obscure public library (in Pompey's
Head, New York), one of those turn-of-the-century brown-
brick Carnegie libraries cast like dull buckram volumes
throughout the country, had such holdings. For once my fas-
cination with libraries paid off. For years I have ferreted
out special collections, no matter how meager, in the libraries
of whatever towns I happen to be in, knowing that old journals,
letters, and other arts from the luscious spread of the past
often reside there.

When I introduced myself to Mrs. Georgina Strew,
the librarian of Pompey's Head, explained that I was a poet
seeking fresh materials for my writing, and asked whether
there were any archival holdings there that might interest me,
she was excited. No one, she reported, during her tenure
of some fifteen years, had ever inquired after such a thing.
She asked me to sit down. Then she disappeared, returning
with a dusty packet of manila envelopes.

She pulled a small worn leather-bound book from one
of the envelopes. The book contained about twenty numbered

---

*First published as a monograph insert for Invisible City (San
Francisco/Los Angeles) May-June 1979: reprinted in The
Independent (March 1980), 18-20.

pages, highly foxed, quarto-sized. The title page read:
Poems of the Ancient First-Century Poet Harun abu-Hatim al-
Farskin, copied out and translated by Percival Harder, M. A.
Harder had actually signed the flyleaf in watery purple ink,
and had drawn a hyacinth, complete with stem and flower,
a simple one-lined swirl of his pen. Inside were Arabic
poems, followed by translations.

I asked Mrs. Strew how Pompey's Head happened to
own this treasure. Her story was entirely credible: "Harder
was an eccentric Englishman ... one of those eminent Vic-
torians." She blushed. "He liked boys, you know." She
cleared her throat. "When he died, in Sussex, in 1896, the
only one of his relations the court could locate was a nephew
whom he had never met. That nephew, Hubert Harder, D. D.,
was the vicar of our local Episcopal church. Eventually the
Reverend Harder received his uncle's books, papers, and
various personal effects. The vicar evidently destroyed most
of this material, keeping merely this slim book of Harun abu-
Hatim al-Farskin's poems, and," she continued, opening the
second envelope, "this packet of letters and notes. The vicar
bequeathed these papers, along with several manuscripts of
his own sermons, to our library."

The packet of letters was neatly tied with a faded pink
ribbon. Silverfish had nibbled a scattering of holes here and
there.

"Percival Harder apparently died of tuberculosis,"
Mrs. Strew said. "His brief story is here, in these letters:
fading health, coughing and blood, trips abroad to seek relief.
Also, he explains the circumstances of his locating the Per-
sian poems, and how he prized them, hoping that they would
eventually find their way into the mainstream of world poetry
--'in some more enlightened times than ours,' he wrote,
'when references to the male genitalia will be regarded as
sane and normal.'"

I told her of my attempts in the past to write well-
turned ghazals, and how I felt I continually failed to capture
the evanescent patchouli-delicacy of these marvelous forms.
And I had spent several months trying to better Edward Fitz-
gerald's translations of the Rubaiyat--without any success.
Despite my failures, though I still find that tossing off a
ghazal in the manner of Hafiz of Shiraz helps me control
periods of turbulent emotional strain, and periods, too, of
that self-disgust (loathing, almost) all serious poets seem to
undergo when they can't write.

After a few sympathetic remarks, Mrs. Strew led me to a table near a well-lighted window, and told me to make myself comfortable. If she could be of further help, etc....

* * *

I read Percival Harder's introduction to Harun's poems. Harun, Harder explained, was a young shepherd, gifted among the shepherds of his day at creating these three-line poems, writing them down on parchment made from sheepskin, and kept in rolls in special earthen jugs. When Harun reached his maturity--seventeen years, he no longer wrote poems; his boyhood had passed. Harun was, it seems, the only surviving poet of a long Oriental tradition, going back centuries, by which young shepherds whiled away tedious hours on the Persian hills composing and singing poems whilst watching sheep.

Harun was evidently greatly successful; for he was transferred from herding simple village flocks to guarding the more prestigious ones of the local emir. Harder laments that so few--a mere half-dozen--of Harun's poems exist. He guesses that there were originally over two hundred. Harder found them in Baghdad, where he had gone on holiday. He had visited a junk shop in a bazaar in the central city, looking for nothing much in particular, when he found a battered, leather-bound copy of the poems. I should say here that since my own discovery of Harun-Harder, I have inquired via the mails and in person of the more prestigious libraries in this country as to the possible existence of other works by Harun. I have unearthed nothing--except perhaps for a shaky allusion in a German work, I. Goldziher's Die Zahiriten (Leipsig, 1884), in the holdings of the Huntington Library, San Marino, California. There is a reference, on p. 293, to an ancient poet "Harun al-Hateen al-Furskin." Even the most careless scholar will doubt any connection with our Harun. I am still continuing my investigations and intend eventually to publish my own translations of Harun's ghabals, plus a life of the poet, plus all of Harder's letters and translations.

Harder calls these shepherd verse-forms Ghabals. Whether the word is his own invention or not, I can't say. Harder explains that the Arabic word means "little beans," and assumes, wildly, I think, that they are really allusions either to the gonads of adolescent human males, or to those of rams. Considering Harder's odd sexual preferences, I am inclined to discount his interpretation as unfortunate, if not downright misleading. Obviously, the connections of the ghabals with the better-known verse form the ghazal are clear; and I prefer to dissociate any sexual overtones, gonadal or otherwise.

Harder, though, seems accurate in the surmises about the general phenomenon of ancient shepherd poetry, and its relation to a tradition in verse, a tradition hoary and prestigious. Recall the practice of ancient Greek poets--Theocritus, Moschus, and Bion--of composing poems on the departures of friends and lovers. A favorite motif was that of the poet and his friends as shepherds. The shepherd's homely musical pipe, or flute, was a symbol for the instrument of poetry. These poets were sophisticated youths, upper-class, educated, who loved to pretend at being shepherds. Why did they masquerade as primitives? We can only surmise: to resolve gamy sexual urges? to complain about an overly complex contemporary culture by employing imagery from simple rustic life?

Harder was contemptuous of these pretenders, including those poets continuing the convention in his own day: Matthew Arnold, Alfred Tennyson (and, earlier, Percy Shelley and John Milton), reminding us, unfairly perhaps, that these men would hardly have known the face of a sheep from its rear-end. Harun was authentic--Harder insists on his shepherdness. Harun knew the solitary, frozen, bone-breaking hours keeping watch over his flocks. Moreover, Harder guesses that like most Arabian shepherd boys, Harun discovered his heterosexuality via the moist, pinkish receptivity of a substantial ewe; and Harder further speculates, that the prevalence of uranianism (we'd say homosexuality) among these youths was directly due to the distastefulness of these ewe-experiences. There's a bothersome hiatus in Harun's logic here. My feeling is that Harder's own distaste blinded him to the truth.

Harder is utterly clear and thoroughly reliable, however, on the requirements of the ghabal. Obviously, it is one of the most demanding of all these ancient verse forms. It is tight, incredibly tight. Here are its features:

> RULE 1: The ghabal must contain 3 lines and 3 lines only. Each of these lines has its gender: the first and third lines are masculine; the second, with its occasional soft run-over pattern, is feminine.

> RULE 2: Every first line of the ghabal must contain and open with the phrase "He smeared. " The remainder of the line must contain a noun, and may contain up

to but no more than 4 accented syllables.

RULE 3: Line 2 of the ghabal must always remain
constant, and must read: "all over his loins, hoping
to attract...." Harder does not speculate on such
consistency as a desirable feminine quality.

RULE 4: The 3rd, and second masculine line, must
conclude with the phrase "his scrotum"; and it must open
with a noun and a simple action verb. The line may
contain as many as 5 accented syllables. Line 3 may
also be more freely alliterative than either line 1 or
line 2. As for the word "scrotum," Harder notes that
a more accurate translation of Harun's original would
be "pouch" or "bag." Harder felt that the ghabal
needed a bit of sharpening here, and that "scrotum"
has a finer, more evocative hang than pouch, sack or
bag.

Here, then, are the seven ghabals, as written by Harun al-
Farskin, and translated by Percival Harder, M. A.

The first ghabal is a marvelous evocation of middle-
eastern rural life. The fact that the bees are wild rather
than tame is a touch of genius, beautifully mellifluous:

> He smeared wild-bee honey
> All over his loins, hoping to attract
> Bees to sting his scrotum.

The second ghabal is religious and sacramental, and
gives us a glimpse into Harun the devout religionist youth:

> He smeared fresh lambblood
> All over his loins, hoping to attract
> A priest to anoint his scrotum.

The third ghabal is outrageously sexual. The object
of the first line, though, is vexed. Harder supplies "estrogen,"
although he is not entirely certain that "estrogen" was
Harun's word:

> He smeared ewe estrogen
> All over his loins, hoping to attract
> A ram to copulate with his scrotum.

"Ram," of course, relates nicely to medieval Christian beast-

fables where Christ is a ram whose sweet breath attracts
wayward Christians to follow Him. Obviously, I do not imply
that a natural genius, like the peasant Harun, had even heard
of Christianity.

In the 4th ghabal, Harun continues the sexual motif--
assuming, of course, that Harder maintains the order of Ha-
run's original sequence. The original verse, we are told,
refers to "marsh animal," rather than to "beaver." Harder
felt "beaver" would be more meaningful to English readers
than "marsh animal." He considered using "otter," but de-
cided that it lacked the nicety of syllabic bounce he desired.
I find this the least impressive of the seven poems; there's
something facile; and, also, one is inclined to associate such
perverts as sniff-freaks with our own bicycle culture rather
than Harun's:

> He smeared beaver castorum
> All over his loins, hoping to attract
> A sniff-freak to smell his scrotum.

To be completely accurate, Harder does say that Harun wrote
"persistent smeller" rather than "sniff-freak."

The fifth ghabal comes as a relief, returning as it does
to religious motifs:

> He smeared angel-dust
> All over his loins, hoping to attract
> A muezzin to canonize his scrotum.

Ghabal 6 gives us a glimpse into an ancient homely
craft, woodworking, and does mirror the birth of Jesus, some
30 years earlier, and his nurturing in the home of Joseph the
carpenter (cf. my comment on the Christian motifs in ghabal
3 supra).

> He smeared woodchips
> All over his loins, hoping to attract
> A cabinet-maker to dowel his scrotum.

Finally, number 7 is a simple excursion into sheer
Persian playfulness. Harun had his congenial side:

> He smeared chicken feathers
> All over his loins, hoping to attract
> A pullet to lay eggs under his scrotum.

Alas, there are no more of Harun's poems. Clearly, the ghabal was useful for giving voice to various of the ancient shepherd youth's frustrations: sexual, religious, and natural. One can easily imagine Harun abu-Hatim al-Farskin and a host of young shepherd ghabal-poets reciting and declaiming their ghabals (erected) on the spot--poems most testeronic, spurting lovely verse matter lavishly over the stark Arabian landscape of beehives, black-shrouded women, olive trees, stunted desert bushes and oases.

ADDENDUM

There are possible values in encouraging young poets today to compose their own ghabals: prestige, the enhancement of the craft, fame. Towards that end, I've tried my own hand at a few ghabals in a contemporary mode. I realize, of course, that they lack the whiff of ancient sheep-ordure authenticity. Perhaps, though, I do not entirely violate the spirit of the ancient shepherd poem.

> He smeared lug-nut rust
> All over his loins, hoping to attract
> Volkswagen mechanics to lubricate his scrotum.
>
> He smeared pyorrhea germs
> All over his loins, hoping to attract
> A dentist to drill and fill his scrotum.
>
> He smeared bat guano
> All over his loins, hoping to attract
> A bat to cling upside down under his scrotum.
>
> He smeared glue
> All over his loins, hoping to attract
> A poet to paste poems all over his scrotum.

PIONEERS OF MODERN POETRY*

The following is a sampling from <u>Pioneers of
Modern Poetry</u>, an experiment in criticism I
wrote with George Hitchcock in 1966. In these
pieces, George arranged most of the "poems"
from various prose texts, and I wrote most
of the "interpretations." These 23 takes were
first published by Kayak Press in 1967 and
saw several printings. The book is now out
of print. Our ripostes were thrust against
some of the excesses of Projective Verse
poets, their adulators, and academic readings
of poems.

PREFACE

In this slender anthology we present a number of
hitherto little-known folk writers who have in their individual
ways contributed to our poetic heritage and who specifically
anticipate the more popular open-verse forms of today. It
has been our intention to explore the roots of the modernism
movement in poetry. Or to quote from Charles Olson, our
collection is a return "to beginnings, to the syllable, for the
pleasures of it, to intermit."[1]

Like most pioneers, our poets are on the whole bluff,
homely and lacking in elegance. Their ostensible concerns
are unpretentious and of practical aim: instructing youths in
the good life, developing writers of shorthand, teaching bird-
whistles, building siloes, treating dizziness in geese, eradi-
cating rats, and aerating potatoes. Unlikely subjects for
poems, the skeptical reader may retort! "Possibly," as Donald
Hall surmises in one of his recent anthologies,[2] "it has some-
thing to do with the Sitwells." However, hostility to new dis-
coveries in poetry is traditional among anthologists and critics
(cf. J. Keats and the <u>Quarterly Review</u>); we do not expect to

*Reprinted by permission from <u>Pioneers of Modern Poetry</u>
(Santa Cruz, Calif.: Kayak Press), 1967.

overcome this hostility at one stroke, but appeal to the un-
prejudiced reader to grant our poets, plebeian though their
apparent subject matter often is, their proper place in the
history of letters.

And what is that place? We are as wary of making
excessive claims as are, for example, Yvor Winters and
Karl Shapiro, to name two otherwise dissimilar critics. But
we cannot conceal our conviction that many of the poems
which appear in this volume are of a truly pivotal importance
in the evolution of modern poetry, particularly of the now
largely dominant open-field or open-face forms. Most of
these poets composed their major works long before those of
more celebrated contemporaries and, while we do not un-
reservedly subscribe to the argument post hoc propter hoc,
it must in fairness be pointed out that Cassell and Miles pre-
ceded Rimbaud by some decades, the anonymous Master of
the London News was coeval with Whitman in his great period,
and Arthur Barnes, concealed in the obscurity of Missouri,
was writing his epochal "Distinguishing Ru from Chu" long
before the birth of Ezra Pound and some thirteen years be-
fore the publication of Ernest Fenollosa's seminal "The Mas-
ters of Ukioye." Yerkes' and Yoakum's "Chairs Sit Are To
On" anticipates the cut-up prose poems of William Burroughs
and Jackson MacLow by at least three and a half decades,
while, as for Dr. William Carlos Williams, who (as a re-
porter for the National Observer recently observed[3]) "developed
an esthetic that exalted new forms; plain talk; 'concrete, '
objective subject matter; and lines measured not by the meter
but by the rhythm of speech itself," it is apparent that his
discoveries in this area are substantially predated by F. W.
Woll's "The Silo" (1915) and Stewart and Mix's classic "The
Experiment" (1917). It is not, of course, our intent to
denigrate the work of the more celebrated modern poets, but
merely to restore an essential balance to literary history.

At first sight many of these poems may, to the unini-
tiated, seem to resemble prose. But the phenomenon of
"plain talk" poetry, of lines measured by breath-units and
speech rhythms, should not disturb any modern reader. As
Wallace Kaufman writes,[4] "What does it matter that ... po-
etry is written in what is technically called prose? It works
like poetry.... Poetry is in the final analysis something that
happens in our mind, an event if you want to call it that."

In presenting these poetic "events" (to adopt Mr. Kauf-
man's felicitous phrase) our aim has been to invent nothing.
The lines are everywhere the creation of the poets themselves;

we have striven, somewhat after the fashion of Mr. Oliver Davie (q. v.) to measure, shape and arrange these poems in the most lifelike fashion possible, prompted in every case by what we felt to be the author's true intentions. Thus by supplying verse lines and stanzas for many of these poems we hope we have released internal rhymes and symbolic echoes from the formidable loam of "prose" in which they have lain interred for generations. But our contribution has been one of discovery not of invention.

For the convenience of the classroom we have appended to each poem or group of poems a brief explication clarifying certain textual problems and suggesting fruitful lines of further inquiry for the student who wishes to grasp the total gestalt or matrix from which the poem has sprung. Our critical work is admittedly fragmentary and tentative; however, should popular interest justify it, we are prepared to add Study Questions, an Index, and a Critical Outline to subsequent editions. Adequate biographical materials are, unfortunately, lacking for most of our poets. Standard reference works have (shortsightedly, we are convinced) shown an historic reluctance to list the vitae of unrecognized poets. We do not wish to berate them; future bibliographers will, no doubt, tip the scales in favor of essential justice. The present editors have merely held up the lantern of knowledge to shed a dim aureole in the surrounding darkness--let those who follow bring the piercing rays of scholarship to bear upon this night of needless anonymity.

Notes

1. From his essay on "Projective Verse" as printed in The New American Poetry: 1945-60, Donald Allen, editor, p. 392.
2. New Poets of England and America: Second Selection, 1962, p. 21.
3. July 11, 1966, p. 24. The article is called "Where New Poetry Finds Fertile Ground: The Men, the Magazines, and Their Presses and Spice."
4. Wallace Kaufman, "Our Unacknowledged Poetry: An Essay on James Agee," Agenda: Special Issue: U.S. Poetry, 1966, p. 74.

LOVE ON THE CANAL BOAT

by EDWIN J. BRETT

1.

Why is love like a canal boat?
Why is a sword like beer?
When is a man a perfect chimney?
What's the latest thing in boots?

   Watchmakers
   When it's turned round
   It's the sole support of man
   Make the trousers first

2.

What is that which works when it plays
and plays when it works?
Why is there nothing like leather?
Who gets credit for good works?

   It's an internal transport
   An urchin
   A fountain
   It's of no use till it's drawn

3.

What's the best way of making a coat last?
When is an egg not oval?
Why is chloroform like Mendelssohn?
What chin is that which is never shaved?

   It's one of the great composers of modern
              times
   When it doesn't smoke
   Stockings
   Make the trousers first.

   (from "Boys of England" magazine, 1882)

   Here is a fine set of "cherry-stone enigmas of anomia,"
as a critic paid compliment to Robert Creeley's poems re-
cently. * They are calculated to please the most fastidious

---

*Michael Alexander, "William Carlos Williams and Robert
Creeley," Agenda (1966), p. 66. The entire paragraph follows:
"That is how they most of them are, Creeley's (cont. on p. 121)

taste which prefers cameos to slabs of marble and, like Creeley's poems, they "have the delicacy" of Anglo-Saxon riddles. Abundant surface difficulties provoke thought, and hence satisfy and seem purposeful once the mind breaks through to the various levels of meaning. And as in all good riddles the unexpected abounds: Who, for example, would think of comparing love to a canal boat, a sword to beer, chloroform to Mendelssohn? A poet might, or a mathematics master introducing his boys to the intricacies of logic, or a girl wiggling out of her dress after her first party. Answers are tantalizingly concealed in the quatrains of the poem, where a splendid variety exists: Some answers are simply names, others are definitions, still others are imperatives. The most telling line of all is one of the imperatives--"Make the trousers first"--which concludes the first quatrain and the poem itself. This is verse at its most playful, in a state of undress, one might say, pursuing the trouser metaphor. The puns are delicious: Both Mendelssohn and chloroform are "great composers"; stockings are "the sole support of man, " etc. It is tempting to report them all; but we resist, leaving our readers to experience their own discoveries.

MEASUREMENTS OF LARGE MAMMALS

by OLIVER DAVIE

    1.
Circumference of neck
  below the head
Circumference of neck
in front of the chest
Circumference of body
behind the fore legs
Circumference of body
before the hind legs

The circumference
      of the
      muzzle

---

*poems--cherry-stone enigmas of anomia. They have the delicacy of some of the Anglo-Saxon riddles. The medieval definition of the rhetorical figure of Enigma was a surface difficulty provoking thought, which provided its own satisfaction and purpose when the mind broke through to the meaning. There is something of that in Creeley. 'Oh No' is an easy example of this; the answer is 'Heaven'. "

is always recorded
also of the head
in front of
the ears

2.
Humerus and femur
measurements:
feel
for the knobs
of the humerus and femur
and measure
the distance
between them

feel for the knob
of the femur
and then
strike
the center line

ONE OF THE MOST IMPORTANT MEASUREMENTS
WHICH CAN BE RECORDED

feel for the knob

should be taken again
after the animal
has been skinned.

3.
Length of the back
is made by beginning
at the base of the skull
along the line of the back
to the base of the tail

Length of tail
is always a
necessary
measurement
when
a mammal
is to be
mounted

by the dermo-
plastic
method.

(from "Methods in the Art of Taxidermy, " 1894.)

"The Measurement of Large Mammals" deals with a
problem which so far as we know is entirely original in poetry.
The subject matter is so basic that the work might well be a
part of a longer poem on Noah appointing the specimens for
the ark, or on Adam and Eve taking inventory in the Garden
of Eden.   Oliver Davie writes with a marvellous unenigmatic
sureness; he knows precisely where the various measurements
of these mammals are to be taken and exactly how one de-
tects say the position of humerus and femur by feeling the
living, as opposed to prehistoric, animal.   There is absolutely
nothing blind here; Davie is not another of those legendary
Orientals mistaking the physical parts of the elephant for en-
tirely incongruous things.   He knows his craft intimately,
whether it be writing or taxidermy.   One of his delights is
the superbly handled repetition of key words and phrases.
The opening stanza is a structural marvel based upon re-
peated motifs combined with sentence units of approximately
the same length and syllabic arrangement.   Further, one is
impressed by the neat logical progression of parts from head
to legs to back to tail.   There is something clean and neat
about this entire performance.   We feel assured in the hands
of this master, and are nearly willing to allow him to take
our own measurements along the lines he describes.   In fact,
his gentleness is so appealing that we may even crave to have
ourselves stuffed by him.   Is this illusion, however, or is it
delusion?   A quality does emerge slowly from these lines not
entirely unlike lust, and one comes to wonder whether sodomy
isn't the writer's true subject.   In fact, the more one con-
siders it, the more anxious one grows.   See the material in
part 2 which advises repeated feelings of the knob, striking
the center line, and feeling the knob again.   And doesn't one
detect a sort of lustful snigger behind the block capitals of
"ONE OF THE MOST IMPORTANT MEASUREMENTS / WHICH
CAN BE RECORDED"?   Davie seems to be cruising for con-
tacts.   The last line of this section--we blush to say it--may
refer to the nasty business of drawing back the prepuce of the
horse, bull, tiger, elephant, etc.   Finally, there is absolutely
no concealment in section 3: by "the dermoplastic method, "
the affixing of skin to skin, the "mammal" (note the wonder-
ful equivocation here--as we suspected, humans are included)

"is to be / mounted. "   Penetration is, of course, one such
"dermoplastic method. "   If it were not for the consummate
artistry of this exceptional poem we would surely have ex-
cluded it.   Our criterion has been throughout that quality of
execution supersedes content; and we can only hope that the
vast majority of readers will agree that we are justified in
allowing this disturbing poem to appear in print.   Finally, it
does illustrate a contemporary principle--that no subject mat-
ter ought to be excluded by the poet, no matter how potentially
disgusting or perverse.

THE DISEASES

of adult bees are but imperfectly
    known
at present four are known to bee-keepers
   by name:

1.
Dysentery

affects bees only in
    winter
after a good cleansing
    flight
the trouble usually disappears
    but
if the bees are unable to fly they
    die
in great numbers.

2.
The So-Called Paralysis

Worker bees are seen crawling
    in front
of the hive with their abdomens dis-
    tended
frequently the bees so affected
    are al-
most hairless.   The cause of this
    peculiar
trouble is unknown and no remedy
    can be
recommended.

3.
Isle of Wight Disease

has recently decimated the adult
           bees
on the Isle of Wight and is said to be
           spreading
in England. So far as is known no
           trouble
of this kind has been experienced in
           America.

4.
Spring Dwindling

is probably due to the fact that the colony
           goes
into winter with too many old worn-out
           bees
dwindling may be diminished by
           keep-
ing the colony warm so that
           all
of the energy of the old bees may be
           used
to the best advantage.

                    --by E. F. Phillips, Ph. D.
               (from his "The Treatment of Bee
               Diseases," Washington, D. C. , 1911.)

        This stunning four-part poem belongs to the genre of
the fable poem, if one includes works dealing with bees and
animals but having no plots as such, but containing themes
touching human affairs. As the title reveals, the subject is
bees and their diseases. There are ramifications of the socio-
political sort one finds in Mandeville's ambitious work, The
Fable of the Bees. Phillips confronts the problem of geri-
atrics in the hive, poor ventilation, and the laboring condi-
tions of the workers.

        It is possible that Phillips might have arranged his
stanzas differently. They vary between reports and descrip-
tions. He might have alternated a stanza describing a dis-
ease with a report (stanzas 3 and 4). The poignant stanzas
are certainly the first two which are fraught with tragic over-

tones. In the first, bees are trapped in a dysentery-befouled hive. Some perish in their own excrement, a substance jocularly known in some circles as honey. Others manage to purge themselves in flight, befouling the landscape in the process. The paralysis of the bees is, if possible, even more harrowing. The disease is peculiar and there is no remedy. One can imagine the intense suffering, to say nothing of the personal embarrassment, of these hapless insects. The image of a mass of hairless workers, suffering with dyspepsia and trying to hide their nakedness from the world, although potentially risible, in these circumstances is hardly so.

DIZZINESS IN GEESE

by "The Poultry Doctor"

(from his "The Poultry
Doctor, Including the
Homeopathic Treatment
and Care of Chickens,
Turkeys, Geese, Ducks
and Singing Birds,"
Philadelphia, 1891.)

a rush of blood to the head
worms in the nostrils
or ears   blows on the head

dizziness in geese
is known as "staggers"
sometimes as "vertigo."

drooping wings
stretched-out neck
body is often shaken
turned around and around
until the bird

falls over
and dies.

a rush of blood to the head
worms in the nostrils
or ears   blows on the head

rush of blood--
    belladonna and
    cool fresh water

```
blow --
    aconite
    followed by
    belladonna

worms --
    give cina
    or a little
    turpentine
    or kerosene
    in the nostrils,
    fill the ears with
    sweet oil or milk
```

<u>a rush of blood to the head</u>
<u>worms in the nostrils or ears</u>
<u>blows on the head.</u>

"Dizziness in Geese" is another poem on a thoroughly unpleasant subject. Dizziness of the mortal sort described is distasteful enough when it occurs in humans; but when fowls are the victims there is bound to be a certain detachment. The poultry doctor, as he calls himself, rubs our noses in it, alas. There is little relief anywhere. Even his efforts to find antidotes scarcely palliate the miserable illness he describes. One has the impression of graves opening and hosts of bleeding wormy corpses coming to life, administering blows to one another's skulls. "Dizziness in Geese" is clearly another of those poems, among the most ancient of poetic genres, dealing with human issues via the animal kingdom. There is something ruthless and Bosch-like about such works. Here the Boschian element is not exactly relieved by the macabre attempt to sweeten the whole through the italicized refrain. Such an obsession with violence is regrettable, despite the fact of its prevalence in the world about us, and despite our rediscovery that the world we live in is in truth like that pictured by Hieronymus Bosch and Pieter Brueghel (the Elder). If we were living in the Middle Ages or the early Renaissance we might feel more comfortable with a dance-of-death literature. But we are uncomfortable and don't want to admit either the chilling justness of such a poem as this or its appropriateness as a subject matter. But the work of this unknown master is too compelling to permit us to escape its strictures.

CHAIRS SIT ARE TO ON

by Majors C. S. Yoakum (1879-1945) and
R. M. Yerkes (1876-1956)

(from their "Army
Mental Tests," 1920.)

happiness lists
     great casualty cause
legs flies
     one have only
gotten sea water
sugar is
     from trees
the fish in swim
harness paper of
made is
     young nurse
their cats and cows
from honey comes
     bread

many toes fingers
as men have
and eat good
gold silver to are
water cork
on float will not
vote children 21
cannot under
will live bird
     no
forever

trees in nests
     build birds
leaves the trees in
     lose their fall
is the salty
     in water
     all lakes
seen
can the moon nights
not be some true bought
cannot
friendship be and

emotions   sorrow   similar
grief
are

tropics is in
the produced   rubber

Alaska in
cotton grows

trees   roses   sea
and in grow they
chairs   sit   are   to   on

It will no doubt come as a shock to modern readers to be told that the poem we print above was published with the official imprimatur of the U. S. War Department under Warren Harding's administration! It is the only known case on record where an American governmental agency has been induced (or perhaps "tricked" would be the better word) into attaching its seal of approval to avant-garde art. The authors, both eminent psychologists, smuggled the poem into their standard "Army Alpha" tests where it purports to be a series of "jumbled sentences" which draftees were to unscramble. It may even be argued that the poetry in "Chairs" is accidental, although we find such a hypothesis difficult to accept in light of the obvious metrical sophistication of the work.

We have given close attention to the textual problems embedded in this poem, particularly to the question of each individual's share in the authorship. After comparing passages in Yerkes' earlier work, "The Dancing Mouse" (1907), with equivalent lines in "Chairs," we are convinced that the more playful conceits (e. g. , "harness paper of made is" and "Alaska in cotton grows") are his contribution, while the overall architectonic of the poem is more probably the work of Yoakum, whose other book ("The Selection and Training of Salesmen," 1925) shows a much slighter poetic talent. The division of labor which we provisionally assign, then, is somewhat along the lines that Elizabethan scholars allocate to Beaumont and Fletcher, the former being generally assigned the poetic passages while the latter is held responsible for the taut dramatic structure of their collaborative efforts. This conjecture (and we confess that, lacking external testimony, it must remain a mere conjecture) is also supported by the imaginative resourcefulness displayed in Yerkes' later book,

"The Mind of a Gorilla" (1927), from which we should quote were there space.

WHAT TO SAY TO THE PASHA

by The Rev. Anton Tien, Ph. D. , F. R. A. S.

> (from his "Egyptian,
> Syrian and North-African
> Hand-Book, A Simple
> Phrase-book in English
> and Arabic for the Use
> of the Armed Forces and
> Civilians. ")

1.

Shall I assist you to alight?
Procure for me a little milk and honey
Pitch my tent and spread out my carpet
The wind is keen today
We may have a storm tonight
It lightens
It thunders

The air is very temperate
The trees are beginning to be covered with leaves
Autumn is the season for fruit
The sky begins to get cloudy
The nights are short and the days are long
The snow is fast melting from the ground
The enemy has advanced as far as Kafr-dawar
Of what advantage will this be to me?

> #### 2.
>
> Whose?
> Not yet
> We want
> I will give you
> Wait patiently
> Leave it alone
> Go away
> Why are you here?

3.

In which direction is the wind?
It is an easterly wind

It is a westerly wind
It is a northerly wind
It is a southerly wind
I have been very much occupied

4.

How many men has the Pasha?

5.

Is the proof of this news strong?
They are hidden behind the mound
They are advancing from the rear
Be quiet
Don't make a noise
It seems that the enemy is restless

6.

Do not the mosquitoes trouble you?

7.

Undo it
Tie it up
Turn it over
I hope you are better
Is it not so?

8.

What is your name?
Who are you?
I am a Bedouin
We are Bedouins
What are you doing here?
We have come to fight and to loot

I am anxious to return to the camp

9.

It is enough
How far is it from this place?
Do me the favour
Do not forget
How do you do?
Mind your business
It is painful
This is painful

10.

Bring in the rebels

Tie their hands and feet
You have done it well
Joseph, bring in the dinner
Will you please to sit next to the lady?

11.

I am wounded
I am shot

Shot in my arm
Shot in my leg
Shot in my foot
Shot in my chest
Shot in my head

Bind up my wound
Give me something to drink, for
I am thirsty

12.

Have pity on me
Spare my life

I surrender myself

The Near East has exercised a powerful attraction to the Western imagination for centuries, but seldom has so much been implied about the Westerner in that world as in the Reverend Anton Tien's dramatic poem "What to Say to the Pasha." Edward Fitzgerald's Omar Khayyam was transplanted to a skeptical-Victorian-bachelor-author's rose garden, while Burton, Doughty and T. E. Lawrence all saw the Muslim world through the glass of their Romantic predilections. How refreshing in contrast to turn to "What to Say to the Pasha"!

Out of the deceptively erotic Khayyamism of the opening lines there develops a world of violence, personal tragedy and typical misdirected Victorian military plans (see any of several frank accounts of the Crimean War and of the indifference of Gladstone's government to the plight of General Gordon at Khartoum.) And note how skillfully Tien prepares for the ultimate Lear-like tragedy: "We may have a storm tonight," he says (Sec. 1, line 4). Yet this note of foreboding is accompanied by a strange onanistic self-absorption, peculiarly modern in its anguish. "Of what advantage will this be to me?" the speaker asks.

As the enemy draws near, the speaker becomes nervous, as the telegraphic set of phrases in # 2 so brilliantly suggests. It is possible to detect also a kind of upper-class British sniffiness in the last lines of this section:

> "Leave it alone
> Go away
> Why are you here?"

These are the sorts of commands and demands a British officer worthy of his rank and trained in the better public schools and at Oxbridge would properly be expected to make. And we must not be misled by what seems a petulant and womanish tone: The mesh jockstrap belies the mailed fist; The Tennysonian concern for wind directions (sec. 3) has nothing whatever to do with lullabies.

The speaker's next question exudes a pustulent irony and reveals the incredible failure of Victorian military intelligence, adumbrating all manner of debacles. Certainly the qualified hero in the midst of such a predicament should know the size of the Pasha's army! But now the enemy is upon him! And here the enviable tenderness of the English character in times of stress appears full blown. The hero solicitously turns to his water-boy (pre-Kipling, we assume): "Do not the mosquitoes trouble you?" he asks. In the keenest danger, there is time for tenderness over those less fortunate than yourself. It is this inspired touch that elevates the poem beyond the level of a Stephen Phillips or Ouida and gives it a truly Shakespearian flavor.

From this point the poem moves with amazing swiftness. Someone is apparently wounded (sec. 7). The speaker, very appropriately in the role now of nurse-medico, advises the wounded man to undo his leggings and tie his blasted calf, or knee, in proper bandages. Once again the hero is solicitous: "I hope you are better / Is it not so?" The exchange with the Bedouin enemy which follows is a brilliant orchestration of hostile voices, while the dinner sequence (sec. 10) is obligatory for protocol. The lady is essential in a different way-- she is the archetypal betrayer. Delilah amidst the sands. The solicitousness of the captured Britisher at the feast cuts no ice with her; she is not taken in by his surface interest in the opposite sex and shortly has him shot--as he starkly reports to us--in "several places." As his life-blood ebbs away the speaker nobly chooses (in the manner of Oedipus submitting to the worst the gods can inflict) to "surrender" himself. What unabashed dignity in that statement! What a triumph for the universal man--the true subject of all poetry worthy of the name--shot full of holes but still the undaunted master of his will. It takes more than a few Bedouin bullets, the poet tells us, to extinguish the courage of a properly-educated, dedicated British officer.

PART THREE

"Never crowd the frying kettle.
You can develop a machine-like
precision by adding one dough-
nut at a time to the kettle, at
about 15-second intervals for
the first six doughnuts."
--Irma S. Rombauer,
Joy of Cooking.

FREUD'S BLOCKS, EINSTEIN'S SIZZLE:

Guy Beining's The Ogden Diary*

In this short poem-novel, Ogden, the hero, scribbles
in a diary in the cellar of a burnt-out house. A second
"voice" assembles the diary entries, and provides opening
and closing commentaries after Ogden's death. Ogden floats
around in the dark cellar, hosting occasional memories (sex-
ual and otherwise) of his twin sister and of his life in New
Hampshire and Florida. His diary begins on April 1 (is the
whole book a fool's joke?) and stops towards the end of the
month. By that time, just before he dies, Ogden has lost
track of dates. He's a very contemporary dude, hidden away
from the conventional worlds of business, war, family, re-
spectability. He scavenges rat-like to keep his sanity for a
few final days. He eats canned sweet-potatoes, thinks of his
dead cat Tom burned in the house-fire, cuts his finger on a
Budweiser bottle, recalls ripping out a car radio from his
sister's car, and realizes that his emotions are "in the
ground." He feels his death approaching as cold soaking
through his bones. He lacks any way not to trace time. He
hallucinates, and is relieved that Freud's blocks and Einstein's
sizzle no longer haunt his brain. Never self-pitying or
frightened, he goes "haiku to bed"--a truncated symbol of
his dying self. Life is "a synthetic bed." To escape, Ogden
must evaporate, "become ambiguous"; his death translates
him into a "worldless void." A final diary entry declares
his joy over reaching the end. He is in a coma, and has
been trundled off to a hospital, where he lingers briefly and
dies. At this point, the second voice takes over and reports
Ogden's hospital stay, with a coolness much like Ogden's when
he was scribbling in his diary. Is voice #2 Ogden's, speaking
from the void? Or is voice #2 another person whose destiny
resembles Ogden's? Is this whole book a parable for our own
spinnings into the void?

I'm intrigued by Beining's book--it leaves a lot un-
answered. The chart and design of Ogden are so elusive.

---

*Reprinted by permission from Small Press Review (Decem-
ber 1979), p. 10.

This is not to say that Ogden is automatic writing; it isn't.
But two bizarre minds speak out here. Perhaps Ogden is an
exercise in a form poets seem to be trying more and more
these days, a bastard form, borrowing both from poetry and
fiction. Ogden kept me thinking and re-reading. The poetry
itself is free verse, tense, flexible. Beining knows what he
is up to. And the prints, by Tom Sutton, provide an uncanny
reinforcement for Beining's story--each picture anchors to a
physical motif in the poem near which, or around which, it
appears. Sutton's sensibility is as engaging, and as puzzling,
as Beining's.

TOUGHENING UP FOR THE EIGHTIES:

James Bertolino's <u>Are You Tough Enough for the Eighties</u>?*

     Through poems laced with a Grand Guignol arsenic,
celebrating various mutants and otherwise maimed folk, foe-
tuses, and beasts, James Bertolino proved over and over
again that he was tough enough for the seventies.   Now,
seeing this new book--although it contains only twenty poems
--I am confident that Bertolino is tough enough for the eight-
ies.   X-rays of teeth crowned with decay appear throughout
this handsomely designed book, providing a mood of sanitized
(via film) but ruthless rot, a premonition perhaps of what we
poor bastards are in for in this new decade.   Bertolino gives
some hope though, by providing us with a new savior for the
eighties, a "genius mongoloid" who comes to lead us to and
through this "new world. "   He's the special creature of a new
and appropriate mythology, a goat-footed turtle, as he de-
scribes himself, epitome of the mutants produced by our D.
D. T. sprayings, gender-fuckings, and mindless hormonal in-
jections.   In the mongoloid poem, our beloved creature, a
"red-faced genius, " comes "like the balloon / of no karma"
to save us.

     How do we appear through Bertolino's eyes?   Well,
we've lost most of our feelings.   The world collapses and the
best we can do is watch.   Our politicians are addicted to
sadism and cruelty.   A senator from Nevada throws a cat in
a closet and sets off cherry-bombs.   Another politician is so
old his armpits have gone bald.   The "nice guy, " shafted in
the seventies, will be murdered in the eighties (see "The Nice-
Guy, " Bertolino's longest poem).   Bertolino is our voice; but
he's "dying / of this language" and wanders in these frigid
"post-literal alps" at the start of a new decade.   Our blood
thins.   We want to walk right out of our limbs and run off,
hoping to survive by becoming once again amphibious.   Bore-

---
*Reprinted by permission from <u>Northeast Rising Sun</u> (Fall/
Winter 1980), pp. 15-16.

dom, love-failures, physical pain are our norms. Like the
old cat after her abortion, we know we've lost something
crucial, yet we continue to believe we are about to generate
a birth:

> In the study, near the bed, near
> the blackened bootstring's
> constellation of knots,
> the old cat lies pulling at
> her stitches. Already the fresh
>
> bleeding has mixed with the orange
> of antiseptic. Already the wound
> has become hers. Now her sharp tongue
>
> probes for the tumor, that comforting lump
> she knew as kitten. But no, her last
> chance to nurse and clean
> has been taken, and now her slow
> body shivers, her head goes down.

This poem is ruthless.

Some readers, I would guess, will find Bertolino un-
bearable. Who wants to meditate on the X-rays of somebody
else's caries? Who wants to believe that poetry can deal
with more than the nicer things of life? Toughtitty, I say!
Bertolino's work is full of Mary Lincolnesqueries. I suspect
he's right in seeing the mutant in all of us. He provides a
memento mori for the times; but I doubt that he really ex-
pects us to take much heed.

GOING NAKED IN THE POETRY WORLD:

Michael Blumenthal's Sympathetic Magic*

I'm glad I finally touched this book. I didn't want to because of the repulsive pink cover, the tint of blood coughed up by someone whose lungs are nearly wasted away. For $6.50, and to celebrate a second printing, I'm sure the publisher could have given us something less malodorous. I had not read any of Blumenthal's poems before; and I now shout huzzahs. Several are stunning. This surprised me; the heavy laying on of hands by Howard Nemerov, Grace Schulman, Linda Pastan, Gerald Stern, and Charles Fishman (in a fulsome foreword); the numerous headquotes from writers as diverse as Merwin, Oppen, Rich, Shakespeare, Hamsun, Duane Michaels, the dictionary, Kirkegaard, Tom Wolfe, and Ezra Pound--all gave the impression that these poems were so heavily blessed and inspired that Blumenthal must be a shameless sycophant. What a delight to find that he's good enough to have gone naked through his own poetry world. I wish he had.

First, he has range. He writes with power of his Jewish background, of his peregrinations away from people who've loved him, of feelings from inside the skins of strange women, of ironic glances towards the world around him. Second, he is a master of the unexpected insight. What poet would find inspiration in a passel of young lawyers all pissing at the same time in a row of urinals while reading briefs (not fruit-of-the-looms)? A realtor is a giant iguana. A man places his head "like a pat of butter" between his lover's breasts. Used condoms weave "like white eels in a Hudson / we dreamt clean as a mountain river." Abandoning your Toyota in a snowstorm is "better than leaving your wife or your nagging lover."

I risk giving the impression that Blumenthal is mainly

*Reprinted by permission from Gargoyle 15/16 (Jan 1981).

a poet of stunning moments. This is not true (and this is
his third quality): He has a sculptured simplicity. He's
direct, in the way that Neruda and García Lorca are. Blumen-
thal is deeply anchored in a life of keen and moving observa-
tions. Fourth, he is one of the few poets I know who uses
the declarative poem well--that mode so befouled, noisome,
and tacky that it pretends to tell you what you've done, seen,
and felt. Almost always, Blumenthal uses this over-exploited
device with originality. Here is how he addresses an old
woman who urinates in the night:

> You would go to pee--
> the bedpan held between your shaking limbs,
> a tired old plumber,
> a wind-up doll
> on its last rotation.

Here, Blumenthal tells an aging Jew, proud of his penis,
what's really going on:

> And then you go to your bed,
> and you make love to your wife like a Jew,
> with your desperate tongue and your mutilated penis
> and your envy of womanhood grown so large
> you are the best lover in the world, better
> than Robert Redford and all the goyische skiers,
> better than the Black athletes with their beautiful,
> round buttocks that turn like greased bearings
> in your wife's Jew-hating dreams.

When he employs that other popular convention, the
"I" voice, he is equally fresh. Occasionally, "I" is Blumen-
thal, at other times it is not (viz., the marvellous "Prosthe-
tics"). "A Brief History of Modern Art" evokes Duchamp:
why not give up poetry and play chess? An image of a heart
suggests Duchamp and Max Ernst blent:

> I open the window, hang my heart
> from a string beside the birdfeeder,
> wait for answers. As I wait, I play chess
> at the table, watch the nuthatch peck
> at my heart, the lightning strike it,
> the dank air invade its vague geometry.
> Weeks of no full moon, no light. Check,
> I cry, sighting a break in the clouds.
> Checkmate, answers my buffeted heart.

Rather than keep raving about Blumenthal, I shall con-

clude by looking briefly at one poem I admire and comment
on a pair of poems which should work better than they do.
In "Night Rocking" the speaker, nude, goes to the living room,
leaving his wife's bed early in the morning. He sits in a
rocker, kills a bottle of wine, and reflects. He imagines the
imprints he makes whenever he moves his body to a new
space: his damp form remains pressed to the sheets he has
left, "the way a victim's blood / holds the shape of an acci-
dent. " The motion of rocking reminds him of tides, of his
restless departures from his woman and of his returns to her.
Finally, he "peels himself" from the wooden rocker and re-
turns to bed, "the way an old beach sleeper returns to the
print / of his body in sand. " A closing, stern image con-
veys his sense of subtle cruelties:

> ... I sleep again,
> knowing you will wake in the morning, stretch
> your small hands towards me, forgiving me
> as sand forgives the restlessness of tide,
> as an old widow forgives the beatings of her dead
> husband.

I shall close with a pair of carpings: in "Manoxylous" the
y endings (constancy, unity, duty, etc.) seem ineptly scattered;
and the second stanza is prosy. "Dining with the Half-Mad, "
in the style of W. C. Williams fails to transcend its abstrac-
tions. These reservations are minor; Blumenthal is an im-
pressive poet. I gather that this is his first book. May
there be many more.

A POSITIVE, POSITIVE REVIEW:

Carmine Lips's Over and Over Again*
(Published by Cat's Ass Press, Up, California
94719, 3½ pp. $4. 50.)

This small, beautifully produced book is one of the
most powerful I've read in recent years and will surely re-
main one of those books I return to again and again through-
out my life. You know you're in the presence of a great
piece of work when it pisses you off. You throw it down, say
"Fuck this, " ... then a day passes and you go back and you
start reading again--and the anger starts all over again.
Lips is also very sensitive, for example, and very, very
funny. There is humor and human concern in the verse, but
also care for all living things. She is also prepared to drive
a Honda into the sunrise with a bare foot touching the ground.
She's trying for the highest kind of self-enclosed lapidary per-
fection. Once, though, you can see into the cover, what is
inside the book will come out to meet you. This is simply
one of the best books of poems I have ever seen. These
poems have so much range and warmth that I cannot pick
isolated passages to quote. This is a book of great subtlety
(something missing from much contemporary poetry), of gentle
profundity, of suggestion that is unexpectedly powerful in its
gradual unfolding. The style, effective and unaffected, is un-
like any I've come across. Praise the book! Praise the
poets!

---

*This collage review is made up of bits and pieces from actual
reviews appearing in an issue of Small Press Review; I as-
sembled it in protest against sugary reviews, thoroughly
positive in nature, which do a real disservice, I feel, to
poetry. Reprinted by permission from Small Press Review
(October 1979), p. 12.

OVINE VS. URSINE POETRY:

Mary Cheever's The Need for Chocolate

On The Need for Chocolate the publishers have spared
no expense. The paper is heavy. The book is well-glued.
Most of the pages are lavish with white space; in fact, most
stanzas or brief parts of poems get a whole page to themselves.
A dozen lines probably required the pulping of several magnifi-
cent trees. The type is primer-big.

I grew increasingly depressed as I read along. I con-
cluded that these poems would probably never have been pub-
lished by a large trade house if the author weren't so well-
connected--mother of Susan, wife of John. And a Sol Stein
took the photo of the author up against a tree. Is he the
Stein of Stein & Day, the publisher? I dismissed these
thoughts as being irresponsible. Casting about for a way of
reviewing such a book, I invented a contrast which may be
useful, one which says much about American poetry, as it
is written by both males and females. The poles of this con-
trast are what I call ovine vs. ursine poetry. Here is what
I mean.

Much poetry I read these days published by trade
houses is ovine, sheep-like, written by poets who write a
competent verse modelled after college and writing workshop
courses. While the competence seldom descends to the level
of work by Susanne Somers, Rod McKuen, Leonard Nimoy,
Ray Bradbury, or Leonard Cohen, ovine poetry remains
placid and cud-chewing. The forage such writers nibble is
made up of poetical wisps (clichés) and fancy daisies (meta-
phors) easily plucked.

On the other hand, there are poets who write out of
an ursine originality and fervor. They rend life with their
claws, and write out of energies seldom dependent on what
safe poets are doing or have done. No placid ovinians these.
Here I include Diane Wakoski, Cynthia Macdonald, and Lyn

144

Lifshin (at her best). You may add your own poets to the list. She-bears are loners except when they are in heat. Their forest-psyche domains are their own--and they strive to keep other creatures away. Even when they write badly their work has an invention and wildness that keeps one reading.

What, then, makes Mary Cheever's poems ovine? I shall be as exact as I can.

In one of her best poems (parts of it are moving), she recalls her son's birth and reports that while he was being born she saw a red sun suddenly slip from a "bottomless vault." This good image quickly disappears in a verbose self-speculation built around being, been, and was, followed by an easy simile (Cheever is a simile addict): Her daughter is "like a wakeful bird over water." The problem is one of artistic tact, of knowing when to allow a poem to be ursine, to let its vigor swell without destroying it via fancy writing, without, that is, striving to make it sound good, like a good poem should.

Another feature of ovine poetry is the overuse of fancy adjectives. These are usually antiseptic, up-tight, pretty. The ovine poet stops the poem for the sake of a chic literary effect. In her "American Cancer Society," Cheever devotes several key lines to describing the exfoliation of a cancer, potentially a power-house motif. But she kills it via arty images and adjectives: aberrant, jeweled, luscious, hoarded. Even during the rare moments when she is sexual (at one point she dares to say fart), Cheever gives us verbal embroidery rather than felt emotions. She describes atomic reactors in terms of male ejaculations, using stale adjectives and the equally stale abstraction "male necessity." But why male? How does she account for that nuclear power maniac Mrs. Ghandi in her scheme of things. Often Cheever drifts into cuteness. In "Skunk Glee" (thanks, Robert Lowell), raccoons are "fur balloons" wearing "tiny tennis shoes" and "dainty prosthetic mitts." The skunk, "absolute / ruler of smell" (here Wallace Stevens turneth over) does a "figure eight rampant on dancers' tiptoes." This is coy Disney. Cheever also displays easy stylistic devices picked up from reading poets, I assume, in college lit courses. Here is a kind of Gerard Manley Hopkins rag:

> wet wet wash wring
> ring roll gash

>   gush tumble spin
>   all your sheets....

And she takes time to evoke Shakespeare, King Lear, and
Beethoven, all to accompany the destruction of an old building
by wrecking ball.

        I am sorry to be rough on a well-meaning but greatly
limited writer.   I merely take her book as representative
of many I might otherwise have chosen; and I am not interested
in over-kill.   Mary Cheever is not about to harm any poet
(or critic), great or small.

        But, this book is yet another expensive example of a
blight on contemporary poetry.   The market for serious work
shrinks by the day, as fewer and fewer trade houses even
read poetry manuscripts.   Hosts of real poets go unpublished
while prestigiously connected folk of minimal talent are heard.
It's enough to send you off to attack the nearest cedar tree
with claws unsheathed.   The ursine critic must at times behave
in ursine-fashion and expose the facile and the sham.   One of
Mary Cheever's lines goes this way: "there certainly are
some wild beastly poems. "   What an irony!   Beastly poems,
yes; wild ones, no!

WOUNDS AND SUBMISSIONS:

Peter Cooley's The Room Where Summer Ends*

     Cooley's new book is among the best on Carnegie-
Mellon's recent list. Cooley, who is poetry editor of the
North American Review, has published his finely-honed poems
in numerous small magazines for several years now. This,
his second book, gathers work written over the past four
years. He is too seasoned a poet to cast forth a heterogeneous
collection. He orchestrates Summer with care, so that the whole
reads as a single poem of several lyric parts. There is a
thematic statement, a development and a resolution.

     Life for Cooley is a matter of wounds and submissions.
The gods aren't likely to appear, leaving us to our medita-
tions, as gnats swirl around us, a dog barks, and we greet
our omissions. Cooley seems to feel separated from other
men, and takes his separations as occasions for reflection
and meditation. As a boy he felt the same way--so there is
a continuity drawing him through his adult life towards
his death. As he ages, his sexual hungers stab and lin-
ger. His body, with all its strangeness, is his best-
observed reference:

                 How strange
at the beach each one of us appears
naked to ourselves & yet a body

Greek deities took on in stone.
While from the surface of the ocean,
at evening, shaking off the foam,
the fixed stars' stare has risen
with their reflections, found their
    names,
light, light & nothing we can be.

*Reprinted by permission from Small Press Review (January
1981), pp. 6-7.

He is a scorpio-spider.   He fantasizes a spider squatting at
his center, usurping his eyes for its own, and luring him to
poetry.   What he seems to say is that we descend into our-
selves where our spiders (souls) wait to trap us.   We fear
these creatures?   No, for we are their match.   Nature is
often Cooley's vehicle for insights.   In human worlds the
natural is a primary reference.   For example, a New Orleans
fruit market is a metaphor for Eternity:

> Under the stars of summer
> tomatoes have squatted, jostling
> the slats of trucks, beside squashes
> secreting their ripe meat
> like the pagan face that shines
> through Christ's in medieval paintings
> at his last breath, and sugarcane sweating
> its white gut and the egg plant
> bursting purples of their wounds.

As one's innerself is replete with spider, so the in-
terior of the physical universe is replete with the arcane
(death, heaven, hell) silently drawing us into its mouth(s).
Again confronting essence, Cooley wonders why he is chosen
to bear witness to this universal spider--why is someone who
feels so unworthy and so unanointed chosen to create poems?
These reflective and doubting moments usually occur at night.
Cooley walks away from his family, "leaving my wife / my meat
half-cut, the tiny cages / my daughters ring the air with, / ca-
naries perching on a song."   He sits and smokes, with his
face towards the stars.   As he waits, if he's lucky, the
stars touch him and he finds his voice.   Here he reaches a
first stage of awareness, and accepts his gifts.

A section of "Songs" follows, celebrating mutes,
idiots, whores, old men, blind men, drowned men, saints,
and hermits.   Each of these persons speaks in a found lan-
guage the world at large would mock and ignore.   One of
the best of these deliverances is "Song of the Drowned Man."
The voice is Cooley's own as the voices in the other poems
seem to be, too.   In an effortlessly achieved mystical rap-
port, the drowned man interweaves, with his double: He
descends into the ocean and drinks "the spume

> tilted to my lips, turning
> the whirlpool's sides,

> my cries breaking on the wheel
> of seaweed, tiny fishes,
> then entering the coral reef,
> the bed of shell I knelt in,
> seconds.
>
>   The tide is out,
> something pulls my bones--
> I know--a fish or human voice?--
> death swimming in my throat
> is all my soul will be
> until the world's end--
> the hooks are lifting me ...
> that figure dressed in fire,
> wherever I am going now
> I pray I never see his like again. "

This excursion into other voices leads Cooley to the third and final section where he returns to his self-examinations: How can he, steeped in his mortality, once summer ends, leave behind any evidence of his having been here? He prizes the effortless task as valuable--feeding small birds because they don't expect or ask him to, talking to the brother he never had, confronting (in a stunning poem "Miscarriage") the presence of a miscarried foetus who inhabits his mind and his family's life. He seems now to have rejected the conscious world, and, when he returns, matches up with the conscious person of his meditations. In the room where summer ends, he gazes out a single window as evening descends and he is not ready to embark on a final journey (from "ARARAT"):

>   I am not ready yet
> though darkness falls from the air
> & I have dreamed of this. I've got to
>   pack,
> I've got to be wished well by
>   somebody
>
> familiar. The animals are darkening,
> calling. They are wading the dark, thrashing.
> And now their ivory fetlocks, their horns,
> demand an answer going down, Are you coming
> before the waves close over us, are
>   you.
>
> So. This is my night to leave
> carrying nothing. . . .

Cooley guides us through a corridor of persons and events enhanced and enlarged by the connections he finds with his own perplexed and meditative psyche. He is a subtle and gentle poet of being and becoming. Filaments reach the stars.

SIMPLE, SIMPLE, SIMPLE:

William Corbett's Columbus Square Journal*

   Corbett clues us in on his book this way: "How bright
of me to live / in an age of full days, short poems." Right
off, questions indecently thrust up their steaming little heads:
What are these days full of? Are Corbett's haikuesque poems
better than his longer pieces? Are jotting down notes and
diddle-messing with one's daily history more than a self-
indulgent journalism? Has poetry become finally the news-
paper of a poet's daily life? I conclude that Corbett's days
should be less full, and his poems longer.

   So many of these pieces are simple lists of details
and events recorded almost for later fleshing out: Hillary
got stung by a bee today, no one phoned tonight, I can't af-
ford to buy Ned Rorem's Diary, my fingers and lips are wet
with sex-smell, I am broke. Part way through, Corbett in-
vites a blessing from Francis Ponge: "...nothing is simpler
than what I have to say." Well, what does simpler mean?
This book has a simple structure, and a few good simple
poems and entries running from Columbus Day of one year
all the way through to Columbus Day the following year.
Simple is too close to simple-minded for comfort. Simple
also describes bits of information appealing to your friends,
the way country folk and other unlettered writers list the un-
reflective details of their lives for the enlightenment of their
kind elsewhere. Simple also thinly veils an unattractive
narcissism--self-obsession with the pickings from one's nose,
the smells from one's rear--hardly momentous. I wish Cor-
bett had thrown out about half this book and kept some of the
really good things; viz., the longer nature poems and poems
to people later on in the book.

*Reprinted by permission from Stony Hills (June 1981), p. 3.

LIFE CUTE-OUTS:

Kenward Elmslie's Tropicalism*

You'll find a lot of things here that don't make sense,
and some that do. You have to respond to a dizzying word-
play, grammar-fun, elusive merryatries (the results of making
merry), and insanities. Also, it helps a lot if you spent hours
during your younger years watching Looney Tunes, Popeye,
and Casper the Ghost cartoons, and your older years at Andy
Warhol movies and at the Whitney and Modern Museums of
Art. It helps also if you practice talking like the transsexual
actresses Candy Darling and Jackie Curtis. Or, if you haven't
seen their movies, listen to some good camp-faggot talk (you
might read between the lines of a lot of old Frank O'Hara
poems). Then try licking the empty bottoms of Bumblebee
tuna fish cans; beat the bees to the final big-lick. Finally,
imagine little Kenward making cut-outs (cute-outs) of his life
with colored scissors and paste -- metaphysical forms in the
matter of Herbert's pulley and altar, and splendid creations
built out of erector sets, glued together with piss, shit and
kum. Do all this without ever seeming dirty or gross or
tertiary. Like the author himself, you'll eventually need a
distance from it all, from the dingleberry critics/poets/net-
grabbers who will trash your poems if you aren't careful.
You may end up feeling about Elmslie's poems as he must
have felt (as he implies) writing them:

> "Delightfully layered so I feel pinioned. Energy
> trip. / Go through puddles, drunk."

*Reprinted by permission from Stony Hills (Spring 1980), p. 7.

CLAYTON ESHLEMAN:

Hades in Manganese*

In Hades in Manganese, Clayton Eshleman returns to
the cave art of the paleolithic era and proceeds through Greco-
Roman culture, modern psychology, his own history and sex-
uality, to these holocaust days. An amazing synthesis.

Eshleman has visited European caves, both well-known
and obscure ones. What an incredible metaphor the caves are
for "the hominid separating of the animal out of" man. Eshel-
man's poems entice us back to powerful pre-psychic forces.

Paleolithic man drew his beasts in black manganese
dioxide mixed with earth, fats and blood, presaging, says
Eshleman, the "Greek god of death" and Hades, the Greek
underworld. The figures on the walls are equivalents for
glyphs (words) scratched by the poet on the cave walls of a
disappearing modern world. "Hades in Manganese" is about
language and the creative process.

Eshleman has never been one to write down to his
reader. He loves private imagery, and addresses friends
and acquaintances. One of his most stirring pieces is an
elegy for his mother. Poets, many of them obscure to lay
readers, appear: Olson, Blackburn, Zukovsky, Rothenberg,
Artaud. There is an ambitious spread of ancient allusions
and specialized diction: Okeanos, Tartaros, Hermes, therio-
morphic, erectectomy, panopticon, urboros, the "branchiate /
heart of this excellent / dryopithecine, autumn...." One is
advised to have an encyclopedia nearby.

At the other end of the spectrum are frequent scato-
logical references; Eshleman writes for the whole man. And
there are stylistic mannerisms: "he volumned her, she fic-

*Reprinted by permission from the Los Angeles Times (May
10, 1981), Book Review Sec., p. 15.

tioned him." He is not above using the occasional split in-
finitive. And here are a pair of easy word associations:
"ordure" begets "ardor"; "erections" begets "direction."
Most of the poems eschew anything like a tight formal
structure; they are open-field poems.

Despite flaws, the book has many splendors. Eshle-
man's energy and inventiveness are irresistible, and there
are elements of humor that seem new. Few poets writing to-
day attempt such grand syntheses. If indeed, as he says,
man is "a maggot on stilts," a creature with "an earthworm
psyche," Eshleman's journeys to these ancient caves remind
us that man has an incredible imagination, one of great daring
and creativity.

MOSQUITOES, DEATH, AND OTHER MATTERS:

Robert Hershon's A Blue Shovel*

At one point in Bob Hershon's new book he says that he takes "great pleasure" in "the exact size of his steps." Two motifs appear here that nicely characterize these new poems. First, there is "pleasure." He loves being alive. He is an affectionate man who sees whimsy in what lesser souls commiserate over. No self-pity here. Second, there is his love for the literal. He cares to know "the exact size of his steps." He never leaves his landscape to pursue fantasy or surrealism. He's like a Thoreau who wants to see what's right there, in the immediate world. And he goes with his eyelids peeled.

Each of these poems is a measuring of footsteps: In the title poem he measures out why it is that nobody really notices him unless he's standing right in front of them. He calls 49 people he thinks of as friends to find that not one is thinking of him. He decides to change, to become a blue shovel by a lake; in other words, he'll expect less of others, be more patient, all steely-blue and pristine, until he is noticed. Another measuring has to do with confronting hostility in others. In "Tin Cans," a crazy neighbor claims that Hershon's kids are stealing her dogs and selling them to the butcher. She retaliates by tossing tin cans in his yard late at night. Since he can't argue with a crazy woman or go to the cops, he decides to use the cans, for ashtrays, pencil holders, geranium pots.

Guilt must also be examined and determined. For ten years, Hershon harbors guilt feelings because he gave a man wrong directions. He comes to question his assumption that his credibility is infallible. He loves his friends. One has the sense that Hershon's values begin here. In "Singing with Friends" he writes:

*Reprinted by permission from Small Press Review (April 1980), p. 12.

> The song always better
> before it has been sung
> but the singing
> better than the song
> and the eyes hit
> this splendid note

In a group of short poems he takes quick shots at
various of his foibles. Here he confronts his own "Macho
Madness":

> the exquisite summer pleasure
> of pissing a mosquito to death

Here, via quoting three scraps of dialogue, he devastates the
boring non-events of a public school teacher lounge:

> Mozzarella cheese is not kosher
> Lots of cocker spaniels get epilepsy
> We were bored to death in Puerto Rico
>
> We were bored to death in Puerto Rico
> Lots of cocker spaniels get epilepsy
> Mozzarella cheese might be kosher

He writes movingly of various pains. "To a Turn" conveys
the pain of a marriage gone to problems. And a pair of
poems--"The Third of July" and "The Fifth of July" are
poignant for what they leave out--the Fourth of July. Antici-
pation, the day itself, and the day after--the latter produces
a lengthy self-examination of the basic sort one does as New
Year's day approaches.

Hershon is one of our better celebration poets. He
feels intimate with himself, his family, friends, and his
readers. "Here's a Surprise," a tender love poem, says it
well, much better than similar efforts by Richard Brautigan:

> here's a surprise
> you and me in your bright little house
>
> and here's a surprise
> you and me in your cheery bed
>
> o you are a prize in the morning

I like the size of Hershon's steps. They fit the large
man he is; they fit his landscape.

ROBINSON JEFFERS:

Marlan Beilke Takes a Look in <u>Shining Clarity</u>:
<u>God and Man in the Works of Jeffers</u>*

There's something intimidating about books as physi-
cally beautiful as this one--lavishly illustrated, imaginatively
produced. You feel pushed towards an uncritical reverence:
This is almost a monument, rather than a book, to a poet
I've always had difficulty appreciating. Too much of Jeffers
seemed (and continues to seem) to me like warmed-over Walt
Whitman and Algernon Swinburne. While he could on occasion
swing a mean rhyme or free verse cadence, he bogs down so
often I want to scream. I end up closing his books, won-
dering again if the fault isn't mine--myopia? For isn't he
California's one and only fantastic first-half twentieth century,
authentic bard? And living in California as I do, isn't it
heresy not to revere every jot and tittle of his works? I do
want to like him, his being a loner, his having built his house
High Tor, his love for his ugly dog, his stoical and gloomy
view of life.

When <u>Shining Clarity</u> appeared, its title put me off.
Even the multi-level embossing of Jeffers' silhouette struck
me as more monumental than accurate. And the size of the
book--$1\frac{1}{2}$ " thick, 5" high, and $8\frac{1}{2}$ " wide--it's almost as big
as a tombstone. Shortly after I began reading the book, I
began to wish that Marlan Beilke had been less plodding in
holding to his central themes: god and man in Robinson Jef-
fers. Apparently Beilke teaches economics, English, Latin,
and drama at Jackson High School in the Mother Lode region.
He has built a twenty-foot windmill and lives with his wife
and three children in Amador City. He journeyed all the way
to Australia to study Jeffers ... where, I gather, most of
this book was written, at the University of Tasmania. Ob-
viously, Beilke is a man of energies. I suspect though that

*Reprinted by permission from <u>The Independent</u> (Fall 1980),
  p. 46.

this book is a self-publishing venture. The press apparently
is in Amador City. This is not necessarily to say that the
book is automatically bad because it is self-published--if in-
deed, it is. Obviously Beilke's admiration for the poet is
something of an obsession, and I can't imagine any trade pub-
lisher willing to foot the bill for so incredibly handsome a
book.

Unfortunately, on critical grounds, this study doesn't
work. Beilke doesn't seem sophisticated enough to explore
more than these two themes in Jeffers--there's a plodding
trip through the works, more or less chronologically. The
book results in a fancy cataloguing job--and such an assem-
bling is not without its value. There's no sense of any par-
ticular sorting out of Jeffers' good things and his bad things.
I find the study boringly repetitious and old-fashioned. Wher-
ever Jeffers said something about God and Man, Beilke quotes,
including stuff from the juvenalia and college verse. Jeffers
did write a lot of awful trash, despite his precociousness.

My feeling is that Shining Clarity should have been
presented as a monograph. And Beilke's writing is pedes-
trian. His pattern seems to be this--start with some clumsy
initial phrase, lengthy, preceding a clumsy main clause, com-
plete with cliché. Here is an example: "Permeated with the
twin sorrows of war and death, the poems of Jeffers' final
years differ in tone and topic from his earlier work ... [the]
verse is often that of a poet with clenched teeth...." Here
is another example of wooden writing: "Scarcity makes value,
and Jeffers who looks down both sides of the mountain of hu-
man existence can see scarcity down the slope of the past
and multitude down the grade of the future." I don't even
know what "multitude" means here.

I complain also that Beilke almost completely ignores
much of the derivative quality of Jeffers' verse--Whitman, the
major Victorians, bad translations of the ancient Greek dram-
atists. Jeffers wasn't sufficiently the artist to triumph over
these models. Understand, that I do regard Jeffers as a
significant poet; but I resist the mindless adulation of him
this book encourages. I wish that Jeffers had been less ad-
dicted to "great themes"--poems dropped like squirming silver-
fish out of some set of Great Books. I wish also that Beilke
had shown more daring and originality in considering his vast
subject. Obviously, I don't care for his book much. It's
as enticing as a piece of furniture--or a monument in a fancy
cemetery.

ROBERT KELLY:

The Alchemist to Mercury*

If Rabelais's Gargantua, that creature of monumental
appetites and sexual endowments, were alive and writing
poetry, his works might sound like Robert Kelly's. In this
latest volume, containing works from the last twenty years,
Kelly has ingested more than any other fifteen American
poets one might name. In keeping with a Titan's appetites,
these poems and other pieces rumble, stumble, and soar like
fire-wheels going off in numerous and unpredictable directions.
Most are a species of poem-journalism, with often mad-
dening and confusing results. Some of these works, letters to
friends, are often self-indulgent despite an occasional verve
and a rampant humor.

At one point, Kelly himself says: "What I do not know
will kill me. " As he ages (most poems here are more than
a dozen years old), he seems less driven to swallow every-
thing he can. The earliest poems are often pretentiously
erudite, as though Kelly were showing off his allusions to
Greek, African, and Asian myths to impress Robert Duncan
and Louis Zukovsky. He even dedicates a couple of clotted,
mannered poems to Duncan.

His central image of the alchemist evokes his own ef-
fort to turn the dross of life into poetry, in imitation of the
ancients. That Kelly never succeeds in the transmutation
shouldn't surprise us; for his medieval brothers never suc-
ceeded either. One conjoining that doesn't work is Kelly's
odd juxtaposition of the mundane and the erudite: Eating
clams in New England engenders thoughts of the European
Enlightenment, Dostoyevsky, and Gurdjieff; his fantasy of
feeling up the dank posterior of a lesbian cab driver, through
a tiny hole in the cab, is creamed over with allusions to

*Reprinted by permission from the Los Angeles Times (August
11, 1981), Book Review Sec. , p. 6.

Charles Ives, Shakespeare, and a "tantric text." Occasional-
ly, the effects are down-right awful: At one point he washes
his hands in cologne. Doing this reminds him of a cathedral
(Cologne?), and he reports that he's busy cleaning his finger-
nails with a cathedral spire. Self-cannibalism becomes a
funny ritual; he eats his flesh, and when he reaches for his
groin finds that his "left testicle is a beehive." Far out!

Also irritating are his attempts to play logician/meta-
physician--an indulgence common to Projective versifier fol-
lowers of old Charles Olson. Like a school marm instruc-
ting us in math (here it's sex), Kelly invites us "to discover
in this proposition" what keeps a woman's legs open for sex.
Is there a randy humor here I'm too dumb to see? These
yokings of disparate tones strike me as affected. Kelly's
paradoxes and enigmas, scattered like dragon's teeth through-
out, are decoys for profundity, and thinly veil platitudes about
love, reality, and milk.

And yet Kelly's zest is contagious. "A man is no
wiser than the book he writes," he says. I'll buy that. I'm
much more impressed by all the dross-eries Kelly rams down
his poet-throat than I am by his tarnished ideas. He's best
when he lets-off acting Merlin, Jacob Boehme, Charles Ol-
son, or Robert Duncan.

A PHYSICAL PRESENCE:

Morton Marcus' Big Winds, Glass Mornings, Shadows Cast by
Stars: Poems 1972-1980. *

   In reading Morton Marcus' new book, his first in four
years, I am struck immediately by the physicality.   For
Marcus, wisdom begins with the body.   Wisdom is achieved,
and conveyed, by touching loved ones, body to body, mind to
mind.   Filaments of connection run throughout lives, con-
necting persons.   Even Marcus' Jewish ancestors are physi-
cal presences.   When he imagines his grandfather leaving
Russia, a grandfather Marcus never saw, the old man, as
a memory or a ghost, appears blind-eyed outside Marcus'
door, affirming a thread of physical life spun throughout gen-
erations.   And the threads carry responsibilities.   The poet's
body turns upon the spit of his own and of his inherited ex-
periences.   Marcus' "Spider" is the best metaphoric treat-
ment of the theme in the book.   His figures, cast in an
Existentialist light, crouch in caves amid broken dishes and
piles of excrement, hammering out their pain and rage with
old bones.   When the bones break, a special metaphysics
transpires: "the planet is a drum, / and when he hammers
on the earth / with a bone or a stick, the sound reverberates
/ and shakes the farthest stars, / just as a breeze stirs the
crystals on a chandelier."

   Marcus' sense of his own body is often humorous.   In
"Some Words for My Belly," his belly's "true prominence"
reveals itself when Marcus lies in his bathtub.   His belly is
"the snowy slope / down which a woman's fingers / swiftly
ski."   More seriously, belly is the childhood he never had,
the bulge that makes him "woman," and a swaying island
through "whose extinct volcano," his navel, his "ancestors
sigh and moan."   Belly is a "life jacket strapped" around
Marcus' soul--a belly he would not, therefore, have shrunken

*Reprinted by permission from Kayak Magazine, Fall 1981.

or trimmed. He wants this "thumping ripe" melon to endure
and remain "a swelling accompaniment" to his end.

His own body is kin to those of cripples and "destroyed"
people. In "Cripples," an ambitious poem, Marcus remi-
nisces about a legless man, a dwarf, a one-armed man, and
a humpback. The legless figure dominates the poem and is
an only partially realized self-motif for the poet. Marcus
has peered beneath the dank and fetid as well as through
trees, flowers, water, and air. His is a special empathy.
He is the poet of the simple gesture as that gesture evokes
metaphysical meanings. In "There Are Some People So De-
stroyed," mutilated souls have forgotten how heroic simple
gestures are--getting out of bed, brushing teeth, stroking the
cat, cleaning the house. To be heroic is to see that mun-
dane events are, in truth, celebrations of life. The truly
heroic people greet others in the street "and leave their fin-
gerprints / like postage stamps / on anyone they touch."
Longings, growlings in "our nerve-ends," leashing us and
dragging us "down streets / we never planned to go," connect
us, Marcus says. We are all, in a sense, maimed and dis-
jointed by life. He observes hippies "carrying blankets and
guitars / to somewhere else, dressed / like apparitions in a
dream" and himself feels connections. We are all wanderers,
possessed of souls--stilled harp strings "tuned to the drone
of silence"--single threads, radiant filaments sewing us up
in Gogol-like overcoats of darkness.

Touchings, then, are both actual and metaphysical.
In "How Would You Touch the Body of God?" Marcus settles
on, as he often does, some concept conducive of reflection
and then embroiders the idea, much as a gifted child might.
This particular poem, most energetic, moves from an overt
gesture to a subtler one. Here a rabbinical voice fades off
and the poem stands stark, gentle, and clear. Marcus
imagines God as a roller coaster track. God is also a
mountain range; and like a blind man you skim your finger-
tips along his base. Then, God's body is the "edge of the
universe," an edge one would finger "like a tailor testing a
fabric." A gentle sardonic note intrudes: Though the likeli-
hood of our finding God is remote, we "keep in practice any-
way." How? By touching each other's lives "as often as
we can," leaving our thumbs "radiant, gorged with static" and
our "index fingers wavering like winds." Marcus's personal
loneliness is also touched with divinity. Here, though, since
he is isolated, he must touch himself, and, in the process,
creates the image of a church: his arms "lie down together."

His fingers form a steeple. He rests his head on his hands
and listens "into" his hands and arms, "where crimson
choirs / are singing my praises."

The voice Marcus renders in his poems, when the
poet-self is sufficiently contained and resolved, acts to in-
struct and bless. Marcus seldom meditates for long; a poem
may begin as a reverie, but shortly it shifts towards dialogue
and imperatives. "Dust" starts as a meditation and concludes
with this instruction: The reader is not to be "misled" by
dust's "drab appearance, / by its silence, by its gray com-
plexion, / for sometimes it sweeps off the edge of the planet
/ and drifts among the stars." The implication, obviously,
is that our dust-lives achieve an apotheosis. In "The Expres-
sion on Your Face," half-way through, Marcus invites the
reader: "Touch this poem. Feel the murmurings inside it."

When he invites his readers into his metaphysics,
Marcus never sounds pompous or hortatory. His need to
touch, to proffer wisdom, is meant to help, and springs from
his affections, not only for the persons he loves who stand
within his immediate radiance, but equally for all humans who
undergo in a life that contains more pain than sense--again,
the Existentialist view.

Marcus loves basics--elemental presences: tree,
bread, salt, cheese, spider, teeth, belly; elemental acts:
breathing, bathing, love-making, dreaming, walking, praying.
There's a poet-peasant's earthiness throughout. Here is an
example of what I mean: "Spilling Salt," the most mundane
of events, but one rich in folk-meanings, is charged with sig-
nificance. As the poet walks through a house at night, he
notices tossed salt grains on the rug. He kneels (adora-
tional?) and lifts grains to his face:

>   they glow,
>   an opaque white,
>   like the dust of bones.
>   And when I put them to my ear
>   they sound like the sea's breathing,
>   although now,
>   with so few of them,
>   I can hear individual voices--
>   the muffled cries of drowned sailors
>   and all those who have died
>   and been drained to the sea,
>   all my cousins.
>   On my tongue,

                    these crystals dissolve
                 with the small lost bitterness
                         of tears.
                And when I enter the kitchen
             the salt shaker is glowing on the shelf,
                    a vault full of voices,
                  a choir of lost kinsmen.

While the "small lost bitterness / of tears" hints of the
cliché, the passage as a whole demonstrates Marcus's skill
in taking what he himself notes as European folk in origin
and treating it in an elemental yet sophisticated way.   In
"What If" he equates the need for poems with hunger.   He
knows that the poor would rather eat morsels of bread than
read "all those words tied into a bundle. "   What if the bread
is eaten, he wonders, and <u>satisfies</u> (stuffs) the word <u>hunger</u>
so that it disappears from our vocabulary forever?   <u>Well</u>,
obviously, there'd be no further need for poetry.   This dis-
appearance, however, isn't apt to occur, for "the shipwrecks
continue on the reefs of the Soul / and the cupped hands of
the poor / remain empty and waiting. "

      Marcus proffers a special communion of bread and
poems--touchings of an elemental, organic sort.   Our cupped
hands (souls) need more poems like his.

THE POET AS MATISSE:

Bert Meyers' Windowsills

Bert Meyers died of cancer on April 22, 1979, at age 51.
He was an immensely gifted poet, largely unacknowledged in
poetry circles, despite his having published books with Alan
Swallow (Early Rain, 1960), Doubleday (The Dark Birds,
1968), and Kayak (Sunlight on the Wall, 1976). Bert looked
with extreme disfavor on the hustling so characteristic of the
American poetry world, and refused to be part of it. He
never had himself listed in the Directory of American Poets,
for example.

Windowsills reflects Meyers' characteristic tones: life
as a series of lovings tinged with threat, the positive beauty
behind common objects--leaves, hands, tools, boats, flowers,
children. I have always felt that his voice was closer to some
of the European, South American, and Oriental poets he ad-
mired than to American poets--Jammes, Laotzu, Akhmatova,
Basho, Tu Fu, Neruda, Kavanagh. He responded especially
to poets who touched life with a philosophic reading of objects.
The flower in the glass, the boat shimmering on the waves,
the blue teapot in the old oak cupboard somehow symbolized
for Meyers the permanent beyond all transiences.

Windowsills is about looking, and about framing views
beyond sills. The poet, the book assumes, is a passive
viewer, a Matisse of poetry. A world of meaning transpires
beyond his windows. Before we can know, Meyers implies,
we must see. Nor is he sententious about this: His book is
full of visual pleasures and delights. His motto, from Goethe,
is apt: "Best of all, merely to look. "

The first section of Windowsills contains a dozen short
"Images. " Bales of hay are "cartons / of sunlight fading into
a field. " Leaves suggest "shreds of a giant eraser"; shadows

are fences; a passing snowfall transforms the windowsills all
over the city.   Frequently, Meyers' vision turns on some
slight disturbance, as his poem moves from metaphor and
scene to metaphor and scene.   Here is VII:

> A flock of crows
> dissolves in the mist--
> a cigarette's ash
> in a glass of water;
> and sunlight
> twitching in a puddle.

The tenth "Image" turns on two metaphors.   Hands are "twin
sisters"

> to whom everyone's
> a wrinkle
> that needs to be smoothed,
> a stranger who should be fed.
>
> Hands, those humble wings
> that make each day
> fly toward its goal;
> at rest, still holding
> the shape of a tool.

The second half of Windowsills is a series of "Post-
cards" from France.   Here a painter's eye regards the sea:

> When calm, the sea's so blue
> you could paint the sky with it.
> Sometimes, it's a green tablecloth
> laid on the wind.

"Island" evokes an exotic, bustling landscape.   Each stanza
is a variation on the theme of the wavering vanishing point.
Dwarfs and hunchbacks load wagons in the heat.   "Gardens
drip ... / Flowers burst from the walls. / An ox appears /
like a hillside in an alley."   This tourist's point of view con-
tinues as we move inside a grocery store: "So poor, a box /
of baking soda's / smaller than a cigarette pack."   Next, a
scrawny young priest follows a double file of boys down a
street.   "Pale girls lean on their windowsills, / framed like
the earliest photographs."   The tourists leave.   We stay be-
hind observing the retreating tourist-ship in the twilight.
People on the pier wave lighted matches.   The boat, "a huge
altar," loses itself in the fog.

A series of village vignettes follow. There are nine of them. Here through strokes as simple as those in a Hokosaui print, Meyers evokes a French village cemetery:

> The cemetery's such a pretty town--
> old, quiet, full of mansions.
> People, flowers, crows, everyone comes.

Here is a street market. Meyers' inventiveness is a whimsical celebration of life. He writes of fruits and vegetables with great affection--after all, they are the basics of life, the "walls of France":

> A market in the street.
> Bananas rest their Midas hands.
> Herbs, those quiet housewives,
> wearing their modest prints,
> were found in the fields at dawn.
> Clods of garlic, the kitchen's diamond,
> hand from every stall.
> Cheese, like the walls of France;
> red peppers with a plastic glow....

This is a rare one-liner. Any poet who has tried to write one of these knows how difficult they are:

> Frogs croak "twenty-one" in French all night.

Meyers' image-making works best in the final long sequence, "Paris." Each of these 18 vignettes sparkles with vibrant seeing, each is a fixing of absorbed impressions. Here is one of my favorites:

> An old dog, a four-legged
> bundle of straw,
> leaves the cafe and goes
> to the gutter for a drink.
>
> When he returns, his footprints
> are a crossed row
> of tiny vases, each one
> with four flowers, on the sidewalk.

No poet has more economically captured the seaminess of Parisian streets than Meyers in this "Postcard":

> And here are also filthy streets,
> leprous walls that sunlight

> never touched, smeared with crud,
> battered like garbage cans...
> the cracks in a stone
> are a landscape of nerves;
> the air's a perpetual fart
> and even the shadows wear rags.

I am tempted to quote all of these poems.   They give the
sense of having been lingered over and honed.   Once Meyers
found the right phrase, metaphor, detail, he applied his spe-
cial fixatives of tone and style.

Because of his death, Meyers' poems assume even
more meaning than when they were written a couple of years
ago.   He seems to say that while our mortality is a horrible
trick, we can rejoice in the sheer glistening pleasure of see-
ing what is direct, simple, and immediate.   Our windowsills
contain incredible meanings within their frames.   I am sure
that Bert knew when he was writing these images how mortal
he was.   He had battled emphysema for years.   These are
wise, beautiful poems; their beauty is intensified by the fact
of his death.

I visited Bert for the last time three months before he
died.   He had been reading a contemporary Israeli book on
how to face your own dying.   As always, remarkably frank,
he said to me that he was afraid of what he had to face.   He
realized that his deep sane sense of life's awful irony made
his doom no less inevitable.   At times he said he was very
prepared, at other times not.   As this small book shows,
there were glorious flowers, sunlight, water, in abundance
beyond his windowsills, past the danse macabre of living, to
some far less ghastly place, of the transcendent spirit.

CAROL MUSKE

Skylight*

Carol Muske is an accomplished poet who writes within
limits. Her free-verse forms are seamless. When she
writes a free-form sonnet her mastery shows. When she
writes travel poems (India, Cyprus, California) her quiet ob-
servations make them hers. There are hints of violence, but
seldom any rage. She has observed, reflected, and, in long-
vowelled, slightly elegiac tones, evokes sensitive and intelli-
gent responses from the reader. Love poems vary little in
their tones from pieces to her family, Ghandi, whores, or
rural Vermont. Poems of girlhood approach some risk-taking.
Muske is the kind of poet trade publishers love; she is pol-
ished and observes non-controversial limits of language and
theme. She looks and sounds the way good poets should.

In "The Fault," which seems very personal, she writes
of having never found roots; she senses that hers are here-
abouts "somewhere." In the meantime, she has "learned to
stand perfectly still / and fill the flower" with her anxieties.
In "Par," where she reports being tacked up at half-mast in
a sand trap on a golf-course, she refers to her "modest col-
loquial speech": It seems to me that the occasion requires
more starch. When she backs off from an overt feminism,
she observes that "everyone loves a crippled debutante."
Here I perk up. I wish she had allowed that crippled deb
some rope. A pretty blessed life--a good education, re-
sponsive teachers and lovers, good publishers and teaching
jobs--does not in itself stimulate the energy and even rage
needed by a poet who aims to be first-rate. I can imagine
Muske writing her accomplished poems for the rest of her
life, unless, in her next book she allows that crippled debu-
tante to wiggle forward, up stage; or, to paraphrase a mo-

*Reprinted by permission from Gargoyle 17/18 (Winter 1981),
  p. 60.

ment from one of her best poems, "Golden Retriever," she
may have to lay about and start breaking a few necks.   I'm
impressed by <u>Skylight</u>, but, I fear, I am unmoved.

A COUPLE OF RABELAISIAN RIFFS:

Opal Nations' The Marvels of Professor Pettingruel
and The Tragic Hug of a Small French Wrestler*

These two brief works by sometime-Vermont writer
Opal Nations reveal a fascinatingly schizophrenic talent. On
the one hand, Nations emits scads of throw-away pieces--
books printed on the cheapest paper, fuzzily executed draw-
ings, poem-doodlings on the torn panty-hose of the universe.
On the other hand, he authors works printed superbly, hand-
set, in limited editions. The Marvels of Professor Pettin-
gruel is of the latter sort. It's the best prose by Nations
I've seen ... surreal, mad, playfully Rabelaisian, stylistically
in the pattern of esoteric English writers like Aubrey Beard-
sley and Ronald Firbank. Surreal events keep tumbling out;
Nations gives the impression he has had some mad friend
concoct collages--of the crazier sort one finds in Kayak--
which he, Nations, then sets about describing.

Here's an example: a butler wears a life preserver
when he goes to bed, and induces dreams of floating through
space "inside a marmalade coloured satin-wood coffin, con-
fessing at length his daily sins to a priest whose presence
from the neck up made himself evident through the bung of
his anal sphincter." The professor himself, who loves sand-
wiches of "cold porcupine spiced with tadpole larvae jelly" is,
I would guess, an image of Nations himself in his more out-
rageous moments. He conducts the show, allows us to trip
with him through his vaguely scatological castle.

I'd like to see The Marvels become a classic for
reading to American preschoolers--we might eventually match
the English as a people possessing a humorous, scary, ir-
reverent zaniness. Peter Koch's illustrations are marvelous.
My favorite is of a cross-sectioned female body seen from
the side. A woeful-looking big baby is cuddled up in the

*Reprinted by permission from Stony Hills (Fall 1980), pp.
14-15.

womb, staring out at us, while out the woman's anus fly an assortment of birds, moths, butterflies, and folded hands.

The Tragic Hug of a Small French Wrestler is an example of Nations' Punk Publishing: cheap paper, cheap ink, cheap graphic shots, and sometimes cheap fun. In general, though, I find the graphics more effective than the prose pieces. The latter hit me as over-written and too often cute. There's a kind of easy surrealist romping.

Here, for example, details seem too easily flung together: "It rained in the basement again, swallows swarmed in through the windows and gobbled up the honey bees, a coconut doormat was hung by the neck, the young virgin secretly married the floor mop and stole away on a far away honeymoon. . . . "

And Nations rambles on. In "My New World Record," Nations announces that he currently holds the "one millimetre free style standing still record." The idea is fine, as a parody of all the record-breaking attempts made by people to get into the Guinness books of records. But the piece could be a lot funnier (and funkier) than it is. "When Ends Justify the Means" is an effective tour de force told to six-year-old Guss Grass. It's a neat political tale.

In Nations' drawings he ridicules many human pretensions with, one feels, a perverse kind of affection. Among the best are "Henry's Ritual," showing Henry seated with cloth over face jerking off into wooden tub and, then, with penis dripping, face freed, reading The Church Times; a marvelous "Corset Trampoline," with corset ready for jumping still attached to woman: a hilarious series of fantastic jock straps.

Nations has a significant place in what has become a Punk-Literature movement. His works, though, predate the movement--if indeed one does exist. Nasty-Naughty Lit may be a hit for a season, and not much longer. I'd like to see some publisher publish a big volume of Nations' best productions over the years; then we could better see whatever dimensions there are. As of now, he seems a very piecemeal artist. He reaches me best when he is less the surrealist and more the satirist. As Professor Pettingruel knows, this insane culture needs all the healthy mind-fucks it can get--Nations is capable of planting an occasional good one.

IT NEVER RAINS BUT IT POURS:

Richard Peabody's I'm in Love with the Morton Salt Girl*

The Morton Salt Girl--I'd assumed she'd passed from
the scene--was a symbol of innocence when I was growing up
in the thirties. Each time you grabbed a box of salt you
grabbed her, as she strolled confidently along wearing her
short billowing yellow dress and yellow slippers, protected
from the storm beneath her big umbrella. She was a darling,
and in contrast to another famous image of the day, the White
Rock Maiden with her wings and apple-breasts, she was ut-
terly sexless. The Salt Girl's little white-stockinged legs
seem so unerotic. Even her knees, badly defined, lacked
sexy dimples.

When Richard Peabody's poems arrived for review I
was a bit cynical about his taking liberties with this pristine
girl, cuts above your basic Brownie Scout in purity. Yet,
when I glanced at Peabody's photo on the back cover, I saw
that he was young, whiskered, mustached, with nice vibrant
fun-hole eyes, clad in one of those heavy dark misshapen
sweaters with a matching knit cap, of the sort fishermen wear.
So, I was ready for youthful iconoclasm by the squirtgun full.
I have not been disappointed. This is Peabody's first book;
he edits Gargoyle magazine, in Maryland.

In the title poem, Peabody does his best to turn erotic.
The girl survives with her virginity intact. My guess is that
Peabody's fantasies about licking her salt and being hung up
by her over a rafter (so that she can pour salt all over his
ham self) has engendered some terrific salty jerkings-off.
It'a a good poem, full of salty spunk.

This book is, then, unabashedly personal and youthful
and fun. Here are some things we know about the author, of
his daily life: He eats cornflakes, canned peaches (they slide

---

*Reprinted by permission from Northeast Rising Sun (Fall/
Winter 1980), pp. 9-10.

into his mouth "like ears ... juicy/sunshine/yum-yum"),
toasted marshmallows, and lots of eggs. He sips hot choco-
late and plays chess. Not surprisingly, his favorite com-
posers, painters, and writers are those you cut your teeth
on: Smetana, Van Gogh of the ear, Dürer, Monet (a canvas
or two), Poe ("The Black Cat"), Gary Snyder, Ginsberg--the
latter two boasting audiences of people who don't read books.
He loves the bizarre folk he meets. One such person is the
laughing maniac who emits his "Dada laughter" nightly:

> The laughing man
> is a ventriloquist
> and we are all
> his dummies.
>
> Does he enjoy laughing?
> I think not.
> It is an affliction of sorts.
>
> Is he happy?
> Would you be?
>
> When somebody laughs
> I turn and walk
> the other way.
> Never can tell.
>
> One of these nights
> I'm going to
> follow him home
> and nail his mouth shut.

Peabody sustains most of his images well. An im-
possible one where he says he'll make a book out of his
woman shouldn't work; but it does, except for the overly long
literary "dark continent at the end" at the end:

> This book will
> make you real to me in a way your words
> never could. It will reach me where
> your love could not. And late at night
> when other lovers are entwined, I will
> pull this slim volume from the shelf
> and caress the downy jacket like a lover's
> soft thigh. Only then shall I open you
> as I never could in life, and read from
> the secrets in your heart's dark continent.

This poem is rambunctious, a quality I enjoy throughout the book. If I had to pick a favorite poem, apart from the title poem, I'd choose the fairly short "Manna." It has the mystery to keep me reading: and I like the closing touch of rocks becoming bread:

> The bread that men make is not fluffy.
> It resembles ancient sun baked walls.
> The texture is rough and gritty
> but the stuff is filling.
> Young boys balance loaves of bread in their arms
> offerings to be eaten with goat's milk and honey,
> or perhaps fish. Sometimes in the desert,
> when the sun is just right, the rocks turn into bread.

I look forward to more of Peabody's work. He's fun to read, a quality not enough poets these days possess; and he produces zaps--often enough to let you know he's alive and you're alive. Some authentic verse runs from his pen, flows from his strong salt-box.

NORMA EGSTROM (PEGGY LEE) IN KANSAS:

Roxie Powell's Kansas Collateral*

1.

Linguistic sensuality, porn talk, re-evocations of those jerk-off pain-halcyon high school days in the fifties and sixties in small midwestern towns never quite destruct some of the pop culture greats. Frank Sinatra. Peggy Lee. Betty Grable. Gary Cooper. Just thinking about them you still slip the old bolt. A not very subtle subversive thought: a reckoning up in sheer cwts of the loads of fantasy kum generated by Peggy and Betty (Patti, Maxine, and Laverne weren't that cute--they were more like your sisters), a neo-French lit'rary-critical method of rating the stars! Roxie Powell's new book Kansas Collateral freshly sings some of those duck-tailed ballads--Peggy's Rox-orchestra with struck wooden bells (balls), muted strings, rubato piano, the Dairy Queen girl's mons veneris flaked into something you can't handle, your gangliness, in the front seat of your Nash.

2.

The fifties car sounds--you can't destruct them either. Even during the movies, the sounds of horns, those easy sex-fantasy blares while Carmen shakes her fruit-hat and Betty's legs scream epics of snufflings and slurpings. The prom queen in your arms. Not always so Lucky Strikes. The prom queen safe at home. Your incredible hard on, an extension of your car, a "racing pride that / anoints and keeps you cool / stroking your phallus point, / pointing it true / like fish gone deep / in heavenly glue."

*Reprinted by permission from Little Caesar 8 (Feb. 1979). pp. 70-71.

3.

The poem as Art, socially and historically.   Powell's
history of his Kansas WASP family: the fat engineer's wife
adept at killing chickens, sublimating sexual cries while her
husband sits "attuned" to the Silvertone radio.   Generous dad
gives Rox the keys to the new car.   Rox busts the car.
Powell's mother's beauty evoked in an incredible poem, "Her
Beauty"--mysterious, lyrical, basic, rough: "She snuggled /
and washed me with / ooze, / she brought me up cold /
called my name wrong...."   Mother and child worry each
other.   She wonders why infant Rox is "corroding her entrails,
/ her hysterical beauty?"   Rox confesses the fact, but with-
out an explanation.   Mother accepts--and this is her deeper-
than-physical-beauty.   She lights his cigar, washes his nuts:
"She wanted me to know that / I am who I am."   Keep the
old farm ethic glued to God's calloused toe.   Listen to good
old Grandma when she calls up on the telephone, from be-
yond the grave, reminding you to put your best foot forward.

4.

A good poem implies subjections.   Verse sentences
never end.   "Juice and death" grow "visually," Powell says.
Many of his poems think sentences spun around the alcoholic
haze of good blues lyrics.   "Winebottle Blues" is one of his
best.   You should sing it, after the tango is over, the wine-
bottle dead--for the cockroach you smashed with the bottle.
Your life subjected to a bottle.   But never quite ... for
"strange angels" hover.   They lift your bedsheet and find "an
empty mind" and a bottle.   Angel-juice, death's continuing
sentence, the winebottle refrain repeating itself.   Tacky sex.
"I'll be seeing you / in all the old familiar places...."   Wine-
bottle Blues.

5.

A roller's worth of blood covers Powell's pasture.
The farm batch of pigeon eggs, drugged, fails to hatch.
No income.   Over it all smears a blue synchronicity--Peggy
Lee, Fred Waring, Doris Day, the drive-in, teen car-cul-
ture, the pin-ups, the sexual gobblings.   Death's artifacts.
Nash Ambassador moonlight.   I can't think of anyone who's
written of this life better.

JERRY RATCH

Jerry Ratch's formative years as a poet occurred in the sixties, the years of the counter-culture revolution, of student uprisings, of mass demonstrations against the Asian wars, of marches on behalf of oppressed blacks and gays. As a young poet, himself scarred by polio, observing and participating in a scarred society about to go up in flames, or so it seemed, Ratch took his cues from the Beats, from underground comic books, from the Kool-Aid acid lingo of the times. Much of the poetry then, written by Allen Ginsberg, Ed Sanders, and Lawrence Ferlinghetti, eschewed formalist writing and shocked the establishment with funky themes and four-letter words. Sanders actually went to prison for publishing his magazine Fuck You: A Magazine of the Arts.

These iconoclast poets were echoed by other artists who developed a tabloid art. Ron Crumb's outrageous Zap Comix led the way, as did Andy Warhol's films with their semi-verbal characters speaking like figures in comic-strips-- if it couldn't be gotten inside a balloon, forget it! And if what was said was mindless--so what? Pretend that a vision had transpired, a vision eluding establishment creeps. Warhol's characters spoke as if half their brains had sizzled away, burnt out by dope. The minimal became a means of protesting a sick culture; to be parsimoniously verbal was to bug the establishment. You were then much less communicative with the enemy, who were unable to reach your depths of conscience and feeling and make you vulnerable.

Ratch's poetry has connections with this protest culture; and it relates also to the Existentialists who were much read and admired at the time. Albert Camus' heroes seem tragic because their minimalist speech entraps them. Samuel Beckett's abstract figures stumble around in a wasteland looking for Godot and the remotest hint that life has any meaning. Both nature and man are utterly wasted.

I simplify. But it does help to understand Ratch's

work, if we recall the sixties as a decade when many revo-
lutionary currents channeled themselves into a vigorous stream
of protest screaming for basic reversals in our mores.

I.

These several currents are reflected in Ratch's earli-
est poems. Puppet X, a doll without a name, operated by
strings only partially defined, speaks of a wasted culture and
seems to avoid suicide by emitting his thoughts in half-formed
gasps. His speech resembles that inside balloons in comic-
strips. He talks as if he's made of cardboard, not flesh.
He employs a crazy, devastating humor that turns macabre
and ironic. Life is a matter of sheer existence amid ir-
rationality and pain. When T. S. Eliot wrote of our going
round and round that mulberry bush as a mindless action in
a world seen as a mindless wasteland, he was envisioning
life in similar terms.

Clown Birth resembles Puppet X in its drift. There is
a central narrative presented with utter economy--Ratch's
clown has little breath to waste, and his observations, while
they are spare in breath, do not spare his culture. Consider
his notion that simply by being born we are born as clowns
(clones?). We are superficial figures harboring enormous
interior deserts of angst. On that surface, our painted-on
smiles and happiness face-dots belie what is really transpiring
in our hearts and souls. A clown's interior life, in its an-
guish, is probably very like a puppet's interior life.

II.

After Clown Birth Ratch seemed to sense that changes
were necessary. With Osiris we can see that that change was
towards a poetry of pure language. The narrative elements
present in Puppet X and Clown Birth have shrivelled into mere
abstract hints of place and event. Obviously, Osiris suggests
ancient Egypt and ritual cults; and our placing the Osiris
poems in this historical context is important. This is in it-
self fascinating, for it serves Ratch as a paradigm for writing
poetry so spare that he seems to have chiselled it on slabs
of stone.

Again, both his grammar and his philosophy merge.
Passion is kept at a distance, except insofar as a play of
language allows it to enter. In one of the Osiris poems,

gouged-out eyes and tomb bats are surprises, suiting an
ancient theme of lost kingly power and maimed pride, per-
haps terrifying us--but only after the grammar of the poem
has asserted itself.

Helen, published here for the first time, contains an-
cient motifs-- Helen of Troy as paramour and destructive
agent. Ratch continues to be parsimonious with his lines.
We read them as if we were reading short breaths translated
from ancient stele. The fragility of the poems evokes a
timelessness, a runic quality. Here, Ratch's earlier comic-
strip humor is gone, as are the Existentialist commentaries.
Art, it appears, now assumes its own reason for being; and
if poet and audience do indeed sit on the edge of a precipice,
just before the final hydrogen blast, to celebrate Osiris and
Helen in such hesitatingly lovely, brief lines generates an
ironic distance.

Ratch's turns towards the old poet Geoffrey Chaucer
and to the modern Ezra Pound are further thrusts towards a
pared poetry. Ratch's art now becomes "Marginalia." If
in his first books he was writing half-completed inscriptions
on stone, he is now writing lists of words as "poems" in
the margins of other men's poems. The poet now seems to
be urging himself out of existence; his presence remains only
as a hand holding a pen, a seemingly disembodied hand scrib-
bling down gasps/words in the murky depths of the night.
Chaucer Marginalia is an experiment towards this end. It is
refreshing, however, to find that yCantos, inspired by Pound,
is a blend of the marginalia mode and the stele mode of
Osiris and Helen.

III.

Jerry Ratch illustrates well what a host of poets of his
generation are doing: viz., the Language Poets in the San
Francisco Bay area and on the East Coast. Ratch, though,
is of no coterie; his poems stand on their own as fascinating
excursions into the contemporary spirit, and into pure poetry.
I hope that numerous readers will find beauty in his work.
Ratch requires that we linger, reading the poems aloud, al-
lowing them to echo, in a kind of advanced listening chamber
equipped with acutely sensitive receiving systems.

Editor's note: This essay will appear as the introduction for
Ratch's Hot Weather; Poems Selected and New, published by
The Scarecrow Press, 1982.

ROCHELLE RATNER

Combing the Waves*

These 80 poems improvise with grace on a central
theme--the woman as mermaid. There's nothing fey about
Ratner's use of the motif. Her mermaid is obsessed with
her sexual role as a woman, with her presence on earth and
in the sea, and with her self-image. She reveals herself,
at times scathingly, in pretty human terms: She is jealous,
she has deep affections, she fears sex, she loves sex, she's
deeply attracted to the land. Once she is on land, however,
her problems, as one might expect, are numerous. How
does she keep her earth husband from knowing she is a fish
below the waist? Once she has entered the city, how can
she return to the water? Is she able to make love to a man
without drowning him while both are in the water?

Ratner's metaphor is complex. It's easy to assume
that a woman's reasons for wanting to be a mermaid are
several: she will be as beautiful as the legendary seductress
singing on the rocks to sailors, luring them to their deaths.
She is also the symbol of an incredible fertility, "spawning
hundreds of eggs/without any real intercourse." She can
escape the difficult trammels of many painful mortal loves
through her fantasy that a fish-woman is not a sexually wholly
useful woman. And, as I've already implied, her fear of
sex can be subverted; being a mermaid is a way of playing
possum--if you'll excuse the shift to land-animal imagery.
Men have enough trouble with the gross image of woman as
fish--our mermaid, though she is beautiful most of the time
and smells good, still lacks legs to spread. It's easy and
perhaps unfair to read neurotic designs here--Ratner knows
too well what she is about to engage in any distressing revela-
tions of her own psyche. She's a poet who loves the persona.
Obviously there are moments when Ratner seems to draw

*Reprinted by permission from Small Press Review (May
1980), pp. 4-5.

directly from her own experience; assuming that all the mer-
maid thinks and undergoes transpires with Ratner is a mis-
take. Ratner is of the mermaid's party and knows it.

Her mermaid has been very stubborn throughout her
mermaid girlhood, both to her parents and her teachers.
There is a moving poem about finally learning to swim, after
having vehemently insisted throughout her childhood that she
would not swim. She also dislikes useless women who sit
around drinking tea and coffee, curling their fingers while
they do so. She hates idle chatter--and believes in achieving.
One poem illustrates the poles of her design. Here we see a
human woman lying in her bathtub, vaguely distressed by her
sexuality, ripe for the erotic "weightlessness" that will en-
gender mermaid fantasies:

SOME NIGHTS

Some nights I sit in the bathtub
and think how one thing lovers do
is take baths together.

The cold white sides close in on me
till I notice that under water
my fingers are short and fat
while my legs stretch smoothly
as I guess his cock would.

My thighs drift apart naturally.
When my stomach's cramped
the water eases it.
The nipples of my breasts
seem to rise and float
as I lie back.

I jiggle the faucets,
first too hot then too cold;
will I never get it right?
It's no longer something I can control.

Some nights my body seems so weightless
that I think perhaps here, perhaps someday.

In "Three Poems of the Dress" she relates her life
with a man who loved her too uncritically, then came to beat

her. The dress becomes a symbol of her self-assertion.
Like a good Ingmar Bergman heroine she inserts a knife in
her vulva:

> I will make my own dresses.
> The same knife I cut cloth with
> I will place inside me
> so the minute he enters
> he cries out in pain.
> I will show him how strong I am,
> how well I can function alone.

Ratner writes for clarity. Her tone is colloquial and
direct. She eschews metrical and metaphysical and metaphor-
ical pyrotechnics. Occasionally she works a direct rhyme of
two, or spins off snatches of lullabies. Her characteristic
style though, which she employs with considerable skill, is a
projective-verse, fairly short-line style. Her enjambments
work. Her verse currents do often draw us under "forceful-
ly," much as her mermaid draws her lovers under.

DINOSAUR POEMS:

Herbert Scott's Dinosaurs*

      This handsomely produced chapbook turns on a pair of
sentimental premises: that dinosaurs, like us, are/were
"true / children / of this world," and that once we are about
to go extinct we hope to engage the new creatures replacing
us with awe and wonder. These obvious themes do not in-
terest me as much as does Scott's use of collage techniques,
and his juxtapositions of details from his immediate life with
the history of dinosaur research. Here are some of the de-
tails from the latter Scott finds useful: Robert Plot, First
Keeper of the Ashmolean Institute, in 1677, speculated that a
fossil bone, quarried in Cornwall, must have belonged to
some elephant brought to England by the ancient Romans. In
1822, Eva Mantell, walking on a Sussex Road, discovered a
dinosaur tooth and gave it to her doctor husband Gideon, gen-
erating his life-long interest in fossil remains. Earlier, in
1802, Pliny Moody found huge bird tracks in some red sand-
stone: Superstition prevented his seeing what they really
were. Waterhouse Hawkins, in 1853, unearthed dinosaurs
from the grasses of Othniel Marsh, England. In America,
Hawkins re-structured the creatures and gave his studio in
Central Park to the citizens of New York. Five years later,
28 vertebrae were found in a marl pit in New Jersey. In
our own time, archeologists have retrieved over 300 tons of
bones near Vernal, Utah. The diggings go on.

      By itself, all this information is neither the stuff of
science nor of poetry. As data it is interesting--but it is
incomplete: poets aren't specialists, usually. They set down
a few sketchy facts, establish a theme, and proceed to write
poems. Even if they are careless, it doesn't matter all that
much. The poetry matters most.

      I have no reason to suspect Scott's facts. I'm far

---

*Reprinted by permission from The Independent (March 1980),
pp. 8-9.

more intrigued by his working of the materials, as they re-
flect news about his own personal life. All of his poems are
brief, rarely of more than a dozen four- or two-line stanzas,
in free verse, with clipped, honed cadences. From what re-
sembles a newspaper or diary of his life, Scott weaves mo-
tifs as unifying agents: A red-haired woman bathing in a
mountain stream turns him on, two boys fishing for trout
stimulate thoughts about aging, his young daughter collecting
seashells prompts father-feelings, and memories of an es-
tranged wife lead to a mild guilt. It's all a noble try, an
impressive olio, damaged finally by Scott's need to sound
momentous, elegaic, and self-important. In a passage of
surprisingly low libido, he strips and lowers himself into a
cold, fast stream, and is, he tells us, startled alive. He
throws back his head, beats the water with his arms, and
laughs (sentimentally, I think) at his own "featherless," "scale-
less" body. He's a "ground-blessed creature" who wants to
fly. Is the implication that dinosaurs too once roamed in
the rivers, felt alive, were sexual, wanted to soar?

Despite a good ear for cadenced verse forms, Scott's
use of personal news is too often mundane, almost banal:
viz., he tells us that every summer he travels along high-
ways from Michigan to California to see his kids; that he and
his daughter like to visit Pismo Beach; that he smiles at his
"foolishness" as he sits down to his evening meal. Perhaps
I am not being fair. Perhaps what Scott demonstrates is
that the mundane and the banal in our lives link us to the
dinosaurs. Their daily news was probably not much more
interesting than most of ours. Or, perhaps, taking another
slant, Scott says that in order to present himself as a sensi-
tive, caring man, he must show us how peaks of feeling gen-
erate from the commonplace. He strikes me, though, as a
lingerer, a writer of attitudes given to generalized feelings
about the eon-esque ephemerality of man.

One other example will demonstrate his personal reti-
cence. He's enamored of the red-haired woman bathing in
the river. Apparently, they make love--but the event, if it
happened, is vapidly recorded. He laughs once more at her
beauty (is her beauty ridiculous?), and then at himself, and,
he tells us, he "was not shy." Later, he seems equally en-
amored of a muskrat--but he finds that he likes being "invisi-
ble / to other creatures," so he does not touch "the wet,
sleek body." What Dinosaurs needs is a few energetic Whit-
manesque thoughts--perhaps the fishing-boys might have been
spied on playing dirty. Certainly, the dinosaurs must have

ripped, snorted, rutted, and farted. Scott's poem, finally, is
too genteel. The inside cover-blurb bills him as a former
grave-digger, factory hand, and supermarket worker. Then,
there's a big hiatus: He is currently an associate professor
in an English department. I wish he had allowed the grave-
digging, factory-laboring voice more scope. Alas, the college
professor takes over most of the way.

SEXUAL ESKIMO QUEEN TEEN FANTASIES:

Jack Skelley's Wammo Amnesia and Juvenile Loitering*

Los Angeles is a vibrant center for punk rock: Darby Crash collapsed here on numerous stages, and X, Fear, Black Flag, and the Circle Jerks have stimulated unforgettable battle-zones. It is not surprising to find a nest of punk and new wave poets flourishing in Southern California. One of the best is Jack Skelley, a 24-year-old Angelino who, in addition to reciting his own poems, plays funk/punk music with a trio called "Planet of Toys." The trio takes its name from one of Skelley's poems. The trio is part of a lively scene transpiring at Beyond Baroque, in Venice, that oasis of live poetry events in an otherwise pretty sterile landscape. In addition to Skelley, other local writers of the mode include Bob Flanagan, one of the musician-poets of "Planet of Toys"; Dennis Cooper, who runs the series of readings at Beyond Baroque, publishes the magazine Little Caesar and books under the Caesar imprint; Amy Gerstler, and David Trinidad. A pair of older writers, Jim Crusoe and Harry Northup, have been writing similar poems since the late sixties; and, of course, there's always the fetid, crazy example of Los Angeles' most famous poet, Charles Bukowski, in the background. Dennis Cooper recently published an anthology featuring new wave punk poets (on both coasts), all under 30 years of age, called Coming Attractions.

Skelley seems to feel that there is much in little. His work exists to date in five pamphlets (available for an s.a.e. from Fred & Barney Press, 1140 1/2 Nowita Place, Venice, CA 90291). His appearance in Cooper's Coming Attractions constitutes a sort of mini-collected poems for Skelley.

One of his most appealing works is Juvenile Loitering, done up like those cheap fliers people retrieve from doctors' and psychiatrists' offices, to instruct them in how to keep

---

*Reprinted by permission from Gargoyle 17/18 (Winter) 1981, p. 67.

their daughters from being raped, their sons away from fag-
gots, and themselves in better shape by cutting down on the
Hamms and the hamburgers. The cover, a linoleum block
print, features a frontal sweet young thing kicking up her
heels in a semi-sophisticated boogie. Inside: The poet is on
the prowl in "lonely places" tying down girls who "don't need"
him. He seems to get his kicks fantasizing that he's set
them up for the pleasure of other "compulsive angels." Cur-
few-arrest, acid-highs, stealing bicycles, and horrible hallu-
cinations follow. Yes, as the smiling necktied and the be-
pearled dad and mom show, their children are very tired.

Wammo Amnesia contains five poems and features a
youth suited and scrubbed, right off the Oral Roberts youth-
choir TV stage, or looking like one of a Mormon duo ap-
pearing at your door, on bicycles, to convert you. Once we
turn the page we find we've been misleadingly sanitized, spit
upon. The poems are riffs meant to be sung-chanted by Xine
or Skelley to caterwauling electric gisms of punk sound. It
is Easter morning. You bite the heads off all the bunnies,
squeeze the yellow baby chickens to death, and crack all the
eggs you can find. Enthroned on the toilet, you entertain
numerous b. m. brown Easter thoughts: "With all this milk
chocolate on my hands / I'll never get a good grip on you."
Is he addressing his sweetie, or his penis?

In poem #2, the poet is abandoned by a lover, just as
he is about to make the supreme sacrifice: He's ready to
give him/her all his punk record collection. He's in the car,
"blindfolded" by his tears. He's a wonderful slob of feeling.
As the rain starts, he knows "there's a big crash coming."
Poem #3, "Helium Kid in Space Mountain" occurs in Disney-
land. Where else? Out of a quasi-mystical dope haze, poet,
by himself, careens towards "science fiction city," and is
brought up short by a pimply attendant seen as a cop. Here
is the whole poem:

> I had the whole car to myself,
> blazing to the bone, science fiction city,
> screaming my head off through comets and clusters
> and the 2-D doughnut that rolls around,
> until, taking that last turn speeding down
> through total black to hit a thousand white
> explosions, my car jerked still,
> all lights frozen and this pimply
> employee with a flashlight and cap was saying
> stay in your seat and no flashes when I knew another

car was speeding down the track to smash
mine if I didn't say OK and get moving,
closing my eyes hard to bring on the black
and opening them again on the dark wind.

"Planet of Toys" presents a displaced, frozen punk hip-
ster in a "metalized" society. He's been frozen and has a
"weekend snow rabbit" for a pet--a sexual Eskimo queen teen
fantasy? Adult world, "cranky elders," tell him to keep
frozen and comatose, and not drift south and thaw out. He's
14. Lured by the fantastic exploding planet of his hot hot
mind, he feels "ages of fire" and the blaze-a-lings of a
blasto-plastic new world. The poem is entirely youth-
fashioned and outrageous. Cops and old folks (apparently
people over 35) are excluded; they don't matter much more
than the lumps of snot one picks from one's nose and flips
away.

In "Art's Shoe Hospital," dad apparently dies, killed,
kaput, mort. Life's a bumper-ride along coke-and-popcorn
sticky floors and white-dust haze air. Dick and Cindy do
their thing off to the side, while daddy-death rides off with
lots of other useless debris--like jobs, neat hair, sex wax,
lotsa money in the bank. As a senior citizen myself (56)
and possessor of those turkey-wattles beneath the chin, and
pubic hair, which if untrimmed, hangs down like Spanish
moss, I'm frightened by the culture Skelley evokes. At the
same time, I feel that I want to take these lovely, naughty
babes in my arms and tell them it's OK, that daddy may be
dead, but that mommy isn't. She's gone out for awhile to
score some cocaine to quiet their laughs and screams; and
she may even fetch back a sequined rabbit-skin to wrap poor
baby in. I'm left amazed though, and puzzled, convinced that
something real is going on in this poetry and music.

Peter Schjeldahl, a New York poet in his forties, who
has been part of a long on-going eastern literary-art scene,
Warholian and funky, and who visits Los Angeles often, con-
cludes one of his poems, "I Missed Punk (Because my Record
Player Was Broken)," with sentiments I share. The poem
appears in Little Caesar #11. This is the concluding stanza:

I missed Punk
but it brushed me in the cultural bazaar
and seemed to drop a hint about virtue
being what I'd always thought:
a readiness to lose, to let go

because only in loss is one not ridiculous
(if anyone notices)
Never resist an idea
Never say no to a contradiction
They have come to help you
smash the ego
which always reconstitutes
(and if it doesn't, well,
your worries are over)

LORETTA LIVES!

Paul Trachtenberg's Short Changes For Loretta*

I don't believe I've ever met Paul Trachtenberg's
Loretta in the flesh.   But, after reading these poems, I feel
I know her.   Trachtenberg belongs to that school of American
poets, self-taught, independent of coteries and schools, best
characterized by that other loner Alfred Starr Hamilton, a
poet Trachtenberg admires.   Trachtenberg is a young poet--
he's just turned thirty, and has been writing off and on for
the past three years.   He's published a handful of poems in
little magazines.   This is his first book.   He lives in Cali-
fornia, where he landscapes, reads dictionaries and books of
facts, and goes to movies.   I am delighted that Short Changes
for Loretta exists, and regard it as a personal discovery.
I hope it finds enthusiastic readers.   But enough background;
let's have a few words about marvellous Loretta.

There are hints of Loretta in Gertrude Stein; as Trach-
tenberg says in one of the poems, Loretta tries hard to be
"a saint in three acts."   She also has some of the style and
class of her namesake Loretta Young.   But, thank God, she
doesn't wear the hats.   She's also kin to Mae West and loves
a sexy velvet couch and being adored.   She has a refreshing-
ly realistic view (most of the time) about her charm--even
her feet are mystically calloused.   Loretta is also a poet,
and may be based on Diane Wakoski; but this I wouldn't swear
to.   My feeling is that Diane would appreciate Loretta's
spearing of the poetry world and her efforts to dazzle the
right man.   Loretta writes laconically, lyrically, and with
surprising images.   She never writes automatically, or by
free association.   Her barbs strike by design.   When her
images zap you, you won't forget them.

There are also hints of Loretta's origins in comic

---

*Note: The following appeared as the preface for Trachten-
berg's book, published by Cherry Valley Editions.

book and cartoon lore. She has something of Minnie Mouse
about her, but nothing of Lois Lane. She's sister to Barba-
rella and shares in her sexual musk. She could be Peggy
Lee, or Craig Russell impersonating Peggy Lee. There are
times when I see her as an archetypal drag-queen, the very
Witch of the West she blasts in one of the poems. Is Trach-
tenberg really Carol Channing seen through an evocative, dis-
solute life? Is the real Trachtenberg hiding from us? And
wouldn't Dolly Parton (at least her image) feel a certain
Frederick's of Hollywood affinity with Loretta?

Loretta seems to have tried a lot; but, yes, there
are things she hasn't done--real estate, podiatry, veterinary
science, motherhood. Her dash through life is incredible.
Even her absurd bout with cancer doesn't delay her--an evo-
cation of the Beatles produces a Magical Mystery Cure. For
me, at least, no matter how affected at times, or incisive,
or cruel, or compassionate Loretta is, she is never Gaboring.
Life may "short change" her. I end by envying the sweep of
her life. And when at the end of her book she is finally
spun into space (where she loses her socks) I give a cheer.
I know that she is off wreaking her funky charm on some
planet as yet unknown to us. There she's busy inventing new
sexual positions and creating new verse forms and new
"changes."

CESAR VALLEJO*:

Selected Poems†

Few foreign poets have fascinated American poets as much as Peruvian César Vallejo (1892-1938). Translations are numerous, and literary battles have been waged by the translators. This book, containing work from the best-known of Vallejo's volumes, is translated by H. R. Hays, who died in 1980. Hays began translating Vallejo in the 1940's.

Why the fascination with Vallejo? Well, his colorful life appeals. He was of a large, influential Peruvian family. His father was governor of a small provincial capital. He attended the University of Trujillo, where he was active in a Reform movement sweeping South American universities. At 28, he began his wanderings in France and Spain--where he endured great misery and poverty, was expelled from France for radical activity, and died in Paris in 1931.

American poets have always admired the Bohemian artist. A Vallejo who starves in a garret (getting stoned on bad absinthe, and writing and reading radical tracts) seems to relieve American poets from similar commitments. They can go on teaching at good colleges, investing in real estate, rearing fat families, and building up their manuscript collections without feeling too guilty. By admiring Vallejo, their hearts are in the right places.

Certainly, another reason for Vallejo's popularity is the poetry itself, and its tremendous human themes. Vallejo reflects a Europe (Spain) torn apart in the thirties. His poems are filled with men dying in prison cells, but beneath

*Reprinted by permission of the Los Angeles Times (Aug. 7, 1981), Part V, p. 20.
†Selected Poems, translated by H. R. Hays. Old Chatham, N. Y.: Sachem Press, 1981. $13. 50 and $6. 95.

the misery resides a potent bedrock of positive feeling.   The
life Vallejo knew as a young Peruvian was simple; its images
were basic: smoke, blood, bread.   No matter how decimated
by poverty and war, Vallejo's folk are survivors.   As Vallejo
wrote: "Today I like life much less / But I always enjoy
living. ... "

His poetry is largely free-verse much influenced by
Whitman.   There's a Whitmanic gusto, a desire to embrace
life with appetite.   There's a quality of gut, or "belly, " as
Vallejo called it; the heavy blows struck by God slam into
our viscera and double us over--but we may still choose to
get up laughing.

Another quality in Vallejo appeals to Americans--his
imagery.   I hesitate to call it "surreal, " because it seems
to derive from hallucinations induced by alcohol and hunger
pangs, rather than from art.   Here are a pair of examples:
"Strange sewing machines" are inside the poet.   His lover
crucifies herself "upon the curved logs" of his lips.   These
images supply a chic that American poets like.   I'm happy
to report that these inventions are minimal here.

The translations read easily, and the Spanish texts
appear on facing pages.   The selection, of manageable length,
provides a good place to start for readers unfamiliar with
this seminal poet's work.

DIANE WARD:

Theory of Emotion and The Light American*

Diane Ward's riff is a Diane Wordriff. I have two of her chapbooks before me, and I have read them, and now I have them behind me. I have caught glimmers of sense in them, also violations of sense, the pair adding up to nothing that I'll remember or want to read again. I want to be fair to Ward, since I like experimentation. But when the experimentation is self-indulgent and seemingly careless I protest. Ward's writing seems spun from a most uninteresting head, one that promises much more. She's hip--on the side of not polluting the environment (I think), for the "homo" (does she consider us weird?), and for acquaintances wrecked by routine jobs (and bad poem-writing?). She feeds dogs great salads and arranges little portrait settings of people who are told boringly what's in their rooms. She spins off a series of what seem to be held-in belly laughs re: a woman of absolutely no distinction, the last new word in poetry-flower-petalism/narcissism. If these pieces enriched my poetry ear, I could go with the non-sequiturs and the dull surrealism of facts wrenched syntactically to make no sense nonsense. Ward employs the dullest of dull devices: repetitious short prepositional phrases, ampersand rashes, verse lines of a plodding length which kill any possible music in favor of a spavined, ruptured cadence. If her aim is to entice us into her peculiar world of sur-real grammar/diction, she's not succeeded, at least for me. I feel irritated. Can even your friends--I assume that the dedicatees for these chapbooks are friends of the author--sit through readings of such writings as these in anything but a super-stoned condition?

*Reprinted by permission from Northeast Rising Sun (Fall/ Winter, 1980), p. 18.

DEATH ETCETERA:

Michael Waters' Not Just Any Death*

Not Just Any Death opens with two good poems: The
first, "Apples," explores the feelings of a speaker who as a
child stole apples from his father's tree and threw them into
a lake, and who today still likes taking things from his father
for the pleasure of returning them.   The second, "In Memory
of Smoke," records Waters' affection for his mother and
avoids sentimentality by the image of the woman down, ex-
hausted, with her head inside the oven she has been cleaning.

Waters is much less successful when he embraces
what seems to be his ubiquitous theme loneliness.   A poem
recollecting having met Judy Garland when he was six is
tossed away with a facile image of "death's face" seen years
later on someone who might have been the aging Garland.
Another poem spins off what being inside a grave will be like
--there's all that "loneliness" under there to deal with.   (I
wish American poets would declare a moratorium on loneli-
ness and variations thereof, for a decade; violating poets
would have their typing fingers chopped off).   "Drunk with
Pavese" is an ingenious piece--in the sense that the writing
of it sounds self-consciously like a gifted highschooler fan-
tasizing over his girl's drooping breasts.   God gets into the
act: In Heaven women's breasts should stand up and "stare
God in the face."

"Instinct" parallels an old dog who by instinct (Waters
tells us that "Instinct is wonderful") prepares a place for his
dying in a patch of grass, and an aging uncle, a "monument-
maker," who sensing his death, by instinct, clutches his
chisel and engraves his name "on the cheapest marker" and
then goes to bed and dies.   I have trouble thinking of the

*Reprinted by permission from Northeast Rising Sun (Summer
1980), pp. 14-15.

uncle as an old dog--and that is exactly what Waters di-
rects me towards. "Snow in the Cellar" is an ambitious
poem--it's ostensibly about a simple task, the shovelling of snow
out of a basement where it has gotten in during a storm. But
Waters must reveal that universe wheel inside him as he fills his
own emptiness. I don't take such wheeling as convincing
evidence of feeling--it's more like posturing. His best mo-
tive is a tingling arm. Again, "Frogs" is another poten-
tially good poem spoiled by Waters' yanking something simple
and stark into Momentosity: His impression of how frogs
appear--"green. / almost shapeless, bits of rotten mushroom"
is fine. And the recollection of himself as a kid trying to
shoot frogs with a gun works well. But the final idea of the
poem, that frogs have minds, that in their "tiny brains" they
"can forgive anything" is of the order of cows on their knees
praying to God, or of minks forgiving the killers who are
taking their furs for women's coats. Old Samuel Johnson
called it the Pathetic Fallacy.

The second half of Not Just Any Death has the same
strengths and flaws as the first part. Waters movingly
evokes incidents from childhood: the bum who peeled apples
perfectly and tossed the skins in the grass where the child
found them and kept them in jars; the country girl with the
luscious breasts who has been out blackberrying; the giant
manta ray transformed into a giant striding over the horizon;
a piece on Frank Sinatra heard while aging and recollected
at a moment of young romantic love. In some poems there's
a facile casualness about insomnia and death--a gloomy but
fashionable motif which has the poet wondering if his brain
will continue to recall pale women when the worms are sing-
ing, in the black soil, nibbling him away.

In Part III, there are more of these death poems.
(A smear of Dylan Thomas' rage against "the dying of the
light" might starch these pieces up some). In "Black Leaves"
we slide like falling leaves into "nothing at all," falling into
an open coffin in a field, beneath the "black shade" of an
oak tree. In "Leaving Tracks" a drunk drives across a lake
at night and, if I read correctly, goes through the ice: Waters
lets me down--what does "I can still hear the wild singing"
mean? The wild song of the drunk? The song of the ice
as it broke? There's a fine image though--"a perfect circle
of ice/ like a steering wheel."

A longer poem than most, "The Blind," deals with

country matters. It seems almost too easy for Waters to
drop into rustic tragedies: A man backs over his daugh-
ter with his pickup truck; a run-away dog returns home miss-
ing a leg. There's an ensuing sentimentality (also see the
poem about the death of Elizabeth Simms--"the silence of
one/ blossoming into zero. "). We are given few details of
these tragedies--the survivors weep their expected tears,
maintain their hurt memories, and feel flicks of sorrow.
There may be something profound in all this; but I don't see
it, and chalk it up to the distressing influence on American
poets of James Wright and that much-admired Iowa Kitchen-
Stoop School of Poetry. What bothers me is the assump-
tion that there's something decent and great about these
folk shuffling under the soggy oak leaves and the spent ap-
ples; and there's something sentimental built-in if these
folk happen to be the poet's ancestors. This cleaning of
the pasture spring allows us more glimpses of these lives.
I think we need a lot more originality and insight.

     This impulse for lathering over the rustic and barely
remembered shares something with another kind of poem,
one poets write about their kids. And Waters has one of
these--"Remembering the Oak. " The pitch is (and I'm talking
about this genre of poem broadly here) that our kids have
done real cute, almost metaphysical things, and that if we
are fathers and if these events occurred near some pine tree,
lake, or mountain, there's a real time-and-theme connection
thrust between parent and sibling. The effect felt is much
like the throb Aeneas must have felt when he thrust his old
dad Anchises up on his back to fetch him out of burning Troy.

     Waters' son has hammered a series of nails "barely"
into an oak tree to help the squirrels with their climbing.
Now, that's a bit precious, although I don't doubt for a mo-
ment that the kid did it.   There's the Christ image too--the
kid has been "hammering his own stubborn/nails into boards,
sweating/like Christ in the sun, thumbs blackening ... "
Waters' hope is that some day when the lad is adult he will
remember this moment when Eternity seemed to sap through
the oak-tree, through the father, and through the son. Please
don't get me wrong--the poem is not bad. But when I read
this poem along with the others on memory, dying, trees,
lakes, ancestors, and berries, and sense the sort of ballad-
eering tone laving over me (and them), I feel robbed some-
how.

     Waters is a gifted, sensitive man who doesn't take

many risks in these poems. These works sound "right," the way good poems should. Obviously I've been an irresponsible bastard for carping about them as I have, and in such detail.

BERNARD WELT

Serenade*

In <u>Serenade</u> I catch the voice of an ingenue teenager
sounding often like an aging man.   Welt lives with memories
of wistful loves, is affectionate towards the people he writes
his poems for (Dlugos, Winch, Benson), conjectures about
directions in his life, and in a wispy, often fey tone doesn't
seem to make many choices, preferring to drift along.   For
Welt, at one point, a fart is as good as a poem or a moun-
tain.   To give up with an "Oh, well," or some such pallid
epithet, when your life is fucked, has a certain winsome
charm though it may be deficient on energy.   The effect is
that of an O'Hara-esque shimmer, with silver-points in your
eyes, a dance of glitter.   Welt is technically very adept
and fun to read.   He loves a kind of swish, hip language,
and uses a variety of stanza and verse forms.   He knows
his craft well.

I wish though that he had more to say.   He seems to
drift along following the minor tunes of his masters--O'Hara,
Elmslie, Ashbery, Schuyler.   "In the Office" seems to sum
up the ambience of <u>Serenade</u>.   He says:

> Today I feel about seventeen years old,
> horny and interested in everything
> and not very profound. . . .
>
> . . . .
> Am I not here much?   Everybody around
> here probably thinks I'm writing
> a poem, but I'm not.

Such coyness, methinks, doth really not become the
Lady.

---

*Reprinted by permission from <u>Northeast Rising Sun</u> (Fall/
Winter 1980), pp. 14-15.

GARY YOUNG

Hands*

      Two strong qualities attract me to this poet's first
book: 1) skill in employing precise natural detail, and 2)
the presence of a primary image, hands, that doesn't swamp
the book. I'm tired of verses, often ruptured haiku, that
parade some minestrone of flora, fauna, and landscape as
momentous event: The reader is kept standing off at the edge
of the marsh looking on at the red-winged blackbird poised on
the cat-tail without ever really entering the mood or meaning
of the scene. I'm also tired of poems built around a gimmick.
One such batch came my way recently, for review, made up
of 52 poems based one each on the cards in your basic deck.

      Young's hands feel and ache and write. They caress:
touching a mother in distress, cupping a wife's soft body,
healing the dwarfed and the misshapen. Hands are a subtle
image rendered with ease. Young eschews gimmickry for
layered meanings.

      The title poem has an illusory simplicity. Hands lift
a curtain, so that the light enters and wakes the speaker. A
woman appears at the window backed by dim light. Shortly,
there will be meeting and consummation:

>Because everything we touch
>lives with us, we have hands.
>
>The contagion of memory
>glows like a lamp
>
>behind the windows in our fingers.
>The curtain is raised.
>
>and the light wakes us.

*Reprinted by permission from Northeast Rising Sun (Fall/
Winter 1980), pp. 43-44.

"The Doctor Rebuilds a Hand, " a vastly different
working of the hand motif, is unforgettable for the movement
away from the horrible condition of the woodsman (who has
had his hand nearly severed in the forest) to the psyche of
the doctor who restores the hand. Notable also are Young's
oscillations between original details and symbolic meanings--
as the doctor works "the red pulp" into a hand, using his
own for a model, he is disturbed by an interior scene of a
whole "landscape of bodies. " The doctor has an uncanny
sense for what the woodsman, lost in the forest and maimed,
endured, and his (the doctor's) psychic needs. Here is the
poem:

> His hand was a puppet, more wood than flesh.
> He had brought the forest back with him: bark, pitch,
> the dull leaves and thick hardwood that gave way
> to bone and severed nerves throughout his fingers.
> There was no pain. He suffered instead the terror
> of a man lost in the woods, the dull ache of companions
> as they give up the search, wait, and return home.
> What creeps in the timber and low brush
> crept between his fingers, following the blood spoor.
> As I removed splinters from the torn skin
> I discovered the landscape of bodies,
> the forest's skin and flesh. I felt
> the dark pressure of my own blood stiffen within me
> and against the red pulp I worked into a hand
> using my own as the model. If I could abandon the vanity
> of healing, I would enter the forest of wounds myself,
> and be delivered, unafraid, from whatever I touched.

Rare here is the poem without fresh visual detail.
"Flag" ends with an image of a battle flag as a rooster's
cockscomb. In "Autumn, " moths presage winter on a cold
night. Seeking warmth, they appear in the shivering room,
like "pilgrims never to be delivered from/their wilderness, "
clad in "ragged, dusty clothes. " In a poem of illness, from
his fever-bed, under soaked sheets that stick to him like
bandages, the poet notices apricot blossoms, losing them-
selves and mixing with some late snow in a windowbox. He
recalls a dream and knows that he is "still running" from
sleep, still "falling behind. "

Humans are seen vividly also, as if Young views the
world around him without eyelids, or with a sharply-focused
telescopic lens. In one of his best poems, "The Cold did not
Break, " an Indian is the speaker. A devastating, prolonged

cold-snap decimates the camp. One old woman is found frozen, "balanced/on all fours like a crab/with huge glass eyes." All the dead (and they seem numerous) are buried in their frozen postures. This, in the final stanza, has a ruthless beauty:

> There was nothing left but to beat
> fertility into our women.
> To beat the children
> that passed out of them.
> That was our strength:
> to torture what we loved, to endure
> ourselves, over and over.

I could continue pointing out Young's merits. He's considered well what it means to be human--the pain is there ("Poem for my Brother" and "Sleight of Hand"), the subtle affections ("My Wife"), and our equally subtle obligations to ourselves and others ("Duties"). He is a gentle poet, of lyric gifts. I found many clearings of the spring in Hands.

PART FOUR

"Folding in is one of the most
tactful of cake-making opera-
tions: the objective is to blend
thoroughly, yet not lose any of
the air you have previously
worked into your materials."
--Irma S. Rombauer, <u>Joy of
Cooking</u>

NOT MUCH FOR YOUR MONEY, MR. MICHENER:

The National Poetry Series: Ronald
Perry's <u>Denizens,</u> Joseph Langland's <u>Any-</u>
<u>body's Song,</u> Wendy Salinger's <u>Folly River,</u>
Sterling Brown's <u>Collected Poems,</u> Roberta
Spear's <u>Silks.</u> *

American Poetry in the early 1950's was elegantly
tooled, formalist, impersonal, full of games.   One such
period work comes to mind, a gathering of poems by John
Malcolm Brinnin in which the poems spelled the names of
friends if you followed the first words of each line down the
page.   An especially popular mode was what has been satiri-
cally dubbed the "Fulbright Poem."   Many former GIs re-
turned from the Hitler war to scribble away, evoking memo-
ries of culture-feelings and culture-sights: on Big Ben, on
the Trevi Fountain, on the Champs Elysees, on the lions of
St. Mark's Square, etc.   The idea was to tinge these Euro-
pean objects with your own melancholy--an eternal wistfulness
passing for original feelings.   Establishment journals (fill in
the blanks yourself) featured these poems.   A poet I met re-
cently made a pitch to get into one of these still-extant jour-
nals--they are still publishing such poems.   He was quite sure
that if he wrote about the seasons and dropped a European
placename he would sell a poem.   He called the piece
"Spring in Catalonia" and it was snapped up.

Now, along comes the much-heralded National Poetry
Series, initially suggested by Daniel Halpern and funded by
grants from James Michener, Edward Piszek, the Ford and
Witter Bynner Foundations, and five large trade publishers.
The fliers promoting the series declare that "outstanding"
books that might not otherwise be published will be published.
Michener himself makes a pitch for "new forms" of poetic
"expression, new ambitions and new types of statement."   I

---

*Reprinted by permission from <u>American Book Review</u> (March-
April 1981), p. 4.

gather that's the kind of poetry he wants his money used for. I am suspicious that the folk actually choosing for the series assume <u>new</u> and <u>outstanding</u> to mean <u>old</u> and <u>safe</u>. Let's consider this first batch of winners, all of them expensively and handsomely produced.

Ronald Perry's stream is the same one, alas, that pellucid poets have been standing ankle deep in for years. He's been diverted our way by Donald Justice. In this, his fourth book of poems, Perry writes gently of his travels. Nature is rendered safely: Peacocks predictably strut and preen, "all eyes." A sanitized hawk catches pigeons by his "talk" rather than his talons. Egrets are busy chanting psalms; gulls, litanies. Line-starts are unabashed throw-backs to Shakespeare and the Jacobeans. Some are in the queenly tone of a writer of quite light verse: "I'm sorry, my dears." "I wish I had something better than this." "It's all too much." There are numerous self-conscious tetra-meter starts: "and then departed: all the ark." Perry's voice throughout is neutered, a vaporous shadow dissolving in urbanity. He is a poet who would never roll his trousers at a party, leave his fly unzipped, say a four-letter word, or go without a tie except when wearing an expensive turtle-necked sweater.

The second poet, Joseph Langland (chosen by Ann Stan-ford), is one of this country's senior poets: He's been teach-ing, editing, and writing for a long time. He writes old forms and meters with some of the joyous obstinacy of an old woman eschewing Sure-Jell in favor of old-fashioned home-pectin methods. In his poems, love is important--but when it's miss-jelled it's no great trauma--nonthreatening cycles of nature just keep on recurring. There's always a spirit in Langland's <u>woods-jam</u>, despite a bit of scum forming now and then on top. Even death is simply a version of that old Whitmanic "earth's compost." Langland is a nostalgia poet, of rural matters seen as benign. Having grown up on a scrub farm in Wisconsin, I know first-hand that women die in child-birth before the doctor gets there, that sows chomp their far-row, that skunks suck blood from hens. Perhaps Langland's experiences were different--easy farts slip out while rocking on the old front porch at twilight, after a day spent hoeing beans. Pretty gray, pretty inoffensive. Although Langland has won prizes at the great American Poetry Jelly-Offs, I can't in this case award him my Poetry Housekeeping Seal-of-Approval.

Next appears Wendy Salinger's verse, selected in
"open competition," we are told, by Donald Hall. When the
book came, I had hoped for more--judging from the picture,
the author is young, vibrant, alert. The poems though are
disasters--they are largely self-conscious, with a southern
bent, lathered with the pomposity of giving second-person
news--"You do this." "You feel that." Or they attempt
flights via the over-worked first-person--that ungainly
buzzard of contemporary verse. Most of her poems would
be improved with most of the i phrases whacked out. These
are mannerisms spawned by Iowa and similar workshops--the
"kitchen stoop" school of poetry, as some critic once called
it. It's a mindless Adam-ese, in the sense that Adam waking
up sees solipsistically and gives the news to Eve as she
stands by lifting up all the drooping flower-heads, clearing
the peach-trees of their extra genitalia. Salinger's poems
mirror soft-ware people against a backdrop of soft-ware
nature--all in a kind of treacly Carolina glow. She is also
fond of a short of breathed fairy-tale (as a Miss America
candidate might breathe one), and there is a limp-wristed
evocation of "gay boys" making "coastal Carolina fair." The
writing is too often creative rather than felt--viz., "Humid
seizures" that "wrestle us out of modern motion"; azaleas
bursting "over the gravestones" in "violent hallucinations"; a
porpoise vaulting "her sleek parabola." She seeks (so she
tells us) what her tongue seeks as it "sucks after a vast/
vocabulary of texture." I do have trouble with that one! And
there are other lapses of taste--one of the worst fails miser-
ably: "A woman so beautiful it made me sad. / So white.
Rose red." Alas, Snow White, how do you feel being de-
prived of your n and w? In another poem, hands lead Mozart
down stairs "to answer the chord, that longed after him in
the dark." My irreverent guess is that he had a full bladder
and was on his way to relieve himself against the roses. I
find it hard to believe that this manuscript was the best sub-
mitted in the open competition portion of this series. Salin-
ger in a bit of whimsical self-irony (I'm not sure she sees
the point though) says it best herself: "Poem, my awkward /
machine, we go on."

With the poems of Sterling Brown I have no complaint.
Here the National Poetry Series performs a real service--the
making available of a life-time's work by an ignored poet.
Brown's first book appeared in 1932, and, as his sponsor
Michael Harper says, most of the other poems, those not ap-
pearing in Southern Road (1932), are appearing in book form
for the first time here. Brown was educated at Williams

College and at Harvard, and taught for over fifty years at
Howard University. The poems are unpretentious, frequently
moving, evocations of the black experience in America, via
ballads, short lyrics, narrative poems. Poverty, prison,
unemployment, prostitution, lynchings appear--as do soul-
singings, splendid love-clamors, and a general joie de vivre.
Brown's poems range from the traditional academic line ("An
Old Woman Remembers") to rag-time poetry ("Cabaret"), to
popular ballads ("Real Mammy Song.") Throughout his long,
productive life, Brown seldom writes merely to be in--no
Fullbright poems, no trendy-sweatered poems, no fashionable
workshop poems. He celebrates a vast often painful, often
joyous life. His presence in the series does much to justify
the series. Brown is frequently awesome, often beautiful.

Finally, there is Roberta Spear's Silks, easily the
most impressive of the honky portion of the Series. Philip
Levine seems to have had his eye out for quality, and not
simply for favoring students and old friends. Spear has a
sure talent and writes simply with what seem to be Nerudaian
twists: An old woman feeds her horse a slice of moon and
disappears over the mountains; ashes from a man's pipe scat-
ter like flakes "the lost seeds of man"; the feet of a corpse
seem to walk, with its steps echoing throughout the world.
Spear has a quiet, hard-seeing way of moving at, into, and
through natural objects, assimilating them into her vision.
Most of the time her surrealism works. A sense of life
(again it recalls Neruda's) flows through: One pauses to re-
member a crazy old woman in her garden, or to commemo-
rate an ironer of laces who is dead--her house decaying, or
to observe men outsmarted by crows in their "greasy suits."
Unlike Perry, Salinger, and Langland, Spear does not write
poems to be writing--she has a vigorous core of need, it
seems. I want to hear her because she is usually fresh.
My one complaint is that she has a pattern of beginning poems
very monotonously--often with adverbial phrases, and most
frequently with "at" phrases. The device becomes predictable.
She's too good a talent to let these flaws persist. She needs
to dismiss some of the workshop mannerisms--the devices
she has seen in the poems of Wright, Levine, Hall, etc.

I would be much less severe on these books if I were
not led to believe that a poetry publishing venture with some
$205,000 behind it (no, I do not misquote the figure) would
sponsor better poems. Sure, four of these books deserve to
be published, as lots of good minor poetry does, anachronis-
tic or not. But in a series pretending to the best in current

American writing?   If these are the best, is there any hope
for verse?   We need less of the flaccid from establishment
publishers, establishment coffers, and establishment poet-
selectors.   The whole project needs more daring and guts.
But I am sure that no amount of fussing by me will shake
these James Montgomery Flaggs out of their pegnoirs (or,
an allusion to Norman Rockwell--that Michelangelo of Satur-
day Evening Post covers--might be more apt).   I do, how-
ever, pray to the vexed poet-gods of the ages, whoever they
may be and wherever they are, that the sponsors of this
series will wise up and toss the aspidistras out the window.
As I finish writing this, I notice that the second round of
titles is just announced; let's hope they're better for more
than cluttering up the libraries.

THREE FROM COPPER BEECH:

Sheldon Flory's <u>A Winter Journey</u>, Henry Gould's <u>Stone</u>, and James Schevill's <u>Fire of Eyes</u>*

1.

Sheldon Flory has a beautifully secure ear, and his sympathies are in the right place--with children, gentle animals, bluejays, and Jesus. He never seems to write a thoroughly bad poem. And yet, something is missing: energy, immediacy, and, finally, anything like a memorable originality. He seems to suffer a disease ("indisposition" is a fairer word) many American poets suffer from--call it Roethke-itis, Hugoitis, James Wright-itis. The symptoms are: (1) a tone of reverie, resignation, mild regret; (2) a basic imagery of contrasting light and darkness--light always slowly appearing or fading, either displacing or allowing darkness to arrive (The two conditions become gentle romantic tags, substituting an easy emotion in place of what should be more profound; perhaps more denotive imagery would help); (3) a keeping of the reader at a remove, by reporting to him rather than letting him into the experience directly, using phrases such as "I remember," "as I drive back and forth," "I always stop here," "I grow/ To fear that all I am is what I've read."

In "Poem on a Fragment Heard Between Sleep and Waking," for example, the title itself is indicative of a passive shadow-land, light imagery becomes a facile device for quasi-metaphysical meanings. "Horizon light" breathing among tree trunks abolishes "time/ In dreams." The poet hears the dog hump in his sleep, and recalls that his mother "has been gone" three months (why doesn't he say <u>dead</u>, if that's what he means; or, has she simply gone bac<u>k</u> to her own home after a prolonged visit?). The poem concludes

---

*Reprinted by permission from <u>Stony Hills</u> (1980), pp. 1, 16.

with the idea that "the light is taking" our speaker some-
where. Vague. I gather that the light moves him on towards
his own death-trip, to his personal dog-thumping hours in
the future. Other poems are spoiled again and again by easy
touches: "Darkness comes down," "mountains of the soul,"
we "all are drowning/ And we all are calling/ And clutching
each other." Perhaps Flory's self-said fear that all he is
is what he's read is, alas, truer than he thinks.

2.

Henry Gould flashes light around and through many of
his poems but he does so unpretentiously. He is an accom-
plished young writer who has a growing personal voice. He
allows what he sees and feels to emerge without much de-
pendence on his masters. The book faults itself, I feel, by
not insisting sufficiently on the title--potent in itself, Stone.
I had expected more thematic explosions, shenanigans, ex-
plorations. There aren't many though. Gould seems to have
pretty much hidden his stone away from us. We can see
each of his poems as pebbles tossed into that moon-bleached
cistern of meaningless existential life.

In "Joshua," a stone thrown into a languid stream
sends out the usual ripples. They almost reach the bank,
but not quite. Does this mean that his poems aren't yet
making the splash he wants them to? The poem falls short
also by producing a little orgy of "light" at the end.

> One of these days, crystal stone,
> you will rise like air through ripples
>   and rings.
> rise beyond boundaries and riverbanks.
> struck by light releasing your song--
> so touched by light, releasing light,
> so quiet rivers roll again.

Stone demonstrates that Gould writes a fairly safe
poem well, deriving a certain freshness from what happens
to him in a young, vigorous life. I'd like to see him aban-
don some of the aging-male poet's obsession with sadly lost
dreams and an easy metaphysicality. "Circus Maximus,"
for me, is damaged by facile motifs; and "Why are the plains
like memory," "Haven," and the title poem (the latter is
chock full of momentatious, literario-historical prattlings)
sound as if they were written by weary, aging, if sensitive,

men. "Armenia" and "Self-Portrait" are refreshingly dif-
ferent though. In the latter we find this vibrant touch:

> I am one
> with the hell of animals.
> weird rhinos, giraffes, gazelles
> trapped in the oven, the bloody
> reservations in the final drought.

I'd like to see Gould forget all he's learned about
what good poetry is; perhaps he should read some rambunc-
tious poets--Duncan, Eshleman, Patti Smith, Michael Lally,
for example. My apologies to him, though, for being pre-
sumptuous; I guess we find to read whatever we feel we need.
I enjoyed Stone much, read it with minimal irritation and
with moments of real delight.

3.

James Schevill has a reputation as a pretty fine poet;
but when I opened this book with its not very inviting title,
and turned to the first full poem and found "The Dreamer of
Light Sings His Song of Sounds," I exclaimed, "Oh, no!"
Copper Beech seems to require plenty of light, dreams,
singing of lutestrung voices from the poets they publish. And
when I read the poem and found it tortured with hissables,
those awful s-sounds Tennyson despised so, I hardly wanted
to go on.

I'm glad I did, for once Schevill gets the ornateness
out of his system and decides to see the Guatemalan life
around him, he is good. The book is straightforward, fresh-
ly descriptive, compassionate without being sententious or
patronizing. In a poem on walls he defines his role as poet
this way: As an American living in a Guatemalan town
separated from the local shacks by a stone wall, he observes
the citizens across the wall and talks to them. The wall is
always there. His poems are his attempts to breach that
wall:

> I write this poem to peer over
> walls that always rise to separate
> social language from solitary song.

His portraits of a weaver, a girl who runs a bar, the
shoe-shine man, a healer, and a gardener ring movingly true.

Schevill eschews needlessly ornate language, seeming to sense that if he is to evoke the stark beauty of that life he must use restraint--and some humor. Rufino Tomayo's paintings come to mind--the colors are flamboyant against the backdrop of earth-browns and death-blacks. The gardener becomes the most crucial of these people; Schevill sees in his labors something of his own industry as a poet. In a stunning 16-liner, "The Essence of a Garden," Schevill's meditation produces the notion of an "illuminating place of order" located "between form and force of color." The metaphor is Edenic--in this Garden, soaring fruit-trees are loaded with fruit. Gladiolas, red zinnias, birds of paradise scream their beauty. Then, as the dry season appears, they wither and go dormant, waiting for the return of rain, and of man, when they will reproduce their beauty and lusciousness. In the life of a poet, poems seem to work this way as well--great periods of fruitfulness interspersed with fallow times.

"The Writer and the Gardener" is a more playful treatment of the garden motif, and is, I think, a fine example of Schevill writing simply and forcefully. Here's the beginning.

> I shut out his world; he shuts out mine.
> To him plants, trees, grass are words.
> To me words are plants, trees, grass.
> Working at the typewriter I look out.
> Working with a shovel he looks in.
> We greet each other when we pass.

I am grateful to Schevill for these touching poems. He entirely avoids the boring Momentosity American poets are apt to produce as imitations of fashionable Latin American authors. Too often they write what sounds like badly translated Paz. Schevill refuses to see an earth-sermon beneath every Guatemalan stone, or in the coils of Guatemalan snakes, or in the embraces of Guatemalan youths and maidens. When his old men or women speak their wisdoms, they are straightforward and unpretentious--no heavy Don Juan-trip laid-on for the edification of American honkies.

A word, finally, about Schevill's forms: They range from free-verse sonnets, to 16-liners, to brief rhymed poems, to free verse poems in no recognizable traditional form. He is a fine craftsman--apart from the sibilant problem early in the book. His sounds, pauses, and line breaks consistently satisfy. This Guatemalan sequence works.

NEW ONES FROM BURNING DECK:

Chapbooks by Barbara Guest, Russell Edson,
Harrison Fisher, William Doreski

In the first of her eight poems, Barbara Guest asks
if we are "caught in the ruts. " After having read <u>Biography</u>
several times (once aloud), I must confess that I don't know
whether I'm caught in the ruts or not. Guest writes what I
call fractured poems; they have fractured lines, moods,
stanzas, and settings. Little follows through. Reading her
is like reading a gathering of possibly good starts. At times
a prevailing voice or tone emerges that is reflective, imagist,
and somewhat personal--though Guest never gives much of
herself away.

In most of her poems, she fractures those hoary uni-
ties (tibias) of time, place, and action with an abandon bor-
dering on the giddy. At the same time, despite her disjunc-
tiveness, Guest seems to write out of a literary tradition of
good, normative language and literary allusions. She invites
us to take a pedantic approach to her work. Her surreal
touches seem invented as literature rather than energized
from a felt and necessary emotion. An aridity bothers me.
When she asks if I've located "the forms in the vests, " or
whether I can tell her when the anemones were picked (shortly
after "the flea entered the garment"?), or if I know the
"year of the prune, " or whose telephone is ringing, I am so
dislocated (bored) that I don't much care. I feel that what
she does is literary jogging. I identify with one of her
speakers who reports being hit by "nuttiness. " Even If I
think of John Ashbery, as a possible clue to what she's
doing, there's not much help. On the surface her poems
seem to share in the disjointedness he likes, and the ennui,
and the presence of a sensitive autobiographer-poet es-
tranged from a culture. But Guest, at least here, lacks
Ashbery's wit, music, play of language and idea, and his
outrageousness. I feel, finally, that I'm a guest at the
wrong party.

More accessible is Russell Edson's gathering of Ed-
sonesqueries, <u>With Sincerest Regrets</u>. Some of them work
well, but most don't. The reason? Though they start off
sounding original and funny and off-the-wall, too often they
don't deliver. These pieces recall Edward Lear's drawings;
their heads and faces are more interesting than the torsos,
and their torsos more so than the legs, feet, and tails; in
other words, there's a moving towards the vapid and the cute.
Strong legs and feet are missing, so the bodies topple over--
humpty dumpty pieces set upon the wrong ends on top of the
wall.

Here are some examples: In "Sautéing," a man
sautés his hat, as his mother had his dad's, as his grandmom
had his grandpop's. The problem is that this lonesome dude
has no woman to sauté his. Alas, he is left incredibly lonely.
"Sautéing is such a lonely thing," Edson editorializes. I'm
let down. Perhaps if lonesome hero had sautéd himself along
with his hat? or had, like one of Charles Bukowski's lonely
men, decided to do something really vivid, like castrating
himself with a rusty tin can, I might care more.

With "The Prosthetic Duck" we are treated to another
cartoon. It's kind of imaginative, but frustratingly coy. I
want to hit the duck over the head with its own breast-bone.
"Sheep" is another potentially good piece that creaks through
its development. Here, though, the start is weaker than the
conclusion. A house full of sheep, moving around like clouds,
or balls of dust, finally pity another sad lonely man (is Edson
a reincarnation of Abner Dean?). Sad lonely man sits in his
kitchen with his face in his hands weeping. Guess what a
kind ewe offers him? Her vagina! Sad, lonely, sex-deprived
man accepts, and does it in the missionary position. But
don't get your hopes up--the effect isn't very steamy or kinky.
In "The Ruined Eclair," a son watches his mother break his
father's bones, as he, the son, is busy eating dessert.
Even if I read the pastry as a penis that has shot its load
all over the sheets, I am still disappointed. Even the
little tale of daughter finding a dirty old man's penis to
pinch and caress, doesn't take the hero's mind off his own
eclair. He remains nice and lonely and self-obssessed.

And so we sally. I referred to Edward Lear earlier;
it may be useful to see Edson's pieces in the pattern of
Lear's nonsense writings. Yet, they are different; for they
are strongly narrative, have elements of the fabliau and they
eschew rhymes and obvious poetic effects. Perhaps Edson

needs a strong infusion of Strewelpeter and Wilhelm Busch--
or even of some of the adrenalin from the Katzenjammer
Kids at their worst-behaved.   Judging from this newest book,
Edson needs a break from what has apparently become formu-
laic--patterns in which rather fresh starts waffle (sally) off
like so many ruptured ducks or mediocre Carol Burnetts in-
tent on skits that don't quite work.   I want to feel more
wildly taken in and more uncompromisingly treated than I am
here.   But I did smile a little, and that's a plus.

To quote him, Harrison Fisher is "of a whole other
order of cheese."   In Text's Boyfriend, he takes risks with
his tongue's blender (another of his images) that Edson and
Guest do not.   He works from a stratum of sense usually;
but he does love fractures and dislocations of a quasi-surreal
sort--and although they do not always come clear, they seem
integrated with their events.   They've aged along with the
basic cheese of the poems and, hence, seem part of it.   He's
also an immensely energetic writer, one who knows how to
charge the first lines and never flag until the end.   Just as
day is the weather's boy-friend, he is the text's boyfriend.
This implies, doesn't it, that he's into lots of cheese where
language and syntax form like mold on Gorgonzola.   He writes
of writing: Literary expression is a form of mass murder,
poems are hawks in a land where the authorities outlaw the
private ownership of hawks.   He writes of Zero, on shooting
his department chairman, on our selves as a "cabal of par-
ticles" adhering out of cosmic fear, and on the metaphoric
ugliness of most children.   The second stanza of "Future
Cooling" reveals his techniques and themes: Here the poet
seems to function as a voice or a presence who loses hope;
yet he must guard those he loves from a like despair:

> The universe
> steps closer all around you,
> hugs you into your next birthday
> like some slower, dirtier version
> of a waltz for the first prize
> of fabulous cheese, but your partner
> is incredible cheese, the cheese
> with something extra, and through
> his head hole
> comes the spirited breeze
> of not having to lose, even
> when you do.

There are many hints in this short book of a considerable
talent.   Still under thirty, Fisher is a poet to watch.

It is William Doreski who strikes me as the most original and exciting poet of this lot. I was entirely unfamiliar with his work--his <u>The Testament of Israel Potter</u> was published by Seven Woods Press in 1976. In <u>Half of the Map</u>, he registers his responses to the often seedy Boston area with powerful and unexpected images. His opening poem contains a warning: He's returned home, and he's not happy: "I flounce on all fours / With a gory rat in my teeth. It was your familiar, its face / Is human, it resembles me." In "Union Square," a roving gang in cars become werewolves "trailing tails of flesh." "Speed" succinctly captures the pure luck of driving a freeway and surviving: The gods are potentially vicious, as they have always been; but for this once the speaker and his sweetie lucked out:

> The turnpike fools us: undressed by speed, our flying
> bodies spell
> "Sweetmeat" on the abutments. No death so much a
> slammed door:
> And honey, I'll take you piecemeal and me a rag--so
> why argue?
> Overhead's the loft where gods sway in drunken pleasure:
> let's sing,
> The radio's loud between us, and of course some share
> of our flesh
> Is flying already, white flag amid the shooting of the
> stars.

A marvellously original poem transpires in a vicious rainstorm: "No one here believes nature's so fierce, / With prongs you can hang your hat on." The candy store starts to float away. He observes a pair of drenched lovers pass, with "Arms twinkling, with rain-drawn creases, breasts and genitals glued to their clothes." He thinks of dashing to his car:

> I could make it to the car if I loved the locking of horns
> The way elk do, or devils whose only sport is torture.
> Now the hills are going. Greylock overhead shrugs and
> almost sighs.
> No one laughs, but look: I'm running with my pants in
> my arms, all fire
> And smoking, trusting to heat the rain's too startled to
> extinguish.

Some of Doreski's poems reflect a proletarian life: "The sweat of the dumb is pure beer, I'll gladly lick a foot or two /To prove good Catholics can share. " In "Evening in Lechmere, " he is bankrupt and sits all evening "chugging wine" near the noisy subway station, and tries to believe that the "clash of railroad iron and locked bumpers mimic human bones. " These are tough, sensitive poems about worlds that matter. Their long lines are sustained with intelligence and skill.

It is possible that some writers, especially Edson and Guest, here don't consider chapbooks as in the major flow of their more ambitious efforts. Perhaps they give publishers of chapbooks inferior work. And the Burning Deck folk may see such books by semi-celebrity poets as sighs in the larger breathings of writers that interest them. Yet, this press is so prolific, and the books they publish so superbly designed and produced, that what they do deserves scrutiny. Burning Deck has been around for a long time--and I value their contributions. They seem to feature a mix of work by new writers and established ones. For me, the really valuable presentations are those by unknowns--these books by Doreski and Fisher should gain them some of the readers they deserve.

TEN SHORT REVIEWS FOR LIBRARY JOURNAL*

BALAKIAN, Peter. <u>Father Fisheye</u>.

Balakian takes many cues from W. C. Williams; he has
an amazing affinity for fish, onion roots, tomatoes, creatures
in pond ooze, fat rainy skies, ice, storm, gray weather--all
seen beside, in, and under many of nature's various red
wheelbarrows. His landscapes contain people he knows, has
known, and reveres: parents, friends, Hart Crane, Vallejo,
Williams. He is both toughminded and gentle. A flaw is that
his poems are all in the same voice, and employ the devices
of a simple subject-verb-object pattern over and over again.
Also, the presence of <u>you</u> in most poems is an annoying
mannerism. Yet, this young poet has gifts and deserves
a reading.

BARTMAN, Joeffrey. <u>Habit Blue</u>.

An impressive collection of free verse poems. Bart-
man deals feelingly and succinctly with monotony, his "blue
ice" personality, the pain of having persons merely drift
through his life, shooting a dog who's been at the hens, en-
during a rain-storm. He writes a very funny prose poem on
cooking turkeys. He sees the discolored and the unusual,
relishing what he sees: frozen bats, a bug on a shank of
ham, an old man's yellowed teeth. Most readers will de-
light in these poems. They are well written, and intriguing
without being obscure.

---

*Reprinted from Library Journal, March 1, 1980 (Balakian);
March 15, 1980 (Bartman); May 15, 1980 (Berrigan); Feb.
1, 1980 (Bruchac); Sept. 1, 1979 (Creeley); Oct. 1, 1980
(Ginsberg & Orlovsky); March 1, 1981 (Heyen); Aug. 1980
(Horovitz); Jan. 1, 1980 (Mazzocco); Dec. 15, 1979 (Polite).
Published by R. R. Bowker Co. (a Xerox company). Copy-
right © 1979, 1980, 1981 by Xerox Corporation.

BERRIGAN, Ted. So Going Around Cities: new & selected
poems, 1958-1979.

    A huge collection, lavishly printed. These poems
pick up the more self-indulgent murmurings of Frank O'Hara
and circle--the cozy friendships, the contempt for the out-
side world, the scattered verse forms, the endless triviali-
zing. Once in a while Berrigan nicely wrenches the old son-
net form, swings a potent image, and manages to transcend
his cuteness--but not often enough. For the hardened New
York School fan and collections wanting everything in current
poetry, Berrigan is nowhere as good as his mentors--O'Hara,
Ashbery, Schuyler, Koch. Fashionable rather than substan-
tial.

BRUCHAC, Joseph. The Good Message of Handsome Lake.

    Bruchac writes of what he knows well--the native
American experience. This poignant series presents the
feelings and visions of Handsome Lake, the Senecan prophet,
who at the turn of the 19th century sought to invigorate his
people against the persecutions of the whites. The poems
are generally simple and declarative, but do suffer from a
sameness of voice--even the Quaker sounds like Handsome
Lake. And it's strange that so good a poet as Bruchac re-
lies often on mannered circumlocutions and clichés, viz.,
"his breath left him" (why not say "he died?"), "the drinking
of rum," "when their time comes to leave the earth."
But despite these flaws, The Good Message is moving and
persuasive.

CREELEY, Robert. Later.

    Creeley's old magic with rhythm, tone, and language
has apparently abandoned him. What remains are the notes
of a perplexed aging man. True, there are occasional keen
observations--but reportage doth not a poem make, no matter
how celebrated the reporter. Creeley's topics seldom es-
cape the facile and the commonplace. Grown older, he still
wants to know why humans are "so torn, so lost." And when
he is painterly, as in "Nature," he supplies old-fashioned in-
terpretations. A handful of poems though do reflect some of
the old splendor. "Corn Close" is the best; and "Peace,"
with its sardonic treatment of bikers, is memorable. In
general, however, the paucity of language, the telegraphic

style (by this time a mannerism), the monotonous rhythms,
the stale Camus-izing, make this book must-reading only for
the hardened Creeley fans.

GINSBERG, Allen & Peter Orlovsky. Straight Hearts' De-
light: love poems and selected letters, 1947-1980.

A hefty gathering by these celebrity figures, ranging
from sophomoric doggerel to some of Ginsberg's best-known
homoerotic poems. The letters are more illuminating than
the poems. Robert LaVigne's line drawings etherealize a
liaison as famous for its sensuality as for its spirituality.
Most of the letters were written during separations, primarily
when Ginsberg was on reading tours and dope and spiritual
quests. Readers will find no holds barred--intimate sexual
details and language to frizz grandma's hair. The book is
for Beatophiles and for specialized collections. Once again,
Ginsberg is his own mirror ... is his own mirror ... is his
own mirror.

HEYEN, William. The City Parables.

These 29 often moving poems range from the destruc-
tion of an anonymous city (a futuristic vision) to Belsen and
Jonestown. Human ruination is symbolized by the pollution
and destruction of our world. In "The Host" a turtle emerges
from a contaminated water-hole amidst old tires and trash.
Odes to Mickey Mantle, James Wright, Wittgenstein, and an
assortment of birds and creatures imply some hope. The
overall design, though, seems out of focus--the city idea
evaporates too soon. Were these poems left-overs from other,
more ambitious manuscripts by this fine poet?

HOROVITZ, Michael. Growing Up: selected poems and
pictures 1951-'79.

These writings are a "belly's slosh barrel" of gob-
bets (echoes) of McKuen, Lennon, Dylan, various rock lyrics
(acid and soft) popular in the sixties, bright kids' versifyings,
puns, kazoo moments: an ant hill crawling with formless
writings and busy drawings. It's hard to squirm your way
in, and you may be put off by the self-indulgent showmanship.
The moments of madness and fun don't quite bring it off.

MAZZOCCO, Robert. <u>Trader.</u>

The speaker in these 30 poems is someone on the
fringes of life; he seems to minimize threats by trading
away excitement. He fantasizes (rather than lives) trips to
headhunters, smelly people, houses, senile parents, brother-
memories, repeated dream-screams. Mazzocco is a com-
petent poet too much in love with negatives--"nots," "nos,"
"nevers." And he also numbingly repeats enervated refrains
(viz., "once again"). The poet is in need of a good editor:
prune the negatives; the "you do this and that" patterns; the
first-person reportage: "I sit, I rise, I walk, I move, I
know, I wait"; and the awkward "that" patterns (one short
poem, "Gigolo," has eight such constructions). Mazzocco's
intelligence (and it is considerable) doesn't save the book,
for me.

POLITE, Frank. <u>Letters of Transit.</u>

Here are dazzling poetic takes on topics revved with
energy: parodies (one splendid one of James Wright), zappy
film scenarios, camp biographies (Rita Violin and Carmen
Miranda), intimate personal scenes (touching love-departure),
Nazis, pollution, fantasy figures (the amazing Fungo), trash
women, talk with friends, blue herons, the miseries of
Minnesota arctic cold, and word poems: <u>punish</u> "is squash
and pumpkin crossed." Many of these poems deserve to find
their way into anthologies. This is one of the best poetry
<u>reads</u> I've come across in a long time.

MALE COUPLINGS:

Brother Songs: A Male Anthology of Poetry,
        edited by Jim Perlman, Holy Cow Press*

        Several things strike me about Jim Perlman's daring
to publish an anthology of poems by men to men. First,
since there is plenty of truth in the macho-sperm of American
males, how can an ambitious publisher expect these same
males to cease admiring their beer-blessed paunches, their
assemblings of CB units, deer rifles, fishing rods, and lawn
mowers long enough to go out and buy a book of poems and
then read it? Second, how does this same publisher hope to
convince an audience of males, other than poets or teachers,
that reading poems is not a brain-softening feminine act: To
the American male mind a poem once read may be as loath-
some as a used tampon. Third, how can same publisher--in
a culture seeming now to have discovered that touching is OK
(and, indeed, possibly necessary), or that your father's
nakedness suddenly made visible, despite old Noah and his
sons, will not do severe brain damage--hope to transcend the
superficiality of all the in encounter groups, Gestalt stuff,
Est ceremonies, etc. and thrust these poems into the world?
Well, I don't pretend to know the answers. I welcome Perl-
man's courage.

        Brother Songs presents connections between men on
various levels: father-sons, sons-father, brother-brother,
friend-friend. The poems are varied. A host of poets,
known and unknown are represented. Among the contributors
are James Dickey, Paul Carroll, Philip Dacey, Donald Hall,
David Ignatow, Ted Kooser, Philip Levine, John Logan, Paul
Mariah, Thomas McGrath, Carl Rakosi, Vern Rutsala, Reg
Saner, Richard Shelton, Gary Snyder, William Stafford, and
James Wright. Many of the poems are elegiac memory-
poems, a fact symptomatic of our Oedipal father-fears.

_____
*This essay was written at the request of the editor of the
anthology, who (when he saw it) decided that it was not
quite in tone with his intentions. It appears here for the
first time.

During our childhoods, our fathers were frightening, nay-saying ogres and bullies--some of the time. We feared dad's genitals, we feared the whack of his flat hand on our rears, we felt distaste for his sexual use of our moms (did we really mean "abuse?"), we despised his niggardliness with money and his frequent indifference towards our rights. And yet we loved him, too. As Brother Songs shows, American poetry is abundant with examples of poems by poets exorcising their fathers. Adults now, these men scribble poems of delayed affection. At last they think they understand dad, and, from the safe distance of years, even love the old bastard. And the sentiment flows--and sometimes the sentimentality. Dad as woodsman, dad as fisherman and hunter, dad of loving (but suppressed) intentions, dad noble and uncomplaining in adversities and in his terminal illness.

Do our early fears and hatreds gray off as we age because we sense that our own children will think of us as we thought of our fathers? Has life so brutalized us that we refuse to allow ourselves the luxury of those earlier hatreds? Whatever the answer, as we age, it seems natural to want to exorcise these feelings. I suspect that beneath all of our father-feelings there are deep unresolved needs to sleep with our fathers. The poems in this collection should stimulate some profound and possibly disturbing feelings about our dads.

Our relationships with our brothers are hardly less thorny than those with our fathers. Notoriously, our brothers abuse us; they lie about us; steal our possessions; call us trauma-inducing names; beat us up; indoctrinate us into kinky sex; send us on errands bound to trap us. Older brother stands feared as a miniature dad. Obviously, what I am saying is simplistic, and my interpretations of these issues may not fit well at all with the editor's intentions in assembling these poems. I hope to stir up readers. For we do have buried feelings about our brothers (and about our sons). And despite the brutalities brothers perpetrate, there is a bedrock of allegiance, and love, instinctively protecting the family against that world of aliens out there. The ordeals of brother-conflict, then, are not finally destructive. Perhaps such conflicts whet our psychic and physical metals. We walk tougher through the world. The danger is, obviously, that we may simply become fathers and brothers exactly in their manner; we were cut from the same cutters as those fathers and brothers were.

The most problematic (because it is the most threat-
ening) male-male relationship is that between non-related
males.   American straight culture is notorious for its fear
and loathing of homosexuals.   That culture, at the same time,
has been just as notoriously blatant in expressing totemic
male sexual feeling: viz., jocks after winning a game climb
and jump all over one another, kiss, hug, slap fannys,
squeeze biceps.   Even the plastic Rotarian backslap is a
modified male sex-gesture.   Where is that incredible edge
between male-affection-for-male and actual homosexual play?
I'm inclined to see a piece, a continuum.   There is, if
this is true, no edge whatsoever.   There is rather a with-
drawing: The jock drops his pants but keeps his strap tightly
in place.   The men on a hunt drink from the same cup with-
out wiping the lip of the cup.   Yes, a sort of communion an-
ticipating that day when affection between all males will pro-
ceed guiltlessly and creatively along whatever Whitmanic,
rosy, fulfillment lines men wish to take, without fear of
violence or rancor.   God knows, we need to change, develop-
ing a greater gentleness.   These poems can help; if they
reach a sizeable audience, there should be awakenings.

UNSPEAKABLE VISIONS:

F. N. Wright's The Whorehouse and The Beat Journey, edited by A. and K. Knight*

Both of these books connect, since The Whorehouse, deriving as it does from the counter-culture mentalities of the late fifties and sixties, would probably never have been written had not the Beats been there first. Spin-offs and derivations can, of course, be good; I am afraid though that The Whorehouse is enough to make me want to tear the Peruvian seed-beads from around my neck, my Volkswagen car key from my left ear-lobe, and my Zig-zag papers from my pocket and flush them all away. The Whorehouse dropped into my mail recently, along with three sheets of "Readers' Comments" intended to make me think that this has to be a masterpiece. Among the quotes the publisher includes (is this a vanity production?) is a negative one, by Bob Wells. Wells says, among other things, "The author isn't Brautigan or Bukowski, but only offensive, and possibly trouble." The publisher's astute comment on what I feel is a thoroughly accurate statement is: "We happen to think Bob Wells is full of shit ..." Monique Chefdor (she's for real?) likes it a lot. Miriam Patchen decided that the dialogue is "amazingly better than life." I wonder what else she said, and if she stayed with the book to the end. Leo Mailman, in the Maelstrom Review, tells Charles Bukowski to move over, and sees Wright's production as "simply a masterful satire on the 'corrupt corporations in the world of American business'-- as the cover states."

I think this book is an incredible bore. I've written three funky novels myself and had a play called Fuck Mother produced Off-Off Broadway; so I do have some experience trying to bring off this Sixties/Beat, Zap Comix, Keseyesque humor. The Whorehouse is for me a post-pubescent snicker. There isn't a single zit that would be fun to pop. "Whore-

*Reprinted by permission from Contact II (Summer 1980), pp. 41-42.

house" is the name of a slick record-selling chain in Southern
California. Tsk, tsk, folks. What a coincidence that the
largest record chain of this type in Southern California is
The Wherehouse. Bob Wells wondered whether there is pos-
sibly legal trouble for any publisher in his use of such similar
names. In addition to Whorehouse there's "Dizzyland." I'd
say the publisher is liable on the grounds of bad taste. Did
Wright work for such a record company, have a miserable
experience, and now try to get even? In order for fiction
like this to work, it seems to me that the humor must be
outrageous ... and there must be some subtlety. There
might even be some great anger underpinning the whole.
None of this occurs here. Even comic books, by leaving
so much out--there are only so many words to fit into speech-
balloons--are effective because they are economical. The
Whorehouse continually parades dialogue of the most boring,
repetitious kind, for 236 pages. Every woman is either obese
and ridiculous and dehumanized, or pert and sassy, craving
to be shafted. The owner's daughters are given transistorized
Japanese breasts so that daddy can tune in when they're in
bed with the employees to see who's loyal and who's not.
Here's more of the humor via names: Los Angeles is Lost
Angels, Long Beach becomes Short Beach, Thousand Oaks
becomes Poison Oaks, etc. The owner of this incredible
business enterprise is Abe Fugumomma. His wife is Willa
Fugumomma. One of the store managers is simply Butthole.
Polly Person is a secretary. Abe's most valued associate
is Bernie Fucking Bastard. The Chief of Police likes to say
"Oink." A punk rock band is Mucous Puss. The No. 1 tune
in the country is "Constipated Emotions." Sounds like a
pretty good riff? It's not. Every page sounds like more of
the same. There's no empathy discernible on Wright's part
for any of his characters. His four-letter words, by page
ten, have the effect of measles spread over every page.
They squiggle like syphilis spirochetes seeking victims and
finally sit as an entirely predictable dead-space in the text.
Perhaps The Whorehouse, with outrageous drawings by R.
Crumb, would have worked better in the early sixties when
people were going to jail for printing the word "fuck," or for
saying it aloud in public. Now, the mindless repetition of
fuck (and related words) is boring. Fuck and shit have be-
come to the late seventies what lilies and roses were to the
1890's. They're exhausted words.

I have said in print in various places that I am for
liberating language in all its forms. No subject matter should
be taboo for literature. I remain, though, firmly against pre-

tentious, self-indulgent writing passing itself off for satire.
I can see why Brautigan's, Bukowski's or Burroughs's pub-
lishers don't have this novel on their lists.   It just doesn't
make it.   There are some things around written in the genre
that do: Kathy Acker's Toulouse-Lautrec and Jean Commeil-
faut's ongoing The Metastatic Octopus are a couple that come
to mind.

* * *

By contrast, The Beat Journey, edited by the Knights,
who publish The Unspeakable Visions of the Individual, is a
source book on Beat writers.   There are interviews with Allen
Ginsberg, Michael McClure, and John Clellon Holmes.   There
is a scattering of letters from Kerouac, Holmes, and Bur-
roughs.   There's a chunk of Herbert Huncke's Guilty of Every-
thing.   Corso and Kerouac contribute drawings.   There are
poems by Joanna McClure and Gregory Corso.   It all makes
fascinating reading.   There is a lot of information about how
Ginsberg wrote various books and individual poems, and much
talk about his feelings and relationships with the primary
figures in the Beat Movement.   Much of what Ginsberg says--
and this is true of the McClure interview--has been said
elsewhere; but that is in the nature of the interview: The in-
terviewers scattered hither and yon aren't all aware of the
overworked questions.   The virtue of these interviews made
at the Beat Writers Conference at the University of North
Dakota in March 1974, is that they are unhurried.   Most of
those who mention and discuss Kerouac are at a loss to say
why he finally drank himself to death and withdrew pretty
much from the world.   Obviously, the affection that Ginsberg
and the others had for Kerouac was intense; and, yet, they
don't strive to enhance his martyrdom.   The Beat Journey
rings its truths like a fire-station bell.   The photographs
are fascinating.   Many are from the late fifties: Dylan,
Ginsberg nude about to wash his hands (or privates?) in
a pan, Holmes, Corso, Cassady, Huncke, McClure ... and
various street pictures from the fifties.   My guess is that
the careful reader here will see Kerouac as a martyr though;
as someone who served as more than a center for other
spirits in the Beat movement.   I don't share those feelings.
Each of us has his ways.   And the fine novels remain.
Americans, though, seem to have a special place for writers
who destroy themselves.   Are we at heart perpetual adoles-
cents?   The Apollonian gift of creativity is both a curse and
a joy.   Perhaps it's time to lay this myth of the necessary
self-destructive babyhood of artists in its cradle-tomb and
forget it.   I would guess that E. E. Cummings and Wallace

Stevens would be far more revered by younger generations of poets and writers now if they had been self-destructive. Well, they can have good old Delmore Schwartz.   And according to rumors, they've lost Charles Bukowski, who is reportedly off beer and cigarettes and is into health foods.

CHOIRING THE VISIBLE-INVISIBLE:

Ten Years of Vangelisti and McBride's Invisible City*

Invisible City, the journal of criticism and poetry
edited by John McBride and Paul Vangelisti, has been around
for over nine years. A hugh triple issue, recently out, caps
an exceptional small-press publishing history. The journal's
iconoclasm remains as vigorous as ever. This fat issue
contains much new criticism and information, plus a review
section, plus a several-page anthology constituted from earlier
issues of Invisible City ("to be pronounced as quickly as pos-
sible," the editors inform us). Many of the poets McBride
and Vangelisti have published since 1970 were later published
in book form by the Red Hill Press, another enterprise grow-
ing out of Invisible City. Because of space limitations, I
shall concentrate primarily on the criticism and the review
sections; i. e. , on the freshly published materials.

I: Criticism

The editors see their journal as "necessarily frag-
mented" and isolated from "both conventional and avant-garde
poetries. " This issue is to be read as "a meeting of infor-
mation and criticism. " And to encourage readers to see
each large tabloid page as an entity in itself, the pages are
unnumbered, something which I am sure must perplex librar-
ians and index-makers. The theory--and there is a theory--
is that the magazine is composed by page and not by "field. "
What precedes or follows individual pieces relates to and
amplifies those individual pieces. The editorial statement,
which one would normally expect following the title page, is
buried deep within, headed by a most unobtrusive "(etc.). "
How refreshing, no matter what one might think of thumbing
through all these crammed unnumbered pages, to find editors
with a rationale behind what they are doing--the construction
of Invisible City reaches towards being an art form.

*Reprinted by permission from Bachy, No. 17 (June 1980),
pp. 149-153.

The central issue, or preoccupation, for nearly all of the criticisms is the struggle between discourse and the word. No current journal I have seen so imaginatively treats issues of language--structuralism, contextualism, verbalism, language-poetry, concrete writing. Each page of this issue teems with ideas sufficient for sophisticated graduate seminars and for generating poems by poets anxious to find a new/next step. Unless the word spreads, though--if one can read "invisible city" as a single word--these seminal thrusts may not enjoy the influence they should. All along, throughout these nine years, Invisible City has been a cantankerous, energetic (I hesitate to say "perverse"), magazine. One never feels that Invisible City comes to you. You go to it. And if you give it your best, its contours and editorial ploys will reveal themselves and amuse and enrich you.

The thematic centerpiece is Julien Blaine's "Epelle." Blaine is a French modernist poet and editor of numerous magazines devoted to what he calls écriture (as distinct from literature). His "exhibits" push the reader's tolerance to its limits. He presents us with an m, for example, then he turns the m on its side, changing is visual impact. He distinguishes between a word's meaning and its value. He comments on his "paramagazines" and parabooks": "one played with words on paper, and then words themselves played on paper and then the readers played with the words on paper; and the one transformed the paper, folded it, cut it up, and the words transformed themselves within the folds, they discovered their own attractions, aversions, neutralities, in the cuttings they perceived that they were different, that they can associate differently, the reader along with the word has detached himself from the sentence, they find themselves together to kiss in the corner of the page. In the cuttings, there were even disfigured words which resembled images, shapes, signs, so then we screwed up the books and we looked at the world, it was full of words: bridges over rivers, towers and windows; the world is well-read, fantastically well-read.... The words the letters, these are the world's constants. " (Approaches)

This reads like a playful romp, but it is serious. Few poets, I suspect, have considered the possibilities for poems of letters of the alphabet, sometimes severed from their loops, serifs and legs. Our traditional poems as sequential meaning-patterns get tossed aside in favor of a playful yet austere purity. Our visual field, it appears,

fractures the contours of objects--we pick up a detail here
and another there, and mentally complete the form.   When
we look at a dog we see something of an instant image made
up of enough salient features to read dog.   There is a kind
of short-hand perceiving of dog then.   So with words on a
page: We may see the loop of a p, or the upper curve of an
o, or the serif of the t, without seeing total letters.   Like
other avant-garde writers and artists, Julien Blaine attempts
to translate this way of seeing into forms.   Obviously such
creators relate to European and American concrete poets--
yet it appears they are more purely linguistic; or, rather,
that they are experimenting with the properties of the in-
dividual letter in a way that most concrete poetry does not.
Blaine says that "poetry is not a dictionary but a system of
values."   And by values he seems to mean purely visual
values as they strike our senses and stimulate responses.
"The proof of white on white suffices," Blaine insists; "the
material proof is nothing."

     Blaine's aesthetics has its political frame of reference,
something which pleases the politically conscious editors of
Invisible City.   Like his poetry and his visuals, his politics
seem minimalist--New Left, I suppose, is as good a phrase
as any.   His magazines have apparently fathered leftist
newspapers, some of them underground, serving "popular
struggles."   Blaine loathes the C.I.A., is obsessed with
Chile and Latin America, believes in the potential of avant-
garde art to stimulate political action.   Perhaps a poetry
of pure vision and sound seems totally extraneous to politics.
There is a connection though, and Blaine makes it: Only in
a non-bourgeois, non-fascistic society, can the poet/musician/
visual artist express himself with complete freedom.   My
own sense is that this New Left moves, not towards Commu-
nism in a classical sense, but towards something more like
an enlightened anarchism where the individual is paramount,
where a private spirituality of ethics and esthetics clears
away the miasmas of traditional rhetoric, concept and mo-
rality.

     The opening interview with Archie Shepp, which I find
to be the weakest feature of the issue, stresses this political
theme.   Shepp finds that black music possesses "certain
dialectical qualities."   He adopts Max Roch's notion that
Afro-American music is "a microcosm of democracy at work.
When the music begins, every man is truly pulling his own
weight--every man is a leader."   Shepp also feels that black
music is the only art form to appear "completely uninformed

by white experience--all other academic forms must be taught
to negroes by white people. If a negro painter is to be suc-
cessful, generally he has to study western painters; if he's
to be a successful writer, he has to study western writers. "
He laments the state of black writing, finding that it hasn't
progressed much since Richard Wright.

Two moving poems by Amiri Baraka follow: "Real
Life" and "Das Kapital, " first published in Invisible City in
October 1976. There is also a fragment of an interview
made in that same year but never published. "Real Life"
is the most bitingly satiric poem on Nixon and Ford I have
read. In "Das Kapital, " stranglers and maniacs prowl
blighted American cities with the rats. In the interview,
Baraka details his experience with publishers who after pub-
lishing his first sixteen books now find him too political to
publish. Julien Blaine would agree with Baraka that "all
art ... represents the class stand of whoever writes. " Po-
etry, thus, is always a mixture of politics and art.

In an essay on Jack Spicer, written in 1966, before
Spicer's work was as accessible as it is now, Gilbert Sor-
rentino makes more sense of Spicer as a language poet than
any other critic has. Spicer built his aesthetic "around lan-
guage itself, divorced from the image. " His poetry, Sorren-
tino explains, reflects three primary ideas: 1. Language,
not its tropes and elegances, is the core for the ultimate
poem. 2. A poem is an instance of reality, not a gloss of
same. 3. The poet is not an interpreter but a revealer ...
things do not connect, neither in the poem nor in the life
from which it springs: They correspond.

Spicer is the true conservative/conservator: He be-
lieved that the world is a place "which yields up its meanings
to that artist who has subordinated his ego to its multiplex
phenomena. " The poet does not impose his will upon objects
in order to interpret those objects--that would be "anti-
humanist. " For Spicer, Sorrentino observes, "the world is
a great rock, and ... it stays so. The artist's job is not
to tell you what he thinks about it, but is to tell you it. "
How different this vision is from Robert Frost's, Sorrentino
says: "We clambered about Mr. Frost's walls, picked his
apples, and thought such claptrap as the thing that art does
for life is to clean it, to strip it to form an instance of
wisdom. " By your intervention in the world's chaos, be-
lieving you can structure and order it according to your
own preconceptions, you simply multiply the chaos--your
"egoism" imposes "a lie on what is true chaos. "

Spicer wanted correspondence between his psyche and the material world. "To connect is to muddy and blur; to correspond is to isolate and sharpen." Baudelaire, the father of correspondences, felt that a pure spirit, through revelation and an exemplary life, can experience the "perfect reality" in an imperfect, commonplace one. Spicer's world, says Sorrentino, is different, is more purely temporal, is one "to be got to in order to understand it." Nothing Platonic and idealized here. Both men relate in that they both insisted on revelation, believing that "the world is there, regardless of what we think it is." The poet must "reveal" that world. Spicer did think by a "poetics-in-action," by negating the image and by positing "separate instances of the real as correspondences." Spicer sought total presentations, not deep images or surrealisms. He sought to bring diamond to diamond, bone to bone, and rock to rock, all towards a totality. His fascination with "language" was the substrata of his highly original poetics.

A lengthy feature on Walter Benjamin includes an account of a conversation with André Gide, written in 1928, and a mini-anthology of pieces from various of Benjamin's works through 1930. The interview with Gide is possibly of primary importance--not only is there a fine sense of Gide as a person, but Gide discusses Proust and his, Gide's, relationship to the German language. Gide believed that his fame would come after his death; his influence was to direct French writers towards other lands and languages. The excerpts from Benjamin's works highlight various moments of his political/literary thinking. One wants to read more. There is this fine touch from Brecht: He and Benjamin were playing chess--Brecht said he wanted to work out a new game--"A game in which the moves do not always stay the same; where the function of each piece changes after it has stood in the same square for a while." This, metaphorically, is exactly what Julien Blaine and Jack Spicer hope (and hoped) to do with language, and with the letters of the individual word.

The most minimalist of the language/letter/image poets are the Italian avant-gardists Giulia Niccolai and Adriano Spatola. Some ten pages of Invisible City are devoted to their work. Niccolai and Spatola early in the sixties sought to continue the neo-avant-garde work of the Italian poets in Gruppo 63, those featured in the famous anthology I Novissimi. (Invisible City has published work by Antonio Porta, one of the important members of the movement.)

They began publishing books in 1968; since then 100 books
have appeared under their Geiger (yes, after the counter)
imprint. Their journal <u>Tam Tam</u> has flourished for ten
years and publishes the most interesting experimental work
the editors are able to find in Europe and America. Giulia
Niccolai's essay "Feminism and Italian Avant-garde Art" was
originally delivered as a lecture at the University of Califor-
nia Los Angeles, in March 1978, with slides demonstrating
the work of various female experimentalists. While Niccolai's
essay may appear too specialized for the American reader,
just the opposite is true. Niccolai provides a sketch of the
state of poetry in Italy, a brief history of the avant-garde
movement, and of feminism in the arts. She finds that few
people ever buy women's books--and her publishing house has
published several books by females. Women themselves rare-
ly buy. Niccolai concludes that women are their own worst
enemies--in the arts as well as out of them. Fortunately,
a few Italian women have been trying to correct matters.
These women, including Niccolai herself, are interested in
"the way of making poetry," seeing exact correspondences be-
tween the making and the meaning. All poems, she believes,
are political acts; and in periods of social crisis making and
meaning merge.

For Giovanna Sandri, a concrete poet, the alphabet,
like the moon, is feminine. In those 24 letters "everything
has been registered." Most meanings, however, we have
forgotten--the great tree of language rises from the earth,
germinated from the seed of signs. In these signs (letters)
reside our own roots. To these we must return. The visual
language of <u>visual poetry</u> is a means towards this important
"perception and communication." By tracing words/letters
to their origins, we release implicit energies from every
sign and letter, from our great "collective unconscious."
Sandri's poems, constructed from ordinary Letraset sheets,
recall patient laboratory work, preparations for deciphering
hitherto lost scrolls.

Mirella Bentivoglio's work, in contrast, tends out-
wards, is extroverted, is endlessly curious about the signs
and objects surrounding her in the everyday world. She
materializes words. For her there are no longer any bound-
aries between the physical and mental spheres. Her <u>Nord</u>,
a poem-object or object poem, is made of Plexiglas. Two
of the four letters have been heated to the boiling point, look
frosted, and conceptually underline the identities of cold-warm
as properties. And she loves puns--as she demonstrates in

"The Heart of the Obedient Consumer"--a spirited play on Coca-Cola. "Oca," here surrounded and embraced, heart-shaped, by generous images of C, in Italian means goose, and is a common feminine insult.

Annalisa Alloatti employs the Braille alphabet for her visual patterns, achieving closure. Her poem, "Cecita" (Blindness), generates pity, guilt and unease. Tomaso Binga is the pen name of Bianca Menna, who purposely uses the male name to satirize the macho privileges so strong in art. She insists that an artist is neither a man nor a woman but a person. Her happenings cover entire walls. In one event she uses her own body as a writing surface, using her naked shape to form letters, thereby "inventing" her own alphabet. Her writing is de-semanticized--it mimes the traces of writing rather than spelling out words. Irma Blank transcribes from a daily newspaper, following its layout exactly. The writing, though, cannot be read. In a sense, she creates "a writing made up of nothing." Betty Danon's Punto linea (Dot Line), praised by Roland Barthes as perfect, creates dots and lines, via typewriter and by hand, enabling the reader to follow the work either as lines or dots. Dots and lines interchange and complement one another. A poem begins with the word punto, or dot, which eventually becomes the stretched out word linea (line). Anna Oberto and Lucia Marucci also explore new writing in special ways: Oberto creates visual poems, incorporating collage bits produced by her son, aged two. Marucci constructs collage figures, feminist in motif, similar to some of the pop-op art inspired by Warhol and Lichtenstein. Niccolai herself creates images out of everyday objects--buttons, pins, typewriters. She attempts to "dislocate" these objects "slightly from the everyday," allowing the "poetic elements" to reveal themselves. Her lecture is nicely supported by well-reproduced photographs of samples from all the artists she treats.

The lengthy interview with Adriano Spatola, co-founder with Niccolai of Geiger Books and Tam Tam, is both descriptive and critical. Spatola has studied language and philosophy on advanced university levels. He finds that visual or concrete poetry is largely a matter of gesture. There's a certain innocence behind such works. He says: "A visual text is only the condensation of one aspect of a larger linguistic reality and, though often generic, it isn't necessarily usable within a community." Our notions of "reading" poems must shift--he aims in his own work to counter the drift of the literal. Nor does the unconscious interest him--and, one

would assume, neither does surrealism or imagism. "There
is the unconscious, fine, but there is also being, and I am
concerned mostly with being, as a phenomenon or a linguistic
trace. "

Rather than enter the unconscious, Spatola says hu-
morously that he goes "only inside the dictionary. " And
what of the dictionary? In the manner of the good visual/
concrete artist, Spatola finds that the dictionary is "a living
organism, " not a "data bank. " Living organisms have trau-
mas, etc. When Spatola uses classical rhetoric, as he does
in his poem Majakovskiiiiiij (published here in full), he is
writing parody. His mentors are not poets, but rather phi-
losophers--Husserl, Nietzsche, Heidegger. The interview
strikes me as a good assemblage itself of put-ons and thin-
ice skating. Here, for example, is an instance of blent non-
sense and sense: "I attempt to have time as my only link
with reality; that is, time as the wear and tear on the words
in the dictionary, for there are words which are twenty years
old and then there are words which predate language itself. "
I feel that I should know what reality and time mean, but I
don't and yet I like the idea of the ages of words. Finally,
Spatola is highly critical of the impact of American poetry,
particularly Beat poetry, on Italian poets. Young Italians
are writing what Spatola calls "translations"; these "poets of
translation" have no sense for the proper uses of the Italian
language. They are busy writing their "translations" in the
manner of the American Beats. This "colonialism, " Spatola
says, "is ponderous, very much commercialized, as if it
were Coca-Cola or something. "

Spatola's translator, Paul Vangelisti, presents a sam-
pling of his own recent work, influenced by the European
avant-garde. Vangelisti probably knows as much about lan-
guage poetry as any American editor/poet. He has written
in relative isolation, generally ignored by critics and re-
viewers who have not known what to do with his concrete/
verbal/visual works. As American poets begin to write more
experimentally again--and there is evidence that they are,
particularly in the Bay Area, Vangelisti may be seen as a
seminal figure, and Invisible City an important vehicle, for
the movement. One of his creations is of a woman in a
cloche hat--clearly she is from the 1920s. He has cut out
her face, throat, and part of her chest, and has pasted in a
piece of a newspaper, turned sideways, excised from the
stock market section. I am amused by the piece. It works
well visually. I have not forgotten it since I first saw it some

months ago. Vangelisti also contributes a perceptive essay
on the impact of Donald Davie on his thinking. Vangelisti
has provoking, if tentative, things to say about Davie on
Pound. Vangelisti's "Scapes," a poem of 21 short parts,
appears, apparently without his knowledge, thanks to John Mc-
Bride, his co-editor. McBride also prints variants and dele-
tions Vangelisti would have suppressed. Yet, faulty as this
version is (Vangelisti tells me he has made revisions), its
appearance fits the idea of language poetry as a means towards
an organic unfolding. The flawed poem resolving its flaws
is, perhaps, yet another form of linguistic invention, of
lingual becoming. The matrix of "Scapes," remains essen-
tially unchanged; the matter undergoes polishings. As the
poem says, peaches do have bumps, horses do rest quietly
against the green choruses of the eye, pe ras cemuln lescul
zuci. That's Etruscan, folks: a hell of a language!

II: Reviews

The reviews are double-edged. At times, they are
simply reprintings of portions from the work being reviewed,
in order, I gather, to stress Invisible City's interests. The
review of Triquarterly 43, the little magazine issue, for ex-
ample, quotes Reed Whittemore and Gilbert Sorrentino, ig-
noring the numerous other contributors to the issue. Whitte-
more sees two literary generations since the fifties and the
period of his influential journal, Furioso: The "apolcalyptic
Beat generation" with its "alternative life style" and a "new
quiet generation, with its attentiveness to its poetry and its
poetry only...." Whittemore confesses that he had little
time for the Beats back then: "The Beats were interested in
culture and civilization, wanted to change it, thought that
literature had a role in changing it, and were even annoyed
with our generation because they found us too literary and
inactivist." The newer generation (among them I would guess
are the Gary Snyderites sitting off in the woods gazing at
bear shit) took themselves off to the forests and wrote a
literature "narrowly conceived" and "at best a craft, at worst
an indulgence." Whittemore calls these folks "woods poets,"
their poems "woods poetry."

Sorrentino is quoted on the quality of Kulchur magazine,
which he says "did not read like any other magazine before
or since." It had its ambience, with each issue full of arti-
cles and pieces complementing each other. A magazine, he
observes, should not be a "hodgepodge of good pieces by good

writers. " William Carlos Williams told him that the only rationale for a little magazine is "its editor's belief that the writers he prints must be presented as a group. Anything else is just a collation of pages. " Yes, something to think about as we try to give good reads to the plethora of little magazines today. Too few of them, unlike Invisible City, have an interior rationale, a reason for being apart from publishing friends and pushing editors' careers. Too many editors are, at the same time, too passive and simply collate their pages--and their poets. Sorrentino calls for more criticism by writers of other writers. He finds the current situation of reviewing (and I heartily agree) "oddly passive. " Issues of magazines are "all charm, gossip, and news notes. " A call for rebellious magazines!

Next, Ken Bullock's lengthy review of Boundary 2 is particularly apt, since the writers he discusses are Baraka and Spicer, who figured earlier in this issue of Invisible City. Boundary 2 devoted their Fall '77 issue to Spicer, and the Winter '78 supplement to Baraka. Bullock sees Boundary's focus on Spicer as the first attempt to register "a broad critical response" to the Black Sparrow edition of Spicer's work. The pattern of change in Spicer is now clear: He moved "further into antithesis and admonition, " and came finally to consider his poems "dictated" messages from the universe. In general, however, Bullock is dissatisfied with the special issue, and with co-editor Spanos' remarks. Spanos wrongly, Bullock believes, "collates Spicer's work with Pound, Williams, Olson, Creeley, Duncan, and Snyder. Most of the essays seem random and lean of information; there is little critical interest in Spicer's poetry for itself. " There is a "free trading in terms" rather than the critical "disclosure" the editors had desired. Michael Davidson's contribution is excellent, however, and distinguishes between Spicer's poetic and the "immanence" theory of postmodernism --as held by Charles Altieri and others. It is absurd to think as these critical theorists do, that until the appearance in the seventies of Heidegger, Merleau-Ponty, and Derrida there were no critical tools for coming to terms with Spicer.

In contrast with Spicer, Baraka has become increasingly polemical. Bullock calls him "a brilliant polemical poet ... perhaps the most important in current American poetry. " In an interview, Baraka recalls his days in New York when he tried to break from the influence of "people like Creeley and Olson. " Then, he said, New York contained "two little warring schools ... what I call the Jewish-Ethnic-Bohemian

School (Ginsberg and his group) and the Anglo-German Black Mountain School. " Baraka was caught between them, because they were "all literary buddies. " His novel, The System of Dante's Hell, was an attempt to break free. Most of the essays in Boundary 2 deal in various ways with Baraka's polemicism. The most pointed essay, by Sherley Anne Williams, is feisty and to the point: "Baraka, by whatever name, is a black dealing with black...." While these criticisms provide a sense of Baraka's "relation to black cultural traditions, and of the importance of his opposition to academic and finally Bohemian Black Mountain poetics, none finally provides a sense of the conditions" of producing these works, "or of the importance of their shifting polemic, " or of what Baraka derived from visiting Cuba: "His sense that the opposition 'New American Poetry vs. the Academy' was false. "

The most provocative of the "reviews, " because it is the most experimental in its design and layout, treats Pier Pasolini's controversial last film, Salò. Invisible City had earlier carried several translations of Pasolini's poetry and an interview. The most fascinating piece here is by Roland Barthes. Barthes says that in Salò Pasolini has "shot his scenes to the letter. " He spares us nothing: the enucleated eye, the eating of excrement, the chewing of sharp needles. Our glance, says Barthes, is "stripped naked"--such is the "effect of the letter. " The letter is "scrupulous, insistent, displayed, over-polished like a primitive painting: allegory and letter, but never symbol, metaphor, interpretation.... " There are obvious connections here among Spicer's, Blaine's and Niccolai's attempts to convey the rock as rock, the diamond as diamond, the word as word, the separate letter of the alphabet as letter. The film is a matter for the semanticist, and for the artist in pursuit of the image as object not as metaphor or symbol. Pasolini himself said in 1966: "Cinema reproduces reality. " This review invites more questions than it answers. We need a speculative essay on the language of poems and writing (écriture) and the language (visual and auditory) of films.

The political theme re-emerges in a page of excerpts from Galvano Della Volpe's Critique of Taste, a seminal book of Marxist criticism totally unknown in the U. S. A. , and recently published in translation by New Left Books (London). Volpe relates the need for examining the semantic or linguistic side of poetry and of art to Marx and Engels and some of their statements in The German Ideology. He arraigns Kant and the romantics for the fundamental error of "mistaking the semantic immediacy of poetic speech for a synony-

mous immediacy of intuition or pure image. " And he mis-
trusts the literate American Left for burying itself in the
writings of Lukacs. Lukacs was absolutely mistaken in pre-
ferring "the refined but second-hand bourgeois art of Thomas
Mann, an occasionally brilliant epigone of 19th-century real-
ism, " to "the poetic originality of Proust, Joyce & Kafka. "

    Brilliantly showcased is a review of two translations
of the Haitian poet René Depestre's A Rainbow for the Chris-
tian West. To Invisible City's credit, they published Jack
Hirschman's translation of a fair chunk of this important
poem in 1972, following that with the entire book (Red Hill
Press) that same year. For whatever reasons, the book did
not find an audience. Once again, Invisible City reprints the
"Aphorisms & Parables" section of Rainbow, as translated by
Hirschman, along with a brief portion of an address Depestre
gave before the Cultural Congress in Havana (1967), plus
Carole Lettieri's assessment of Hirschman's and also of Joan
Dayan's translations. What a model for other journals to
follow--the poet in question substantially represented in poetry
and prose, the critique ensuing. To simplify Lettieri's es-
say: "Hirschman's translation participates in the excitement
of the voodoo dance, yet is at times sadly misinformed
as to the real meaning of the French. Dayan's trans-
lation accurately pins down the content, but almost com-
pletely misses Depestre's form. Hirschman needed a little
bit of Dayan's information, and Dayan needed a lot more of
Hirschman's poetic spirit. " Again, the problem of language
is central.

III: The Anthology

    Part III of Invisible City is a showcase for earlier
numbers of the tabloid, spread over some nine years. A
two-page spread precedes a catalogue, an anthology, allowing
readers to taste, smell and see something from every book
Red Hill Invisible City has published. The books are all in
print. Poems by Eluard, Bukowski, Guillevic, Russo, Paso-
lini, Fortini, Hirschman, John Thomas, Shange, Huidobro,
Aragon, among others, grace these pages. Among the books,
Helmut Maria Soik's Rimbaud Under the Steel Helmet makes
available work by one of the best, yet hardly known, con-
temporary German poets. Alvaro Cardona-Hine's translation
of César Vallejo's Spain, Let This Cup Pass from Me has
been reprinted. Charles Bukowski's selection of Los Angeles
poets who interest him is a special book. Three books by

the brilliant Stuart Perkoff amount to a Collected Poems for this poet who died young. Many other books merit individual comments; in the interest of space, however, I shall simply give here the address of Red Hill Press's distributor (Red Hill Books are distributed by Small Press Distribution, 784 Shattuck Ave. , Berkeley, CA 94709), and Invisible City (PO Box 2853 San Francisco, CA 94126), where lists of books and issues currently in print may be obtained, and I hope that readers may want to order them.

NOTE: I wish to be entirely clear regarding my own connections with Invisible City and The Red Hill Press. Two of my books, Holy Cow and Hawthorne, bear the imprint. A sequence of my Shaker poems, The Gift to Be Simple (Liveright, Inc.), was first published, in selection, in Invisible City. For nearly nine years I have kept silence in print about what I feel is the excellence of this journal. Now, since it is obvious that no other critic intends to herald this fat commemorative issue--it requires the attention one would give to a demanding book--I have decided to risk accusations of nepotism and provide what I intend to be a more or less descriptive rather than judgmental account of the contents of Invisible City. Obviously, I will be delighted if my remarks do send good numbers of folk to the tabloid itself. There's a lot of visibility here, and the streets are well-paved and full of unexpected delights.

SCRIBBLING IN JOURNALS AND OTHER POETRY MATTERS:

The Streets Inside: Ten Los Angeles Poets: Momentum Press
(Deena Metzger, Eloise Klein Healy, Kate Braverman,
Dennis Ellman, James Krusoe, Holly Prado, Harry
Northup, Bill Mohr, Peter Levitt, Leland Hickman)*

Imagine the United States poetry world as an enormous
beehive regionally divided. Each poet-bee works more or
less in isolation, filling his (or her) cells with poet-nectar
distilled into honey. When a poet fills his allotted honey
cells, he must evict other poets from cells near him, by
bad-mouthings, put-downs, outright hostilities and vicious
stings. The means for such poet-destruction are various.
But warfare in the hive doesn't interest me as much as the
efforts of poet-bees from various parts of the forest to form
a new bee community, to set up their poem-honey caches, as
a means of advertising the presence--and the quality--of their
fresh honey. Yes, by such clustering, poet-bees have a
chance of robbing already established bee-clusters of some
of their market: East Coast poets, Athaeneum poets, Wes-
leyan University poets, San Francisco North Beach poets, old
Beat poets, Nairopa poets, Iowa Writing Center poets (and
their numerous swarm-offs), Bolinas poets, etc. This is a
given: The demand for poet-honey around the U.S. is a con-
stant; the poet-loner-bee, or the bee members of a fledgling
hive must somehow entice poet-honey consumers away from
their accustomed feeding sources.

One way to do this is to publish a handsome anthology
of poems by poets you know and like, thereby fashioning your
own apiary. This William Mohr of Momentum Press has
done, and most impressively. He makes quite clear that his
swarm is not representative of all poets living and writing in
Los Angeles. He has chosen ten persons, all of whom have
either appeared in Momentum or in books published by Momen-

---

*Reprinted by permission from Bachy, No. 14 (Spring, Sum-
mer 1979), p. 138-141.

tum Press. Most of these poets are under forty. Four are
women; six are men. In a town noted for its superficiality,
The Streets Inside is welcome evidence of quality. I have the
feeling that most of us writing in S. C. have assumed that the
best way to flourish here is to get away as often as possible.
Do your writing in New York or San Francisco. Poets in
Los Angeles rarely seem even to talk to one another--and
apart from the poets who've swarmed around Beyond Baroque
in Venice for several years, nothing much by way of a com-
munity seems to exist. What do you hear of anything vigorous
going on in Kessler-land (UCLA)? at Stanford-land (Cal. State,
Northridge)? at Coulette-land (Cal State L. A.)? Sure, there
are separate poet-bees zinging around, inserting their stingers
here and there--and a fine critic or two. Apart from Paul
Vangelisti of Red Hill Press and KPFK, Clayton Eshleman,
who has tried to originate a community of poets, and John
Harris and Bachy-folk, most writers pretty much seem to do
their own thing, keeping their eyes fixed on national and in-
ternational reputations, politicking with the Poetry Society of
America or with the National Endowment for the Arts. Poli-
tics should begin at home, one would think. But poetry-
politics seems to begin in New York, San Francisco, or
Frankfurt, Germany.

Obviously, I welcome The Streets Inside as an impres-
sive effort towards defining a hive-geography for Los Angeles.
A hive-map. What is this new swarming like? Has it
swarmed well? Will its honey sustain us? Yes. Yes. Yes.
For, despite the different zingings (no two voices here are
that much alike), the pollen has been gathered from shared
flowers: weed-blooms as well as cultivated, hothouse ones.
The greenhouses of ten selves.

This is a most readable anthology, of that rare kind
you can begin at the front and read through. The layout
makes for inviting reading. The type is strong and dark.
The book is readable also because of the permeating frank-
ness present in almost all the poems. These poets are self-
obsessed ... or, rather, the limits of their worlds are condi-
tioned by what they themselves can see, touch, smell, taste.
The danger, in a few instances, is that the poems are narcis-
sistic and self-indulgent. The first-person pronoun swings
around like irritating hornets seeking soft places on your skull
for their landings.

Perhaps the poetry-as-journalism (or journal scribblings)
owes something to Charles Bukowski and Diane Wakoski, both

inordinately fond of that ego-pronoun. They generate poems
by giving you the news of their lives, frequently humdrum
news: Poems begin with the news that poet B or W is sitting
at the breakfast table, or on the head; and they may be pick-
ing their noses, hungering for a lover, eating their toasted
English muffin crumbs. Poems get cranked up; they aren't
inspiritedly launched. Gab Poetry, I've called it elsewhere,
writing of Bukowski. The Newspaper of the Poet's Life, Ive
said, coming to terms with one of Diane Wakoski's recent
books. Both of these poets, incidentally, are masters of the
form--I admire much about both of them. But imitators are
another matter.

DEENA METZGER is the most blatantly newspapery of
these ten poets. Her poems read mostly like prose chopped
up to look like poems. They generally lack the tenuosity and
inventiveness of poems by Kate Braverman or Holly Prado.
Metzger writes much too slackly, I feel: She gives too much
commonplace information: "The women I know are so soft/
they have breasts to cry against...." Does she know women
without breasts? Are these the hard women? I feel senti-
mentalized--and illogically so. Another sample of writing
that seems over-trivialized are numerous sections of prose/
poems strung out with "ands." And overused is reflective of
a boring child's mind--the child hasn't yet learned to sub-
ordinate information, but rather strings it all together in a
continuous babble: "But you have lived almost a year in one
house and have another year to go in it and have two cats
you hate but they live and require food and that is important
for all of us to remember that creatures live and require
food and that we feed them and...." I am sure I will be
damned as pedantic if I suggest cutting drastically and getting
some subordinate elements in--and even an image or two.
Can the ands and feed them to pussy along with her Meow-
Mix. Metzger talks too much--talks at me. Some poetry is
talking, true: but such writing should still have concision,
inventiveness, originality--or we are bored. Humdrum lives,
boring to the people living them, must be boring to people
expected to read them.

ELOISE KLEIN HEALY also often fails to turn ordinary
prose into poetry. Here are a couple of passages from her
lengthy poem "Furnishings." Since her line breaks don't
seem to matter all that much, I am simply going to let these
passages stand as prose, although they are printed on the
page to look like poetry:

> This is our difference. I always ask for more and
> more specifics while you have already answered to
> the general catagory (sic).

This one, though a bit more interesting because of the allusion to Bosch, is still mundane and cute:

> I think if I hung the Bosch over the bed I would
> fall into it. I would hit my head on the dancer's
> knees just like the time I fell in basketball. Barabra's (sic) knee came up at me very slowly. I
> thought, "Here it comes again. I'm going to hurt
> my head." But I was not afraid, really, only for
> my glasses.

It puzzles me that Healy can't seem to tell what writing she should throw in the wastebasket and which publish. For she can write stunningly. "Like a Woman in a Short Story" has power, and an imagist, nasty intensity. Here is one of the best moments:

> But there was a magnetic element
> in all the tensions that kept them circling
> and gathering small things wrong between them:
> metal filings, turning from metal screws, shavings
> from cylinder heads, chips from aluminum borings
> and ugly ugly flint
>
> they kept striking together as they mated.
> Yes, she thought, they mated--two animals
> who smelled each other and mated
> and because each animal knew it needed
> to get what it needed
> their bodies sometimes spoke a vicious language.
> "I take I take," his body sometimes said.
> And often she turned on him and grasped him
> and her body said, "I take what I want."

Bringing off an ego-poem is immensely difficult. My complaint with many poets is that they scatter I's like bits of bee-dung dropped throughout the hive, defiling both the honey and the comb. A personal journalism rather than poetry. The newspaper of the poet's life. Because an event occurred, no matter how dull it is--that seems to justify its use in a poem. To succeed with ego-poems, a substratum of image, obsession, invention must exist. Hip language on its own won't make it.

KATE BRAVERMAN is one of the several I-poets here
who succeeds. When it comes to pulling out surprises from
her flamboyant life, she is her own woman. One feels read-
ing her that her zingings-along to various flowers (thistles,
weeds, Venus-flytraps, dahlias, gardenias, roses) are re-
solved in taut writing. She avoids the breathy kind of padding
I find in some of Holly Prado's prose poems. Braverman is
a master of the opening line. She draws you in, and her
poems become in a way symbolic Venus-flytraps. I feel read-
ing her that I may be sucked in and devoured. I like the
feeling. Here is a sampling of her openings: "The wood is
ripped in a thin patch." "I was the rag doll / you wanted in
childhood." "The women are leaving slowly / hobbling on
broken feet." "I have dropped like bait / and hung in the
foam."

DENNIS ELLMAN is a gifted poet whose poems--at
least in this collection--are damaged by the oversimplified
declarative ego statement. Here is a sampling: "I bowed
my / head. My loneliness, / I offered, is the / same un-
changeable force / that whitens the space / between my words.
/ My loneliness, he said, / is my loneliness." Perhaps the
triteness of the bowed head would seem less trite if we didn't
have to be told all the stuff about loneliness too. Here is
another randomly chosen moment needing, I think, a good
pruning: "I stand in the yard / with clippers and saw." Or,
these opening lines seem needlessly dead: "I hear you come.
/ I watch through the window." There's sort of a Dick-see-
Dick quality here--a sort of primer language and sentence
structure. My guess is that this kind of writing went over
better in the late Sixties than it does now--when nearly every-
body was strung out on good dope. We set out to inform
people who know what they are doing, what they are doing.
If that makes sense! "You sit upon / an upturned crate."
Or, "You / grunt and write me about disgust...." There's
an implicit naivete here--and it is defensible; an elemental
positioning, almost as if the poet is an Adam starting off his
poem with most elemental news. In one of Ellman's poems,
"Tomatoes," I count "I" a dozen times in seventeen lines.
Visually, these pronouns leap from the page, dance before
your eyes, and damage the poem. Ellman's announced models,
Philip Levine and Charles Wright, both lovers of the first-
person pronoun, skirt destructing their ego-poems by avoiding
banal statements--but not always. Ellman does have some
gifts--and I want to hasten to say so. He has a special
poignancy in evoking his childhood and exploring male con-
nections in his family. "The Man" is a highly original poem,

unspoiled by <u>pronoun disease</u>.   His handling of the long verse
line is consummate.   Here are a few lines:

> The man demands the company of pregnant women
>   who lie on him and squeal.
> He feels the thumping in their loins and thinks
>   it is the thumping in his loins.
> He wants their lips upon his breasts, their hands
>   placed strong between his thighs.
> He smells sometimes, the milk that sleeps behind
>   their nipples.
> He wants their nipples to jar his nipples.
> He wants the milk to seep into his own dry glands.

JAMES KRUSOE resembles Kate Braverman in his
tough, intense responses to life.   He wields that simple,
first-person line with the confidence of a veterinarian with a
scalpel.   His ear is taut and lyrical--he knows how a poem
should sound.   And he realizes, too, that inventiveness (or
originality) helps to keep readers awake.   He's full of sur-
prises.   He can run off a chant-poem: "I Was the Mean
One," and move it around painful childhood memories, evoking
a proletariat culture: "Joe loses his stomach; it comes out
in bits / Through his throat." "Bill loses twenty years of
Christmas calendars, / His teeth in a bar, loses jobs, more
jobs." "On Saturdays I watch cartoons, / The rabbit cuts
the fox in half, / I buy a knife." A bitter child's life shapes
itself.   "Hydra" conveys more of Krusoe's proletarian feelings.
I thoroughly believe in his nonsentimental sense of the tragic
in life--and he doesn't need clichés and phoney, pretentious
Dick-and-Jane stances.   I believe his wisdom:

> Bad things happen but there is consolation
> In the singularity of death, and even torture's
> More like a baseball game where most of the time
> The players stand around and scratch.

Krusoe's new book, <u>Small Pianos</u> (Momentum Press), contains
much more of the same skill and acuteness.

HOLLY PRADO'S poems seem to derive from Jungian
dream-journal passages and assorted <u>I-Ching</u> castings.   She
adopts the voice of the sensitive woman in a kind of ongoing
encounter group with herself as the only member.   Occa-
sionally, she allows someone else in.   The drift of her
writing is always towards triumphing over pain and betrayal.
Meditation becomes a means of licking her wounds.   She

seems to hoard pain as a primary means of self-awareness.
As she says, "The giving up of grief is the hardest thing I've
ever had to do. " While I admire Prado's intelligence and
clarity, I am put off by the self-obsessions seemingly justi-
fied by the journal-entry form of poem.   Here is an example
of solipsism, as she drags her diary around in the Los
Angeles dust:

> this week you say you've dreamed of me
> how I leave your house to walk
> you find me in the streets and I wear blue
> like streams like brooks you say.

This strikes me as stuff from a letter ... not boring, not
exciting.   A personal obsessiveness shuts readers out:
Friendly addresses to friends who have shared intimate ex-
periences we can only guess at have the effect of making us
feel that a poem may be gestating, but not for us.   It's for
Eloise, or Jim, or Martha, or Matt, or Bill, etc.... but
it's not for us.   Well, then, I wonder, why put it out into
the world?   Why not send it to the friend in question via
special delivery ... or parcel post?   And, of course, there
is always the telephone.

Prado is too good a poet to limit herself in this way.
I would urge her to get on with the good poems she can write
(and has written).   "Marla: A Tumor in Her Breast" is
Prado at her finest.   Her empathy is real and moving; and
the poem lacks the indulgent emotions and wasted phrases of
the journal-entry ego-poem.   Also, Prado's final three poems,
two of them to a lover, are celebrations.   They demonstrate,
I hope, that Prado has discovered that she has exorcised
much of her pain, and can let go, and love.   She is a medi-
tative poet who can cut to the bone in cauterizing feelings.

HARRY NORTHUP, poet and actor, is a wild language
explosioneer.   He has dated his numerous poems; and if there
is a progression that makes sense, his language grows in-
creasingly energetic, exorcistic, baffling.   The words seem
more important for their syllables than as single constructs--
a storm of neutrons and protons spinning madly around.   The
result?   a flamboyant psyche in flames, fast knives flipping
through fire, hip-hits, eagle-shits, shock-flocks, exorcisms
(mother's cunt, the cock of Jesus), eroticisms, sperm and
sexual juice, and poetry--always poetry.   I prefer his later
poems to the earlier ones; in the latter, too much smacks of
automatic writing; in the former, there's an awesome energy,

sometimes out of focus, but mostly in. Here is a sample of
Northup at his most inventive:

> thrones, flights, far below, far happy below, far sen-
> sation below
> love love sex
> when, those, weeks, violins,
> raid, winded, you don't have to call me sir,
> you can call me emperor
> usually, it's been quiet, then it gets multiple & violent
> when those weeks, rained.

BILL MOHR has an uncanny ability to select fascinating
poetry material. He is in the mainstream of the experimen-
tal ego-folk; but Mohr perceives that poetry is more than
journalism. He experiments with verse forms, stanza pat-
terns, line breaks. Perhaps his training as an actor and
playwright has tuned his voice--there's always control--and
fascinating modulations move from poem to poem, and within
single poems. He knows how to keep an audience awake.

Here, encapsulated, a single stanza evokes Mohr's
childhood:

> My mother's hair, rinsed red, her hips
> of six births; in every room religious calendars
> and statues; an eighteen year old altar boy
> not believing women want to touch.

"Apartment # 6" deserves to become a classic. A youth dies
under mysterious circumstances--he seems to have rammed
his head through his window, slicing an artery. His mother
appears to retrieve her son's clothes:

> No suicide note, no hit-and-run driver, no drunken
> riptide,
> no excuses. A sudden death
> is a myth and I am tempted
> to believe a swirling mass
> of insects smashed his window,
> dragged him to its edge,
> his fingers squeezing cold
> blood from their buzzing
> guts, his mouth spitting broken
> antennae, until his wound was sucked into the burning
> air.

"The Bulldozer" is another powerful poem. Mohr has a
special gift for weaving his own intense interior responses
around the sinews of events. His ego never smothers a
poem; even when he tries his hand at the prose poem he
maintains an intriguing, original flow: "The tongue must
grow again. Edging from the tip between the teeth back to
the throat. When full, the tongue will dig into the top of the
throat. The first word, a blood-word. Each nostril will
widen mouth-wide. "

I have trouble with PETER LEVITT'S work--except for
three poems: "There Must've Been a Million, " "How the
Forest Grows" and "The Web. " His work in general, though,
gives me the feel of <u>writing</u> (and overwriting) rather than
work coming from some spirit-need welling up, foaming from
mouth and penis. There's not much sense of shaping and
forming. He wastes time telling us too much; and in a sense
he fails me since he doesn't think I'm bright enough to fill
in his blanks. Here's an example: He's describing a love/
sex scene:

> I've held my lover, beneath
> the arms, her
> legs drawn up,
> and together,
> my body's full
> length on hers,
> we made a butterfly,
> with softly arched spine
> an arc of pleasure.

The butterfly image strikes me as cute, unnecessary, and
wipes out any erotic intensity otherwise generated by the
poem. I don't object to an image succinctly employed; but
Levitt can't resist overdeveloping his, bludgeoning us with its
meaning, telling us that the butterfly's body and wings are
really "a human soul. " It's a question of tact, aesthetics,
maturity. And the break of the fifth line is wretched.

LELAND HICKMAN requires a large part of this Los
Angeles honey hive for himself. Here are five long sections
from his almost epic-length poem in progress, Tiresias.
The modest price of this anthology is worth it for these
poems alone. They are real discoveries--and I gather that
Hickman has not circulated his work much; finding it so well-
represented here is a rare treat.

Like his compeers (most of these ten poets are friends),
Hickman is intensely autobiographical. Tiresias is his on-
going history.   His premise seems to be that once you under-
stand your sexuality you will comprehend your spirit, and why
so much pain is necessary.   Living is to be blind--as the old
prophet Tiresias was; but it is also to see.   Yes, Walt Whit-
man, of course, knew the linkages between spirit and sexuali-
ty--and old Walt is one of Hickman's fathers.   Another is
Ginsberg, follower also of Whitman, and creator of some of
the most sexuality-freeing poems in our century.   I'd also
toss in Arthur Rimbaud and James Joyce.

Hickman's first poem is an exorcism of his father's
brutality.   Pain-words scatter across the page as father re-
turns home from his job at Lockheed Aircraft:

                                            & bitter   hisses
belt out of belt loops   lashes ass often   how I
must cringe   hate   breathe it in
secret   grow nervous ecstatic Hidden   set fire
to ladybugs   weep   hurt fat girls   weep   seek
                                             boys to
scorn me   dig in my dark my shovel snaps breast
bones   & how out loud wd I shout it   shout it out
fierce   whip me dad whip me whip me til he crumples

In 1961, aged 26, he wanders Selma Avenue, the notorious
Hollywood street for hustlers.   The poem "O Blue Temple"
seems a recollection of a sexual encounter with an incredibly
powerful, fantasy man (who is nonetheless real) who has sex
with Hickman the youth, but who won't allow him to repro-
cate:

                          .... I lie
        in subtle husht boy-thin
body beneath numinous ill gaze under lamplight, undoes
cufflinks, tie, I reach out to touch, no you can never
                               touch me, doffs
        shirt shoes socks unbuckles belt-
buckle my cock up bright o hoist me higher in my harsh
                        malign fire this
        ragged rasa for stern aloof beauty whose
tight black slacks inch low down slow over hard
                        rock silence be
ginningless ignorance sprung music-muscle gleam-tippt
                        at large & at
        lung-top crowing all
        child all child all child....

"Hay River" contains a "prayer dream." Hickman imagines
himself aged nine, in the old black family jalopy. His dad
wearing a black overcoat is dead in the front seat. His mom,
invisible, drives them to the movies "in my night / time not
on any road but high up, out / in my sky where meteors /
shine thru her...." Hickman's central image merges with
an insane, storm-crashing wilderness (the Great Slave Lake
region). The storm symbolizes Hickman's sexual anguish.
The blend of violence, human struggle, and nature is in-
credible. This is how the poem ends: Hank

> bolts forward, breaks
> thru my final
> trees I am pulled, skulled
> thru my wrencht Woven-Here down stark hard
>   sand Great Slave
> Lake's gnarled uprushing roar
> shudders daemonic its groan thru me my night sun-
>   light gleams blood-rust on my waves, gleams
> off floating tree-hulks far out adrift sinking &
>   heaved huge black in
> slow moiling cry wind squalls sand, leaves, over
>   weatherbleacht tree-
>   trunks washed up on
> shore ragged roots flare gaunt against lightning
>   I gaze I gaze
>   long into my night how lost my light goes

The final two poems are also memorable. Hickman's vision
of the poet in the wilderness (life) as an Indian caulking his
boat rings true. Hickman's wildernesses are his own forests
and orchestrated lung-fires. He is a slave, and is beaten,
screwed, pummelled--as virgin forests are in vicious storms.
Hickman is writing an incredible symphony of the tortured
self. I have attempted to give a personal and, I hope, fair,
assessment of each poet. God knows, a critic should do all
he can to encourage such stirring signs of poetry-life in Los
Angeles. I hope I have suggested that these poets do share
an ambience--as a circle of friends seen against a shimmer
of Los Angeles and Hollywood Hills. They have foraged well
for nectar. Their poetry-hive is sweet, nurturing, and pro-
ductive. The Streets Inside brings them together at a crucial
moment in their lives. Most have already published separate
books, some with large houses. Others have books forth-
coming. There will probably never be another time in their
lives when they will celebrate their poetry, and one another,
in a second anthology. And that is how it should be. An-

thologies seem to me to fulfill two primary functions these
days: First, they gather up and reflect the best-known es-
tablished poets writing in a culture, the poets universities
like to teach; and, second, they assemble works with a view
written by young writers on their way. The latter collection
interests me much more than the first. It's the difference
between petrified wood and a living jacaranda tree.

CRITICISM AS FICTION:

The Mouth of the Dragon

Note: In a conversation, Andrew Bifrost once
told me that he regards each issue of his poetry
magazine Mouth of the Dragon as an ongoing
"novel," that he structures the contents of every
issue around that pattern.   He was sure, he said,
that his readers generally weren't aware of this.
I found the idea intriguing, and so have taken the
current issue (Vol. II, 1979) and have invented a
"novel-in-progress," based on the poems therein.
The theme is the growth and nurturing of the
speaker's self-hood.   Various persons flicker
through the novel, some in actuality, others in
memory and fantasy.   The initiating moment is
Frank O'Hara's death in July 1966.   I am sat-
isfied that Bifrost does what he says he is doing.
I do caution the reader, though, against the bio-
graphical heresy: The protagonist is not Bifrost.
I hope that my experiment is a useful way for
reading other poetry magazines.

PEAKS AND TROUGHS

"Bring me my doll; I must make contact with something dead."
--Frank O'Hara

Chapter I

        I wander Manhattan looking for you.   I finally see you
across the street, naked, in your apartment.   I crave you.
If I am a pirate and cross a gangplank to you, I'd leave the
shades undrawn.   Someone might need the view, as I do.
Look, I have nothing up my sleeve.

Chapter II

We are fishing. You are knotting your leader, as a
body darts past you in the water. The eyes that meet yours
are mine. I can't maintain the tension. You hook me. I
jerk against the line, unraveling, red, in the current.

Chapter III

Returning from war, we are men. We get drunk,
near that blazing river we knew as boys. You once put my
hand over your back--I smart still, recalling. You've caught
some tropical disease, you tell me. You are fragile. I love
you. I soak my shirt in the cold water and rub your back
and buttocks. You say you know where I live, and will go
with me. You are a poet. In laughter, I forget my body.
Your orgasm shakes me loose.

Chapter IV

My happiness has turned into a painful illusion. You
say that a robin knows he is to sing, not to cluck. Why do
you upset me? Chickens of life! I wander hurt, delirious,
dreaming. Thinking of the corpse in the airplane (would he
have loved me?) and of aging Margaret (she's 31) who keeps
trying to get a man. In life, in those National Geographic
pictures, nothing is visible ... no genitals, a few well-turned
posteriors. Here, down 8th Avenue, in the sun, men are
shirtless. I am shirtless too. This is weather for going
naked. Why are we so addicted to "good taste?" If I were
a smoker I would settle for someone merely to light my
cigarette.

Chapter V

I seek escape. I try fantasies of others, of Arthur
Rimbaud during his first trip to Paris:

> You like boys, sir?
> For twenty-five I suck.
> For fifty and what I can steal
> My ass is yours for the night.
> For ten you blow me in the alley.

I'm at home in Sodom, and hope, like you, to survive in a
pile of ashes. Handsome boy, let me hold your shoulders
awhile.

Chapter VI

In San Francisco, I think of Walt Whitman.   Then, I
am in Nova Scotia, with you, in a sleeping bag, observing
the moths pollinating the white orchards.   A peach orchard.
In a lightning storm the orchard is electrified.   Each peach
is briefly incandescent.   The storm subsides.   A metaphor.

Chapter VII

Oh, these peaks and troughs!   I watch a tanned boy
on the beach.   I see a silver protractor sparkling with sea
salts.   I measure the magnificent undertow of the lad's body,
the bouncing triangle of his bathing suit, as a vortex.

Chapter VIII

Vince has found a wealthy lover on a Greek island.
I remember some of my own previous lives: In ancient
Rome I was a secret sensualist, licking around the edges of
young men or elderly boys.   In Alexandria, I romped with
steamy, naked, shaggy stevedores.   In Byzantium, I slept
with Constantine's grooms and jockeys, their hind-quarters
as full and fleshy as the steeds they served.   These I always
rode to the finish line.

Chapter IX

I hunger for a burglar to enter my unlocked door and
ravish me.   Fantasies of an athlete's juice breaking in my
mouth, "sweet at first bite," returns me to the unfinished
business of my family and my youth.   My brothers engender
children for their treasures; my lover's bowels (I have a
lover now) contain the precious pearl necklaces of my in-
heritance.   When we were children my brother, sister, and
I had small sailboats.   Theirs sailed with the stream.   I
held mine back from slipping away from the dock.   Shortly
there was a fire in my room.   My mattress smouldered;
otherwise, dear family, there was no danger.   Still later,

there was another fire, in the Organ mountains, in New Mexico. I watched them burn out of control. It was so hot. Thinking about our lives keeps our minds off the heat.

Chapter X

I recall also going down with Robert at night, into the lake. He dragged me under, surged against me, until he came. I imagined this, I confess. I simply wanted it to happen. Now Robert is celibate and studies Yoga--and I am at least ready. I go to the baths. I feel alone there, since I see that man again with his boy. He has so much more than "towels and wishes."

Chapter XI

Here are some ideas I must change, soon: 1). I used to think that straight boys were such good trade for what they bring. I was wrong. 2). Your charms have felled many, and, you think therefore that you have felled me. 3). I want to be a good boy; keep on giving me advice. 4). I tell my plumber that finding a muse and losing one are never the same. 5). Take less than you can get; there may be richer meat tomorrow. 6). I would rather eat cake than screw a salesman.

Chapter XII

I'm fed up with changing my ideas. Spring is here. Yes, I love the green horizon, the crickets, the meadowlarks. I want men. Obviously, spring is not enough. I am horny. I go to a meeting--Robert's Rules. I see _him_ over to the right, shirt open, luxurious hair, bulging cro<u>tch</u>. I want him. He smiles. I am on top of him. He's screaming with delight.

Chapter XIII

Alas! I can't see it all.

Chapter XIV

At Fire Island, Adonis of the Surf, so summer-golden,

summer-perfect. I'm recalled to myself--to feces, fur, and flesh.

Chapter XV

Personal questions: could I get a hard-on in Korea? Does the Merton College pinnacle spurt semen? How many petals does your basic star-flower contain? Why do I want a boy to hold both his arms around me?

Chapter XVI

I eat cornflakes. I am not filled/fulfilled. Perhaps if Larry were once again standing naked here ... No, I'll try to cultivate a vision, a mystical vision. I'm sick of these electric sex jolts. But Larry still drives me crazy. I write: "The eight eyes on Mt. Rushmore go insane watching us fuck."

Chapter XVII

I said "noise." I said "image." Neither is enough: barefootedness, revolver, "urn of the mind." I try to sleep. A pail of water explodes. So, you can see where I am. The revolver again. It must go off. Juice for the handkerchief. I love walking with you in the snow.

Chapter XVIII

I can say, "It was nice to be among so few ... like survivors on a hill." But would I mean it? How long can we take it? How long can we fake it? How long shall I keep on hiding you under my bed when my family comes to the door unannounced?

Chapter XIX

There are no words for love. There are no words for hate. And if, as you say, flesh is an illusion, I can still see God in the other, God in my lover. Mystical? Oriental? I'll go down on you, down your spine slowly:

your ass
won't stop me as I taste spots
the wife-to-be avoids
on religious grounds.
an apostate, I'll remove this time
the dab of yellow tissue
you missed this morning.

Chapter XX

I seem to end where I began this novel. I am twenty
again, and am making love with my little brother. I bathe
him and rim him. We promise never to go with girls.
Brother is fuel, brother is fire. My alcoholic father, my
mother a wracked woman. I drank fast, as my manhood rose
in me. Why? Because he drank? I would be better than
he was.... These lips I touch are my father's! What passes
between them passes between his! Now, reader, you may
think you know something about me.

DISCOGRAPHY AND OTHER MATTERS:

John Giorno's Sound-System Poetry Records*

A fascinating spin-off of public poetry readings is the recording of poets on tape, video cassettes, and records. Most tapes and records I've so far heard are big bores-- either ego trips for the poets involved or a drizzling effort to enrich our culture-archives with the voices of deceased writers. The earliest of all, I guess, was a scratchy brief recording of Alfred Lord Tennyson reading "Come into the garden, Maud." Now, that one is valuable: Hearing it, even in its gravelly state, one can sense well how his magnificent voice managed to keep Queen Victoria awake during the reading of all 133 parts of In Memoriam. So, I have contradicted myself--there is that occasionally stunning record--Ralph Bellamy reading The Rubaiyat of Omar Kayyam, Dylan Thomas reading anything. For the most part though, unless you are interested in having your ears tickled by voice-hairs from the past, ignore the recordings, and let your own brain hear the poems as you read them on the page.

The Giorno Sound-System recordings are different. I did listen through them, all five albums, all twenty sides. I have even forgone eating lunch and answering the telephone. This is not to say that I am never vexed, insulted, or irritated. Many cuts are flaky. Poetry becomes an event rather than something embalmed for the school Parps and Marms. The Giorno pieces are almost always performances--and this is what good poetry readings should be.

As most poetry readings go in this country, they are bastard art forms. You may hit a true performance, and you may hit some vapid, stumbling, mumbling, ministerial intoning. You may experience something unforgettable; you

*Reprinted by permission from The Poetry Reading: A Contemporary Compendium on Language & Performance, edited by Stephen Vincent and Ellen Zweig. San Francisco: Momo's Press, 1981, pp. 260-262.

may find yourself in such misery: Any boils on your rear swell
enormously and burst out of boredom and vexation. Have you
ever had the guts, dear reader, to walk out of a poetry read-
ing? Most poets are such terrible cowards.

Those of us who give public readings--I've probably
given three hundred or so in the past 12 years, do so out of
many motives. We may hope to get our books heard. If we
publish with small presses, distribution generally stinks, and
the reading is a way of distributing ourselves. Some of us
like the Celebrity Trip--and no matter how minor the stir
we have made in the poetry world there is always apt to be
some lovely, innocent sweet young thing in the audience who
will treat us as if we were W. S. Merwin, Anne Waldman, or
Galway Kinnell. There's an Instant Fame, then--or at least
the illusion of it. Some of us hope eventually to find our-
selves on records and video tapes. So we keep on reading,
accepting any and all invitations to stand up there and amaze
the world.

Giorno records do work well, and include an amazing
range of poets (I'll give a sampling shortly). Most of them
cluster about St Mark's Church, and the reading program
there. A second center is the Naropa Institute in Colorado,
the poetry center nestled-over by Ginsberg and Waldman.
Occasionally, someone not of these hubs will wander through
the wax--Merwin, Charles Olson, Frank O'Hara, Gary Snyder.
There is also a good spread of sound and language poets.
John Giorno himself is generously represented in performances
of a tripartite Giorno voice, thanks to tape-recordings. There
are folk from the former Warhol crowd who funk-up--Jackie
Curtis, Taylor Mead. Some punk stuff appears--Patti Smith.
Much Burroughs ... one album of four sides is a recording
of his famous Nova Convention. The engineering on all these
albums is impeccable, and the prices, thanks to assistance
from the National Endowment and the New York State Arts
Board, are cheap, less than you would expect to pay for an
album by a rock star.

Here are a few of the high points--and the list is much
abbreviated. Peter Orlovsky yodels the joys of his compost
pile and rhubarb patch. Jim Carroll hustles a homosexual
in a public john, and is turned on. Trungpa Rinpoche in-
tones "teeth" and breathes heavily. Giorno performs a
Suicide Sutra, and almost takes you in; he also subdues
demons in America, and wipes his wrists in blood, shit,
brains and pus. Spicer reads from Billy the Kid and The

Holy Grail. Ginsberg, accompanied by Bob Dylan and other musicians, sings a wonderful ballad to New York City newsboy Jimmy Berman; later he recites "Please Master," allowing sado-masochism to exude all over your ears. Michael McClure reads a bit of beast language. Frank O'Hara eats a pair of "Lunch Poems," endures Marilyn's death, and helps the Film Industry in its time of crisis. Tom Clark licks not too celestial assholes with hash on his lips. Paul Blackburn does "The Once-Over" woman. Joe Brainard tells us that he shoots big loads. Ron Padgett asks for a lot of pity --even his pen weeps black ink; he feels "totally fucked." Waldman is a Fast-Speaking woman, Diane di Prima is Loba, Diane Wakoski devastates a man and then exorcises his presence in her life. Corso rips through marriage and obscene honeymoons. Creeley, Olson, Robert Lowell, Cage, Wieners and Levertov appear among the daddies and mommies of poetry. More delicious than almost any other reader is Helen Adam reciting her grisly apartment-on-Twin-Peaks poem, and her junkie ballad. Charles Bukowski is on cloud nine wearing two horse-collars and lamenting the closing of topless bars. Sylvia Plath licks daddy all over and then eats him. William Burroughs tells us he never wanted to be president. Jackie Curtis wishes herself/himself a Merry Xmas, evokes his/her lucky star, and takes off after Betty Hutton. Jerome Rothenberg is a Navajo chanting a horse-song. Kyger is full of French ideals, a little bruised, but nicely mellow. Bill Knott murders poetry in a plate of beans. Denby examines boys' shoulders, wrinkled crotches, smokeless moments in Manhattan, and the cranky woman inside him. Robert Duncan articulates "the progress of the syllables." Gary Snyder sings his wild mushroom song, celebrates dharma as avocado, finds aluminum foil inside a ground-squirrel, eulogizes the Queen of Crete and other bare-breasted, bare-footed folk who wouldn't be served in today's restaurants. Elmslie sings "Woolworth." Sanders tells us what Lesbian dwarfs are like and what cocaine suppositories do. And on and on, for about twelve hours of listening.

This quick run-through, almost a riff in itself, is meant to celebrate these recordings. Young poets in writing programs around America should listen to them. When they put themselves together afterwards they should be better poets than they were before.

PUNK AND PURISM: SOME RECENT BAY AREA POETRY:

Paul Vangelisti's 2 X 2, Jerry Ratch's
Chaucer Marginalia and Osiris, Louis
Patler's An American Ensemble, Larry
Fagin's Stabs, Opal Nations' The Tragic
Hug of a Small French Wrestler, Dan
Dolan's The Last Days of the American
Dream, and Bruce Hutchinson's Benthos
(Lab Partners). *

Every so often a veritable snow of books arrives for
review. Sometimes these works are of a piece, sometimes
not. The most recent batch have a couple of obvious con-
nections: They are either written by or published by folk in
the Bay Area, and they reflect in at least two ways language,
or word, or grammar poetry. Vangelisti and Ratch are
purists of grammar and word; they will appear esoteric to
some readers--there's a kind of cerebral intention akin to
that of some French and Italian structuralists and minimalists.
Patler, Fagin, Nations, Dolan, and Hutchinson spin words
and drawings around in a blatant Punk manner. These guys
are young, hip, and aggressive and offensive with vary-
ing degrees of success. Their words and images have multi-
colored coiffures, the hairs (syllables) standing straight out
from their heads (poems): jolts of electricity. If you are
into eye-shadow and lurid flesh-tones, you'll dig some of this
poetry. Once the patina of merde is scraped away, these
men, like Ratch and Vangelisti, are obsessed with language:
personality rather than profound personal feelings. Word-
riffs rather than neat conventional poem-structures-lines.
One-shot effects, single takes, rather than poems you want
to take home and re-read. I am tempted to use New Wave
as a term describing what these poets are up to; but there
are too many connections with old-fashioned dadaist, collage,

*Reprinted by permission from San Francisco Review of
Books (Dec. -Jan. 1979-80), pp. 25-27, 36.

surrealist, minimalist, cut-up, and concrete poets. No matter how effective some of these books are, though, they don't finally appear sufficiently new, as a group, to merit their own label. They may represent a couple of fashionable trends; and what seem like Bay Area events are like a lot that is happening in New York City and elsewhere. They may be creating work that gives the illusion of being new but is in actuality an almost instantaneous dead-end. I hope my examination of these books will stimulate readers to make up their own minds, after, of course, getting hold of the books and reading them through.

I.

Invisible City, with its emphasis on Italian avant-garde poetry, fosters language poetry. The current triple issue is a feast of such work. And the co-editor Paul Vangelisti writes poems based on various semantic devices--transitional words and phrases, for example, become poems. If we seek comfortable sequential readings of his work we are taken in. His poems on the surface sound the way good poems should. He likes to sound conventional, reflective, narrative, old-fashioned even, as a means of intensifying the language game. When we read one of Vangelisti's works, say 2 X 2, we soon find ourselves engaged by his rational tone and seemingly clear observations and reminiscences. In the epilogue to 2 X 2 he reveals his preoccupation with grammar and language. The big armored fish of traditional poetry, once the poet wakes up to see what the creature is really like, requires little water for swimming, and it needs no face. Poetry is like that--the poet invents his own grammar. The play of correct tenses and numbers become his preoccupation:

> So that it won't
> become just a
> matter of crossing
> out lines trying
> to keep in mind
> what tense or
> number trying to
> recall what is
> being said when
> what is not has
> become a preoccu-
> pation. Yes, lines and
> the armored fish

```
that waking up
one realizes is so
big it needs no
face and little water
to swim in.
```

He invents concrete images--objects--based on photo-
graphs of himself as a child and of his family. In one xerox
copy of a snapshot of himself as a boy wearing a sailor's
suit (it's a frontal portrait), Vangelisti cuts out the entire
face and throat and covers the area with a detail from a map
of the region in Italy where his ancestors came from. The
snapshot now becomes something else, an image of sorts,
but an oddly literal one in which the image of the boy "speaks"
the map, and reflects the entire map in his face. The re-
sult is an anti-poem, which is to the language/grammar poet
a poem.

Vangelisti tells me that he enjoys trapping us within
his words and in his syntactic play. Discourse, he says, is
merely an illusion. The verbal spin-off is the primary rea-
son for the poem's existence. The subject matter (as it is
in 2 X 2) may be the deterioration of a marriage; but that
subject matter is ancillary to facts of tone and grammar.
The ideal Vangelisti seems to be after is what Julien Blaine
calls Ecriture (Writing). Blaine is a leading French expo-
nent of language poetry, and a poet in his own right. The
current Invisible City features Blaine's theories and a sam-
pling of his writings. Writing, then, rather than Literature.

Jerry Ratch, who lives in Berkeley, has since the ap-
pearance of his first books Puppet X and Clown Birth moved
increasingly towards a poetry of pure language. Here is a
portion of a poem from Osiris (1977):

```
what does he feed on
only what he sees
what does he feed on
only what he sees

what does he live on
what he eats
what does he live on
what he eats

who are his attendants
tomb bats
that fly in the night
```

      o who has
gouged out his eye

      and who has made him
not to speak

      that he might diminish
decrease
& gradually lose power

Like all of the poems in Osiris this one has a central narra-
tive; a traditional reading is possible. But something else
occurs: In the numb effect of the recitative (question and
answer) Ratch conveys grammar. It's as if he's providing
us with a beginner's primer for acquainting us with a foreign
tongue. I have heard Ratch read several times: He reads
usually in a very quiet voice, pausing significantly after each
line so that each of his lines has the force of a separate
phrase-poem, a piece of skeletal verse, grammar, idea,
spinning slowly in our minds. The ordinary rush of a poem,
with enjambments and quick turns of phrase and meaning,
does not seem to matter much in his poems. The repetition
too, a form of serial poetry, provides an odd effect of gram-
mar revealing itself before us. Ratch numbs us, so that a
coldness ensues. Passion is kept at a distance, except in
so far as his play of language allows it in. The gouged-out-
eyes and the tomb bats come as a surprise, suiting a theme
of lost power, perhaps terrifying us--but only after the gram-
mar of the poem has unmistakably asserted itself.

    In his newest book Chaucer Marginalia, a superbly
designed and manufactured book, Ratch moves all the way
over into a pure language poetry. The entire work depends
on an original interplay of words. He takes passages from
Chaucer, drops all words from the lines except a few that
interest him. These he disposes of as visual constructs on
a page; then, by way of marginalia, provides a list of his
own inventions, verbal associations stimulated by the words
from Chaucer. Here is an example (most of the poems are
longer). I shall try to convey a sense of Ratch's page by
spacing Chaucer's words as Ratch does. He determines
spacing by leaving the word where it was positioned in the
original (now absent) line. In a sense, therefore, Chaucer's
entire lines are still intact--by implication. Lines that don't
exist, do exist. A nice matter of epistemology, folks!
Ratch's own poem then becomes a gloss on the Middle Eng-
lish poem. Some of the modern words associate clearly with

corresponding Chaucerian words; others do not. By relegating his poem to the margin, Ratch makes a statement on behalf of anti-poetry, or a-poetry (as in amoral); his poem is subservient to the stimulus for the poem. Here is the piece:

rennen			runs
kinde,			the natural
		stevene	voice
briddes			birds
fil	cas		befall chance

rethor			rhetoricians
saufly			safely
also			dwell
		woned	as
		hegges brast	hedges burst

Obviously it is possible to find meaning in this bit of marginalia, in the contrast between the hap-hazardness of natural order (birds and hedges) and the self-serving rhetoricians (they would not admire language poetry, one feels) who keep themselves "safe" from natural energy.

When Ratch's poems work they are tied to Chaucer's words, and don't seem happenstance. Chaucer thus controls Ratch's diction and reins him in. At one point (and I shall simply list Chaucer's words without giving the pattern they form as they arrange themselves in a shape on the page), envined becomes wine stocks in the margin. I find this doesn't work so well. Wine stocks seems a clumsy and easily gotten equivalent for "envined." Here is the entire piece:

"plein/hoomly/dayseye/delit/
plein/envined/plenteous/snewed. "

The Marginalia: "one/entirely/unpretentious/daisy/of/sensual delight won't/fill/wine stocks/with/plenteous/snow. " Here, on the other hand, is a set of words that work superbly around the themes of pleasure, lechery, and death:

"liking/ouche/likerous/for/al-
gates/leve/cors/upright/bithinke. "

The Marginalia: "pleasure:/the/lecherous/trinket//that/con-stantly//dear//imagines/the/corpse supine. " It is possible to fault Ratch for not always being as inventive as he might be. But what he has tried is impressive. I see his work as

double-edged--a work invented entirely out of the word and
disjointed connections of words, fashioning poems, skinny to
be sure, but poems, nevertheless, which make comments on
nature, life, death, and love--and on language.   If we take
the time to read his poems carefully, we enjoy a special
verbal experience.   There's a winsome modesty in his at-
tempt; by generating poems from a classic poet he does not
imply that he is the venerated writer's equal.   The fact of
"marginalia" keeps the distinction clear.

II.

Two books, handset and beautifully designed by Ala-
stair Johnston, in his Poltroon Modern Poets series, are
attempts, I think, at Punk, Language Poetry.   The less
daring is Louis Patler's An American Ensemble.   "The Wink"
seems to present the semantic problem:

> The ghosts
> tell jokes
>
> on the masts
> of faluccas
> at high tide
> in high seas
>
> which cannot lift
> the language
> one iota
> up or down.

How then, do we move language up or down--if that is the
problem?   Patler tries via the humdrum object: this is
from the title poem:

> Red napkin   cloth napkin

Patler likes automatic writing, which isn't all that new, or
that interesting.   "The Prism," despite its linguistic halts
between stanzas and sections strikes me as a series of self-
indulgent associations.   Here is a sample moment: "Among
the herds/of dirt roads//her fist is in/her mouth//completely/
wet//making circus noises//among others.//Have a look see./
Have another."   The Dick-and-Jane simplicity (again, that old
grammar-examples manner) doesn't work--and I have trouble
with the nymphette with a mouth big enough to jam her whole

fist inside. Patler also likes jokes. I suppose, to be gen-
erous, you can say that he implies a world-view, a Punky,
latter-day existentialism, where jokes tossed into the inane
provide a kind of sanity, an antithesis to self-pity. Alas,
Patler seldom hits home with more than a single take; viz.,
"Be generous/with the short guys://they're the last/to know/
it's raining!" Here he seems caught between a purely visual,
denotative image (rather nice) and a coy simile trapped in its
own syntax (who is cooking the pens and pencils?):

> So many pens and pencils
> in the ceramic cup
>
> like mom's way
> of cooking spaghetti.

These, I think, are fair examples of Patler's writing. I
wish he knew how to be more outrageous, Punkier, more
purely verbal, more obnoxious than he is. An American
Ensemble seems a work caught between modes.

Larry Fagin's Stabs is more successful because Fagin
knows exactly what he is up to. Reading him is a bit like
reading Ratch--without the Chaucer, and with more humor.
Again, the book is superbly made--handset, quality paper,
well-designed. I gather that these are almost anti-poems or
a-poems (again, in the sense of amoral or apolitical). The
book is made up of one-liners, with half a dozen spaces be-
tween the lines. As a result, one reads each line and lin-
gers over it before proceeding to the next line. Sometimes
there are connections between lines. Most of the time though
I have the feeling I am reading an intelligent man's scrap-
book of thoughts culled from journals and notebooks, and
printed for my delectation. Some of the lines (are they
"poems"?) are freshly seen moments of the world we all
know: viz., "The projector's reels are the mouse's ears."
I wish I had said that. Or, "Sound is a kind of pain to which
all pain replies." Occasionally, Fagin spawns an atrocious
pun: "get your grandma goblin shot." If there is a mode
unifying all of these--it is that of the advertising slogan, the
imperative that pushes us out to buy or to do something.
The poem as standup comic: Fagin impels us towards lan-
guage, and destroys our notions of the traditional poem.
Some of the best of these bits (and as poems they do over-
lap) have a Magrittesque quality: In "Ladders hook together"
one has the image of one ladder hooked to another, that one
hooked to another, etc., and on into infinity. A nice visual

treat--I almost called it "surrealist." But I don't think sur-
realism interests Fagin much.   His primary force is visual
and comic.   He tries to give us objects from his world in and
of themselves.   What we do with them from there on is our
responsibility.   These object poems are his purest language
poems.   Here are a few taken at random: "beer bottles in
branches," "inertia nutcracker," "boys wrestling under flash-
ing orange light." Fagin sustains his inventiveness well
throughout these 28 slim pages.   And that is no mean feat:
The trouble with poets as stand-up comics is that unless their
material is consistently good they aren't invited back for an-
other gig.   I'll look forward to Fagin's next.

III.

Some of this poetry appears in books as important for
their graphics as for their texts.   Three of these have just
appeared under the imprint of The Fault Press, another
California publisher.   The first, by Opal Nations, is The
Tragic Hug of a Small French Wrestler.   The indefatigable
and outrageous Nations assembles a series of prose pieces
(parody-stories mostly) and a number of Opalesque drawings.
I don't feel that the prose works very well.   Nations too often
settles for the cute rather than the madness-inducing, and
he's too enamored of a boring English style (Saki stories,
whodunits, etc.) to avoid being boring himself.   The old
principle for stand-up comics again applies here--if your
material isn't consistently good you won't get more gigs, un-
less you hire your own hall or publish your own books.   Na-
tions' drawings, though, are another matter.   There's a
clever jock-strap series: barbed wire and strap, strap with
soap and sponge holder, strap with Kotex band and cute rib-
bon.   In another scene, two men hang by chin straps from
ceiling hooks--"Naked Subway Commuters with Fractured
Jaws."   There's a rather ruthless series of a nude woman
whose breasts slip gradually lower, until they drop from her
body, leaving her in tears.   One of the best is of a corset
trampoline.

I'm interested in these drawings as poems.   If as a
writer you set out to deny traditional metaphor, and seek to
capture the isness of your world, why not move from writing
poems over to drawing pictures?   You'll then have annihilated
the verbal, creating in its place a perfect anti-poem.   Most
of the time, though, Nations requires titles (verbals) to guide
us along through his pictures.   When Nations' irreverent

forays work without words, the viewer must create his own
language whilst (to use one of Nations' words) being zapped
by the drawing. Technically, Nations' graphics are pretty
nonprofessional--which is, I would guess, part of the act's
irreverence.

A less funky work is Don Dolan's The Last Days of
the American Dream, a sequence of 100 excellently con-
ceived and executed full-page doomsday drawings with a line
of text (as a poem) beneath each drawing. The texts, if as-
sembled and presented by themselves with plenty of space
around them, would have more impact than Lary Fagin's
Stabs. For Dolan's view of the world is intensely grim:
earth holocaust; boredom ("Working at a gas station. What
a life. What a death. "); alienation ("There was something
lacking, though. We washed and dried our minds away. ");
brutality ("Men beat their wives because their bosses yelled
at them"). At times, the graphics seem indebted to Escher's
drawings, at other times to Edward Gorey's. Usually, how-
ever, Dolan's works exude their own powerful ghastliness.
I have called the captions to his pictures poems. And, if they
are seen as yet another slant on what I call anti-poems, or
a-poems, the label works. We move, once again, towards
no language at all--in a literary sense. Dolan's minimal,
comicbookeese becomes Ecriture, writing, and not literature.
Adopt the simplified dialogue, create a language for mongo-
loids, rubes, and retardees. Obviously, to sound stupid and
lobotomized is a way of reducing your responses to an alien,
existentialist, purposeless existence. You needn't go to an
art school or university to write the necessary language. With
skill, Dolan uses this mini-language for enormous themes--
war and the destruction of capitalist society: "Ambushes
were everywhere. We gradually took control of the country-
side. " Like the good comic-book artist/writer, Dolan leaves
out what would take a novel to cover. His humor and origi-
nality make the device his own, viz. , "Killing angels became
an infantry exercise. " "Work hard! Good old American
know-how. Build a better mouse trap. Build a better terror
weapon. " Finally, The Last Days of the American Dream
seeks to mirror the destruction of capitalism. The "fat cats"
--their police have failed to protect them and are killing one
another--desperate, retrieve their old World War II weapons.
The rebels know they have won. Ecriture with balls. Anti-
poetry with an intense political design.

More overtly poetic is a stunning book of text and
drawings by Bruce Hutchinson: Benthos: Lab Partner[s]

Part 2, also published by The Fault.   Hutchinson has been
drawing his disturbing, scatological, penis-o-logical works
for several years now--they turn up in the little magazines.
And he has published chapbook collections of them.   He is
one of the wildest of small press artists working today.   He
worked in the Bay Area for a time, but has now moved to
New York where he pursues an intense life.   All of his books,
I believe, have been published on the West Coast--and they
are outrageous delights, if you are able to find them.

        Benthos owes much to far-out fantasy fiction and to
puns.   (I see the pun-poem as another form of anti-poem).
Benthos, Hutchinson's invented land, surrounded by a cyto-
plastic sea, has a population of six.   The sixth Benthosian
is IL (read both Illinois and ill).   Il's journal provides the
poetry for Benthos.   The other inhabitants of "the Genetic
Pool Sharks and Plasma Donors" are N. DAK, who lives on
Snare Dream; CA is on Spinal Tap; TX is on Embryo (drip-
drip) Eavesdropper.   UT dwells on Jungle Logarithms, and
NEB is on Beatniked Memory Blocks.

        Obviously, these samples of Ugh-language are take-
offs on States--a nice irony in itself.   IL writes of his birth:
"I was scooped from the BROTH, I emerged from my BIRTH
a CAUL BOY.   My head bubbled underneath a HAIR NET.   I
was cut apart.   TX handed me 2 things.   The Stake from my
heart and A Diary.   I was to record the life of Benthos.
This way there would be proof we didn't exist. "

        I can't do justice to Hutchinson's drawings: dope-
crazed (krazed) eyeballs, maggots and worms, drops of blood,
bandages around heads and skeletons, loathsome tendrils and
octopus tentacles, threatening amoebic forms, cauls, after-
births, fish for eyeballs, embryos, sharks, skates, hairy
insect legs, etc.   To turn the next page involves some psychic
risk.

        Bucolic Benthos is threatened by Dodoists (are they
artists? extinct birds? both?).   IL bleeds and sings pre-
paring to fight them.   He writes this poem on the threat:

                Why do the DODOISTS come?
                Do they sleepwalk out of extinction?
                The crumbs stick to their fingers.
                Why do the DODOISTS come?
                Do they tiptoe out of a S. O. S. ?
                The submarine sticks to their igloos.

> The submarine sticks to their igloos.
> Why do the DODOISTS COME?

Obviously, Hutchinson here bows to the formal poem--see the
refrain and the repetitions. But the result is what I call
writing rather than literature. The craziness, the irra-
tionalities disturb our sense of the well-made, nicely crafted
poem. Hutchinson's language is immersed in loathsome blobs
of pun-threat, punk-threat.

IL continues, telling us that the other folk don't know
the Dodoists are on the way, because they are so "Busy
nailing OVARIES to their rhythms, preparing for my SUDDEN
disappearance." IL disappears; it's his turn to clean the
bottom of the CYTOPLASTIC SEA. He will be gone for eleven
days:

> **11** days between
> the **2**
> IMP
> PLANTS.
> Diabetic Playmates
> M n'EMANATE from
> toot shoots of these
> INSULAR herbs.
> I emanate aching
> cavities.

He returns, does a swift merging act with an invading Do-
doist, finds that absorbing one isn't too bad after all. He
next meets a Grrr, a strange musician girl who played for
him "all afternoon PLUNKING and PLUCKING ticklish (p)omens
from her SIGH-LO-PHONES." She calls herself "Scuffed
Shoe Horn of the Foot Hills." Two sets of curtains hang
from her head, two "unsettling certainties shedding threads
into the constellations." IL wants to marry her: "She
sighed, her eyes swimming upstream." Then "she plucked
the last notes, tucked them into" his bandages, "tugged on a
loose thread and...." IL seems to forget her without much
trouble, diverted now by finding a "PREHYSTERICAL BURY-
GO-ROUND" where he seeks his ancestors. He finds two
frozen specimens, which he hopes are his "foster fossils":
"A MOSS Heart beating me to the MosKular core-puscle of
my blood-line." He desires that they adopt him for RE-
TURNITY. In one of the fossils, he finds the shape of an
ancient priest. He pulls off some bandages. "His spirit
seeps through. Smell of low tide." As usual, IL seems not
to have gotten very far.

The most outrageous of IL's poems is a celebration of
the hut he lives in.   His lines sound like parodies of the long
line used by James Dickey, W. S. Merwin, Ginsberg and
others:

<pre>
              8:13: I have returned to my hut to
                    hoot hoot hoot hoot hoot huff
                    and hum hum.
              I am back in my room making noise
                    and a noose-ance of myself.   I
                    am making wallpaper
              from plankton and knotted rope.
                    Flooding prevents me from
                    trimming the shadows
              on the door.   NAPS stored beneath
                    the floor have mildewed.   And
                    the roof--the ROOF!
              The roof, with its soft leather wings,
                    has chewed a path thru the
                    thunder storms.   It
                       will migrate
              soon.   I will have to restructure the
                    antennae to get good reception
                    on my
                          BLACK-AND-WHITE
              WOMB-VIEWER.   (I like the
                    cartoons.)
              Oh I love my little hut and I love my
                    tiny LAWN, AND the Lawn
                    Ornaments--the
              LAWN ORNAMENTS! I found
                    them giving
                    off sparks in a STAR PIT,
                       covered in TEE PEES of
                       dust and dandruff.
                    I carried them home on
                             wobbly tippy-
                             TOES! And
                             before I go
                             away I will
                             STUFF them
                             with
                             SHINY
                             ERASERS
              OH I LOVE MY LITTLE HUT my
                    little hut
                          MY LITTLE HUT
</pre>

I should note that Hutchinson's verbal texts are calligraphic, not printed or typed.

Hutchinson incorporates several characteristics of New Wave or Anti-Poetry, as I have been describing it. He reduces speech and language to insane babble, baby-talk, comic-book speech. (IL loves watching cartoons on TV, he says.) He likes bad rhymes (hut-hoot) and puns (noose-ance, STAR-PITT, A Moss Heart). He is indifferent to normal poetic forms; his line races along dictated by its own non-sense and flashes of sense. His world is intensely deranged--at least in normal, nonschizophrenic terms. Out of this derangement he fashions a weird order, which is his alone. Finally, his visuals work as anti-poems, as they exchange their energies with verbal texts. His spirit is like that one finds in Punk explosions and outrageousness; and it teems with scary private allusions.

I remain puzzled by much of this work. I am irritated, bored, amused, outraged, bemused--a whole melange of responses. The fact that I am stirred means that these works are effective. But I can't say though that my suspicions of minimalist and punk poetry are lessened. Too much of this writing is one-shot--it doesn't bear repeating, as few ethnic jokes bear repeating. We are titillated. Flashes without much smoke. Vangelisti and Ratch do lead me, though, to consider the problem of poetry's traditional limits. They seem to aim for a purity of statement and form concealing any overt echoes of their own personal undergoings and preoccupations. Poetry becomes perhaps a chess game, a pure mental gymnastic--in itself no mean feat.

A note finally about the energy, the zaniness, and the willingness to take risks characterizing these poets: In a period of thoroughly bland poetry issuing from the Iowa school, the few New York trade houses still publishing poetry, APR, and the university quarterlies, these books are indeed welcome. And it is great to see such energies on the West Coast. I wish these poets well.

PART FIVE

"End the beating with an in-
creasing speed and gradually
add, while continuing to beat
at high speed, 3/4 of the sugar
called for in the recipe. "
--Irma S. Rombauer, Joy of
    Cooking.

m.peters

THE MACDONALD-EDDY NATURE POETRY SNYDROME:

Judith McCombs' Against Nature: Wilderness Poems*

As a rule, male poets have seen far more sermons in stones, intimations of immortality in tors, tarns, and teepees, more arousals of passion induced by Alpine storms and exploding volcanoes than women poets have.   That men have had this edge on affinities with Nature puzzles me.

None of the great 19th-century Nature poets were women.   Men alone removed Nature's clothing (was not Nature "the living garment of God?" as Thomas Carlyle said it was)--and the removals were not necessarily erotic.   When Wordsworth in his skiff was frightened by the louring presence of Mt. Skiddaw he was responding to incredible forces he imagined beyond himself, forces he read as a Universal Consciousness innately responsible to and caring for him, even when its moods were hostile.   Following Wordsworth and Carlyle, Emerson and Thoreau set the pattern for generations of Yankee men to find their Transcendental buckwheat in the wilds.   Despite her personal noisiness, the American female transcendentalist Margaret Fuller was pretty much left out of it, albeit she did own one of the more cantankerous heifers at Brook Farm.   Transcendentalism has been a man's province.

Nature's nymphs and seraphs, in their diaphanous gowns and slippery garter belts, continue to lure male poets to twitch their last garments off; and poets in our time have continued to yank, snap, pull, and tear, revealing hints of warm nature-flesh: viz., Gary Snyder's peregrinations up, into, over and through the Rockies, feasting (metaphorically) on centipedes, lizards and manzanita berries; Howard McCord's ultimately romantic returns to the navel of the universe, that primitive omphalos located somewhere in Iceland;

*Reprinted by permission from Western Humanities Review (Summer 1981), pp. 153-157.

my own poems inspired by northern Wisconsin forest and lake
settings, by arbutus patches in snow, scenes of deer drinking
at quiet lakes; William Stafford's and Wendell Berry's arrange-
ments of domesticated landscape scenes.

What I'm probing is what strikes me as an arrogance
in these poets (and others who take their cue from Nature);
they assume that Nature cares! A useful term for the phe-
nomenon, perhaps, is what I call the MacDonald-Eddy Nature-
Poetry-Syndrome. It's an old but not very well understood
disease. Let me explain. There's an unforgettable scene
in the movie "Rose Marie" in which handsome Canadian
Mountie Nelson Eddy seats himself on a Rocky Mountain peak
at night beneath a scintillating full moon. He begins to sing.
Across a sizeable valley rift sits Jeanette MacDonald com-
fortably positioned on another mountain peak. She's wearing
one of those marvellous hats and some gauzy frock. They
sing to one another, and like gypsy moths sending sex signals
in a similar, though silent-to-human-ears fashion, they bathe
the Rockies with delicious chocolate-covered sound. Nature
herself is immersed in human love trills, lilts and vocables.
The bears forego rending stumps for ants and honey, deer
perk up their ears and interrupt the flow of fecal droppings,
martens allow the freshly caught partridge to flop free....
The singers inspire Nature; Nature inspires the singers.

There's something sentimental here, of course; and
the treacle is male induced. (Wasn't Jeanette an Indian
maid?) The question persists--why does the male artist
rather than the female call these mountain tunes? Women are
generally back at the main camp, brewing up the coffee in
tin cans, whipping up biscuits, or taking saunas with one an-
other and their kids. Here are some possible explanations:
Since Nature is female (Mother Nature) women might feel re-
pelled by getting it on with her. Lesbianism? Also, if Na-
ture is female, a woman might feel that she already possess-
es whatever estrogens it is that attract men to Nature. Also,
traditionally American males have had a rough time displaying
emotions; women have not. Women are supposed to be sen-
sitive, drizzly, and emotive, even if they have to force these
feelings as a display for their males. Nature for these re-
pressed men serves as a kind of female safety-valve; emotions
they fear to display for living persons in their everyday lives
here receive a sanitized sanction. Exhausted burly linemen
and tough oil-pipe conduit builders and fire fighters, as they
guzzle down their Coors, look up at the wilderness and are
stunned. The mountain-side trembles, momentarily chilling
these hunky males. Nature as safety-valve.

Which brings me to Judith McCombs' poems.   How
refreshing they are!   At last, an American poet has put the
thumb-screws to Nature, and a woman has done it.   No filmy-
gowned, floppy-hatted Jeanette is she.   McCombs has earned
her right to be "against Nature. "   These poems should be re-
quired reading in all writing programs throughout the country,
and should be framed and hung at all Sierra Club shelters
and recited in the main lodges of the U.S. Forest Service as
parties of back-packers take off for the wilds.   McCombs
herself is an indefatigable woods-person; she's gone on sur-
vival outings in winter.   She teaches wilderness classes at
the Detroit College of Art and Design.   "Against, " in her
sense, has at least two meanings: the one I've already im-
plied, that she opposes Romantic notions of Nature; another
is that she reveals herself as a minutely observant peregrina-
tor of the wilds and projects herself "against" the immense
backdrops of trees and mountains.   This second view is the
dominant one.   Let me illustrate.

Here she nags a male friend who is hiking with her
and who finds glaciers "messy. "   In the face of massive
glacial shifts, human warmth is slight and fleeting:

> Why can't you take Nature as offered?
> Shut up & be grateful, you can't afford
> your private dynamite, so don't interrupt
>
> Out on the ice it's our one chance to listen
> to whatever the glacier is muttering, to see
> how this great swollen hunk & its Neanderthal drains
> are ploughing the bedrock   Here we can notice
> how accidentally the glacier creates
> soil & water, valley & life
>
> Look, we are mammals, tramping the surface
> The warmth we have
> is small & not lasting

She is satiric about the equipment hikers think they need, so
that they'll survive in the wilderness--a mark of their vul-
nerability and their exclusion, finally, from the Nature they
idealize:

> What are you proving, importing yourself
> & your gear to the wilds?   Your daily calories
> exceed the environment   What you can gather
> is sour, or breaks, & besides you are queasy

about killing
             You stop on a ridge & the safe water gurgles
out of your plastic container into your mouth
In your left breast pocket the keys to the car
are jingling
             You can always go back
You can always go back

Earlier in the same poem, McCombs exposes the common
Romantic fallacy that we can talk to stones and babble along
with brooks. Here, I think, she neatly dumps several manure-
cart loads of American poems in which poets carry on in this
naive way:

        The hawks don't want you out here, they're too
               ignorant
        to beg for your garbage   The bears & the clever
        mammals avoid you   The trees are just trees,
        they all look alike   The stones have no numbers
        no shapes you remember (but they seem to multiply)
        Did you come all this way to gibber with stones?

        The main trope for most nature poetry, I'd suppose,
is the Garden of Eden.   If Adam and Eve were up to it
then, and if God were giving Pulitzers for poetry, chances
are that Adam's efforts would resemble Wordsworth's or
Snyder's; Eve, if she wrote at all, would treat the small
disasters of rose petals, flies trapped in spider-webs, the
deaths of raspberries.   Here is McCombs on the matter of
Paradise:

        Nature is not like you & me, dear,
        whatever its virtues it doesn't have hands
        & it isn't our garden   If the inhabitants
        squeak to each other, if the stones understand
        what hooks them to earth, that does us no good
        The clever things hide when they hear us, & the
               rest
        move so godawful slow, we can't notice, or follow
        A strange kind of time is elapsing, outside
        of our watches   We can't make the mountains
               conform
        to the lines on our maps   They slide in the night
        & when we're not looking   Between boulder &
               boulder,
        forests & scree, summit & summit,
        There aren't any numbers   There is only the earth
        . . . .

There's a perfect night view of the mountains
      behind us,
a real panorama, just like the brochures,
but it's bigger & colder & harder than us
Let's talk about something more human: my hands
in your pockets, you're ticklish, & who left the
      grease
in the stewpot again, & why is the bedrock
on my side of the tent   My watch says it's 8
& here comes the moon with her merciless light
so where is the flash

No matter how far in we go, how long
we are what we are

                        unnatural, human

Her realism is refreshing.   On one of her backpacking trips,
she tries to retrieve an old table she finds, for her camp.
When she rights it, it collapses into the lake.   Conclusion?

                                    Aristotle was right
(& my shins are learning):   a thing is its usage:
& a table that is through with being a table
is not a table at all

How refreshing!   A female Thoreau!

     Lest I misrepresent McCombs, though, let me say
that she never chucks out the transcendental possibilities.
Only after she has dispelled the arrogantly sentimental read-
ings traditional for Nature can she celebrate the mysterious
"natural flowing" of the world "which feeds on life & tends
ever towards life."   She praises this "flowing," both with
"gratitude & bitterness," because humans are so minuscule
against Nature's indifference.   McCombs performs basic hu-
man acts: feeding her baby, loving her man.   Her celebra-
tions are consistently Aristotelean, and she reminds us of the
basic problem: We feel that mountains want to be loved--but
they do not:

          the mountain is there, a mountain.   It is not
          inside you.   It has all it can do
          being a mountain.   It does not want
          to be loved.

She is a small but potent figure on this earth; her lovings are intensified by her unblinking realism. She celebrates the human need for succor and comfort. She lights a match in the dark--a paradoxical act, since her brief flame (her life) prevents her from <u>seeing</u> what might possibly be surrounding her in the dark forest, as an envisioning:

> In the blackness a lapping
> of water or muzzle; the air says something,
> gibberish or warning, & quits when I move,
> matches in hand, to strike open the fire
> that stops me from seeing.

McCombs' songs are far more moving than Jeanette MacDonald's. They evoke an incredible dignity and beauty. McCombs writes with impressive skill. If this book receives the wide readership it deserves, American poets will have to see Nature in a far less sentimental way. Those in need of change may turn to the best of Frost and Lawrence for some clues. They may memorize a few of McCombs' poems and kick the traditional nature-habit of male poets--those prurient pokers and probers of Nature's parts. I'm nagged (and pleased) by the idea that it took a sensitive women to get things right.

WRITER MEETS CRITIC:

William Matthews and Robert Peters

ROBERT PETERS

Rarely does a poet have a chance to meet his critic on common ground--and, you might say, that's just as well; for the exchange could lead to deflations, knifings, the disruptions of friendships, and life-long animosities. There are safeguards in setting distances between the reviewer and reviewee; the real drift of an assessment won't be dissipated in the flash and onrush of the moment. And yet, as a critic who employs considerable energies writing about contemporary poets, with special emphasis on the small press writer, I've sought ways of breaking out of established critical formats-- via a sometimes funky slant on the writer in question, via essays written in the manner of the poet they are about, and via a drift towards the outrageous and the provocative. My hope is that I have so far engendered more good-will than animosity, and that my critical perceptions have been sufficiently fearless and sufficiently sound to serve that useful, traditional critic's function of discerning fresh talents languishing out there unnoticed and unsung, of defining the strengths and weaknesses of established poets, and of raising flags against some of the holy-cow/bull poets currently in fashion. Certainly there is no end of matters to write about.

How does this bring me to William Matthews' Sticks and Stones (Pentragram Press, PO Box 379, Markesan, Wis. 53946. $3.00)? Matthews strikes me as one of the most quietly passionate, intelligent, and technically accomplished poets of his generation. His two earlier volumes, both published by Random House, have established him as a considerable, growing talent. His contributions to the pizzazz of Lillabulero, that too short-lived journal he co-edited with Russell Banks, revealed his critical acuity. In its brief ex-

istence <u>Lillabulero</u> was one of the top journals in the country,
in terms of class, and also in the array of writers show-
cased. Then, of course, there are the Lillabulero Press
books and chapbooks. Finally, Matthews earns brownie points
with me because of his enthusiasm for small presses and
little magazines--this despite a period of disaffection he ex-
perienced over his column in <u>New</u> (the Crossing Press). Few
poets today are as involved in grooming that monstrous Pega-
sus of contemporary poetry--part dray, part stallion, part
palomino, part shetland, part sawbones. Matthews is a de-
lightfully political writer--he personally knows more poets
than almost anyone else. Amidst it all he keeps his humor
and a semblance, at least, of sanity.

I can think of few other poets with whom I would
rather exchange views on a recent book. Matthews is judi-
cious, and will lay out as good or better than I have to give.
He is a fine bull-shit detector. He is also a thoroughly com-
mitted professional. He's as attentive to the varieties of
poems around, the noxious ones as well as the rare, as he
is to the plethora of flower and plant life around his house.
What I hope to avoid here is pushing him into any sort of
defensive position; he may want to comment on matters quite
apart from those I raise specifically over his book. He
should in no way feel committed to holding himself to the in-
terview form ... this is meant to be an experiment in some-
thing other than the interview. Perhaps an exchanging of en-
ergies between poet and critic is what I'm after. So, what I
propose to do is to comment on <u>Sticks and Stones</u>, sometimes
addressing myself to Matthews, sometimes not. I am writing
in California. I shall send my commentary to Bill and ask
him to respond, improvise, further develop whatever and
wherever he chooses.

Sticks and Stones

Of the three sections of <u>Sticks and Stones</u>, my favorite
is the first, "Love Poems." The understated pain, the numb-
ness of a man who has left his house over personal difficul-
ties with a lover gets to me. Here, too, the mildly surreal
images work--written down as they are with the ease of di-
rect reportage. Here is what I mean: Matthews maintains a
special logic even when his images are from dreams and
nightmares. He likes to present his details as they are--
factual, no-nonsense. Here is an example from "Goodbye
Again":

> I fill one pocket with bats
> because a pocket is dark.
> I fill the other with stones
> because they make devoted pets.

He doesn't literally put bats in his pocket; yet, if he were to, his reason for doing so makes sense: Bats like dark places, a pocket is like a dark cave, etc. And the idea that stones are pets says a good deal about the speaker's psychic state-- nervousness, stones as worry-beads, the fact of an earlier "good-bye. " If the world (lover) isn't in tune, stones won't break my bones or hurt me, especially if they are pets. There's no self-pity here, though. And the freshness of the images allows the poem to sail off, as it does, becoming one of the best poems in the book.   The mood continues:

> Because my words flow
> downhill I follow them there.
> Let the wind go through their holes;
> it's the holes I love in them.

Where a lesser poet would have dropped the stone/bat images, Matthews employs them to structure the remainder of the poem, maintaining the surreal qualities of touch and space:

> In one pocket the stones
> are laying their eggs.
> I throw my breath
> over my shoulder.

> In the other pocket
> the bats have lowered the dark sails
> of their wings
> because it's always night

> in my pocket
> and you have to sleep sometime.
> Everything goes from itself,
> a dandruff of seeds.

Generally, I have trouble with Surrealist poems. As they are written today (Tate, Simic, Codrescu, Valaoritis, etc.) the need to be flashily original takes over, at the expense of a deeper seriousness. Automatic, clever writing. The sur- realist enthusiasts will see what I say as red-neck criticism, I know. But the mode is risky when a poet ensnares him- self in his own cleverness. Matthews avoids the trap, and

yet most of his poems make connections here with current
surrealism. To paraphrase his "Your Dog and You," his
paws do click along on the pavement as he lopes home.

In many of these poems the person they mirror is in
the process of withdrawing--from a love he is with, or from
the world. One would assume that withdrawal always has its
passive side--the withdrawer, unprompted or unforced by
violence, moves towards bland catatonic states of his own
devising. One way to improve our lives is to walk away with
them to our own private caves, beachhouses, nests. In "The
Portrait" a photographer, bored, photographs an engaged
couple--a cryptic situation of a man forced to be in the world
yet finding his way out via his "darkroom trance, air in an
inky lung." His withdrawal is from the stiffening couple who
anticipate the shutter-click and straighten up, their energy
zapping the photographer as a "lapse between a lightning-bolt
/and thunder." Perhaps the photographer is jaded because
he's taken so many pictures of engaged couples. Perhaps
he can't allow himself to move into their anxious joy because
his own life is a failure and, alone, he is incapable of in-
tense personal connections. "The Portrait" turns on psychic
states, and the final image of moths ricocheting against the
colored glass lampshade symbolizes the photographer's glassy
psyche in its only partially successful withdrawal into non-
feeling:

> And in the hall
> outside: bell-shaped, its lipped rim
> pressed to the ceiling, a cream-
> colored glass lampshade
> is rung by ricocheting moths.

The second section of Sticks and Stones, "Food for
Thought," is much less directly personal than part one.
Matthews likes the parable/prose poem; and he's pretty good
at it. My sense of the prose poem generally is that poets
write them when their own wellsprings are drying--the prose
poem allows for a sneaky indifference to formal matters, an
excuse frequently for bad associative writing. Most of the
prose poems I read sound like fragments of cute and/or bad
dreams. I find the genre a contemporary affliction. Yes,
you can say, it's better than spending your energies writing
book reviews--at least it's creative. Whatever!

The irony of "Money" turns on "our common life" and
the worship of money. Matthews implies that currently we

are blinded by money, and that eventually we'll clear up our
seeing.   Ironic.   He advises that we return to early texts
written "before we were us."   These texts are all about
money.   The last text is a neat ironic nod towards Yeats:
"for money's pitched its tent in the place of increment."
Perhaps this shouldn't work, but it does.   And it's nicely
ambiguous.

While this section is less personal, the presence of
the persona is either withdrawn or withdrawing.   They are
losers: An explorer dies in snow meadows after scratching
his farewell poem, by knifepoint, on the toe of his half-eaten
boot.   There's Eric shorted out by lightning on a golf course,
and a witness who is numbed by the experience, as he re-
flects on it.   A protagonist who drinks beer after playing ten-
nis is a stunned bloke who drives home finally to feed his
dog.   This is the same voice who regrets his marriage, one
(so bad that) "the kids won't believe we fought for their
sakes."   The voice once more, this time playing basketball,
aware of his aging, hating his "decadent grace," pleading:
"Body, come back; all is forgiven."   There's something
lovely, dead, and muy suburban about these poems.

The final poem of the group, "The Waste Carpet," is
a brilliant four-pager about ecological pollution.   It shouldn't
work; what's new about pollution?   But Matthews' twists of
perception, style, grace bring it off.   He juxtaposes the mo-
mentous (literary) with the mundane: The poem opens with a
formal line and then moves into the common and the imme-
diate.   Something like tripping from Yeats over to The En-
quirer:

> No day is right for the apocalypse,
> if you ask
> a housewife in Talking Rock, Georgia,
> or maybe Hop River, Connecticut.
> She is opening a plastic bag.
> A grotesque parody of the primeval muck
> starts oozing out.   And behold
> the plastic bag is magic,
> there is no closing it.
> Soap in unsoftened water, sewage, Masonite shavings,
> a liquefied lifetime subscription to the NEW YORK
>   TIMES
> delivered all at once.
> Empty body stockings, limp,
> forlorn, like collapsed lungs....

> Also,
> two hundred and one tons of crumpled bumpers
> wrapped in claim reports,
> liquid slag, coal dust, plastic trimmings,
> industrial excrementa.
> Lake Erie is returning our gifts.

Matthews' humor is telling as he writes about fields of abandoned cars. References to bishops, choirs, and to historical explorers are delicious, first-rate. These images collect as pieces of "the new flood." Cars, waste, detergent sludge are "the stiff gods we have made," dooming us:

> The amiable cars wait stilly in their pasture.
> Three Edsels forage in the southeast corner,
> a trio of ironical bishops.
> There are Fords & Dodges,
> a Mercury on blocks,
> four Darts & a Pierce-Arrow,
> a choir of silenced Chevrolets.
> And, showing their absurd grills
> and trademarks to a new westward expansion,
> two Hudsons, a La Salle, and a De Soto.

Farm animals wait frightened and amazed by the encroaching slick:

> Hair along the hog's spine rises,
> the Holstein pivots his massive head
> at dusk toward where the barn was.
> The spreading stain he sees is his new owner.

The slime "crests towards the Mississippi." We had assumed the world would end in a fire-storm; but we were wrong. Facing the disaster, poets must keep on writing, muttering their lifetimes of words. They prepare elegies, among other ones, to California, possibly the last refuge for self-demolishing man:

> We're all coming west
> inexorably, bringing our ruinous
> self-knowledge,
> quoting Ecclesiastes.
> We'll be there Friday, early,
> your time.

Again, Matthews' touch is sure, as he blends the formal

(literary) with the colloquial.   <u>Inexorably</u>, <u>ruinous</u>, <u>self-knowledge</u> elevate the tone; the final two lines reduce the tone to the informal.   Such contrasts are among Matthews' most characteristic traits; and he wields them extremely well.   He's learned paradox from masters--Thomas Hardy, Yeats, T. S. Eliot, Frost.   Not that he's imitative; he isn't. His voice is his own--distanced, involved, quizzical, in-formed, and seeing.

"Landing on My Feet" is the least successful part of Sticks and Stones.   I sense a lack here of a solid rounding-off.   I think of books like this (special small-press books) in the framework of a considerable poet's larger career as sub-ject to the same requirements as more ambitious books. Therefore, I expect that the final section will provide legs, solid bases, landing strips, security positionings for the earlier sections.   Apart from the superb title poem "Sticks and Stones," I feel let down.   "Singing the Blues," the final poem, deals with teen-age cruelty and sexuality.   Predictable, if well-written.   The speaker looks up Kelly Nesbitt's skirt and grooves on her pearl-colored panties.   He holds a dime over a Bunsen-burner flame and drops the dime for creepy Norbert to find.   There is one far-out line: "In comic strips teenagers use a juke box but in real life it's the phone."   As a windup though this poem seems trivial; it's a panty sniff-off rather than a blast off.   And the final line is good encounter-group therapy positioning: "I go singing, getting better, get-ting confident, going, going, gone."   Perhaps a problem is that there are too few poems here--five as distinct from nine and ten in the earlier parts.   Also, there's an imbalance formally--the poem-prose modes back here are slack.   There's little urgency.   I'd have taken the remarkable "The Waste Carpet" from Part Two and set it back here to close off the book.   I'd feel happier that way.   Yet, "Sticks and Stones" is a superbly funny poem about contemporary poets, and about the narcissism of poetry-readings.   Here is a section of it:

> Will there be a party
> after the reading?
> Who will be there?
> Moonrock, the anthologist.
> A woman poet
> afraid of living on her looks--
> may she grow older.
> There will be groupies--
> may their pubic hair

clog the teeth of bad poets.
There will be the poet
whose marriage poems
are really about his writing students--
may his divorce poems
be better.
There will be the poet
overlooked by Moonrock--
may he turn in his sleep
like a lottery drum.
The Dark Prince will be there
in a dust-jacket,
sexual strip-miner and Dust
Midas, a love only
a mother could face.
Someone will know a cruel joke
so funny he'll tell it anyhow.
Will Twitch the Ironist be there?
Will the best young poet
in America be there?
Dervish will be there--
may his disciples
return to him
the gift of himself.
We don't need each other.
We need ceremonies of self-love
performed without witnesses.
We need to leave the party,
like a car starting across the fields
. . . . .

So Sticks and Stones is good Matthews, with much pleasure
among the pain.

--robert peters

WILLIAM MATTHEWS

When I sat down in Colorado in 1978 to do my half of
Robert Peters' interesting experiment in criticism, I found I
couldn't get it right. One draft was too contentious: I
wanted to explain what I thought I'd been up to, wanted to
defend the poems where Peters had poured anything thinner
than a syrup of admiration on them. Another draft was
more theoretical than I liked, once I'd done it; one problem
with the chatty, enthusiastic and personal critical style Peters

uses is blurred terminology, and I wanted to address that
then, as I do now; but then what I'd written seemed pedantic.
I let it drift and didn't write another draft, promising my-
self that after the book seemed less fresh to me, I could do
my part better.

And now it's 1981, I'm writing from Seattle, and I
want to add to Peters' lively commentary on Sticks & Stones
a few cavils, footnotes and responses.

* * *

I think I know what Peters means by a "currently
fashionable surrealism," though with hindsight we can see
now how by 1978 that fashion was nearly exhausted.   There
was a kind of poem in the air then, written as much by the
zeitgeist as by an individual poet, which I'll describe for our
purposes here as a blend of William Carlos Williams and
Pablo Neruda in translation.   I don't think surrealism was
the right word for it for two reasons.   One is that we never had
a period of native surrealism; it was always an exotic im-
port.   And the second is that if you adopt, as Peters has,
a kind of wave-of-the-hand, you-know-what-I-mean use of
the word, a sort of shorthand such as active literary people
would use in conversation--and this is the method of his
criticism, that it resembles serious, excited conversation
about new books--you begin to lose, in order to gain the
fluency of shorthand, the discipline of exact terminology.
And the begged question has two parts: Perhaps the reader
does not, in fact, know exactly, but only sort of, what the
writer means; and perhaps, too, the writer has never worked
out exactly what he means by using a term, so that the
shorthand threatens to become, however unintentionally, a
kind of slur and laziness.

Whatever Peters means by "surrealism" here, I can't
understand it if the term must cover, like an amiable blanket,
all the poets he names as examples of it.   Tate and Simic
seem to me among the most interesting, intelligent and dura-
ble poets of my generation; neither of them seems to me a
surrealist (though I know both of them have read widely among
European surrealist poets); and I'm sorry to see poets whose
work I value so highly so roughly undervalued.

* * *

A second interesting question Peters raises has to do

with what makes a poem "personal." At times he seems to
mean that the poem is spoken by an "I" who is more or less
the poet, rather than a persona. At other times he seems
to mean that the poet is writing about his actual biographical
experience rather than imagined experience. And at other
times he seems to mean that the most personal poems are
those in which the poet has invested the most emotional risk,
that this is a kind of hallmark of authenticity, and that it can
be true of poems whether or not they are spoken by the poet
or by a persona, and whether or not the poem refers to ac-
tual or imagined experience (though how would the reader
know, in most cases, except by gossip or accident?). I think
Peters uses the term more or less the way most readers do,
in several overlapping ways, all of them favorable when com-
pared to impersonal, and without stopping to think hard or
signal when one of the overlapping meanings is abandoned,
even in mid-sentence, and another slid into its place.

A long and useful essay needs to be written by some-
one--it will not be me--on the words personal, private and
public as we use them in talking about poetry. All poems
are all three, in important ways. They are public because
published, written down. They are private because no reader
can guess what the relationship is, very exactly, between the
public text and private curiosities and emotional pressures
that produced an urge to work on and perfect that text. Even
a poet who wanted to explain that relationship to us, an ele-
mentary knowledge of psychology might suggest, could not
except naively provide an authoritative explanation: Part of
the poem is private even from the poet. All poems are in
some way personal because some person made them, and im-
personal because they are made, expressed, pushed out of
the self by the work of making.

Once we have a poem before us, we have other prob-
lems to deal with. Is "I" also the poet? Suppose we are
wary, sensing a trap in these questions, and say "No." Does
it make sense, then, to say that all poems are spoken by
personae, even those in which the persona hides behind the
anonymous name "I," and that no poem is, then, really per-
sonal? That's a neat move in logic, but not in psychologic.

There is, surely, an important emotional difference
between the "I" of Lowell's "Skunk Hour," let's say, and
Whitman's "I," and any theoretical sleight-of-hand that makes
it harder to talk about that difference, one the poets have
worked hard to create, is simply foolish.

I'm not going to offer any solution to the problems I'm raising here; I don't know them. I want simply to point out that there's something full of common sense about the slurred ways Peters uses the word "personal," and that there's something wrong with that slur, and that the adoption of a more formal and academic vocabulary about personae is not in this particular area (in some areas, it is) a bracing precision, but another kind of confusion.

In the particular case of my poems in Sticks & Stones, I'd wanted the book's title to carry a lot of weight.

> Sticks and stones
> will break my bones
> but words will
> never hurt me.

The title is ironic, of course. Anybody who works with words learns to respect and fear their power to determine, to hurt, to be memorable in a way no bruise can be, nor even a broken bone.

"The understated pain, the numbness of a man who has left his house over personal difficulties with a lover gets to me," Peters writes about section one. Well, who would leave over impersonal difficulties? And there's that word personal again. I think Peters is right to see the primary tension in the book as one between speech and silence, glibness and discretion, response and numbness, explanation and acceptance, myth-making and bland catatonic states of one's own devising. But he puts too much weight on personal. Sure, it's my misery-wracked divorce that is in part behind those poems-- there's got to be some emotional urgency behind poems-- but the poems are not about the divorce, they're about urgency, the continual need to re-imagine.

If you have the good luck not to be an accomplice in a misery-wracked divorce, you are still subject to the question whether it is better to make up new stories about your life and suffer the consequences of those stories' inaccuracies, or better to live out the consequences of the old and beloved stories you've been so loyal to, or to pretend that these stories don't matter at all, or that they mean everything. None of these possibilities is true without the others, and none of the ways Peters uses the word personal is true without the others. Since he uses the word more or less the way we all do, and since he has developed that habit from

wanting to talk about poems that make use of that ambiguity,
maybe we should pay attention to this problem.

* * *

"There's something lovely, dead and _muy_ suburban
about these poems" in section two, Peters writes.   What I
think he must mean by _suburban_ is inert, materially imposing
but spiritually empty, maybe even a little complacent.   The
characters seem, as Peters shrewdly says of one of them,
"numbed" more than complacent, and they may share with
what Peters means by suburban this trait: They wanted to
be emotionally secure, sealed off from the shocks and loss
of being alive, and they traded for such impossible security
the ability to respond to shock and loss when it came, as it
inevitably does.

"Losers, " Peters calls them.   Right again, I think,
looking back on them; to the people in these poems, their
fear and fate, both, is always loss.

Section three, now that I look at it through Peters' re-
marks, does seem weaker than the other two.   Maybe that's
why I couldn't get my response right in 1978; one of the early
versions I wrote of these comments explained the structure,
as if I had only to say what I had in mind in order to correct
what I might well not have got on paper.

I think the title of section three gives the game away
a little: "Landing on My Feet. "   It's a "personal" title, in
a way the first two section-titles are not.   It's as if I hoped
to cheer myself on.   At the time I assembled the book it was
hard to know what prediction for myself I could believe in,
and I should therefore have resisted the impulse to make one.

I wanted the book to be a "special small-press book"
only in the sense that it was printed by a small press rather
than my commercial publisher.   Too many poets use the
small presses the way baseball clubs use the minor leagues;
in this light, "special" can be a condescension.   So when
Mike Tarachow of Pentagram Press suggested the book to me,
I said that I'd reprint none of its poems in later commercial
editions, that it would be a book by itself and a rehearsal for
nothing else.

The last poem should have been, I see now, "Sticks &
Stones. "   I think that if I'd switched the position of that poem

and "Singing the Blues," the section would seem less over-
matched by the first two. It would be less "personal," and
centered more on the work of the imagination, by which facul-
ty all the various overlapping and over-contradicting meanings
of "personal" that I wrote about earlier in these notes are
united.

That's what I wanted the book to be about, the work
of the imagination.

Above I've discussed a few reactions I've had to
Peters' remarks-- digressions, exceptions, reservations.

I'll end by mentioning the pleasures of this format.
Breathes there a poet with soul so dead he doesn't love to
have a bright and engaged reader pay attention to his work?
That poet isn't me.   I'm grateful for the passage about the
diction in "The Waste Carpet," in particular, and the list of
masters Peters gives seems to me exactly on target for the
time in my writing life when I wrote that poem (the inclusion
of Hardy, a favorite poet, seems pleasingly exact).

Most reviews are not useful to the poet.   I'm not sure
which is worse, a stupid positive or a stupid negative review,
and given the perfunctoriness of most reviews and the low
state of poetry criticism we endure, most reviews fit into
one category or the other.   The third useless category is the
review that refuses to commit itself to judgment; this is
journalism at its worst, all the "objectivity" of news reporting
and, since the news is poetry, it has either no news value or
is, as Williams had it, the news without which we languish
and die.

But now and then somebody writes something that is
like a meeting, and Peters has done so for Sticks & Stones.
I'd be very pleased by that fact alone, and am doubly so by
his offer to let me respond.   Thanks.

JOSEPHINE MILES:

Coming to Terms*

Josephine Miles' 10th book of poems appears 50 years
after her first published poem, and 40 years after her first
published book. Her life has been long and productive: in
addition to writing poetry, she has written on literary theory
and poetics. Miles has received a University Professorship,
a prestigious award going only to a handful of teachers at the
University of California.

Coming to Terms strikes me as the most accessible
of all of her books of poetry. This is not to say that she is
always an easy poet to understand; she still swings an elusive
theme with grace, moving off to the right a jog where the
real pendulum of her meaning scintillates. The scope of her
new book is vast, moving from childhood poems recounting
her pain when the crippling arthritis she has endured all her
life struck, to moments as a young teacher, to the troubled
decade of the 1960s and the student demonstrations she wit-
nessed first-hand at Berkeley, to the literary life she has
enjoyed on the West Coast for so many years. I find this
book the most engagingly personal of her books. There is
no sense that she will ever know stagnation as a poet.

Coming to Terms opens with "Trip," an account of a
long train ride she took as a child through the American South-
west. She moves easily to poignant insights about our lives,
the great hurting scope of them, rendered through an image
of a vast western landscape:

> And I see, what do we see, all of us,
> Stretching my gasping eyes without air
>   or kindness,
> Sandy ranges of an infinite distance

*Reprinted by permission from San Francisco Review of
Books (March 1980), pp. 17-18.

> Under a white hot sky under
> Infinite distance
> Beyond a plain, a sea, a life of sand
> Of infinite distance
> No place to end.   A breadth
> Hurtful to any small heart
> A scope which beached our débris on
>   its shore
> Abandoned, lost from a tide of life.

"Before" recalls her childhood when the first "small flame of arthritis" struck.   Bed-ridden, in a cast, she rejoices over a gift of six bottles of perfume: "Oho!   There is something to life!"   "Doll," one of the best of the poems, gives an unselfpitying glance at herself, as a doll in life, resembling the play-doll broken beyond mending:

> It turned out Lillian had been knocked
>   to the floor and
>   broken
> Across the face.   Good, said my mother
> In her John Deweyan constructive
>   way,
> Now you and Lillian can be mended
>   together.
> We made a special trip to the doll
>   hospital
> To pick her up.   But, they can't fix her
>   after all, my father said,
> You'll just have to tend her with her
>   broken cheek.
> I was very willing.   We opened the box,
>   and she lay
> in shards mixed among tissue paper.
>   Only her eyes
> Set loose on a metal stick so they
>   would open
> And close, opened and closed, and I
>   grew seasick.

The straightforward manner here has an unforgettable authenticity.

Miles began publishing poetry early in the 1930s, and several of her new poems are about various poets and artists she has known through the years.   She writes affectionately

about a California poet who grew Swiss chard and kept a black
coffin in his livingroom, with a papier-mâché lady beneath a
glass cover, holding a bouquet of orchids: the "freshness,
savor,/Sweetness, suitability" of the chard "seems to prevent
/ Any comment on the orchid bouquet." The poem is a
beautiful testament to friendship. She dines with visiting
European writers. One poem is a short meditation on Aldous
Huxley and her beliefs as contrasts to his. In another, Sea-
mus Heany visits Berkeley. And there is a highly moving
account of a fund-raising party for the Black Panthers in a
Berkeley home, featuring Jean Genet. Genet was hostile,
irritated people; and someone threw a bottle, hitting Michael
McClure's young daughter, who was left sobbing.

Her "tally of poets," in the poem "Makers," is her
recounting of the poets she has seen come and go, including
several who influenced her: Brother Antoninus was there
early, and Yvor Winters with his Palo Alto airedales. When
Miles arrived in Berkeley she was part of a gathering of
poets, some of them now obscure: Marie West, Genevieve
Taggard, Hildegarde Flanner, Sara Barnsdale, Charles Wood,
and the Caldwells. Robinson Jeffers and Kenneth Rexroth
were also crucial figures. A younger, pre-Beat, gathering
appeared, a flowering of a San Francisco poetry renaissance
during the late forties and early fifties: Madeline Gleason,
Robert Duncan, Jack Spicer, James Schevill, George Elliott,
Archie Ammons, and William Stafford. Finally, the Beat
Movement happened: "Ginsberg late prescribing /Dog piss in
gardens."

During these years Miles was pressured to abandon
traditional sounds and forms in favor of vers libre. She
manages, I think, to incorporate the best of both worlds:
Her free-verse poems are as good as any around; at the
same time, she never abandons her sense of meter (though
not necessarily regular), or her belief that craftmanship has
a form and order that really counts. She is amused by "the
black interests" of poets who will do almost anything to get
published: Printers make poets' hearts "go." She is amused
by younger poets who flee the cities, hippie-wise, to find
"change" in the land. But, she wryly notes: "Sometimes
they move back, now they come /On motor bikes, wife and
child and manuscript / In the hip pocket. Here they are!"

About a third of Coming to Terms is devoted to Miles'
life at the university. One of the most poignant of these
poems is "Memorial Day." The police invade the campus

with rifles and tear gas.   Miles is in class trying to teach
<u>Paradise Lost</u>.   Choking from the gas, she manages to in-
form her students that the next meeting will be off-campus,
at her home.   One student, with that engaging irrepressibility
of students, says: "OK, we'll bring the wholegrain wheat
germ raisin bread. "   She urges the students to educate their
parents, "even if they believe in the war you're protesting. "
They tell her they have tried; but most parents won't listen.
The poem concludes:

> The army helicopter
> In its regular rounds of surveillance,
> drops down low--
> Our twenty figures in a courtyard may
>   mean trouble.
> Couldn't we pick these flowers to
>   throw at them?
> All these camellias overgrown and
>   wasting?

In "Officers" she recounts her feelings for campus
policemen, a series of them, as they have guarded the cam-
pus gates over the years.   During the riots, the police turned
vicious.   On one occasion, Miles was being escorted to cam-
pus, as she had to be because of her physical condition, by
a student with a van:

> Then on a dark night a giant officer
>   came up to the car
> When we were going to a senate
>   meeting, strikebound by pickets,
> And smashed his billy club down on
>   the elbow of my student driver.
> Where do you think you are going?   I
>   suddenly saw I knew him.
> It's you, Mr. Graham, I mean it's us,
>   going to the meeting.   He walked
>   away
> Turning short and small, which he
>   was, a compact man
> Of great neatness.
>
> Later when I taught in the basement
>   corridor,
> The fuzz came through.
> Running, loosing tear gas bombs in
>   the corridor

> To rise and choke in offices and
>   classrooms,
> Too late for escape. Their gas masks
>   distorted their appearance
> But they were Mr. O'Neill and Mr.
>   Swenson.

> Since then, I have not met an officer
> That I can call by name.

In a different vein is "Bureau," an amusing satire on
campus bureaucracy. She made a mistake in a letter of
recommendation for a student and tries to retrieve it. The
Placement Bureau, once they find her letter, won't return it.
In "Bureau 2," she finds the SPCA even more difficult, as
they procrastinate about catching the skunks fighting under
her house. The "colloquial remedies," mothballs and tomato
juice, fail to deter the creatures. After great run-arounds
from various city and county offices, she finally reaches the
secretary of the County Health Officer. The secretary says:

> What makes you think Mr. Simms will
>   speak to you?
> What makes you think Mr. Simms is
>   interested in skunks?
> Mr. Simms is animal health officer of
>   this whole county
> And his chief interest is wolves.

An easy, yet deep compassion emerges from these
poems. Miles turns aside from any pity people express for
her, redirecting that energy towards her visitors. Those
who have the privilege of knowing her personally know how
authentic her caring is: She's very tough-minded, yet gra-
cious, about her own condition and ours--she resembles
Thoreau. In "Album," her father, as he watches her scratch
her knee-cast with a paper knife, tells her that according to
"laws of compensation" (good old Emersonian term) her "old
age should be grand." She observes:

> Not grand, but of a terrible
> Compensation, to perceive
> Past the energy of survival
> In its sadness
> The hard life of the young.

One of her hallmarks is a keen vision for people and
for landscape details. She is in an airplane when the pilot

announces trouble with the landing gear.   There is much loud
jolting and shaking inside the plane.   Instead of recounting
her fear and the fear of the other passengers that they will
crash, or of rehearsing the state of her sins as she pre-
pares to meet her Maker, she reports what she sees in "De-
lay":

> Then many of the ladies and
>   gentlemen
> Moved from where they sat in holiday
>   or business absorption
> Over next to some child and engaged
> In a great deal of peaceful
>   conversation--
> Reminiscences of their own, sighs,
>   questions of the children,
> Till the gear
> Jolted itself into landing, and the pilot
> Came on again, to regret the
>   inconvenience.

In "Lone," her VW stalls with a broken axle.   She
and the driver are in Nowhere Land; but they keep on driving,
scraping the split axle, the car "dragging its rear end like
a dog."   They find an oasis, evoked by a few salient details:

> And there appear a leaning porch and
>   pump.
> Three signs: Gas, Nehi, Wrecking
>   Crew.
> They stand by the pump, the bottles in
>   their hands.

I detect few false steps in Miles' poems.   Her crafts-
manship is sure.   She writes out of a long tradition of English
and American poets without being stifled at all by that tradi-
tion.   Few of her lines appear unfelt.   And she perceives
that all good poems have complex appeals.   She eschews the
journalese poem, the self-obsession poem, so fashionable
these days.   Her poems are full of precise observations
which are nearly always about some symbolic telling of our
lives--and hers.   An immediate, warm humanity springs from
her work.   Her ear is deft, her tone is her own.   She cele-
brates life objectively, seeing its crippling pains, frustrations,
and defeats.   Her lengthy closing poem, "Center," reveals
much of her practical and non-flinching, celebratory meta-

physics.   We are here, she writes,

> To err,
> To fail and attempt as terribly as
>   possible, to try
> Stunts of such magnitude they will
>   lead
> To disasters of such magnitude they
>   will lend
> To learnings of such magnitude they
>   will lead
> Back in enterprise to substance and
>   grace.

BURN THE MOVIES!

The Gargoyle Interview with Robert Peters*

Robert Peters was born October 20, 1924, on a scrub pine farm in northern Wisconsin. His dad was a farmer, lumberjack, mechanic. He attended a one-room country school, the in-town high school, and after three years in the Hitler War, enrolled at the University of Wisconsin where he earned three degrees in six years of intensive schooling (Ph. D. , 1952, in Victorian literature). He has been a Guggenheim Fellow, a Trustee for the American Society for Aesthetics, a National Endowment of the Arts Fellow, and has had several visits to the Yaddo Foundation, Ossabaw Island Project, and the MacDowell Colony. He has published books on Swinburne and John Addington Symonds. He is a contributing editor for The American Book Review, and consulting editor to Bachy and Contact II. He reviews regularly for numerous small press periodicals, and for the Library Journal and for the Los Angeles Times. He was recently appointed editor for the Scarecrow Press American Poets Series.

He is a professor at the University of California, Irvine, where he teaches courses in Victorian literature and contemporary poetry, and in the MFA program.

INTERVIEWERS:† You have a penchant for coining words or phrases to describe directions in modern poetry, hence: "feminismo, " "the snigger, " "catatonic surrealism. " Is there a

*Reprinted by permission from Gargoyle, (January 1981), #15/ 16 pp. 21-25.
†The Interviewers are Eric Baizer and Richard Peabody.

need today for a new definition or theory of modern poetry--
specifically dealing with the poem that can't be notated?

PETERS: We need better poems and fewer theories. Theo-
ries abound, particularly fashionable ones--Derrida's, her-
meneutics, etc.   I teach in a university full of theories
about literature.   Not much current poetry is read by these
theory-professors.   They seem to stop with Stevens and Wil-
liams.   When my Great American Poetry Bake-Off appeared
and I was reviewed by my colleagues for a pay-boost, one
beguiling colleague said to me: "We didn't know what to do
with it; why do you write about people we've never heard of?"
I'm not much given to paranoia, but want to stress the real-
politik of English departments, including good ones, like
mine

        So, I'd like to see less theorizing about and more
reading of contemporary writers.   When I make up names
like "feminismo," "momentosity," "the snigger," "catatonic
surrealism," and "gab poetry," I am trying to call attention
to a point via a lively tag--other more conventional terms
would be less lively, and I fear my reader would nod.   When
I write essays, whenever I can I try to keep my readers
awake, rubbing in a little sand and ground glass if I have to,
or giving a well-placed pinch now and then.   And since I
belong to no schools or groups--New York crowds, Iowa
kitchen-stoopers, or the San Francisco siblings--I feel I can
say what I please, within the bounds always of responsible
criticism and good taste.   So, to answer your question, I
don't think we need "a new definition or theory of modern
poetry"--we need more poets full of energy, risk-takings,
iconoclasms, intelligence, lyric sweep.   And we need more
readers of these poets.

INTERVIEWERS: You wrote that most literary criticism is
"chokingly entwined with the Virginia creepers of traditional
critical prose." Which contemporary critics do you find ex-
citing?

PETERS: I enjoy reading my own criticism as much as any-
body's.   That sounds narcissistic, but I just don't find much
criticism being written that revs up or blasts off towards the
tree-tops.   I struggle to experiment and make art forms out
of my essays.   Recently, Greg Kuzma published a gathering
of critical pieces published by him in Pebble Magazine over
the past few years.   It's pretty boring, most of the essays
being quite interchangeable one with the other.   This is pretty

typical of most criticism--well intentioned, genteel. Dave
Smith's features in APR are like this.   About the only theo-
rist around who has something new to say is John Vernon--
yet, his seminal book Poetry and the Body goes unreviewed
and largely unread.   Get it, and take a look ... University
of Illinois Press.   And, of course, there's Robert Bly.

        There are critics I don't always agree with but usually
read: One is Richard Kostelanetz--he's bright, iconoclastic,
tenacious, and hairy.   Marjorie Perloff is another.   Add
Hadyn Carruth and Merritt Clifton (he jabs his readers in
good places).   And Bill Zavatsky calls fearless shots, al-
though I feel he trimmed a bit in his recent commentary on
the Naropa Poetry Wars in The American Book Review.   The
critics I like constitute a mere handful.

        Criticism seems to be in as it has never been--wit-
ness the plethora of recently launched review journals: Three-
penny Review, Meridian, The Independent, American Book
Review, Northeast Rising Sun (revived), Contact II, Bachy,
Stony Hills.   We need fearless critical writing.   Too many
critics are afraid that if they scowl they'll never get their
books published in the National Poetry Series, win prizes,
or appear in the New Yorker, The American Poetry Review,
Poetry Chicago, or get invited to read at Iowa or at St.
Mark's, or be invited to teach at Naropa.   I hear this from
the juicy mouths of some critics: "If I can't say positive
things about a poet, I won't review him. " My god! As
Robert Bly wrote recently in a letter to Bachy magazine de-
fending me against a pair of vicious attackers: "It's a critic's
job to be nasty; he's [Peter's] not a mother or an uncle. "
Models?   The old ones include Thomas Carlyle, A. C. Swin-
burne, D. H. Lawrence--a trio of fantastic, iconoclastic ener-
gies!   Contemporary ones?   Robert Bly as Crunk, in those
classic pieces from The Sixties and The Seventies.   James
Dickey, as he was in The Suspect in Poetry.   Kenneth Rex-
roth who says more in three or four pages than other critics
say in a book.

INTERVIEWERS: History plays a dominant role in your own
poetry.   You've dealt with Ann Lee, founder of the Shakers,
in one book; Byron and his circle in another; King Ludwig II
of Bavaria; Elisha Kent Kane, the American Arctic explorer;
Hawthorne; Van Gogh.   Because of this, do you feel affinities
with W. D. Snodgrass's Führer Bunker and William Meredith's
Hazard, The Painter?   Why the historical approach?   Do you
find it easier to speak through a persona?

PETERS: I'm glad you got around to asking me about my poetry. After all, that's my priority. My criticism is an adjunct, despite my efforts to create, as I've said, a critical art form. Dickey is my immediate model. I have the feeling that his The Suspect in Poetry, scalpel-like, was so upsetting to poets that it was better known in the sixties than his poetry. My fantasy is that poets fearing that Dickey might review them adversely, thought that by reading and admiring his poetry they'd send good "don't review me, please," vibes his way, thereby protecting themselves. That's how, possibly, Dickey got known as a poet. I'm hoping something like that will happen to me--that poets may read my criticism and then pick up some of my poems and read them with care--some of them at least. I write many different kinds of poems, I think, and each book is generally different in style and conception from other books. I don't want to be pigeon-holed.

Well, I'm afraid that this is all outrageously personal. I greatly appreciate the chance, though, to get some of these things said.

But back to your question. One explanation for my interest in history is that I'm a frustrated novelist (I have actually written five novels, none of them published). Another may be that the scope of history suits my own energies, which seem larger than life-sized, so I'm told. I often end up scaring people off, including some I want to nuzzle. I'm physically a big man ... huge chest and arms (I've been liftin' those weights) ... 6'3" tall, big neck, etc. But despite my appearance I am actually a panda.

Each of the figures I've treated historically do relate to my own psyche. As Clayton Eshleman has said, "Peters inhabits these figures." The Shaker mystic Ann Lee lost four of her children in infancy. I started writing poetry at age 39 when my own $4\frac{1}{2}$-year-old son Richard died of a one-day meningitis. And Ann Lee was celibate--an experiment I was interested in at the time, and one, I might add, I shortly abandoned. King Ludwig was an esthete and homosexual--two strong drives in my own nature. My Ph.D. dissertation (U. of Wisconsin 1952) was on the late Victorian Aesthetes and Decadents--Oscar Wilde, Hubert Crackanthorpe, Arthur Symons, Ernest Dowson, John Gray. And I published a prize-winning book on Swinburne's esoteric theories of literature and art. I also spent eight years co-editing and publishing three fat volumes of John Addington Symonds' letters.

Symonds was a Victorian homosexual poet and historian, and indefatigable letter-writer. And I'm shortly off to England, on a grant, to complete an edition of Tennyson-family letters.

Ludwig also fascinated me because of the juxtapositions of beauty and disease in his life. He was one of the handsomest men of Europe; yet, through choice, he was seldom seen in public (he became king at age 17), and just past thirty years of age, his teeth turned black and fell out. He grew fat. All this while, until his murder (?) suicide (?) in his late forties, he was building incredible fantasy castles. He was a great eccentric and non-conformist. I'd like to have the wealth he had, to dispense diamonds and rubies to men just for being attractive.

The Arctic explorer Elisha Kent Kane is a different case--except that he was felled in his mid-thirties by illness --rheumatic fever and its ravages; so, beauty and disease are linked again. I never felt that I was Kane, as I had felt I was Ann Lee and Ludwig. But he did allow me great motifs of ice and snow--continuing the cold of Ludwig (titled The Picnic in the Snow). At the end of the book, Ludwig, disappointed because King Louis XIV of France failed to show up for dinner (Ludwig believed he'd appear, although he'd been dead over a hundred years), stood out in the snow behind his castle. He was gradually covered up, becoming a snow/ice man, and would have frozen if his young groom-lover had not found him and taken him inside.

The snow and ice are also extensions of my own early life in northern Wisconsin--semi-Arctic conditions in winter, short summer season, badly insulated house built by my father, but never completed, incredible poverty, nail-holes covered by frost melting and dripping into my face as I lay in bed reading the Bible. The Sea Horse Press is publishing a long book of my poems about this period of my life, to be called What John Dillinger Meant to Me.

Hawthorne doesn't fit this picture, perhaps, although he's always been one of my favorite writers, one of those (young Tolstoy is another) I would like to have had as lovers. Seriously, though, Hawthorne's style (the esthete emerges again) is so incredible! Richard, my dead son, was named after Hawthorne (Richard Nathaniel Frank Peters); so my Hawthorne is a double-edged commemoration/homage. The Byron sequence, available in The Poet As Ice-Skater (and to be included in a new Red Hill Press collection of my work, Brueghel's Pig), is a series of monologues by various persons who've just heard of Byron's death--his wife, a schoolboy at Harrow who commits suicide, and a lousy poet he had lambasted. I found a book in England saying that Byron's tomb had been opened in the 1930's and that he was in a perfect state of preservation ... turned to marble. This set/suite was my first excursion into voices. Looking back at it over this interval of years, I think it still works.

The Van Gogh poem, "Gauguin's Chair," the title poem for my Selected Poems (Crossing Press), is intensely personal. It mirrors my driven need to love and be loved at the time ... c. 1966. When I saw Van Gogh's painting in Amsterdam, where I had gone with a young lover (the relationship was one of those complex pleasure-pain deals), I saw in the picture how by slashing purple paint up the arms and legs of Gauguin's arm-chair Van Gogh had expressed his own love/rage against Gauguin's having left him. The painting contains G's chair, a couple of G's favorite books, and a lighted candle. I saw there my own frustration, hurt, rage; and I was afraid of the violence I was feeling towards my lover, who was finding it rough to deal with my horrible intensity. In "Gauguin's Chair," I try to capture my own (and Van Gogh's) self pity, attenuated psyche, the need to use art as therapy, and the juxtapositions of love and violence. The full details of my own experience are in the "Interview" at the end of the Selected Poems, and in the Cool Zebras of Light section in the middle of the book.

You mention Snodgrass and Meredith. Actually, I don't care much for Snodgrass' renditions of the Hitler crowd. I say in my essay that they are stagey, pretty monotonous monologues. It's as if Snodgrass had seen his poet's voice as something declaimed by a hammy Shakespearean actor. The work, I think, is a failure. As for Meredith--he interested me because I wanted to see how this elusive, much-lauded poet, author of a slender body of work, reflects himself through a persona. Hazard, The Painter, despite some fine writing, is a slight performance. What I'm saying is that I often review books I don't intend to get anything much out of for my own writing. I review books for various reasons--sometimes because I know the writer and want to give him a hand, or because the book is by some mindlessly praised poet who writes a lousy book, or because a book will illustrate some illness or problem I see in contemporary poetry (viz., the negative pieces on Malanga and Waldman in

the first Bake-Off, and the treatments of Quasha, Dickey,
Wagoner, and Strand here).   I don't attack them so much as
I do the Celebrity Syndrome in poetry, or because I feel a
kind of Octopusian (sounds like J. Swift cooked this one up)
urge to wrap my delicious tentacles around all American
poets, dragging some of them under, allowing some to make
it to the rocks where the sirens wait.   I also feel I can use-
fully inform my readers of good neglected writers, or new
writers of note--Lyn Sukenick, Katy Akin, John Thomasson,
William Wantling, Paul Mariah, Alfred Starr Hamilton, Paul
Trachtenberg, Lee Hickman, Ted Kooser, David Fisher.

Finally, I do not find it easier to speak through a
persona than through my own voice.   Hiding things about my-
self has not been one of my virtues ... quite the opposite,
I'm afraid.   The first seven or eight of my books are all
unabashedly personal--and the undergoing is all there.   Billy
Collins of Mid-Atlantic Review calls me an "entrailist."   I'm
very fond of that.   Most of the early books were written out
of my belief that the more you suffer the better your poems.
The Beats had a different equation--the more you fuck the
better your poems.   And I am sure there are also other
equation-possibilities.   But remember that I didn't start writing
poetry until I was 39, and my entry was cataclysmic.   When
I finally got my act together and was no longer into Romantic
suffering, I needed some distance on my ego--and figures
from the past seemed an answer.   Moreover, I have always
been a history buff.   I remember writing an awful novel in
a wallpaper book (that would make it pretty), as a highschool
junior, about the destruction of Lidice, the Czech town, by
the Nazis.   I loved history, but I never finished the novel.

Visits to my friend George Hitchcock resulted in the
books on Ludwig and Kane--he made me aware of these fig-
ures.   Also, George and I had worked voices in a successful
little book we wrote together, Pioneers of Modern Poetry--
Kayak Press saw it through several printings.   We assumed
the voices of pompous, academic critics who had discovered
incredible beauties (poems) in old books for farmers, on
how to destroy rats in turn-of-the-century shorthand manuals
and intelligence, army intelligence, tests.   The book em-
ploys humor, parody, and put-on to undercut some of the ex-
cesses of projective verse poets.   Alas, the book is now out
of print.   I wish we could find a publisher to reissue it.

INTERVIEWERS: You seem obsessed with rituals, surfaces,
masks and voices.   Can you elaborate on why they play such
a large role in your work?

PETERS: I wasn't aware that I was <u>obsessed</u> with rituals, etc. Do you refer to the butchering poems from <u>The Sow's Head</u>, where the kid, defying his father, takes the sow's head back to a lake, chops a hole in the ice, and drops the head in? a pact with sacrificed creatures and his own responsible adolescence? That is a ritual--sort of Jungian, I guess. It was something, an event I sensed and lived, not something I had a theory about. I seldom think of rituals though, in the way that Robert Duncan, Robert Bly, Gary Snyder, Charles Olson, Clayton Eshleman, or Robert Kelly might, or the Lutheran Church. Yet, I guess I'd have to say that <u>The Gift to Be Simple</u> is a book of rituals.

Surfaces, that's another matter. I love details, minute concrete stuff from nature. I used to fantasize that I could be just as good a nature poet as Roethke. That's hubris, of course. There are times when I feel like Adam first discovering the physical universe. And there is a mystique-- the more objects you can love and value and incorporate in your work, the more your own mortality, symbolically, becomes a lie. Of course, I know that I won't take any of the detritus I love along with me into the waves (I plan to have my ashes disbursed in the Pacific); but while I'm here naming and describing, I feel close to a metaphysics, physics. As for masks and voices--I guess I do enjoy being both straightforward and elusive--learned it from Swinburne, Carlyle, Browning, and Thomas Hardy. Like James Dickey, they were geniuses at putting on other people's helmets.

INTERVIEWERS: You profess a bias toward "energetic" writing. You are a university professor; but many feel academia tends to stifle progressive and original writing. Do you see a conflict between your occupation and your literary philosophy, and, if so, how do you resolve it?

PETERS: I have always resisted academe's rituals of dress and behavior, observing the codes in relation to my students --keeping my hands to myself, knowing my subject, trying to be fair. As a grad student and young teacher, I early found that conforming in ways of dress and being obsequious didn't earn you the Brownie points you needed for promotions--I tried to be good, but was almost fired from Boston University (my wife saved my job by writing anonymous letters to a stupid chairman, protesting my rumored firing--she wrote in different hands and on different typewriters, so that he would think numerous students were writing him); and I was fired from that sinkhole of the middlewest (or so it was then ...

riddled with hypocrisy) Ohio Wesleyan University.   Fortunate-
ly, when I skipped west to California (Univ. of Cal, River-
side) eccentricities of dress and behavior were tolerated.

A lot of my energies are spent though away from
campus--writing, reading, keeping up with my enormous
professional correspondence, going to work-outs at the Holi-
day Health Spas.   I often entertain the idea of stopping my
writing and becoming a geriatric weight-lifter--didn't Du-
champs turn from painting to chess?   Rimbaud to gun-running?

I've never felt that simply by being a professor your
talent (testes) will shrivel up like dried beans in a gourd.
If you have talent it should survive, and may even be en-
riched.   I owe UC Irvine a good deal--I teach little, have
few committee chores, and am free to write, to travel and
give poetry readings.   I feel I'm blessed.   I can't imagine
another profession so congenial--and I had to put myself
through incredible chores and frustrations to reach today.
I've labored for what I have.   Most of the complaints I hear
of academe, and attacks on poets simply for being professors,
come from sour-grapes have-nots.   People like Mark Strand
denigrate universities, and reveal--as he does in an inter-
view--that they are pissed because no campus will give them
tenure.   Charles Potts, I understand, used to hate univer-
sities because they wouldn't invite him and pay him to read.
And, so it goes.   Let 'em suffer, I say.   Academe won't
destroy you as a writer unless you let it.

INTERVIEWERS: Earlier this year, James Atlas discussed
"New Voices in American Poetry," in the New York Times,
and included such poets as James Merrill, Adrienne Rich,
Robert Bly, Philip Levine, and a few others.   Whom do you
think are the half dozen or so most important American poets
writing in the last two decades, and could you briefly explain
why you selected them?

PETERS: That's a big order--but here's a try.   My listing
is not a ranking:

Denise Levertov: One of the rare women writing in
America who has really been significantly touched by Black
Mountain/Projective Verse.   Most other women sound like re-
treads of Edna St. Vincent Millay (I first heard this compari-
son in a splendid talk Marjorie Perloff gave at an MLA ses-
sion in San Francisco); or, they are apt to be semi-literate
journalists.   I have been very moved by Levertov, and was,

long before she chose my first book Songs for a Son (1967)
for the W. W. Norton Poetry series she was editing. She is
the first contemporary poet I heard read who sent chills
through me and made me feel that I should write.

Galway Kinnell: He taught me that you could extol
"body rags" and visceral matter--gross, painful, sensuous
details; viz. , suffering porcupines and bears (and humans).
Body Rags is a major book. I learned a lot from him about
being ruthlessly honest regarding your life.

James Dickey: He was the first professional to say
that I had possibilities as a poet--but it is not for this kiss
that I list him here. His Wesleyan Press books are original
and stunning--the work of a zooming, loner-poet, an authen-
tic voice speaking through a Roethkian pattern of moving lyri-
cal writing. He's spun me around. I owe him much.

Robert Bly: Magnificent energy-mover, risk-taker,
stirring writer. He's escaped the doldrums of early success.
He is Growth. Bly is one of the very few poets of my gen-
eration who has not fallen off from his early achievements.
Few poets keep me guessing as much as he does--and that's
how his energies flash forth. The fact, too, that so many
half-assed poets and critics leap on him is evidence to me
of the sha-zam-bam power of his life and work.

Robert Duncan: The best poet of his generation of
Black Mountain/San Francisco Beat-and pre-Beat Poets. He
refuses to play the macho, ill-educated brainless games some
of his contemporaries play. He never writes down, and com-
mands the attention you give to the most difficult poetry. I
don't feel that he is imitable--which simply means that his
voice is his own. More than any poet on this list, he feeds
numerous literary traditions into our current poetry--from
the Middle Ages and the days of the jongleurs and maidens
forward.

Kenneth Rexroth: The daddy of many of us ... whose
powers remain undiminished. I don't understand why he is
so neglected by younger writers. He's a first-rate poet--and
critic--and translator.

John Ashbery: He's a fascinating reversion to Words-
worth--a refurbished, chatty, neo-Romantic. His humor,
brains, creative forms, all drawing from a vast array of
experience (art, trash, travel, regrets, past writers) are

impressive. And I admire his unpretentiousness--I feel he's sitting beside me as we both dangle our feet over the ABYSS, and he's caring and beautiful. As he says in Litany: "I am the poet; I want to talk to you. " He can talk to me anytime.

Charles Bukowski: Great dirty old man of American poetry, given to the narrative poem almost exclusively. He writes what I call "gab-poetry. " He took my eyelids off when I was first writing poems in the sixties. I couldn't believe that any poet could write so freely about beauty, disaster, drunks, whores, screwing, touting and get away with it. I read him first while attending a boring string quartet concert. I had to leave the music--I was overwhelmed. Bukowski makes one's genitals purr and not many poets do that. When CB is appointed Consultant in Poetry to the Library of Congress, for at least three terms, I'll know that American poetry is in good shape.

Cynthia Macdonald: She's been there with the outrageous and the misshapen. She has immense lyrical gifts, brains, and a stunning sardonicism. Her poems jolt you into intense reflection. She's the Diane Arbus of American poetry. Energy and great originality, and a fearless view of life.

Helen Adam and Alfred Starr Hamilton: A pair of superb, neglected talents. I am not hinting that they should be lovers, by grouping them here. Both in their ways reflect the trend of the poet as primitive. Adam returns to the great folk ballads of European tradition; Hamilton, sadly neglected, is the Charles Ives of American poetry.

So, perhaps this is pretty long-winded, but I don't see how I can shorten the list.

INTERVIEWERS: It seems impossible to understand modern literature without at some point looking into literary politics. Are you disturbed by the increasing monopoly of the book industry and growing relationships between publishing and films? Have small presses and cooperatives adequately provided alternatives for innovative writers who might not fit the instant movie tastes of many big publishers?

PETERS: I'm not disturbed so much by the monopoly you mention--let the movies burn! I find most movies an utter waste of time, and the chances of my selling a book of poems to the movies ... well? In Germany, maybe, but not in the U. S. Chunks of my Ludwig have been translated into German and performed in a castle north of Frankfurt--and will appear on German TV. Generally, I'm much more bothered by the literary politics transpiring among poets. Someone, for example, should do an American poetry map tracing the influence of the Iowa Workshop Program, in terms of writing program teaching positions held, prizes awarded to Iowa grads by committees of Iowa grads, etc.; the puff-reviewing of friends by friends. The in-bred Eastern poetry scene (fill in your own names, folks). The stodgy and glossy APR, Quarterly Review of Lit, etc. And out here, the ambitious language-poetry clones: They seem to have sat down and said: "How can we form a school and get noticed? Well, we can publish one another, give public talks via theorizing about what we are doing, boycott readings by poets not in our crowd, spread the gospel of the syllable and the hyphenated-gesture all around the East coast." Well, that's not fair ... but it may not be too far off the mark. So it goes.

When I raise these issues and complaints, I am frequently asked: "But hasn't poetry always been a matter of cliques?" Perhaps so. But that don't make it right. And consider the yearly flaps over the NEA and CCLM awards. Buddies look after buddies. And the screaming by the passed-overs and the left-outs is obscene.

There's no good answer, I guess. But I believe that one of my functions as a critic is to expose some of the crap as I see it; hence, my controversial pieces on APR and Poetry Chicago in Bake-Off; and the piece in this book on the pretty boring new National Poetry Series launched with James Michener's generous bucks.

INTERVIEWERS: Do you think American small presses are in a period of renaissance or stagnation? How would you compare the present state with small presses in the sixties?

PETERS: I don't know really what American small presses are doing--there are so many of them, it's hard to keep up. I do see small press books and magazines, and most of my own 15 or so poetry titles have been published by them. In the sixties, small press stuff seemed less sanitized than it does now--trashier, more mimeographed, badly put-together work. More of a raw, iconoclastic energy then. Now, because of all the money pumped in via government and state support, mags and small press books look sanitized and arty. I'm glad that Kayak is still around ... for it has maintained

its vitality and appearance through over 50 issues--a grand
longevity. It's a magazine that hasn't glossied itself up,
either in form or content. With some exceptions, I'd have
to say that American small presses are stagnant. These
exceptions include Jonathan Williams' Jargon Press, Bill
Truesdale's New Rivers Press, Plymell's Cherry Valley
editions, John Harris' Bachy Press, Mariah's ManRoot,
Cooper's Little Caesar. One fantasy I have is that all sup-
port-funding should dry up. Declare a moratorium on sub-
sidies for three or four years.

INTERVIEWERS: In the foreword to The Great American
Poetry Bake-Off you described criticism as a participatory
art, like sexual congress. Do you think that the poetry of
what you call "catatonic realism, " a phrase you use to de-
scribe the work of Charles Simic, James Tate, Victor Con-
toski, Bill Knott, Andrei Codrescu, and George Hitchcock,
might be participatory poetry? As linear thinking appears
dead in the 1980s, what trends do you foresee in tomorrow's
poetry?

PETERS: I don't see much evidence that linear thinking is
dead, despite Ashbery's poems, and some of the productions
of the so-called "language poets, " and the Ted Berrigan
acolytes. I don't see any particular trends going--just more
of the same--new generations of safe poets getting the prizes,
teaching the workshops, holding forth in the big invitational
summer fests. What I hope is that a handful of energized
poets will continue to appear who will deny the genteel solip-
sisms of Merwin, Levine, Kinnell, Hugo, Olson imitators,
and go their own way. Kill the "I" poem for starters.
Sweep poems off that kitchen stoop into the chick-weed thistles!
Perhaps poetry should return to the scope of some of the
19th-century writers--more long poems? History? Large
preoccupations--Bly with his major archetypes, Eshleman
with his jaunts through the prehistoric European caves; Dun-
can with his complex, horny transcendentalisms; my own
portraits from history. I'll pass on that "catatonic" phrase--
it works for a kind of surrealism, I think; but I find other
problems in Knott, Tate, Codrescu and Simic. Screw the
movies!

INTERVIEWERS: How does a critic keep an open mind?

PETERS: I didn't know that was a virtue for a critic? I
like to think that my tastes are fairly catholic, that I can
spot pretentious and/or good writing in any genre or style.

But, finally, the business of the critic is to have opinions and
to make fearless judgments--sometimes, yes, even making
sexual congress via the work critiqued and the published as-
sessment of it. Too, a critic should make a fair amount of
noise--be outrageous if he has to in order to make points.
Hurt even if he must. Swift and Swinburne and Lawrence
understood the values of exaggeration. At the same time, I
hope always to be fair, and don't see the critic as a Venus
fly-trap (or Mars fly-trap) juicing up poor books of poems
as a way of keeping himself alive. The critic's role has
always been a rough one--viz. the poor reviewer for the
Quarterly who supposedly killed Keats. Let's take the re-
viewer's side. And I know that when I publish naughty words
on some publicized poet I enter the lists of clubs, venoms,
and knives. My sincere hope though is that some of what I
say is valuable. I like the kind of letter that appears in my
mail now and then saying: "I'm glad you said that about so-
and-so; I've always wanted to say that about his work." Well,
why didn't you, you coward?

ON SITTING ON ONE'S THOUGHTS
TO KEEP THEM WARM:

George Quasha's Giving the Lily Back Her Hands*

George Quasha's book-blurb, plus his concluding note, plus the generous size of the book, plus the obviously loving care expended by author, wife, and friends on this self-publishing venture, led me to expect a lot more than Poetry Yum-Yum. Quasha apparently sees his book as an erotic delight; he (or his voices) and his readers (voices as partners) copulate over the text (God, that fashionable word!). He "mates" the Text and the Reader, he informs us, in a "marriage of syntax." Then, after copulation, the Text reverts to its unground from whence Lily and human hands draw power for discourse.

Well, this may be a lot to claim for a book that seems evaporative, hence, quite un-groundless. Quasha seems to believe in a concealed poemics available to a listener waiting for bleeps from poems in hiding. The bleeps constitute the Book. How effective is Giving the Lily Back Her Hands?

As a reviewer, I'd rather praise than carp. Buddy tongue-lickings and puffery require, nay demand, that a few of us who value fearless judgments make them. Jonathan Swift knew that the act of poetry--and by implication all art --is a form of defecation. Quasha himself supports the idea by telling us that he sits on his thoughts to keep them warm --an event that suggests anal retention, as does another of Quasha's remarks that a thought can cut a hole in one's sleep. The unfortunate word is cut, since in folklore "cutting a fart" is a common timeme, numereme, loceme, mudra-eme expressed best after eating beans. But, I digress. Let me confront some other issues engendered by Lily. Quasha's book is merely the occasion for my explorations of something noxious in contemporary verse. He is, in fact, a better poet

*Reprinted by permission from Contact II (Fall/Winter 1980), pp. 21-23.

than my ruminations may suggest, and I apologize for seeming
severe with him. Someone else's book may just as easily
have provoked me; but Fate operates in the lives of critics
as it does in the lives of poets--the mail produced two copies
of Lily in a single week for review; Apollo himself, I feel,
has commanded me to write.

Quasha displays some impressive learning, culled
primarily from structuralist and post-structuralist works on
language and literary theory, a smear-smorgasbord of sources.
Some terms seem invented; others are adapted from various
fashionable offal-fields; viz., Charles Olson, Roland Barthes,
Jacques Derrida, William Blake--lit-semanticist game-playings
and poetry trail-befoulings which drop words like these along
the path: phonemes mudra daimon eopoteia impersona
koan largeness muthos koanish gno mystes pression
teleos amphigologos tropofolio thememe dyslineation
loceme somapoeia sonnetistic moira eschatoerotica tmesis
engrammar paginationality a fisherman's amphibole. Dic-
tion like this spangles and glitters at the expense of real
thought and lyric qualities. There is little sufficiently finite
or concrete to retrieve deposits from that ungrounded cloaca
in the sky. Images and concepts are soon carried off by
noisome, if fashionable, zephyrs, and are soon forgotten.

Another quarrel I have relates to the first: Quasha's
poems are much about the writing of poems, without providing
us with notions fresh or new on the hoary topic. In one pas-
sage, for example, Quasha equates the writer's "length" with
his "longhand," the latter responsible for his poems or "de-
signs on time." Poems, therefore, aspire while they suspire
--that's how lyric meditations occur, folks. In another pas-
sage, evocative of Gertrude Stein trying to clear an awful
lower colon blockage, what seems an interesting, circuitously
presented idea lacks a necessary lubrication/lucubration.
Quasha is both "Anglo-Saxonistic" and "Sonnetistic" in his
"emprise." But his darling Muse, Somopoeia, gives him the
slip from her hiding place behind language.

Quasha informs us that his poems arise from Visions,
and once again he drags in poor old William Blake. I have
the feeling that American poets striving for the visionary
(and this includes Ginsberg, a sort of Babs Hutton of the
Visionary/American Dime-Store) manage to give Blake kisses
without really having read him all that well. Blake becomes
the occasion for mantras, chants, sentimental excretions, and
paste jewelry. He's a sort of organ-stop, a facile toot (tout)

for poets who want to appear more visionary than they are.
Quasha actually lets Blake off easy--he soon spins off to an-
other matter; i.e., the role of voices in a poet's work, yet
another persistent, old, Romantic notion. If voices do in-
deed dictate to us, and if as poets we are merely jotters and
notationeers, we aren't really responsible when the ideas we
receive are insipid and the writing bad.

Meditation leads Quasha to his visions. One path is
the koan, riddle. Riddles scatter all over Lily like sparrow
droppings on an unpaved schoolbus parking lot. Some of the
riddles are humorous, others are tedious: What sound does
one hand in two pockets make? How, in a world lacking
edges, do we find all things on an edge? etc. Here is a
koan employed to comment on how poems are written: If a
poet creates out of a "para-attentional intention," how can
he guarantee at all that his "sentence" will continue as he
thought, according to how it began? There's a basic con-
fusion, I feel, in Quasha's borrowing of the Master and Dis-
ciple motif. He won't make up his mind as to which of the
roles is the more congenial. At times he's the Master ad-
vising the Acolyte and dishing out koans: think a thought
about a hand writing thoughts about a hand. At other times,
he's the Acolyte forming his notions. And then there are
moments when Quasha plays both Master and Student. "Get
moving," seems to be the message: The Acolyte Master de-
cides that he doesn't care to keep on talking in koans. So
he gets up from his cushion to recapture his youth.

Quasha's apparent oscillation between controlling his
writing or being controlled by it, between being Master or
Disciple, has a disquieting ring. I don't quite trust what
he's up to, apart from demonstrating that the creative proc-
ess, despite the fancy language-grunts, and the effluences
wafting toward the sky, is somehow coprophiliac, in the sense
that the issue of writing as a mystery, as a Romantic-poet
syndrome for being seized by inspiration remains fossilized.
Quasha even goes back to Caedmon, that old Anglo-Saxon
monk-daddy of English poetry, and implores him to give it
a try.

Whenever Quasha assists my basic metaphor of writing
as defecation, I am troubled, though cheered; for he sees the
word as a half-heard sound (a fart?) with a hole around it.
From this hole a GIANT emerges, the Giant we kept from
view, as we keep hidden what we flush away before other hu-
man eyes can be offended. It is fascinating to picture Charles

Olson, the Giant of Gloucester, as Quasha calls him, emerging from said hole. Nor do I find Quasha's basic concept of his magic L, the Lily and the I (who eschews "the ordinary" --a nice moment of self-criticism), a sufficient resolution of Quasha's indecisions about the poet's role. Operatively, I and L together sound suspiciously close to Ill, a risky Aesculapian knot of petal and sinew (or vagina and penis). Lily is the muse, wife, center, who seems to birth pronouns for the poet, so that he can construct a textual We. The sexual-textual union, described as Writing, is one of the most original moments in Lily. Poet connects with Lily via the juices of an "inconclusive syntax." He craves to conjoin, but is too pursued by Furies of the Text. Lily shrieks to him in tmesis. As he bends over the poem (anus? penis?), he grows "long in the hand."

Quasha's imagination seems exciting here; but, finally, easy concepts and a monotonous breath-grouping of sounds take over. What Quasha produces is a tour de force of linked energies male and female. There is a problem, though, since sexual differences, as Lilith mounts poet-Adam, are undifferentiated. Do they exist on an "unground?" If Lily-Lilith is the femme fatale inspiring the poem, she is also capable of giving the poet VD or shredding him slowly to pieces between her steaming teeth. Perhaps, Quasha is saying, the male-female roles aren't all that dissimilar: Can you really tell a female anus from a male anus? Charles Manson liked to conduct demonstrations in which his stripped followers would lean over a bar so that squeamish acolytes could observe that we are indeed alike, anus-wise, male and female. What Manson sought was an easy sexual congress between the sexes. If this is what Quasha is saying, more subtly than I have, terrific! There's originality here after all.

Though I have carped much about the many faults of Lily, there are pleasures to be found. And I write not out of distaste for Quasha himself, or of his blend of fashion and tradition. What I complain most of is the Myth-Malady, Milady, and of the Semantics Hang-Up so prevalent in current American verse. It's as if American poets--many of them lack advanced academic degrees and seem to need compensations--are trying to prove that they are not after all untaught, ignorant slobs. Their pursuit of the arcane becomes a means of infusing poetry with cultural starch, learning, and brains.

I applaud these efforts; American writers, both poets and fictioneers, have too long played the rube and the oaf, despising the intellectual tradition of Europe by pretending that the imagination is at its best a form of natural genius. Quasha, in his favor, has brains.

Obviously when the pursuit of the arcane goes mad, when the bowels are too loose, vapidity, Ladogonian project-poetry, mind-fucking verse results. Sounding cerebral, rather than being cerebral, and settling for what amounts to little more than Automatic Writing, as dictated by Lilies and Hands and Raptures, denies the lyric thrust of good poetry. The bowels of the reader, like those of the poet, compact, and the straining to be free produces hemorrhoids.

Walt Whitman boasted that he kept himself clean about the bowels, as evidence of his reverence for his body.   I realize that to remind my readers of this gross side of Whitman is not the best way, perhaps, to conclude this essay. But we are possessed of rectums, useful even when soiled; and, as Whitman knew so well, the writing of poems is of the intestines as much as it is of the brain and heart.   We need well-lubricated poet-colons.   Let the structuralists, post-structuralists and their kind plug themselves tight with El-mer's glue as they sit on their thoughts to keep them warm. What they come up with has little to do with awe-thentic poetry.

POLARITIES:

Wendy Rose's Long Division: A Tribal History and
Elizabeth Marraffino's Blue Moon for Ruby Tuesday*

Here are two new books by young American poets:
Wendy Rose is an established Native American poet and
artist; Elizabeth Marraffino is a New Yorker appearing in
book form for the first time. Both women write of personal
obsessions. But beyond this vague connection there are many
dissimilarities, ones worth discussing since they touch di-
rectly on the matter of political vs. personal poetry.

I.

Wendy Rose is in her early thirties and has an im-
pressive list of books to her credit. Her ancestry is both
Hopi and white; but as one reads her one soon finds that her
Hopi blood generates her joys and angers. Her Anglo-Saxon
self is almost entirely subdued. And I welcome this; for
many poets I've read, writing in the voices of primitives,
be they Indian, African, or Eskimo, write a kind of Tarzan-
talk. Their leapings about the primitive poetry-fire lack a
sophistication of word and feeling, and undercut, I feel, the
complexities of primitive oral art.

This is not true of Rose. Her opening poem, "Mis-
sion Bells," is an indictment of white exploitations of the
redman, rendered in subtle imagery and diction. The Cali-
fornia Mission, the scene of the poem, is, of course, Roman
Catholic. Indian poets, Rose writes, have not guarded their
tribal "copal incense" well, and have allowed it to "slink
nearly visible" into the dank corners of the church. A white-
man enters, sniffs, and declares that the interior "smells

---

*Both books are available from the publisher, Contact II, at
PO Box 451, Bowling Green Station, NY 10004. Rose: ISBN
0-936556-02-1, 42pp., with drawings by Meredith Peters,
paper, $3.00. Review of Rose's Long Division appeared in
The Greenfield Review: American Indian Writings (Winter 1981-
82), pp. 212-214.

like a Catholic Church. " He is reassured, for he has hoped
to elude the "native wind" of Hopi hostility "rushing" to sim-
mer in his beard.   Yet even there he can't escape; and this
is why, Rose says, that the Hopi must continue their barely
audible singing--Indian venom must never die.   As a people,
the Indians remain threatened, as Rose's stunning closing
image reveals: the presidio bells, symbols of the religion
of the white destroyer, can

> ... still ring
> and swing in the air
> smashing us
> like so many red bugs
> between the silver clapper
> and the sound.

The poem is prefaced by a pair of early nineteenth-century
remarks.   One is by a Catholic priest who compares the
Indians to monkeys who do "naught" of interest but imitate
the whites, "whom they respect as being much superior to
themselves. "   The second, by F. W. Beechy, urges the
government to keep the missions thriving, as a means of
guaranteeing national prosperity.

Rose's title poem, "Long Division: A Tribal History, "
displays invention of a high order.   Metaphorically, the skins
of all persecuted Indians merge into a vast, rent hide on
poles, a kind of burial tarp, stretched over a desert-mountain
expanse.   The tribe itself appears utterly dead.   Rose apoth-
eosizes her lost people; their skins have become the land,
lending it their hues.   Their blood has spread from their
bodies to fray "the sunset edges. / It's our blood that gives
you / those southwestern skies. "   But tribal hope persists,
though tribal songs and poetry have evaporated, leaving the
poet embittered and grieving:

> Year after year we give,
> harpooned with hope, only to fall
> bouncing through the canyons,
> our songs decreasing
> with distance.
> I suckle coyotes
> and grieve.

In the next poem, Rose turns sardonic towards anthro-
pologists.   These folk, one assumes, would have compassion
for the exploited Indian.   But, to the anthropologists, Indians

are "pottery," watched over for any forthcoming "exotic pots
of words" spilled from their "coral and rawhide tongues."
A sardonic chant-like couplet follows: "O we are / the Na-
tives." The poem closes with a stanza loaded with details
from nature. The "sounds" of Indian silence are "juniper
essays," and may be "read" only in the hardy branches of
that hardy tree. To catch these ancient sounds, one must
first enter the vastness of a southwestern landscape. One
must then listen for the "reverse snap" of a leaf at 30 degrees
below zero, the sounds of a squirrel leaping from tree to
tree, and the tired "bending round" of cactus loaded with snow
ready to fall--these evoke the sounds of a lost culture. On
this aging planet Earth--Rose sees it as "a leaf with bent
edges beginning to turn color"--some "old and pagan" part
of the world continues to hold on, as tenaciously as the wood-
ticks clinging to the speaker's skin. Hopis must sharpen their
ears, Rose says, if they are to persist.

The ensuing poems celebrate love, and move from the
wrath of the first poems to fresh personal discoveries of self
and friends. "Old ones" appear to Rose in a vision and sing
and dance for her. They have the vividness of wood shavings
sparked with fire.

In "Between the Guitar Strings," a musician sings a
desperate tale of murder and love:

... We are between the guitar strings

hearing of the young man
who lives through his woman's torment,

whose song has bloody and murdered words
that rushed from lips trying to mold

crescents and squares into the thighs
of lost and brown women. And the one woman

who was drawn to him, who drew away from him,
who smeared her pain and early-birthing blood

onto him where stained like an ancient prophecy
it sings in his throat

and looks out from his eyes. It's this way
the poet gave life, with both hands raised up,

to an infant
two years unborn.

Another singer and musician, Ron Tanaka, sings the pain of
his people. To know his "soul" is to know ancient caves.
As he sings, his hearers tell him:

In our sleep
we are layered with your pain.
How you sing
those old mountain songs.

The closing section, "Serenity," reflects Rose's sense of
herself as she ages, when, she hopes, her poems will remain
vital for all Indian children who will create cat's cradles out
of them; i. e. , will absorb them into their daily lives, for
sustenance. In "The Parts of a Poet," Rose relates herself
and her art to an earth-force: Parts of her creative-spiritual
self she finds "pinned to earth"; other parts are spread over
water, form beautiful rainbow bridges in the sky, and follow
the sandfish through the streams. Readers interested in more
of Rose's poetry than this chapbook contains can obtain her
Lost Copper (Malki Museum Press, Morongo Indian Reserva-
tion, Banning, California 92220), a large collection of work,
lavishly illustrated with reproductions of her paintings.

II.

Elizabeth Marraffino's world is much more limited
than Rose's; and to introduce Ruby Tuesday I was ready to
say that a Third World poet is obliged to reflect political-
social conundrums that a white poet is not. The latter seems
freer to pursue the private trammels of the heart. Of
course, my conjecture is silly, for whites have plenty of ills
to write about. Possibly, a poet like Marraffino who seems
in full withdrawal from social ills is, in fact, protesting--her
need to hide may in itself be a comment on the times. But
I'm pretty nebulous. Marraffino writes in her own clear voice,
with a special vividness, and does not need my theorizing
about her lack of grand intentions. She writes, in this book
at least, out of private hurts. She is a poet of wounded love.

Ruby Tuesday has three sections. In the first, Marraf-
fino describes her persisting hunger for a lover who left her
some three years earlier. She writes to him that she is
"more interesting now. " She dreams of him perpetually, pro-

jecting his image, idealized, beyond a "swarming / meadow of stars." In another poem, he is the sun, and she cools him in her arms. She sees his face in the faces of several current lovers.

Her hunger derives from her hurt over Danny's rejection of her. Her psyche craves to have a chance to do better, to be less naive in bed, less afraid of abandoning herself sexually. She was "not the woman" she seemed, she now tells him. How could he know that she was ignorant? She fantasizes their rejoining in earthy terms. They now meet under the ground, tunnelling their way as "strong roots growing finer and finer." They will know an incredible joy at "the first touch of tiny hair to tiny hair." In contrast to the earlier turbulence of their loving, this new connection will be utterly simple:

> only the barely reaching heat of the sun
> the shifting dampness from distant rain
> will feel us tremble as we join
> at last so simply.

The second section, of 14 poems, is much quieter. The poems move easily, and, except for three or four, are self-evident in their themes. In one of the best, the mother of the lover watches her son copulate. His archings and grindings recall his being born. The idea is effective, especially in the final pair of lines where Marraffino's voice takes over and ridicules the lover for the ineffectual look of his penis after orgasm:

The smell of cradles.

A man I know remembers his mother's breast, his hands kneading it, his first hungers. Do you remember, or does your mind reach further into the half-light, red chapel, the water candle, food dancing into your belly, direct, warm, wet.

> As you press against her underskin
> your lover
> lets you be born, biting through her womb
> you slit her belly, the arteries
> ruptured by your small white teeth.

> And shining through the light bulb, your mother
> watches you once more
> arch your back, slip, thrust, leap, dart forward:
> a dolphin. The completed double helix
> discovers first light:
> new son, red naked
> skin rough as your cock
> lying outside the vagina, spent.

Marraffino's primary issue--how to deal with the pain of a lost love--is universal. The problem is almost a cliché. In this image, though, Marraffino is quite fresh: That terrible ache becomes a fish-shape which goes through a scary transformation:

> When your love leaves you pretend
> your body's made of empty places
> to be furnished by a fish-shaped thing
> that nests there, gnaws,
> expands into a human face
> right out of you
> until it sheds your womb
> onto the beach with the useless pretty shells.

In Part III, "Bondage," Marraffino returns to full-scale wrath, with a vengeance. She hides in her lover's veins "like ice or asphalt." When he asks what bearing a child is like, she shouts that it's "near to being a cannibal." He isn't listening. She's enraged. His "pulse rains blood and salt water" over her. She imagines that she flutters into his throat, as "a hemorrhage, or hummingbird." She wants to destroy him. A truce follows. He says she isn't beautiful, that he dislikes her black hair, feels threatened by it. She considers combing it all out and going bald, for his pleasure. More argument. She fantasizes nailing his skin over the window so that the sun-heat will shrivel it. What we hear now is an awful desperation as Marraffino tries to force the male back into loving her. She seems to want to let go, but she can't. While she sees her pettiness, and declares that she is plankton inside a whale's jaw, she doesn't lessen her fierceness. She vows to become "a blind shark" and eat the pupils out of his eyes and hang them like grisly beads from her throat. Her life, finally, becomes a drowning. The book closes on a beachscape, beneath an exploding sky, as a tidal wave roars into New York City. She runs along the edge of the wave seeking her two-faced lover before she goes under.

The irony is that he goes under. When she sees him as a speck out in the waves she seems no longer his victim; but her letting-go seems uneasy:

> Again he leaps out, pulled far and far
> a pale bobbing cork
> grows small on the edge of wet sun.
>
> Breaker after breaker shakes him off.
> Weak flea on water's back.
> Wave snaps round to unlatch his mind
> holding on, holding on, like a weed.
>
> Washed up, broken, completed in sand
> his salt-bleached skin piled on gray pebbles.

Marraffino's tenacity in pursuing what appears to be a single event so single-mindedly may leave her open to charges of a greatly limited vision. Certainly, it is easier to prefer Wendy Rose's poems because of their large expansions. Marraffino's book reads as a single poem; and I am sure that she has more books coming. My guess is that she will broaden her vision. She writes cleanly and well, and she often strikes an authentic hammer-thud.

TWO FOR SCHUYLER:

James Schuyler's The Morning of the Poem and The Home Book

The Morning of the Poem*

Schuyler's new book contains 14 "New Poems," 11 "Payne Whitney Poems," and a 60-page "The Morning of the Poem." While some of the shorter pieces are memorable-- there is a stunning elegy on W. H. Auden, a brilliant flower-passage poem ("A Name Day"), and a set of personal history poems--most seem to exist for the gloss they provide for "The Morning of the Poem." "This Dark Apartment," relating his finding his lover in bed with another man, anticipates the interwoven theme of a helter-skelter gay life. "Growing Dark," "Korean Mums," and "Heather and Calendulas" reflect his love for flowers, dogs, and pastoral settings. Other poems present the history of his reading, his friends, and his nervous breakdown. In one poem he retorts when a "clunkhead" thinks he is congratulating him by saying his poems have opened up:

> I don't want to be open,
> merely to say, to see and say, things
> as they are.

We discover, those of us not in the Schuyler, O'Hara, Koch, Ashbery, Rivers circle, that his first lover, now dead of cancer, was Bill Aalto--and in a sense the long "Morning" is an elegy for him.

So, certain themes and motifs unify Schuyler's poems --as does a certain unique tone. He writes a passage of Keatsian beauty, then puffs it with a colloquialism, often a

---

*Reprinted by permission from Northeast Rising Sun (Fall/ Winter 1980), pp. 38-39.

fey one. I suppose he does this to prevent any self-pity
over his aging, breakdown, disappearing sexual life, and
troubles with his aging mother. In "Afterward," a nice pun
on hospital ward, he recounts some of his recent physical
and mental turmoils. His conclusion? "It's funny to be free
again." In another place, he calls himself "worm food."
Of Human Bondage, written, he says, "by one of the most
over-rated writers of all time," converted him to atheism.
In the first mental hospital poems, he finds that at 51, he
("Jim the Jerk") is still alive and breathing--a miracle.

In my commentary on "Morning" I'm going to develop
a motif from the very end of the poem as an overall motif.
I'll call it the "Golden Shower" motif, which has to do, of
course, with giving pleasure to people who like to be urinated
on. The sixty pages of "Morning" conclude with Schuyler re-
porting that he has to piss, and, as so often happens through-
out these lines, a reminiscence is triggered. He returns to
Paris and his having to urinate so badly he can't wait--al-
though there is a pissoir across the street. By holding his
penis, he makes it, but can't pull it out in time. So he
stands there with the piss drenching his pants. He regrets
that he hasn't worn dark clothes, so the accident wouldn't
be so visible. But then, he figures, he'll move on: It's
their problem if they stare and are offended.

Well, what does piss have to do with his poem?
Since he writes with a beautiful urgency throughout, as a
means of coming to terms with his aging and eventual death,
and of recollecting important events in his life from child-
hood forwards, the poem reads as something he could no
longer retain--his poetry-bladder is filled to bursting.

In a sense, the joke is on him; for he is clothed during
this poem, seated in a window, while a young friend (who
doesn't want to be touched), a sexual turn-on, paints him.
The writing of the poem, then, is a self-drenching; and, as
part of Schuyler's unique, winsome playfulness, it's a drench-
ing of us, too.

Before the reader dismisses my idea as too odious,
and evidence of my own desire to sit in an old bathtub sur-
rounded by beautiful men, let me hasten to say that the urine
motif, as scatological as it may seem, does here work with
an almost metaphysical showering--life with its gross complex
of pain and pleasure, milk and urine, peanut-butter and feces
adds up to as much, metaphorically. So it seems to work

for Schuyler--and so it possibly works for us, in our lives.

The poem approaches the idea of Schuyler's eventual death in various ways: The lead image is of Baudelaire's skull. Baudelaire, Whitman, and Heine gather around Schuyler's death-bed to say goodbye. A superbly moving passage commemorates the death of his friend Bill Aalto. This passage recalls some of the best, more intimate, traditional pastoral elegies--those of Shelley, Tennyson, and Arnold. Among Schuyler's events are these: A young Virginian, despised by his family, eats crushed castor beans and supposedly dies. Various people Schuyler has known as a child are gone--Mr. and Mrs. Blank, a virile youth crushed by a car against a wall. His nagging mother, a bit dotty, ages and finally dies.

The animal world, as well, impresses him with its mortality--another stark evocation of his own fears. There's an incredible image of a bloated Holstein cow floating in water: "a ship of furry flesh, its udder like a motor." His pet whippet, Whippoorwill, is evoked. And when Schuyler meditates on the possibility that some day on this planet some living creature will be granted immortality, his choice, if there is to be a single one, would be Whippoorwill.

When his own mortality shivers his bones and brain, he's sometimes funny, and never maudlin. He's a sensitive, courageous man who feels his death as "currents of damp air" on the back of his neck. When he dies, he wants "no cremation, thanks, worm food,/soil enrichment, mulch." After nights of storm, bad dreams, and hospital pills, he's amused to find he's still alive. He protects himself from hurt by saying that he knows a lot of dead people, but that he doesn't "think about them much." An irony perhaps. When he slips and smashes a kneecap, catches syphilis and Herpes simplex, he's rehearsing for that final urination. He's a bed (grave?) lover: He likes to lie there reading and feeling himself-- "shoulders, armpits, chest, belly, crotch." That way he knows he's still alive.

By stressing death in these poems as I do, I risk ignoring much else that is positive and stirring. There's a whole essay to be written on his sympathetic treatment of his (and other men's) gay sensibility. His brilliant nature writing deserves description and praise. And there is much that is positive and stunning--the long poem reads as a magnificent race with death, with much good-feeling, fun and love

along the way.   He has many times pressed joy's grape against
his "palate fine":

> Letting the oozy grape meat slide
> down my throat like an oyster: grapes,
>   oysters
> And champagne: bliss is such a simple thing.

Schuyler is a tonic to read.   By making something of
a talisman of death, as Walt Whitman did in "Out of the
Cradle Endlessly Rocking," when he exorcises his own fear
of death by repeating it often throughout "The Morning of the
Poem," he seems to say "piss on death."   "And, folks,"
he seems also to say, "if you don't want to piss on it, I will
for you."   Thus the Golden Shower of this poem is both
Danäesque and urinary.

The Home Book*

This folio of poems, journal entries, brief fictions
and other prose pieces reads like a homage of love from an
editor to a poet he admires who didn't get around to assem-
bling his own writings.   These are, apparently, various sorts
of Schuyler-writing left over from the years 1951-1970, as
edited by Trevor Winkfield.   As I read through the melange,
I kept wishing that the editor had thought more about the in-
tegrity of the book as a whole.   I'm afraid that it reads like
a sensitive and intelligent man's scrapbook of writings, rather
than any discerningly organized and structured work.   Per-
haps I miss something obvious; but I don't think so.   I end
up feeling I'm an old scarf or a pair of worn boots being
worried by a salivating white poodle.

Much of this is finger-exercise work, stunning in a
bravura way.   "The Picnic Cantata," a lengthy piece, is
representative.   It is too precious--or at least it hits me
that way.   When it ends I feel Toodle-oo-ed.   In other poems
Schuyler criticizes a sterile middle-class life.   In yet others
he seems to parody a middle-class faggot life--see the camp
rhymes ("I never miss the garden section./It describes heaven
to perfection.") and the Three-Kittens-Who've-Lost-Their-

---

*Reprinted by permission from Stony Hills (Spring 1980),
   p. 7.

Mittens ("Oh, dear, look here, we forgot all about/the rad-
ishes/and the relish").

      There are other preciosities: A poem about his post-
cards <u>must</u> have a French title: "Voyage au tour de mes
cartes <u>postales.</u> "   Now, this may be nicely in with the Whit-
ney Museum crowd, but to those of us out here <u>in</u> the hinter-
lands munching the "tumescent weight" of drago<u>nfl</u>y wings and
gazing through the "Gothic tracery and spires" of our lives,
we can't much dig it.   Poor slobs!   The clue piece of the
volume, I'd say, is "Four Poems: for Frank O'Hara, " where
Schuyler wonderfully captures O'Hara's more faggoty tone,
all camp and queeny.   O'Hara was indeed an <u>adverb poet,</u>
one of our finest (as Creeley is our poet fot <u>it,</u> Hemingway
for <u>and).</u>   <u>Very</u> and <u>really</u> hinge his flip-poem wrist bones
toge<u>ther.</u>   A<u>nd</u> the ca<u>sual</u> obscenities make one want to wash
the little lad's mouth out with soap.   This is, then, I feel,
an aficionado volume--if you love Schuyler's work already
you will want to own this book.   It's a handsomely produced
piece of publishing--a coat of many colors, in pastels.

TIME-STOPS OF THE SPIRIT:

Carolyn Stoloff's Swiftly Now

In this, her fifth book of poems, Carolyn Stoloff's
primary motifs are sun, wind, seeds, and small creatures--
ants, moths, and birds. The landscape is New Mexican. As
resident of Taos, she considers and absorbs scenes and events
with unusual clarity. She scales herself down to the minute
in nature. Her emotions exfoliate from seeds of feeling; like
desert weeds and wild poppies germinating from hard seeds
in the baked earth, caressed by wind and thunder-storms,
these come to fruition as a wealth of petals.

Stoloff, a New Yorker, is entirely at home in her
Western locale; and she might have lavished her time ren-
dering the vast, monumental sweeps of deserts and mountain
ranges--scenes so vast one can gaze for miles of an after-
noon and observe half-a-dozen vivid thunderstorms transpiring
at once. She might have echoed the painter Georgia O'Keeffe,
who has spent a long life evoking Western grandeur. Even
her close-ups of bleached skulls and flamboyant flowers are
monumental; we respond as we do to vistas of great land-
scape reaches. But Stoloff's approach is different. While
O'Keeffe works for the grand transcendental form, Stoloff
prefers the more Aristotelian look--her vision is of the patch
of earth rather than of the expansive sky. Small birds and
insects peregrinate over, under, and through her scenes.
Seeds burgeon. She is content to scrutinize moments of ex-
foliation. After a vigorous afternoon rain, pupae unfold into
butterflies, and a weed-stalk bursts forth with an ephemeral
blossom shimmery with beauty. She is a poet of the intimate
close-up. Her takes define her immediate space; and, at
their best, her definitions evoke psychic landscapes of force
and beauty.

A short poem, "Vespers," effectively displays her
mode. Present are both vastness and restriction; the former

337

makes sense only in terms of the latter. A bird flashes past,
and, for a moment, "mars" the "lustrous rose" of the sun-
set. A meadowlark sings. These swift impressions lead to
this potently expressed wish for a deep union with the earth:

> I'd like to thrust my spine
> like a spear in earth
> let it leaf!

The wish itself, via a natural germination and flow, eventually
glides "like sound" into the horizon, into its "running gold"
wound. The result is spiritual botany; the transcendental oc-
curs via the germinative, from the loam upwards. And since
the flow in "Vespers" occurs within four short stanzas (eleven
lines), the result suggests time-stop photography: the ten-
sion of the poem moves from spine to plant to flower to the
sunset.

In "Evening Meal," the sky is a "banquet of color."
Stoloff's small house has become "all window." She smells
the spiced aroma of sage, as she steps (a concrete act) into
the "still balm" of evening, a balm that soothes the motions
of ants on their hills and the birds roosting in trees. With
her feet "firm on the land" she regards the sky, discerning
"radiant pheasant-clouds" and lambs "from the fatted flock."
She devours this rich feast, washing it down "with a cool
quart of sky," and is restored in spirit. The clouds turn to
"peach fluff" as the twilight falls.

One of her longer poems, "A Piece of Light," inter-
weaves her motifs in complex ways. An ant attempts to carry
a fly, "big as a truck," up a wall. The ant never succeeds.
He climbs part-way, drops the fly, and has to start all over
again. As she observes, Stoloff recalls an acquaintance, a
counter-culture pilgrim, who reports on her two-year trek
towards "light." The woman's tough bare feet reveal her
life. She's lived under pine-branches and tarps in the moun-
tains. Axes, she says, are "more honest" than chain-saws.
People, particularly Indians, have been good to her. She's
lived off nuts, beans, grains, and boiled lily-buds.

As Stoloff remembers the woman, a sense of the
present weaves in. A car passes, throwing dust all over
the phlox outside her window; and she returns to the ant
struggling with the fly. Why does the creature make its
home up in the beams of her house? She casts some of the
light she has used to illuminate the ant and the hippie over

herself now. Her seed-plantings are equivalents for the re-
petitions of ant and woman. Whether the seeds will produce
light, i. e. , germinate, is always unclear. Stoloff plants in
good faith, and is nervous as she searches the soil for signs
of sprouting; but she sees none. She must learn patience,
as ant and woman have had to. Her urgings of the seeds
to sprout lead to this partly-wry observation: She also shells
her "particular nut / for a piece of light." Experience, then,
is a matter of repetitions performed on the hard, resistant
plane of this mineral-vegetable earth. Our destiny is to
foster growth, to believe that our plantings will result in
flowers. Each of us has his seed (his nut) to nurture.

In "Passage," vividly rendered particulars lead Stoloff
to a kind of transcendence. The sunlight she walks through,
on a desert road, is "solid butter." Pebbles, "barley size,"
impede her walk. She observes a rosebush and imagines its
feet drinking deep down in the desert soil. She walks all
day. At noon the hills "slip" into a "yellow skin." When
afternoon arrives, Stoloff feels a sense of someone (a lover?)
absent. The glaring yellow light reflects the actuality of her
days. And the days, like pebbles, resemble barley-grains
in the sweep of time. Dusk arrives with its "shadow-spills,"
followed by "night's ocean." Interesting here are the hints
of a private longing, one that might easily have turned con-
fessional. But Stoloff is too much the artist to allow this.
Resolutions of personal doubt, longing, and pain appear and
almost immediately shave off into some natural event (light-
fall, shower, storm, sunset). In a sense, she steps aside
from her own private cravings in order to gaze at them with
a clarity similar to that she expends on birds, insects, and
plants. The result is a largeness, a universalizing of her
experience that satisfies us greatly.

One of her most effective concretizings of vastness
appears at the close of "Behind the Hour." Once again, she
focuses on a patch of light. In the "fine flour" of this light,
numerous "ragged locusts crawl," symbols of old private
"quirks." At the same time, desert gusts vigorously shake
a tree. "Green-gold clusters" of ripening plums fall. Stol-
off takes up a bleached animal skull, one she has probably
found on a walk, and observes it:

> four firm teeth
> no strings attached
> no sour grass scent
> or mobile lip

> sawdust from broken rock
> spills
> from its holes

If there are "poor Yorick" tones here, they are greatly un-
derplayed. The memento mori is Stoloff's own:

> dry bells rustle
> I exchange breaths
> with the dark nostrils
>
> behind every hour

"After Labor Day" is an evocation of human mortality
envisioned through a natural image. The poem is a medita-
tion on a grasshopper about to deposit her eggs and die.
Stoloff's excitement and affection for the delicate creature
arises from a lyric energy, evidence again of Stoloff's ability
to feel herself into an object she describes, in a few deft
strokes. She is not a word-painter, or an embroiderer of
purple passages. Her techniques are more akin to those
found in the paintings and drawings of Paul Klee or Joan
Miró, where a precisely but quickly-rendered detail evokes
an entire bird, flower, or landscape.

Stoloff observes grasshoppers proceeding "this way or
that," all "up ... around ... and under" pigweed stems. A
hopper in flight excites her. There's a "gasp of vermilion
skirts," as the creature leaps. Another hovers nearby,
"clacking her castanets," before plopping to earth. One hop-
per will shortly "sink" her "ovipositor" into clay, and, once
her eggs are laid, will become a "tatterdermalion," will
crawl beneath "some dry rosette," and there will die.

The concluding stanza is affectionate; and in the sim-
plicity of its tone produces a chill--for Stoloff is really
writing about us:

> I used to wonder where you go
> I guess I know
> a spring   a summer   and one fall
> that's it

"Swiftly Now," the title poem, embroiders this same
theme, of the grace of our dying into nature, as a smooth
natural process. Distant horses seem like small "piano ham-
mers" silhouetted against "chill gusts." There's another bril-

liant sunset. Nearer, " a bird drops / to a brown fist / asway
on its hairy stem / to tug a seed from its cell. " Heads
of flowers, "darker" than night, fall to the asphalt as a "lit-
ter" of notes. The poem closes with this composed moment:

> what won't give gracefully
> breaks I guess

Stoloff's perceptions make her a sort of botanist-
biologist of the spirit. Her special curiosity emerges from
her fascination with life's concreteness. She never gushes,
and knows when to rein in a visual effect in order to suggest
symbolic properties. While she is primarily a celebratory
poet, her wonder leads her to a tough-minded view of the
cyclic sweep of natural events. Her time-stops on nature
occur with the shutter of her camera always wide open. Be-
cause she is never pre-programmed, her surprise (and awe)
often unsettles her. When this occurs, Stoloff is merely
doing what painters and poets have always done who have
guided us to see their visions in the minute forms about us.
Holbein observed a pink in a man's hand, Dürer a hare,
Burns a mouse, Dickinson a robin eating a worm, Rossetti
a three-cupped woodspurge. Each of these seeings generates
its own conundrum: Is the man holding the pink greater than
the flower he holds? Is the flower more than the man? Is
the poet observing the mouse or the robin larger than the
event witnessed? It is exactly such conundrums that Stoloff
confronts. My conclusion is that she is larger than her
events because she contains them all. She has seen, heard,
tasted, and felt them, and she knows their profound over-
tones. These latter she has generously shared with us in
her new book.

COFFINS OF WIND:

Mark Strand's The Late Hour*

1.

My pleasure in any good poet transcends conflict: I
don't see poets as enemies. But, for better or for worse,
the critic must play wolf-roles, especially when poems gen-
erate in him little else than a tedious conjugality. I wish I
could help Strand feel less lost, elegiac, submissive, self-
pitying. How many times an hour, dear reader, can you
face mirrors of snow and fading light, little stabs of sorrow,
wind-coffin miseries and not feel dulled? A body of bliss?
We find on our tongues instead: "Ah, poor me!" We are
"such small beings" travelling "in the dark/with no visible
way/or end in sight." I want Strand to burst graves open,
to make his flesh dance, to scream out his negations in
tornados, to rev up his moon-pallor with rainbows, to cease
graying his quasi-visions into ashes before they are born. I
miss seams in most of The Late Hour. And, seamless poems
lack savor. A bored God sits in the Celestial Armchair spin-
ning out seamless poems. Though laced with ambrosia and
frosted with ichor, God's saliva might better impress us if
there were an unseemly trace or two of a passing oyster.
In The Late Hour no thrill zooms from foot-sole, up perine-
um, past navel and nipple, to one's topmost hair follicles.

2.

It follows, as surely as Atheneum Inc. follows Strand,
that literary criticism is a form of speleology. Our entry
into the subterranean world of the book is its cover, cave-

*Reprinted by permission from American Book Review (Octo-
ber 1979), p. 21.

cover, an adit. In The Late Hour, we find 25 poems, two
of them adaptations from Charles Dickens and from de Andrade,
for the price of $6.95 Speleologically speaking, it's an over-
priced cave. Inside Strand Cavern stalactites and stalag-
mites, like geriatric lion's teeth, are worn down. In this
"kingdom of rot," there's much room for roaming. Some 25
poems sit around as shrouded ashen tombstones. "About a
Man," "Exiles," "Where are the Waters of Childhood" by
contrast have a tenuous grace. Clearly, Strand has not lost
his special meditative lyric gifts. This handful of poems al-
most redeems the others. In these, your face shines back
at you--for these are glimmering pools rather than tomb-
stones. As in most good caves, the mystical is very misty:
glimmers disappear at the very moment you think you've
caught them. Can you be sure of their depths? Can you
wade through them without drowning? Do they contain eye-
less fish? Where is the guano?

3.

When poems lacerate language, energy booms. Ameri-
can poets (Merwin, Kinnell, Strand, Snyder) confuse easy
stances as philosopher poets with poet-wizardry. Alexander
Pope gave the lie to the act: Poets can't be philosophers:
if they try they merely warm over yesterday's lentil soup
and old fried chicken. When Strand complains that in "these
days ... there is little/to love or to praise," or refers to
that "place/beyond/beyond love,/where nothing,/everything,/
wants to be born," I feel conceptually underprivileged. Nor
does his cutting up these pallid thoughts into macaroni lines
achieve for me the momentousness and originality he seems
to want them to convey. Camus and Sisyphus have tainted a
lot of creative minds. And there is no booming when Strand
"mirrors " well-known moments from other poets, viz., the
trivialized Rilke of "Pot Roast" when Strand almost changes
his life and no longer regrets "the passage of time;" or, the
nod towards Roethke's far field in "the field's edge" ("Poem
of Air"); or, the trivializing of de Andrade by the lather of
first-name allusions to a list of friends; or, the Eliotesque
tones throughout "White"; or, the echo of the birdlessness
of Shakespeare's "bare ruined choirs"; or, finally, the Dylan
Thomasese of "in the drift and pitch of love." His "adapta-
tion" of a passage from Chapter XLVIII of Dickens' Bleak
House, since it raises general problems about such adapta-
tions, is worth some scrutiny. Always, there is the prob-
lem of quality: Is the adaptation an improvement over the

original, be it poetry or prose? Strand's adaptation, I find,
is generally inferior in diction and force to his model.   Here
are a pair of instances: Strand substitutes the flat "on de-
serted roads and hilltops" for Dickens' "dusty high roads
and on hill-summits"; Strand substitutes "thousands of stars"
for "a multitude of stars," and dissipates energy by adding
a pretty vapid passage not found in Dickens:

> It is a still night, a very still night
> and the stillness is everywhere.

This seems an echo of the stale, vapid diction of one of Matthew
Arnold's more spectacular failures, "A Summer Night."
What Strand contributes of his own is the ecology theme mere-
ly hinted at in the original--mildew, oil slick, urine, empty
bottles, tires, rusty cans, etc.   The rich-poor contrast con-
cluding Strand's adaptation is, I feel, much more energetically
and imaginatively handled by Dickens.   My guess is that C. D.
would not much appreciate this easy passage: "And the poor
in their tenements speak to their gods/and the rich do not
hear them...." For me, Strand fails to generate the imagina-
tion to match or surpass Dickens; he drops between trying to
evoke Dickens and trying to be himself.   There's an implicit
problem here: If you write "adaptations" and the result is
mere "writing," needed to fill up an already slim book, why
not try an original poem of your own instead? Let the splen-
dor of Dickens remain intact; don't whittle away with pen-
knives.

4.

The casual critic/reader, anxious to be fashionable,
uncritically accepts new books by poets widely-revered, no
matter how derivative, enervated, pompous, slight, or ex-
pensive.   These poets are fetishes, and fetishes demand little
of us except admiration, a good belly-stroke or two (particu-
larly if they are popular on the female-college reading circuit),
and some cash.   Fetishist Fun keeps a lot of American poets
in motion.   Fame rests on a prostatory glow--you rub mine,
I'll rub yours, etc.   If poems were girl-scout cookies, poets
would spend most of their days brushing crumbs from one an-
other's faces.

5.

Alas, memorable images are rare in Strand's poems.

He seems to have whitened most of them away. When such
images appear, a reversal towards excitement occurs: We
feel we are in the presence of talent. In "Poor North, "
Strand's wind "beats around in its cage of trees. " I perk
up. In another poem, a woman in bed beside her lover
"stares at scars of light/trapped in the panes of glass. " In
"Snowfall" snow is "the negative of night. " Poetry makes it
after all. In "Seven Days, " the person addressed appears
inside "a glass pillar filled with bright dust. " Yet another
fine image is of gulls wheeling "in loud broken rings. " But
isn't that a near-steal from old W. B. Yeats?

6.

A poet too-easily traps himself inside a kind of insidi-
ous heroism when he sees himself as an Ur-Mensch, as
Adam, exteriorizing the universe ur-ly. He thinks there's a
pregnant voice behind everything he writes. He spews forth
narcissistic little phrase/word droplets, personal pronouns--
as in this random assembling from "Pot Roast": "I gaze up-
on the pot roast ... I spoon the juices ... I sit by a window
... I do not regret ... I see no living thing ... I bend ...
I think ... I tasted a roast ... when I finished ... I remem-
ber the grave ... I taste it again ... I raise my fork ... I
eat. " Or, here, in a briefer poem, "Lines for Winter, "
Strand narcissitates for Ros Krauss: "tell yourself ... you
find yourself ... what you know ... your bones play ... you
will be able ... you cannot go on or turn back ... you find
yourself/where you will be at the end ... tell yourself ...
you love what you are ... " Certainly, to be fair, there's
an implicit courage in locating selves precisely in les deux
glace of existence--physical ice, spiritual ice. The insidious-
ness transpires when the proportion slips off, when the per-
sonal pronouns dull by their omnipresence and the poem be-
comes a Chinese water torture experience. No poet is an
Adam. An Eve, perhaps? Feeling spreads like cream over
a Proustian madeleine. In fact, one can read "Pot Roast"
as a verbal play on "Proust, " the chunk of meat triggering
Strand's memory, much as Proust's famous cookie triggered
his.

7.

Birds have a way of appearing far less ungainly in
flight than when they waddle on the ground. As a critic, I've

tried in this experiment to ground the elusive goose of poetry
in the snow, without clipping its wings.   Towards worrying
my bird, I have chosen Strand's book--but without explaining
it.   Poems are not isotropic.   Another critic would approach
the goose differently, either pressing numerous golden eggs
from its anus or wringing its goose neck without any delay
for the sake of pressing its liver.   Perhaps, reader, I have
merely been dream-reading, and Strand did not write the book
I've critiqued.   I leave the last word to Strand himself, who
sees the problem most perspicaciously in "No Particular
Day"; he writes of "moves of the mind/that never quite/make
it as poems. . . . "

TEXTS OF PLEASURE, TEXTS OF BLISS:

The shortcomings of Helen Vendler's
Part of Nature, Part of Us*

I.

That prestigious critic of the seventies, Richard
Howard, stroked and kissed his subjects in order to parade
his own sensibility--the tentacles of his prose maintained their
jelly well above the creatures suspended below them, and sent
their filaments down to stroke, play, and secure themselves.
In general, Howard seemed more fascinating than the poets
he discussed.   Even the obfuscations were a way of enticing
us into the Text of Howard.   Howard presided over his Canon
of Poets quite isotropically, as a grandly mitred Archbishop
of Taste and Style.   He was of the breed of critic (his in-
fluence seems currently on the wane) who creates his own
body out of the bodies of poets he examines.   To shift the
image, the critic is a kind of mother; the poets are his babes.
The mother swells with pride as her offspring, nurtured by
him/her, pule, mature, and make places for themselves
(and for their mother) in the world.

Helen Vendler is less the Archbishop than Howard is.
She maintains a relationship with her poets that is more
shaped from a low and informally placed pulpit.   She can
graciously allow her charges to be themselves--but, as we
shall see, within limits.   Once she has blessed a writer,
she may kill his talent with kindness.   Like a fiddler crab,
Vendler inhabits the shellhouses of the poets she writes of,
while these poets remain resident within their shells.   There's
an interesting congress going on within that shell, after which,
of course, the poet may become transmogrified into a poet

---

*Used by permission of American Book Review (forthcoming).

more to Vendler's liking than he or she was before.   Vend-
ler's kiss is not necessarily a kiss of bliss.

II.

 Roland Barthes notes in The Pleasure of the Text (p.
37) that language is the mother tongue.   Mothers love to al-
low their infants to play with their (the mother's) bodies (lan-
guage), and mothers in turn love to play with their children's
bodies.   Both seek to dismember one another by pulling off
limbs and biting off tongues and noses.   Vendler is a subtle
version of Robert Bly's great Indian myth-mother who de-
vours her young.

 But Vendler is also a mother who constantly proffers
cookies and compliments.   The poets she prefers are well-
established, with jobs in nerve-center writing programs, or
in good literature departments.   Most have appeared in the
New Yorker, have poems in slick poetry magazines (Poetry,
APR), or have big trade publishers.   It is true that she
writes of O'Hara and Ginsberg.   But O'Hara is dead and
greatly in fashion; and Ginsberg has become an institution
loved almost everywhere outside the Moral Majority, so can't
be ignored.   I find her treatment of Ginsberg a bit school-
marmish.   Nearly all of her poets write good lines, with
nice soft literary turns of phrase and literary attitudes.   They
like to celebrate aging, death, their families, and the bucolic.
Their sires are Stevens, Pound, Lowell--a pretty safe, if
accomplished, American canon.   When they sound like Whit-
man, it is of a Whitman de-sexualized and warmed over.
There is hardly a carbolic note anywhere.   The living poets
she likes are middle-aged.   She fails to see any poets of
promise in their 20's (Keats and Rimbaud?).   She eschews
poets not on the academic toboggan slide--there's no Duncan,
Snyder, or McClure; there's barely a mention of Black Moun-
tain poets other than Creeley; there are no language poets;
no Wakoski, Eshleman, or Bukowski; no surrealists; no new
practitioners of the long poem (except for Robert Penn Warren,
whom she likes, who writes of Audubon in predictable ante-
diluvian forms).

III.

 Vendler is best, and less dangerous, writing of dead
poets.   She has a gift of feeling herself into a poem and ex-

plaining and judging its quality. She's enjoyable to read. I
understand Elizabeth Bishop better because of Vendler's con-
trast between the domestic and the strange in Bishop's poetry.
Her stressing some dark motifs in Stevens is also eye-
opening. She is at top form on Lowell's nihilism, his need
to subject women, and on his shift from the early "gorgeous"
writing to the "threadbare" writing of the final books. These
essays contain insights most critics would envy and wish they
had expressed as well.

IV.

Without the New, Freud observed, there is no orgasm;
rather, there are simple, tired re-runs. Part of Nature,
Part of Us fails to engender orgasm because it too feebly
seeks the New. Vendler's additions to her canon almost ex-
clusively include poets deep into middle-age or fast moving
there. These poets she keeps closely tied to her, through a
penchant for saying nice things (cookies) while being critical.
She wields the ferule with such grace that a knuckle-rap sel-
dom hurts. A few examples will reveal her technique: David
Smith provokes "sharp disappointment." Well before Smith
can drop a tear, she races on to say that this provocation is
merely "a measure of the satisfactions he gives." The bad
and mediocre seem to produce the good and the superior.
Again she applies the ferule gently: Because Smith's "explicit-
ness" is often "flat"; because his allegorical poems don't
work well; and because he is not always able to manage his
violence effectively--he is still a splendid poet. Vendler's
praise is fulsome--more cookies come from her jar than is
good for the baby's health.

Of Charles Wright she seems a bit more in awe; and
her complaints are even more sugary. Wright's "almost too-
familiar conventions of quiet, depth, and profundity" are saved
by the "oddity of his imagery." This is a pretty fancy way,
it seems to me, of saying that Wright uses clichés well.
She complains also of Wright's obsession with the dead and
with being dead, which results in monotony--"an unrelenting
elegiac fixity." If she means to say that Wright is boring,
why doesn't she say so? She refers, instead, to Wright's
"deliberateness," of his "slow placing of stone on stone,"
which (and I feel she's a real trimmer here) produces a
"consistency" of "incremental power." When she writes of
Adrienne Rich, she does the same thing. Rich concludes
"Study of History" sentimentally, Vendler observes; but, she

hastens to add, the river and mind of the poem "are heavy with truth." With Charles Simic she isn't quite so kid-gloved. One of Simic's flaws is a "weakness for climax" which leads too easily to "known" or predictable shapes. Here comes the pacifier: Simic has a "watchful eye" and uses a "candid language." With W. S. Merwin she administers a wrist-slap or two, complaining that Merwin doesn't let his poems play in the sun enough; he reflects "elusive pallors." She's right; and she concludes with some advice: Merwin should try harder. This, though, is proffered only after she compares him favorably with Wallace Stevens and T. S. Eliot.

V.

When I see Vendler as a mother hen of criticism, I am not being sexist, rather I am being genderless and descriptive. I can easily cook up a list of Mother-Hen male critics. Vendler is better than most critics of this mode. By comparison the eructations of Dave Smith and Tess Gallagher, in the pages of APR and elsewhere, are sanitized. Both boast that if they can't say good things about poets, they won't say anything at all--viz., Gallagher's recent pontifications in Coda. For me, this criticism (or failure to be critical) short-changes readers. The true critic of the past-- Carlyle, Swinburne, Lawrence, Wyndham Lewis, Rexroth, James Dickey, Robert Bly--has called shots fearlessly. A Vendler, Gallagher, or Smith, by refusing to say anything negative, does a disservice to poetry. We need to know when widely-touted poets like David Wagoner or Marvin Bell publish mediocre books, or when the National Poetry Series wastes money publishing safe poetry; or when considerable poets like Merwin, Kinnell, and Rich start repeating themselves. Sure, the fledgling poet of minimal talent should be ignored. But writers of some reputation who are mindlessly revered, or who are given prizes because their friends are on committees (the Lamont, I am told, is fairly notorious in this regard), need to be exposed. If there aren't critics around willing to do this, poetry is in bad shape, and the toadies and sycophants prevail.

VI.

When an authoritative critic writes glowingly of a really gifted unknown poet, the chance of the Freudian orgasm via the new is enhanced. Alas, what I get from Vendler are pretty dull bed-sessions; the talk floating up from the pillows is quite marvellous, but the libido is down and the ejaculation is itself a series of whimpers: <u>pleasure</u> vs. <u>joy</u>. When the Text of Contemporary Poetry is <u>set up as</u> a canon (canonized) by Vendler and the other highpriests, archbishops, and rectors of criticism (essentially the handmen and handmaidens of the Political Father), then let all dissenters and lovers of <u>joy</u> drop their pants and shove their behinds in the face of <u>the</u> sycophants; and let these dissenters behave most noisomely, with a great roaring of winds. No matter how informative and glowing, a Text of Pleasure, like Vendler's, is not enough. We need Texts of Bliss--iconoclastic exposures, celebrations, wolf-howls, and anatomies of the best (and worst) in current writing.

THIRTEEN WAYS OF LOOKING AT
DAVID WAGONER'S NEW POEMS:

<u>Landfall: Poems</u>*

"The blackbird whirled in the autumn winds.
It was a small part of the pantomime."
                    --Wallace Stevens

I.

"David Wagoner seems to me one of our best poets,
perhaps one of the best we have ever had in this country."
--Robert Boyers, <u>Kenyon Review</u>, jacket blurb for David
Wagoner's <u>Collected Poems: 1956-1976</u>, Indiana University
Press, 1976.

II.

David Wagoner is one of the country's most prolific
poets, and probably is in line for a laureateship, if indeed
such a post should ever materialize in America. <u>Landfall</u>
is his eleventh book of poems. He is also the author of ten
novels, the editor of Theodore Roethke's Notebooks, a chan-
cellor for the Academy of American Poets, and the editor
of <u>Poetry Northwest</u> and the Princeton Poetry Series. He was
twice nominated for the National Book Award in poetry, and
once for the American Book Award in poetry--so the jacket
blurb informs us. He has yet, however, to receive an
ermine tippet. We'll have to be patient.

III.

What is David Wagoner's poetry like? Little, Brown

---

*Reprinted by permission from <u>Western Humanities Review</u>
(August 1981), pp. 267-272.

touts it as "timeless and arresting." Let's have a close look at this blackbird of American verse as he wings through the air. Like most blackbirds, he dips and soars with such professional grace he scarcely ever misses the nest or the twig he selects for a perch. A blackbird's behavior is not as stunning, however, or as inventive, as an egret's, or a macaw's, or a hummingbird's, or a shrike's. I must resist, therefore, expecting more of this fairly commonplace bird than I would of a more flamboyant species. The Britannica characterizes a blackbird's song as "mellow."

IV.

Wagoner reflects a middle-class sensibility as that sensibility approaches middle age. His emotional responses fall within the framework of the entirely possible, non-controversial, and secure. He falls asleep in gardens, he stands around in swamps and in woods and on lake shores, and he evokes the fairly pleasant circumstances of a calm, productive, and pleasant existence. Life, one feels, has been pretty good to him; and his meditations on man and nature evolve from a nicely fixed center. A faithful wife is often nearby, asleep in her bed while he writes his poems. Spiders, moths, and gentle birds await his attention. His nights and darknesses contain minimal threats, and are occasions for reverie and a gently probing metaphysics. His imagination is largely a domestic one. He never seems far from home. He's seldom off a moderately well-beaten path. One has the sense that survival trips are not for him--he likes the stroll or the day's excursion, all within a whistle-distance of the boat-landing or the look-out tower. His creatures seem pretty noiseless and patient. We recall that Jonathan Edwards was not all that far from his home either, when he observed those spiders drifting out to their deaths at sea and started a fad among American writers for the minutiae of the botanical and biological realms.

V.

The Poet of Middle Age reflects a superiority towards the younger generation. Alas, Poetry of Middle Age is often written by the Young, and is published by prestigious houses. In "Elegy Written in a Suburban Churchyard," Wagoner observes the young "living it up" to Beatles music: "Ringo instead of bingo." The young, he says, have a bad habit of

leaving squashed beer cans littered around. The Poet of
Middle Age loves to reflect on his own rather pallid aging.
In "Elegy," Wagoner writes his own elegy, as he feels him-
self on that downward side of life, as a tomb-chill sets in.
His energies may not diminish; but he is apt to move slower,
be a bit more urbane, and he avoids being excessive in either
feeling or language; in short, he takes few risks. His ex-
panding middle requires new protective antics--he sits around
and observes and meditates a lot. I'm now writing meta-
phorically; judging from Wagoner's photographs, he is in ex-
cellent physical shape.

VI.

Looking back at Wagoner's poems since 1953, a Middle-
Aged sensibility was there from the start. Wagoner's never
been a really inventive poet, though a good one; and he has
generally worked within the confines of various restricted
themes and formal motifs. He's been an onlooker rather
than an activist and experimentalist. Perhaps that's why he's
become such a good editor. He's an easy poet to read and
admire, as the chorus of general praise for his work shows.

VII.

Wagoner belongs to a group of very vocal American
poets who love to write about their proletarian and agrarian
backgrounds. The middle-aged poet from Tennessee, the
lyricist of the mid-western trapper-farmer ancestor, the
family historian of the Detroit assembly plants.... These
poets, aging, bestow back-handed self-compliments by showing
how sensitive their progenitors were, despite their having
been brutalized by industry, the farm, and lost opportunities
for education and the business world. I challenge the reader
to find one such poet whose progenitors were stupid, callous,
mean, and despicable. Wagoner's father, a smelter in a steel
mill, sought to prevent his brains from melting in "those
tyger-mouthed mills." I don't much like dragging in old Wil-
liam Blake's tyger--a clichéd poetry beast of the first order!
Wagoner's dad brought flowers home from the mill: gears,
cogwheels, ball-bearings. I am moved by Wagoner's mem-
ories of his father--a pair of poems about him are among the
best in the book. Wagoner sees his own "fire" as generating
from his father's (viz., "My fire.") He eschews the senti-
mentality that often goes along with the subject.

Such fascinations with roots may reflect a poet's un-
easiness about his being insufficiently macho in a culture
that hates faggots and expects men to act like men. If your
daddy was a hunter, miner, smelter, or welder, the chances
are that he's invested you with good macho genes. Wagoner,
to be fair, does not linger over his sexual identity; I don't
feel that he has doubts of his manhood, or of his poet-hood.
Reading him is a bit like reading William Stafford--you feel
secure with the iron content of their blood. Geritol is pres-
ent in the right amounts.

VIII.

As I read Wagoner's new poems, I see them stitch
together into an afghan of verse. Many afghans, of course,
are beautiful; but all do fall short of being works of art.
They are cheery, well-crafted pieces hooked together by fairly
easy formulas (patterns). About half of the poems in Land-
fall are naturals for anthologies (afghans) assembled for peo-
ple of unsophisticated tastes--books used in grade school and
secondary school poetry classes where the visuals are as
crucial as the verbal, and in giftbooks meant for the mass
reader to buy on holidays and give to friends. In such poems
(and they do require their own hermetic life and shape)
there's often a wry humor which turns precious; and there's
nary an off-color word or event. The diction is usually sani-
tized. Nature, particularly in its small manifestations,
flourishes; viz., Wagoner's menagerie of squirrels, spiders,
moths, cuckoos, etc. A number of his poems here are good
fun; Wagoner is generally able to pick up some uncanny attri-
bute of the creature or plant he scrutinizes and relate it to
humans. He writes a quietly didactic bestiary (plantiary) of
sorts.

IX.

Take a look at "Cuckoo." Everybody loves cuckoo
clocks. Wagoner's is frozen, "kaput," and belongs to "the
Black Forest of our nightmares." Its parts are stuck. This
well-crafted poem is likable, frosted as it is with good feel-
ing: there's a "slaphappy" doorway, the house itself is "a
flop-house for gnomes," and the cuckoo is "bird-brained"--
effects uncomfortably close to the worlds of Dumbo and Thum-
per. Wagoner invites us to like him--for he emerges as a
perceptive man, full of Gemütlichkeit. His sentiments are

always appropriately poetic and kind; he spares the cut worm
by tossing it over the fence rather than squash it; the spider
goes on about its business unharmed; and the moth is an oc-
casion for empathy rather than distress or squeamishness.
As Wagoner goes about his landscapes, reciting the names of
plants and birds, he's more like Eve than he is like Adam;
he tends, one imagines, "the droop'ng flowers all. "

Our most successful (widely accepted) poets, I assume
have always tried to be inoffensive and ingratiating.   Charles
Bukowski is one of the glorious exceptions, as Ginsberg was
for a time.   Though Wagoner's poetry is cuts above light
verse, he seems to wish for our comfort and belly-glow as
we read him.   He wants us to like him; so he displays some
of the patience and gentleness we'd all like to possess more
of.   He's a good man.

No poem is more revealing of the poet with his heart
in the right place than "Note with the Gift of a Bird's Nest. "
Here a gray-haired poet and his wife (her hair is still golden)
cut off tresses and put them where bucktits can retrieve the
strands and build a nest--which they do.   The poem devolves
into a rather corny love compliment, a compliment the poet
declares after admitting that the whole idea is in "poor taste, "
a literary lapse.   It's all very ingratiating and mellow.   God!
How far this is from Donne's bright hank of hair about the
bone.   Let me be clear: I don't fault Wagoner for writing
lightly--I am suspicious of his adulators who may not see
this poem for what it is, despite Wagoner's own warnings.
On a certain level, it is fun to read; on another, it is self-
indulgent and coy, and might better have been restricted to
the eyes of his wife or of his friends.

X.

Coy moments in Landfall (and there are many) usually
reflect some form of the pathetic fallacy--that device so loath-
ed by Samuel Johnson when he found John Milton's use of the
device, in "Lycidas, " to be "easy, vulgar, and therefore dis-
gusting. "   Here's what I mean: In "Return to the Swamp, "
Wagoner describes a striped bass as "a splashing-master /
Ringmaster of refracted light. "   A bullfrog, in the closing
lines, bestows on Wagoner "his green princely attention. "
Thumper and his friends, again.   In another poem, swamps have
"an underlying answer"; burreeds have "good lost lives"; wrens
"decide" what the poet is and "slowly excuse" him.   (Dylan

Thomas could be awful at this sort of thing, too). Such coyness is a needless luxury. In a marvellous poem, "Sleeping on Stones," Wagoner demonstrates that he needn't settle for the ingratiating effect. In "Stones" he describes a dog-salmon "flailing her tail-fin / To shreds" as she fashions a spawning place in a stream. I'd place this poem among the very best American nature poems I know.

XI.

One of Wagoner's hallmarks, as I have already reported, is the naming of plants and creatures: scarlet sporophytes, clubmoss, bittercress, rush, sweet-after-death, quillwort, spikerush, lobelia, milfoil, caddisfly, etc. He strikes me as a Ewell Gibbons of poetry. He does our nature-living for us, and his naming of plants and creatures absolves us of some of our guilt over our having so thoroughly urbanized ourselves; we need to start all over like tiny first men, Adams, giving names, or matching up what we see in the marshes with our field-guides. As stimulating and as reassuring as it is to know that we are still not totally exiled from nature, we must see the residue of the superficial in this device. To name an object is not to invest it with magic, or to see profundities behind it. The profundities may be there, but saying so doesn't make it so.

In his closing poem, "Landfall," Wagoner attempts to derive enigmas from the mode: Once we've gone about naming and renaming the trees, birds, plants, and animals, they turn nameless again. We must then look to our hearts, renaming and naming them. In Wagoner's next book, I assume, he'll start the process all over.

XII.

Carole Landis, in the forties, was noted as the Ping Girl; Wagoner, I suggest, can be called the Ing Poet. I am not being Confucian; rather, I stress a recurring formal device that mars many of these poems. Present participles produce an easy mellifluousness which most poets eschew. Whitman, I'd guess, remains the model for this dubious practice. Many of Wagoner's poems would be better if he threw out some of the gerunds. Within six brief lines, "Dipper" contains these: skimming, standing, dipping, dipping, staring, drowning, wing-swimming, wing-walking. Three of these ap-

pear in important end-of-line positions. The opening stanzas
of "Algae" and "Cutworm" are similarly marred. Even a
poem I admire, "Song from the Second Floor," turns to this
facile device an inch or so below its navel. A poet with as
fine an ear as Wagoner's doesn't need to settle for such de-
vices.

XIII.

Wagoner, finally, looks and sounds the way a good
traditional American poet should--gentle, a bit melancholy
and introspective, wide-eyed, enamored of first-person re-
portage, eager to name the objects in his Eden (there's rarely
a whiff of Hell), he's positive in his nostalgia--the natural
cycles of seasons and generations are greatly worth celebra-
ting. The commonplace and the minute carry large meanings:
We are these moths, cutworms, spiders. If our roots are
smothered we will survive. I see no evidence that Wagoner
strives to be innovative, or pioneering, or to chill us with in-
sights, as his mentors Frost and Roethke were so capable of
doing. It is probably unfair of me to expect more of this
widely praised and frequently lovely poet. He'd have to risk
disturbance, grotesqueries, and failures if he were the poet
I want him to be. Nightingales do after all have their neces-
sary places in the sky. But you're not apt to find Wagoner
sitting down beside Henry Thoreau on a log eating a wood-
chuck raw.

Note: I have purposely not quoted much from
Wagoner's book. In my experience, Little,
Brown, (and sometimes Doubleday) has proved
intractable in refusing to allow critics to quote
at all from their books without paying substan-
tial fees--this despite the guidelines suggested
in the recent copyright code. This policy does
hinder the reviewer, particularly if the poet
under scrutiny is not as well-known as Wagoner.
Little, Brown dislikes sending out review copies.
I received a curt note from them saying that they
don't send such copies to "free-lance reviewers."
A letter of protest I sent to the President of the
company produced the book. I don't feel inclined
to take such trouble in the future.

STELE POETRY:

Rosmarie Waldrop's When They Have Senses*

Imagine contemporary poems chiselled into stelae--
those stone tablets erected by various ancient cultures to
carry news and messages. Imagine these stelae set up in
shopping centers (modern agorae) for the public to read.
Imagine further that time has obliterated portions of these
inscriptions; the residue offering mere hints of connected
meanings. Time has effaced words from the stelae. The
result is minimalist writing. Individual words still intact
are forced to carry more meaning than if the original lines
were still whole.

Several readings of Rosmarie Waldrop's new book
convince me that what she writes is Stele Poetry. I eschew
"runic," because the drift of her work is demotic (public and
informal) rather than hieratic (mystical). Armand Schwerner's
lost/found tablet poetry is an earlier modern example of
Stele Poetry; and some of Zukovsky, Pound, and Creeley may
be read this way. Waldrop's immediate models are a trio
of contemporary French poets: Edmund Jabés, whose Elya
and The Book of Questions Waldrop has translated; and the
minimalists Claude Royet-Journoud and Anne-Marie Albiach.

In a recent letter to me, Waldrop acknowledges a
kinship. She feels "close" to Albiach and Royet-Journoud,
both of whom she knows personally, both of whom have been
translated by her husband, Keith, of Burning Deck Press.
As for Jabés, she says, she tries to defend herself against
him. And Jabés is a powerful force. His books are hieratic,
grounded in a mysticism of space-ground-language. Words are
"the preferred prey," he writes, "of the nothing" around
them. We emerge from the Void; our utterances, therefore,
also emerge from that Void (or, Infinite), and are, like us

*Reprinted by permission from Sulfur 2 (Winter 1981), pp.
251-256.

on their trajectory back into that Void.   Through the white
margins (the white silences) around our words, the Void
speaks.   We have mysterious ties to the Void, Jabés says;
and it is here where that Universe of hints and secrets
"waits to be discovered" that our poetry occurs.   That Uni-
verse contains a "white light" which never reveals itself
through our work; yet, it makes our writing possible.   Each
of our words is a "determined stone" in the "impregnable
fortress" of our selves in the Void.   The book is scripture:
"God leans on God, the book on the book, man on his shadow, "
writes Jabés.   The book is also "the place where a writer
sacrifices his voice to silence. "

      Obviously, a thoroughgoing imitation of Jabés would
oblige none to treat the grand hieratic, metaphysical prob-
lems he loves.   (One thinks of John Cage rewriting John
Milton's Paradise Lost.)   Jabés has little patience with such
mundane matters as the relationship between the sexes, or
the ephemeral shifts in nature, or in evanescent Ashberyean
moods.   His books read like portions of an Existentialist
Torah.

      Waldrop's intentions are more modest.   She adapts
Jabés' notions of silence, light, and white space for her own
concerns.   If I read her correctly, she is a poet of ordinary
lives rendered in brief, fragmented lines.   She builds with
stones; but the messages she chisels are more private and
lyrical than those on Jabés' edifices; and they are more
truncated.   She seems preoccupied with male-female rela-
tionships.   Along the way she arranges forms and words to
reflect frozen qualities; her words often seem remnants of
some larger lost whole.   Jabés seems much more assured,
and seldom sounds unsure of himself.   Let me show what I
mean by examining a portion of one of Waldrop's longer
poems.   First, though, a brief comment on her titles: The
disposition of the final letter of her title, dropped a bit be-
low the line (When They Have Senses), appears to have slip-
ped from its affixed position on stone.   What does she gain
by this?   Dual meanings emerge: When "they" have sense
then they shall have insight.   When "they" have senses they
shall come to feel, touch, see, hear, and smell much more
acutely than they are now able to.   They should then better
comprehend these elusive poems.   William Blake saw the
fall of man as the loss of a vast angelic set of senses; Wal-
drop implies a similar loss.   I must not overstress this con-
nection, however.   Waldrop is often more playful than Blake;
viz. , her series of poem-titles which read as if Gertrude

Stein, that aficionado of the adverb, had written them. Waldrop's adverbs, in eurythmic gowns perform gladly, ecstatically, flowingly over the page. Gertrude would be pleased. Here are a few of Waldrop's titles: "The Senses Loosely or The Married Woman," "The Senses Continuously," "The Senses Barely," "The Senses Dumbly," "The Senses Visibly," "The Senses Touchingly," etc.

In "Senses Barely or The Necessities of Life" (Part 3), Waldrop writes with maximum stelic effect, once the poem is underway. The opening trio of lines appears to deal with the rupture of a love liaison (a marriage, perhaps) elusively developed in Parts 1 and 2. Here, the pair move into exile, hurrying like Lot and his wife through a cold town:

> they have no street in their hurry   1
> but leave with the cold
> and few household goods

There follows a hiatus of half an inch or so, which suggests that we have moved over to the next stele--to a pair of phrases set over to the right. The visual placement is important:

> a body of pure salt
>
>   2
>
> stationary abode

Has Lot's wife (or the abandoned modern wife) here turned to salt, her future abode ironically fixed forever, until rain and wind wash the salt down to nubbins in the sand? The Stele Mode seems to work here, as the reader strives to complete the sense and flesh out good clause/verse lines from Waldrop's hints.

Then follows another hiatus between slabs/stanzas--this one a space or two longer than the first one, suggesting again that we are at a new stele. To give an accurate sense of the placing of the poem on the page, I shall here give the remaining stanzas, meticulously observing the spacings. The numberings of the stanzas (stelae) are mine:

> preceded
> by repetition   3
> by empty bottles

the time it takes
to mix
the male and female   4
matter

none of the steps may be   5
omitted

        changes into
        unrecognizable   6
        straight lines

        "she was with him"
        the day after   7
        in relative order
        whereas

the necessary eye
of the sun
overgrows   8

Fragment 3 is cryptic, despite its seeming to flow
grammatically within its form.   A possible reading is that
before the wife turned to exile, her life was salt.   It was
boring--a matter of repetitions and empty bottles.   Mr. and
Mrs. Lot were like bottles emptied, drained of love.   After
another break, a new inscription informs us that when the
"mix" of male and female was complete, the marriage was
over.   The Mystery had lost its mystery, had become com-
monplace.   Stanza 5 is an observation, almost Orphic in its
insight: There is no shortening of the route that linked males
and females must take, towards becoming salt.   This moment
of commentary is forceful since it is set off by itself and has
a stele all of its own.   We linger and meditate on the writing;
and the burden on us is enormous--like deciphering sphinx-
like riddles.   Even though our own lives are not in jeopardy,
if we fail to decipher accurately, the lives of the poem and
the book containing the poem are.   For, if we dislike the
book, or resent the obligations Waldrop imposes, we may
throw the book in the trash.

I read # 6 as three fragmented lines with minimal link-

age between them. "Changes into" sits by itself and seems
to relate to changing into salt. "Unrecognizable"--yes, the
human figure once alive and now salt is unrecognizable; also,
the changes in the pair's love-life creating these results are
also unrecognizable. Whatever the meanings, the word sits
isolated. The other words that might illuminate it have fallen
from the stele. The "lines" are straight--which means that
they can be recognized; and this is why I don't take "unrecog-
nizable" as an adjective modifying "straight lines." Waldrop
seems to be saying that our peregrinations away from por-
tions of our lives that have chilled are indeed the primary
(straight) lines of our lives.

A foreign voice next intrudes, expressing amazement
that she is no longer with him. Obviously; for she has re-
mained behind, turned to salt, and is no longer recognizable.
If I were to suggest the words lost from this stele, they
might go this way. My additions are in brackets:

"she was with him" [the day they left the city.]
The day after [they left the city]
in relative order [he preceded her, in customary fashion]
whereas [now she is no longer with him.]

The final fragment presents a dazzling close. Light shim-
mers over the entire event, "overgrows" it, and reduces it
to the minuscule but poignantly human. Beneath the glare,
the potency of the event (the destruction of a love/marriage)
is reduced to a minor crescendo.

My metaphor of the stele, I hope, does give some
idea of how Waldrop's difficult poetry works. The burden on
the reader is most of the time welcome. Waldrop assumes
that her reader, willing to decipher her meanings, will relish
the hunt and the verbal play. For, finally, these poems turn
on verbalism--the word is as important as the message. And
my efforts to wrench a continuous prose meaning of a narra-
tive sort is possibly a violation of Waldrop's intentions. I
don't feel though that I am entirely perverse in trying. I
need to register some sense as I move through this book.
And if I am old-fashioned in this, I refuse to apologize. I
have merely tried to explain via a metaphor what I have found
useful in reading Waldrop. I will say, however, that I find
her intriguing and stimulating; I hope I am not one of the
"cannibal spirits" she mentions who do "violence to words."
Read the book and make your own judgments. All of the
poems do lend themselves well to my stele metaphor. Per-

haps the motif may be useful in defining and reading other contemporary poets.

Because of her preoccupation with a special experimental poetry being written in France, Waldrop is an unusual poet. Most American poets seem to revere Spanish and Latin American writers, among foreign poets, perhaps because these writers create more continuous, less-truncated poems, with more straightforward images. If one sees Vallejo, Neruda, and Paz as beef-red; Waldrop and Jabés are white-- their neutral tones reveal an obsession with moving poetry into worlds of abstraction and meditation, worlds where furniture is largely absent and from which we are invited to fashion a private metaphysics of silence. Jabés wrote: "I do not exist except in relation to the space of a word uttered.... Between the word heard and the word to be said, in this half-silence which is the last refuge of the echo, there is my place. "

ON MADELEINES AND TURNIPS: OR, WILL THE REAL LEON EDEL PLEASE STAND UP?

Aram Saroyan's Genesis Angels

When John Keats coughed up his blood and saw that special shade of red and knew he was dying, he hadn't willed the piecemeal destruction of his body. When Jack Kerouac boozed himself to death, and when Lew Welch, another alcoholic given to breakdowns and depressions, disappeared into the mountains with his gun, ostensibly a suicide, their self-deaths stimulated buckets, nay torrents of tears from the eyes of biographers and reverential poets. Kerouac and Welch took their own lives; Keats did not. And yet this trio fulfills that Romantic dictum about poets and gifted men of talent and beauty, too sensitive to live in an indifferent or hostile society, who kill themselves.

How much pity do Kerouac and Welch deserve? I'm afraid that I can't see them as "Angels"--bastard or genesis --but rather as self-pitying men of an elusive charm incapable of withstanding booze and beat-hood. Booze, it seems, for both of them was a substitute for mother's milk. Mother lingers in the background, pulling a home life together for her middle-aged son. She is a convenience. As Jack hears her fussing in the kitchen or flushing the john, he can love/ hate her for causing his pudgy gut, the fact that he's stopped writing, the perpetual wash of beer down his gullet, his eyes crazed from watching endless TV commercials. Welch's mother was, it is true, away from him most of the time--yet she sent him money when she could, and he stayed with her in Reno and elsewhere when his debts piled up and he was afraid of being busted and thrown in the slammer. Throwaway lives.

It is not my immediate business to speculate on the

mysticism of the gifted writer dying prematurely. The business at hand is to comment on Aram Saroyan's recent treatment of the Lew Welch and Beat Generation "Saga" (Soap Opera?), as it appears from Morrow, Inc., illustrated. When the book arrived, I was standing already knee-deep in tears wept over American writers dying young, waiting for a boat to ferry me over to dry land. Even a leaky raft would do. But, alas, Saroyan's book, I fear, is yet merely another contribution to the great flood (hepatitical) shed over the Beats. And surely writing about these figures from the immediate Literary Past has become a sizable industry (cottage or yurt) attracting both large and small publishers. In the forties and fifties, the industry was devoted to James Joyce and Dylan Thomas. Today, it is the Beats who are mythologized as outrageous angels of death and art, the like of which has never been seen in American literature.

Welch, as he appears in the new pair of volumes of letters to and from his circle (see the last essay in this book), edited by Donald Allen, was anything but the dull, mother-fixated alcoholic Saroyan depicts, destroyed by a world he never made. In the letters, it is poignantly clear that he made his world, chose his directions, and determined his modes of self-destruction. The letters read like a moving epistolary novel.

Saroyan treats most of the Beats as if they were Blakean Los-figures (Lost-Figures), or great Prometheans of contemporary letters. Certainly, if hype rules, they may figure so. Ginsberg in Genesis Angels is seen in a glorious neon-plastic light as a "survivor," a poet-conscience and visionary larger than the ball made up of all the jockstraps of life rolled together, that smelly ball waiting to be pushed eternally up Mt. Tamalpais, that eminence of so many legendary life-forces and so disappointing once one has actually wandered up it. Philip Whalen, too, is stroked for having made his death-to-society choice by moving over into Zenhood. Gary Snyder emerges as the most human, brainiest, and best-informed of these super-folk; he warms his kidneys and sphincter with flushes of manzanita berry tea. As Snyder writes out of a bedrock mind and conscience, Mr. Natural chuckles over his shoulder.

Saroyan's title more than hints at the sentimentality of his book. "Genesis" means start, right? But the start of what? American poetry? Life? Hippie-dom? A new Bible? The reformation of Diana Trilling? Via Ginsberg's

Howl, angels appear in various guises (they are always male)
--boytricks, boychicks with huge streaming cocks; Hell's
Angels; outlaw poet-youth-emigrés from New York City hoping
for numerous thrusts up the butt from men in lumberjack
shirts and cleated shoes; junkie cut-up novelists shooting ap-
ples off women's heads and missing; quester-angels after
various oriental mysticisms. What we get is a big globby
olio of life-experiment in the Wertherian, Byronic, Teufels-
dröckian Carlylean manner.

By squinting a little, it is possible, I think, to see
the Beats as largely self-destructive angels, revving up their
angel anuses (Yes, Virginia, Beat Angels have anuses as well
as hairy belly buttons), all spurting spunk--soft runny loads
over the heads of the hostile conformist, non-art-loving East-
ern Establishment World, thereby transforming American cul-
ture. Without Ginsberg's public disrobings, the exorcism
processions around the Pentagon, the pilgrimage to Senator
Joseph McCarthy's grave in Appleton to plant commemorative
marijuana seeds there, the counter-culture thrust of the six-
ties and seventies would have lacked balls, and may not even
have occurred, Viet Nam war or no Viet Nam war. But even
if one casts a squint-slant towards the Beats then, one feels
that Saroyan hasn't done these innovative, outrageous folk
much justice.

Saroyan writes with a simplicity bordering on guile.
He's picked up what sounds like compost-heap writing, where
you dig out little wriggling, squirming comic book sentences
and throw them into your garden where your chapters are
struggling up like so many anemic cabbages. The worms
feed and are dissatisfied, and hunger for the hulking veggies
grown by Peter Orlovsky on the Cherry Valley farm. Here
are some samples of stuff in Genesis Angels that really put
me off: The Beats, Saroyan informs us, "were the shock
troops, the very pioneers of love in America." Well, where
was Walt Whitman? Where was Thomas Wolfe? Here's an-
other simplistic germ: "Allen wouldn't jump; he has the
semitic skepticism the others would need and value in him
later." Was it really "skepticism" Ginsberg possessed, or
was he, as he reveals himself in "Please, Master," an anx-
ious, culture-avid, gifted young man who craved as many
masters as possible (dope, gurus, Blake, whips, cocks,
farms, towns, the whole of America and Europe, S T A R -
D O M)? If you crave all these masters, and find some of
them to demean you, you won't be so apt to kill yourself--un-
less you believe in an old-fashioned Christian Hell rampant

with punitive masters. Self-preservation, then, via the fixes of fame and fortune, becomes a laudable way of life.

In another passage, instead of comprehension we are served more glossy hype--Ginsberg is a visionary who sees "everything," who carries "the conceptual center of the universe around in his belly." Ginsberg is like some man on a hindu mystical chart with a mystical belly-button as the key (clue), the fake orifice for universal concepts to enter and squirm around therein maggot-wise. The problem with such hype is that much of it is based on legend, much of it self-managed by Ginsberg in his journals, letters, and interviews. For example, we have no reason to disbelieve Ginsberg's tale of his visitation from William Blake, who recited some of his Songs for Ginsberg when the latter was depressed. We must accept Ginsberg's word. I'm suspicious, though, since there are kinds and kinds of hallucinations--some of them being little more than self-projections and wish-fulfillments. It's a matter of voice, isn't it?

Every time I read poets or novelists I greatly admire, (Yeats, Roethke, Lawrence, Firbank), I feel they are reading to me. I hear their voices long after I put down their books and sit staring out at my parsley and tomatoes. It may seem irreverent and down-right mean to question Ginsberg's visions --but if he is presented to me as a visionary and man of impeccable truth, I owe it to myself to be skeptical. I don't even think that Blake was a visionary, in the sense that St. Theresa and Mother Ann Lee were. At any rate, I shall insist on making my own choices among the mystical men-women I wish to carry concepts for me around in their bellies. If Ginsberg, why not the porn stars John Holmes or Linda Lovelace? Why not Moms Mabley or Richard Nixon? Poets are basically such liars, as Oscar Wilde said so well.

Here is Saroyan writing Dick and Jane notes regarding Ginsberg's love for Neal Cassady:

> And Allen Ginsberg fell in love with Neal, and they
> became lovers (because Neal wanted love and harmony
> and complete trust in everybody)--he was insecure and
> wanted love, too--and Jack was left wistful wondering
> about the deep day and night long conversations and
> ramifications of Neal and Allen in the Columbia apart-
> ment night.

And why was Kerouac so obsessed with this pair of unlikely

lovers? Was he considering turning faggot-for-life, fearing he was missing something if he didn't? Was Genesis Angels talked out on tape in Mary Worth's living room? Let's phone up dear old Mary and ask.

Saroyan is also simplistic in explaining Burroughs' cut-up techniques as Burroughs' way of dealing with having missed the apple on his wife's head and shooting her between the eyes. Here is Saroyan in his comic-book seer's role: Burroughs "will cut up his mind with a typewriter and scissors" as a way of dealing with the tragedy. Perhaps. But I'm not convinced.

Saroyan is not much more perceptive writing about Welch. At one point he says that when Welch read Gertrude Stein's story "Melanchtha," "he becomes a writer." This I don't believe. There's no evidence in Welch's letters to prove it. Rather, his becoming a writer was an incredibly slow process, met by numerous blocks. My guess is that his meeting with William Carlos Williams at Reed College, and his friendships with Snyder, Whalen, and Kerouac were more influential. Despite his thesis on Stein, written at Reed College, and read and praised by Williams, Welch never got his act together to revise and get it published, despite Williams' offer of help. And it was probably a pioneering work, since few people were writing on Stein at the time; but an academic chore, however much the author likes the subject, does not necessarily make that author a Writer.

What I resist, finally, is the sentimental inflation of details from personal lives at the expense of the poetry and prose itself. When writers are as touted as the Beats, it is difficult even to hint that they may be and have been mediocre writers, at least some of the time. The personal fallacy, folks, becomes a variety of mindless jerking off. I resist also the general exclusion of women from the scene, except as sex objects and housekeepers. While Joanne Kyger, Carolyn Cassady, and Leonore Kandel, white-stoned maidens all, drift through the background, they seem always ancillary to the macho dudes who do the real writing. The general pattern here is a bit derived from Walt Whitman, and a bit derived from that awful closet-case Ernest Hemingway. Fucking and Art: Welch and company seemed to feel that there's a real equation between the quantity and quality of one's writing and the quantity and quality of one's fucking--ideally, when both are carried on with equal intensity, whether with males or females, your art really percolates. It's time, I think, for some fearless critic to blast away at the perpetuation of the American Male as Great-Writer, Chest-Thumper, Erectile-Tissued author, one whose gifts for both fucking and for writing, for boozing and for doping, are so enormous they may lead to many delicious self-destructions. This seems to have happened to Welch and to Kerouac.

I'm sorry to have been so severe with Saroyan's book. Ginsberg, Welch, Snyder, Whalen, and Burroughs are of my generation; and I have learned greatly from them all about writing and about my own liberation. I expected much more when I first saw Genesis Angels. The book reminds me of a boomerang thrown after angels in flight, the flinger expecting that when it returns to his hand there'll be bags of publisher's gold attached. The photographs, though, are good. The final one is of Lou Welch's rifle, Marin City 1968, leaning against a living room wall, ready to be picked up and fired.

Dispense with hype-books on the Beats tossed your way. Read the primary sources instead--the novels, poems, plays, interviews, letters. If you have read Genesis Angels, as a corrective, return and take a dip in Leon Edel's monumental biography of James; it's an art form in itself. But I'm afraid that's another mess of worms; for are any of the Beats matches for James? or for Proust? Or am I unfair, comparing madeleines and Hostess Twinkies?

LEW WELCH:

I Remain: The Letters of Lew Welch and
the Correspondence of His Friends*

Truman Capote and Norman Mailer have made docu-
mentary "novels" fashionable. Critics anxious to see some-
thing new transpiring in American literature rush to proclaim
In Cold Blood and The Executioner's Song innovative master-
works. It's not my purpose here to explore the excessive
zeal of critics, or to carp about contemporary imitators of
Daniel Defoe, but rather to declaim the recurrence of an-
other old form--the Epistolary Novel. It appears as a two-
volume edition of Lew Welch's letters, affectionately and un-
obtrusively edited by Donald Allen, comprising almost four
hundred pages of fascinating poet-document history. And for
critics seeking new forms, and realistic ones, this gathering
of letters should please them, detailing as it does the middle
and end of the life of a haunted American poet.

Welch resembled a figure out of Dostoevsky, given to
personal excess, but without the snivelling one associates with
lost Russians. Welch had charm; and his numerous letters
to Whalen, Kerouac, Snyder, and his mother reveal a non-
whiner who made gargantuan efforts to right his derailed life.
He worked at (and for a while apparently liked) a job in ad-
vertising for Montgomery Ward (he was eventually fired).
He looked forward to his marriage and his liaisons with
women with a winsome hope that at last he could control the
booze and attract enough money to live on, so that he could
really write. There was a tall element of the procrastinator
in Welch. He taught workshops for menial pay at the Uni-
versity of California Extension, and was enthusiastic and
thorough about his courses. He put his considerable talents
into his singing/poetry readings, once he had moved to San
Francisco and was a vital part of the on-going Beat scene.

*Reprinted by permission from The Three Penny Review
(Winter 1981), p. 11.

He tried to make a go of driving taxis and working on salmon-fishing boats. He resolved to start a new life all by himself in an abandoned shack in the California mountains. At most of these efforts he failed, maintaining a child's optimism over every reversal. Bleary with booze, he would pick himself up from disaster and proceed to carry his considerable energies off to some new locale. He was tormented by incredible conflicts, conflicts similar to those destroying other authors, ones better known and more widely published than Welch: Fitzgerald, Hemingway, Faulkner, Plath, Dylan Thomas, John Berryman, Theodore Roethke.

Among these conflicts and their causes is the belief that if you are talented you don't need a nine-to-five job: just write, and editors and publishers will reward you with money and fame. Then, there's that tremendous pull (my guess is that this is indigenous to American writers) between Thoreau and Wallace Stevens--between the semi-isolated life spent roughing it in the woods and the city life of the successful businessman. This split alone would stimulate enough schizophrenia for a whole battalion of poets. Add next the myth that boozing and copulating produce your best writing. This ideal Welch seemed to have absorbed from Kerouac, Snyder, and Ginsberg--when you're at the top of your fucking form you are at the top of your writing form. Finally, there's that macho fascination with guns as a reflection of your masculinity. Welch loved guns. As I read these letters, I see Welch trapped by these contradictions and powers, in various combinations at various times; he must have felt that he wandered the earth split right down the middle.

Despite his good cheer and his frequent reassurances to his friends that he was a survivor, he seemed always ready to fall into some final sink-hole of failure. He seemed to loathe most failing the friends who cared about him. When he wrote his thesis on Gertrude Stein, at Reed College, William Carlos Williams encouraged him to publish it. This was before anyone in academia was taking Stein seriously. Well, Lew procrastinated, and the revisions he intended to make were never made; the work was never published. It was as if he couldn't face the possibility of the book's not being good and hence, a disappointment for Williams and others who believed in it.

Welch's final, most poignant failure was the building of his house on the land at Kitkitdizze that Gary Snyder had arranged for him to have--a piece on the tract Snyder, Gins-

berg, et al. were settling. Welch tried to borrow money
from his mother, his former wife, and Ginsberg so he could
proceed with the building, but he was never to read their let-
ters saying they would help. He hired a crew to help him
build, and on May 14, 1971, moved to the site where he in-
tended to camp until the house was up. On the 23rd of May
he disappeared, leaving a note behind: "I never could make
anything work out right and now I'm betraying my friends.
I can't make anything out of it--never could. I had great
visions but never could bring them together with reality. I
used it all up. It's all gone.... I went Southwest. Goodbye.
Lew Welch." Reading the final note leaves one feeling jolted,
suddenly directed back to the enormous life-pressures on this
sensitive, gentle man. No hair or tooth has ever been found.
It was apparently the alcoholism, always symptomatic of so
much else, that destroyed him.

Amidst all the outpouring of books on the Beats and
related figures, these letters are in a category all their
own--they transcend cult and gossip, and belong with other
gatherings of the world's truly moving letters--Jane Welsh
Carlyle's, D. H. Lawrence's, Oscar Wilde's. Call these
two volumes an Epistolary Novel, if you will. But that,
finally, doesn't seem all that useful. Welch's letters prove
again that letters constitute a literary form in themselves;
when they are as moving, and as disturbing as these, they
don't require special labels.

LIST OF BOOKS REVIEWED

Guy Beining. The Ogden Diary. Box 715, Newburyport, Mass. 01950, 1979, $2.50.

James Bertolino. Are You Tough Enough for the Eighties? New Rivers (Small Press Distribution: 1636 Ocean View Ave., Kensington, Calif. 94707), 1979, $2.

Michael Blumenthal. Sympathetic Magic. Water Mark Studio: 175 E. Shore Road, Huntington Bay, N. Y. 11743, $6.50.

Sterling Brown. Collected Poems. Harper & Row, 1980, $12.95.

Mary Cheever. The Need for Chocolate. Stein and Day, 1980, $12.50.

Peter Cooley. The Room Where Summer Ends. Carnegie-Mellon University Press: Pittsburgh, Pa. 15213, 1979, $4.50.

Dennis Cooper. Idols. Seahorse Press: 307 W. 11th St., New York, N. Y. 10014, 1979, $4.95.

William Corbett. Columbus Square Journal. Angel Hair Books: Box 718, Lenox, Mass. 02140, 1976.

James Dickey. The Strength of Fields. Doubleday, Inc., 1979, $6.

Don Dolan. The Last Days of the American Dream. Fault Press: 33513 Sixth St., Union City, Calif. 94587, 1979.

William Doreski. Half of the Map. Burning Deck Press: 71 Elmgrove, Providence, R. I. 02906, 1980, $2.50.

Robert Duncan. "Night Scenes" in Roots and Branches. New Directions: New York, 1964.

Russell Edson. With Sincerest Regrets. Burning Deck Press: 71 Elmgrove, Providence, R. I. 02906, 1980, $2.50.

Kenward Elmslie. Tropicalism. Z Press: Calais, Vt. 05650, 1975, $3.50.

375

Clayton Eshleman. Hades in Manganese. Black Sparrow Press:
P. O. Box 3993, Santa Barbara, Calif. 93105, 1981, $20 and
$5.

Larry Fagin. Stabs. Poltroon Press: 2315 Carleton St., Berkeley,
Calif. 94704, 1979.

David Fisher. Teachings. Back Roads Books: Box 543, Cotati,
Calif. 94928, 1978, $2.95.

Harrison Fisher. Text's Boyfriends. Burning Deck Press: 71 Elm-
grove, Providence, R. I. 02906, 1980, $2.50.

Sheldon Flory. A Winter's Journey. Copper Beech: Box 1852,
Brown University, Providence, R. I. 02192, 1979, $4.50.

Paul Fussell. Poetic Meter and Poetic Form (revised ed.). Ran-
dom House, 1979, $5.95(paper).

Henry Gould. Stone. Copper Beech: Box 1852, Brown University,
Providence, R. I. 02912, 1979, $4.50.

Barbara Guest. Biography. Burning Deck Press: 71 Elmgrove,
Providence, R. I. 02906, 1980, $2.50.

Alfred Starr Hamilton. The Poems of ... The Jargon Society: High-
lands, N. C. (c/o Jonathan Williams) 28741, 1970.

Robert Hershon. A Blue Shovel. Hanging Loose Press: 231 Wyckoff
St., Brooklyn, N. Y. 11217, 1979, $3.

Lee Hickman. Great Slave Lake Suite. Momentum Press: 512 Hill
St. No. 4, Santa Monica, Calif. 90405, 1980, $5.95.

Bruce Hutchinson. Benthos. Fault Publications: 33513 Sixth St.,
Union City, Calif. 94587, 1978.

Robinson Jeffers. Shining Clarity, by Marlan Beilke. Quintessence
Publications, 356 Bunker Hill Mine Rd., Amador City, Calif.
95601, 1977, $25.

Donald Justice. Selected Poems. Atheneum, Inc., 1979, $7.95(pa-
per).

Robert Kelly. The Alchemist to Mercury. North Atlantic Books:
635 Amador St., Richmond, Calif. 94805, 1981, $7.95(paper),
$30(signed boards).

Arthur and Kit Knight. The Beat Journey. P. O. Box 493, Califor-
nia, Pa. 15419, 1978, $7.50(paper).

Kenneth Koch. The Burning Mystery of Anna. Random House, 1979,
$4.95.

Joseph Langland. Any Body's Song. Doubleday, 1980, $8.95.

Judith McCombs. Against Nature: Wilderness Poems. Dustbooks:
P. O. Box 1056, Paradise, Calif. 98969, 1979, $2.95(paper),
$7.95(cloth).

Cynthia Macdonald. W(H)oles. Knopf, 1980, $5.95.

Morton Marcus. Big Winds, Glass Mornings, Shadows Cast by
Stars. Jazz Press: 17930 Highway 9, Boulder Creek, Calif.
95006, 1981, $4.95.

Paul Mariah. This Light Will Spread: Selected Poems. ManRoot
Books: Box 982, South San Francisco, Calif. 94080, 1978,
$4.95(paper), $12(ltd. signed).

Elizabeth Marraffino. Blue Moon for Ruby Tuesday. Contact II:
Box 451, Bowling Green Station, New York, N.Y. 10004, 1981,
$3.

William Matthews. Sticks and Stones. Pentagram Press: Box 379,
Markesan, Wisc. 53946, 1975, $3.

Bert Meyers. Windowsills. The Common Table Press: 216 Crown
St., Room 506, New Haven, Conn. 06510, 1979, $3.95(paper),
$7.95(boards).

Josephine Miles. Coming to Terms. University of Illinois Press:
Champaign, Ill., 1979, $3.95(paper), $8.95(boards).

Carol Muske. Skylight. Doubleday, Inc., 1981, $5.95.

Opal Nations. The Marvels of Professor Pettingruel. Blackstone
Press: 190 South 3rd West St., Missoula, Mont., 1979.

Opal Nations. The Tragic Hug of a Small French Wrestler. Fault
Publications: 33513 Sixth St., Union City, Calif. 94587, 1977.

Louis Patler. An American Ensemble. Poltroon Press: 2315
Carleton St., Berkeley, Calif. 94704, 1979.

Richard Peabody. I'm in Love with the Morton Salt Girl. Paycock
Press: Box 57206, Washington, D.C. 20037, 1979, $3.

Ronald Perry. Denizens. Random House, 1980, $5.95.

Roxie Powell. Kansas Collateral. Cherry Valley Editions: 14200
Pear Tree Lane, Wheaton, Md. 20906, 1979, $2.50.

George Quasha. Giving the Lily Back Her Hands. Station Hill
Press: Barrytown, N.Y. 12507, 1979.

Jerry Ratch. Chaucer Marginalia. Sombre Reptiles: Box 265,
Bolinas, Calif. 94924, 1979.

Jerry Ratch. Osiris. Cloud Marauder Press: 6397 Colby St., Berkeley, Calif. 94618, 1977, $3.

Rochelle Ratner. Combing the Waves. Hanging Loose Press: 231 Wyckoff St., Brooklyn, N. Y. 11217, 1979, $3. 50.

Wendy Rose. Long Division: A Tribal History. Strawberry Press: Box 451, Bowling Green Station, New York, N. Y. 10004, 1981, $2. 50.

Wendy Salinger. Folly River. Dutton, 1980, $7. 95.

Aram Saroyan. Genesis Angels. Morrow, 1979, $7. 95.

Scales of the Marvelous (essays on Robert Duncan), edited by Robert J. Bertholf and Ian W. Reid. New Directions: New York, 1980, $4. 95.

James Schevill. Fire of Eyes. Copper Beech: Box 1852, Brown University, Providence, R. I. 02912, 1979, $4. 50.

James Schuyler. The Home Book. Z Press: Calais, Vt. 05650, 1977, $3. 50.

James Schuyler. The Morning of the Poem. Farrar, Straus & Giroux, 1980.

Herbert Scott. Dinosaurs. W. D. Hofstadt: 606 Ulster St., Syracuse, N. Y. 13204, 1978.

Jack Skelley. Wammo Amnesia & Juvenile Loitering. Fred & Barney Press: 1140 1/2 Nowita Place, Venice, Calif. 90291, 1981, S. A. E.

Roberta Spear. Silks. Holt, Rinehart & Winston, 1980, $4. 95.

Carolyn Stoloff. Swiftly Now. Ohio University Press: Athens, 1982.

Mark Strand. The Late Hour. Atheneum, Inc., 1978, $6. 95.

The Streets Inside: Ten Los Angeles Poets, edited by William Mohr. Momentum Press: 512 Hill St. No. 4, Santa Monica, Calif. 90405, 1978, $4. 95.

Paul Vangelisti. 2 X 2. Red Hill Press: P. O. Box 2853, San Francisco, Calif. 94126, 1978, $6.

Helen Vendler. Part of Nature, Part of Us. Harvard University Press, 1980, $15.

David Wagoner. Landfall. Little, Brown, 1981, $9. 95.

Rosmarie Waldrop. When They Have Senses. Burning Deck Press: 71 Elmgrove, Providence, R. I. 02906, 1980, $3. 50.

Diane Ward. The Light American. Jawbone Press: 927 O St.,
NW, Washington, D.C. 20001, 1979, $2.

Diane Ward. Theory of Emotion. Segue Foundation: 300 Bowery,
New York, N.Y. 10012, 1979, $2.

Michael Waters. Not Just Any Death. BOA Editions: 92 Park Ave.,
Brockport, N.Y. 14420, 1979, $4.50.

Lew Welch. I Remain: The Letters of Lew Welch and the Corre-
spondence of His Friends, edited by Donald Allen. 2 vols.,
Grey Fox Press: 161 Grand View Ave., San Francisco, Calif.
94114, 1980, $12(boards), $5.95(paper).

Bernard Welt. Serenade. Z Press: Calais, Vt. 05648, 1979,
$3.50.

F.N. Wright. The Whorehouse. Young David Press: 1290 White-
cliff Road, Thousand Oaks, Calif. 91360, 1979, $5.95.

Gary Young. Hands. Illuminati: 8812 W. Pico Blvd., Ste. 203,
Los Angeles, Calif. 90035, 1979, $4.